OXFORD MODERN LANGUAGES AND LITERATURE MONOGRAPHS

Diaries Real and Fictional in Twentieth-Century French Writing

SAM FERGUSON

OXFORD
UNIVERSITY PRESS

OXFORD
UNIVERSITY PRESS

Great Clarendon Street, Oxford, OX2 6DP,
United Kingdom

Oxford University Press is a department of the University of Oxford.
It furthers the University's objective of excellence in research, scholarship,
and education by publishing worldwide. Oxford is a registered trade mark of
Oxford University Press in the UK and in certain other countries

First Edition published in 2018

Impression: 3

Published in the United States of America by Oxford University Press
198 Madison Avenue, New York, NY 10016, United States of America

British Library Cataloguing in Publication Data
Data available

Library of Congress Control Number: 2017955388

ISBN 978–0–19–881453–5

Printed and bound by
CPI Group (UK) Ltd, Croydon, CR0 4YY

This book is dedicated to the memory of my father Peter Ferguson.

Acknowledgements

This book derives from work undertaken in the course of my doctorate at the University of Oxford, and I am extremely grateful for the supervision I received there, first from Professor Toby Garfitt and later from Professor Ann Jefferson. The work subsequently benefited from the insightful comments of my examiners Professor Michael Sheringham and Professor David Walker. A number of colleagues at Oxford and elsewhere very kindly devoted time to reading work at various stages of the project: Dr Marie-Chantal Killeen, Professor Diana Knight, Professor Dame Hermione Lee, and Dr Jennifer Oliver. I am indebted to the meticulous reading and invaluable suggestions of two anonymous peer reviewers for Oxford University Press. This study has also benefited enormously from conversations with colleagues in French studies at Oxford and elsewhere, who are too numerous to list individually. This work would not have been possible at all without the generous financial support of New College, the Faculty of Medieval and Modern Languages, and more recently Christ Church, where I have been a Junior Research Fellow since 2014. In many other ways, I have been supported throughout this long period of work by my family, my partner Dr Daria Luchinskaya, and my cats.

Contents

List of Figures

List of Tables

References and Abbreviations for Primary Texts

André Gide, *Les Cahiers d'André Walter* (*CAW*) ([first published 1891]) and *Les Poésies d'André Walter* ([1892]), in André Gide, *Romans et récits: œuvres lyriques et dramatiques*, ed. by Pierre Masson, 2 vols (Paris: Gallimard, Bibl. de la Pléiade, 2009), I, pp. 1–166.

André Gide, *Paludes* (Paris: Librairie de l'Art indépendant, 1895).

André Gide, *Les Faux-monnayeurs* (*FM*) ([1925]), in *Romans et récits*, II, pp. 173–517.

André Gide, *Le Journal des Faux-monnayeurs* (*JFM*) ([1926]), in *Romans et récits*, II, pp. 519–82.

André Gide, *Journal 1889–1939* (Paris: Gallimard, Bibl. de la Pléiade, 1939). Reference will also be made to the most recent edition of Gide's *Journal*, ed. by Éric Marty and Martine Sagaert, 2 vols (Paris: Gallimard, Bibl. de la Pléiade, 1996–97).

Raymond Queneau, *Les Œuvres complètes de Sally Mara* (*OCSM*) ([1962]) (Paris: Gallimard, 1979).

Raymond Queneau, *Journal intime de Sally Mara* (*JI*) ([1950]), in *OCSM*, pp. 13–187.

Raymond Queneau, *On est toujours trop bon avec les femmes* (*OETTBALF*) ([1947]), in *OCSM*, pp. 189–337.

Raymond Queneau, *Sally plus intime* (*SPI*), in *OCSM*, pp. 339–51.

References to works by Roland Barthes will refer, when possible, to Roland Barthes, *Œuvres complètes*, ed. by Éric Marty, 5 vols (Paris: Seuil, 2002).

Works by Annie Ernaux will be referred to in their individual publications.

Note on Translations

Throughout this book, translations into English are provided after most citations of text in French. The exceptions are when a certain citation is repeated within the same chapter, and when the French text is deemed sufficiently clear on its own for a reader with limited knowledge of the French language. All translations are my own, and these translations were undertaken with the sole aim of assisting the reader's comprehension of the cited text. Clarity of meaning has therefore been prioritized over matters of style (inasmuch as they can be separated), and the translations tend sometimes towards the literal, sometimes towards the explanatory. For a more enjoyable and well-rounded translation of the text in question (in most cases), a reader is directed towards the complete published translations of these works.

Introduction

The study of diaries has suffered from a strange oversight: whereas the real and fictional forms of autobiography, biography, or letter-writing, are generally considered to have developed in tandem and in a process of mutual imitation, the equivalent relationship between real and fictional diaries has scarcely even been acknowledged.[1] This book follows developments in both real and fictional diaries, and their frequently complex interactions, in twentieth-century French writing. The aim is not to demonstrate the existence of this relationship—it will soon appear self-evident—but to gain a clearer, fuller understanding of the significance of diary-writing as a form of life-writing, and in the literary sphere more broadly. It has emerged over the course of this study that, while the popularity of the diary in France has waxed and waned, and its forms and practices have varied, it has played a perennially important role in calling into question the very nature of the 'author' and of the literary *œuvre*. Paradoxically, this questioning is often more a result of a diary's presentation or status (its relation to an author's other works or diaries, its function in constructing a textual author-figure, its claims upon a form of literary status) than of its actual content. Having said this, there are a number of authors whose finest work is contained within their diaries (again, either real or fictional).[2]

The terms 'real' and 'fictional' each pose problems of their own, which I shall soon address, but the first step towards the desired clarity and understanding is to identify what we mean by the 'diary' itself. Indeed, the diary's many permutations seem to spread into several neighbouring genres, whether it is judged on the criterion of its writing practice (regular or sporadic, with lengthy or brief entries, written in any number of different formats), or that of its subject matter (past, present or future events, introspection, philosophical or artistic reflection, social commentary), or of its principal function for the diarist (confession, self-portrait, chronicle, a tool for reflection, or a literary exercise), not to mention the intentions

---

[1] With regard to autobiography, see Philippe Lejeune, *L'Autobiographie en France* (Paris: Armand Colin, 1998), pp. 42–3. For biography, see Ann Jefferson, *Biography and the Question of Literature in France* (Oxford: OUP, 2007), especially Part V, 'Inwardness, Experience and the Turn to Fiction', pp. 219–64. For the equivalent relationship for letters, see Ian Watt, 'Private Experience and the Novel', in *The Rise of the Novel: Studies in Defoe, Richardson and Fielding* (London: Chatto & Windus, 1974), pp. 174–207, and Deirdre Dawson, *Voltaire's Correspondence: An Epistolary Novel* (New York: Peter Lang, 1994), pp. 16–19.

[2] Henri-Frédéric Amiel (1821–1881), Marie Bashkirtseff (1858–1884), and Renaud Camus (1946–) are all undoubtedly best known for their publication of real diaries. André Gide (1869–1951) and Valery Larbaud (1881–1957) are the most egregious examples of authors for whom diaries are central to their novelistic writing.

or attitude accompanying its possible publication (be it anthumous or posthumous). For example, Jean-Paul Sartre's *Carnets de la drôle de guerre* contain a long retrospective, autobiographical account, while Maria van Rysselberghe's *Cahiers de la Petite Dame* provide a biographical account of André Gide, and Eugénie de Guérin's *Journal* is primarily addressed to her brother in the manner of a written correspondence. Conversely, Philippe Lejeune suggests that his own interest in autobiography was partly due to the presence of a diaristic element within autobiographical works (the ongoing present-tense perspective of the writer).[3]

Not only is the diary nebulous, but writing in English about French diaries involves an additional problem of translation, which has contributed to the existence of a large gulf between Anglophone and Francophone criticism on this topic. Among Anglophone critics, the inclusive, ahistorical, universalizing concept of the 'diary' is epitomized by Alexandra Johnson's claim that 'the instinct to record daily life and thoughts is as ancient as handwriting'.[4] The category is often extended far beyond canonical Anglophone diaries such as those by Samuel Pepys (written 1659–69), James Boswell (written 1762–95), and the diary novels of Daniel Defoe, to include Sei Shōnagon's *The Pillow Book* from late tenth- to early eleventh-century Japan, and the *Meditations* of the second-century Roman emperor Marcus Aurelius.[5] In contrast, Francophone critics generally consider that the 'journal intime' (this term remains dominant, despite the existence of variants such as 'journal littéraire', 'journal personnel', 'journal de voyage', or 'journal de bord' [logbook]) emerged around the end of the eighteenth century, as a form associated with—if not strictly defined by—secrecy, psychological interiority, and reflection. The linguistic situation causes blind spots for both parties: Anglophone critics tend to underestimate the specificity of diary-writing in France and the influence exerted on Francophone diarists by a widely read canon of diaries published in French (both real and fictional), whereas Francophone critics neglect the broader history of forms of daily writing, and the interconnections between

[3] Jean-Paul Sartre, *Les Carnets de la drôle de guerre: septembre 1939–mars 1940*, in *Les Mots et autres écrits autobiographiques*, ed. by Jean-François Louette (Paris: Gallimard, Bibl. de la Pléiade, 2010), pp. 143–679, pp. 351–71. Maria van Rysselberghe, *Les Cahiers de la Petite Dame: notes pour l'histoire authentique d'André Gide*, 4 vols (Paris: Gallimard, 1973–77). For the addressees of Eugénie de Guérin's *journal*, see Françoise Simonet-Tenant, *Journal personnel et correspondance (1785–1939) ou les affinités électives* (Louvain-la-Neuve: Academia-Bruylant, 2009), p. 77. Philippe Lejeune, *Signes de vie: le pacte autobiographique 2* (Paris: Seuil, 2005), p. 64 (Lejeune gives the example of Michel Leiris's 'tressage poétique d'une écriture sans fin' [poetic interweaving of a writing process without end]).

[4] Alexandra Johnson, *A Brief History of Diaries: From Pepys to Blogs* (London: Hesperus, 2011), p. 17.

[5] Pepys' diaries were first published in 1825. Boswell published travel diaries in 1768 (Corsica) and 1785 (the Hebrides, with Samuel Johnson), and his other diaries were published from 1950 onwards. Defoe's *Robinson Crusoe* contains a fictional diary (1719), and *A Journal of the Plague Year* (1722) is a fictional account apparently based on a diary. Sei Shōnagon's *The Pillow Book* (*Les Notes de chevet* or *Les Notes de l'oreiller* in French) were first published in substantial translations in English and French in 1928. The view that Marcus Aurelius's *Meditations* are the 'first surviving diary' (Alexandra Johnson, *A Brief History of Diaries*, p. 18) was promulgated by Gilbert Murray's work *The Four Stages of Greek Religion* (New York: Columbia University Press, 1912), which projects onto this text several of the persistent, mythic ideals of the diary: 'Marcus possessed [...] the power of writing down what was in his heart just as it was, not obscured by any consciousness of the presence of witnesses or any striving after effect. [...] He has revealed himself in that short personal notebook almost as much as the great inspired egotists, Rousseau and St. Augustine.' (159).

diarists writing in different languages. My own approach to the problem is to make a virtue of necessity, by using the term 'journal intime' to denote the relative coherence and historical reality of this form in French writing (which is the focus of this book), and the terms 'diary' and 'diary-writing' to denote the broader formal possibilities of daily writing practices.

Clearly, such generic categories are blunt instruments, and the texts under discussion will be considered precisely because they are exceptional cases, drawing on established forms but treating them in new ways, towards new, programmatic ends. For example, André Gide's *Journal 1889–1939* (1939) will be examined as the unprecedented publication of an almost lifelong *journal intime* by the author himself as part of his literary *œuvre* (in Chapter 4), and Annie Ernaux's *Journal du dehors* (1993) is considered as a project that adopts the forms of the *journal intime* to observe the lives of complete strangers (Chapter 7).[6] There is, however, a common feature among *journaux intimes*, and diaries more broadly, which greatly facilitates the task at hand. Just as Philippe Lejeune found that autobiographies consistently include a statement of their particular 'pacte autobiographique',[7] diarists too unfailingly address the terms of their own writing projects, often with great lucidity, and with frequent reappraisals as the project develops in new directions. The terms of these writing projects may be even more exceptional when they use the experimental potential of fiction, such as in the case of the complex and structurally unstable *journal intime* in Gide's 1895 work *Paludes* (Chapter 2).

This book therefore follows the history of diary-writing in France through a series of chapter-length readings of texts, by Gide, Raymond Queneau, Roland Barthes, and Annie Ernaux. These texts have been selected, not because they are the most typical or well-known diaries from the period in question (indeed, some of the texts by Barthes have only recently become available in posthumous publications), but because of the light that they cast on particular historical developments.[8] The chapters can be read individually, as relatively free-standing studies of the texts and issues at hand, and some have already given rise to separate article publications,[9] but in total they allow an overview of diary-writing across the twentieth century, which I discuss in a concluding chapter. However, before

---

[6] Annie Ernaux, *Journal du dehors* (Paris: Gallimard, 1993).

[7] Lejeune, *L'Autobiographie en France*, pp. 17–18.

[8] I have no desire to set out a canon, either for real or fictional diaries, which would inevitably involve making assumptions regarding the literary status or a generic narrative of these works. Bibliographies of French diary novels can be found in Valerie Raoul, *The French Fictional Journal: Fictional Narcissism/Narcissistic Fiction* (Toronto: University of Toronto Press, 1980), pp. 114–15; Lorna Martens, *The Diary Novel* (Cambridge: Cambridge University Press, 1985), pp. 282–6; and Yasusuke Oura, 'Étude sur le roman journal français' *Études de Langue et Littérature Françaises*, 52 (1988), pp. 100–17, pp. 116–17. A list of real published diaries is found in Michel Braud, *La Forme des jours: pour une poétique du journal personnel* (Paris: Seuil, 2006), pp. 297–306. More comprehensive bibliographies of real diaries (and other forms of life-writing) can be found in the 'Inventaire des inventaires' maintained by Philippe Lejeune at <http://www.autopacte.org/inventaire2.html> [consulted 29 February 2016].

[9] Sam Ferguson, 'Metalepsis and the Auteur Supposé in Raymond Queneau's *Œuvre Complètes de Sally Mara*', *French Studies*, 66/2 (2012), pp. 178–92. 'André Gide's *Paludes*: A Diary Novel?', *French Studies*, 68/1 (2014), pp. 34–47. 'Forgetting Gide: A Study of Barthes's "Ursuppe"', *Barthes Studies*, 1 (2015), pp. 17–34. 'Diary-Writing and the Return of Gide in Barthes's "Vita Nova"', in *Deliberations: The Journals of Roland Barthes* (= *Textual Practice*, 30/2 (2016)), pp. 241–66.

embarking on this history, I will need to address two preliminary tasks. The first is to take account of the valuable critical work that has already been undertaken in this area, in spite of the shortcomings mentioned above. Previous studies of the *journal intime* by Francophone critics have already indicated some of the key phases in its historical development, and the critical issues that it has raised, while existing studies of the diary novel (mostly formalist and international in their approach) have developed some useful critical tools. I shall summarize the ways in which I draw on these earlier studies, while also suggesting a new way of thinking about the *journal intime* in parallel with the history of autobiographical writing.

The second task is to address the most pressing theoretical issues that are raised by the history of the *journal intime*. Most fundamentally, the diary will be considered in terms of an essential 'otherness', which might well be a condition of all language, but here becomes particularly problematic. The history of the *journal intime* is accompanied by a persistent, comforting myth, of a self-identical, self-knowing subject writing spontaneously and expressing a unified 'self', but this assumption is found to be untenable even when a diary is written in absolute privacy without any thought of publication, and all the more so when it is addressed to particular imagined or real-life 'others' (God, the diarist's self addressed as 'tu' or 'vous', perhaps a sibling, as in Eugénie de Guérin's case), or when it is published and encounters a generalized literary 'other', or again when an author fabricates a diary attributed to a fictional character (this relationship is manifested with great complexity in Gide's *Les Faux-monnayeurs* and *Le Journal des Faux-monnayeurs*, discussed in Chapter 4). Evidently, it will be necessary to qualify the terms 'real' and 'fictional', since a 'real diary' cannot be assumed to possess an absolutely objective truth or authenticity (although some diarists have espoused these as ideals to aspire to), and the concept of 'fiction' has at times been extended to include any construction of a self in writing (I shall use the term in a more narrow sense). In approaching the 'author' and the '*œuvre*', I shall avoid attributing any fixed meaning to these terms, for the very reason that they are both functional elements of literary discourse whose nature is repeatedly contested by the *journal intime*. They should be considered a part of the object of the present study, rather than a critical tool in themselves. In order to examine how this contestation is carried out, I shall adopt the Derridean concept of the 'supplement', which provides a useful model for understanding the common structure by which a published *journal intime* acts as a destabilizing addition to the supposed self-sufficiency of a literary *œuvre* or author-figure. Finally, the role of gender in diary-writing must be considered, particularly in comparison with its role in autobiographical writing (which has previously been studied in much greater depth). Unlike the other theoretical issues already raised, gender will not be central to the readings that make up this study, but it must nonetheless be acknowledged as a factor in all these diarists' self-constructions.

PREVIOUS APPROACHES TO DIARY-WRITING

Given the absence of any synoptic approach to real and fictional diaries in previous studies, this survey necessarily follows the development of two separate strands of research, which have been conducted largely in isolation from one another. There is a considerable body of work on what is perceived to be a coherent and relatively independent tradition of French diary-writing, largely concerning the history of the *journal intime*, whereas fictional diaries have been treated by a more limited number of critics, mostly Anglophone, and with reference to an international collection of diary novels (mostly in English, French, and German).

Real Diary-Writing in France

A wave of commentary appeared after a series of diary publications in France in the 1880s and again after the 1939 publication of Gide's *Journal 1889–1939*, but a more modern and systematic treatment of the *journal intime* began after the end of the Second World War. Much of the critical discussion at this time was centred on the recently published French translation of the diaries of Franz Kafka,[10] but the first book-length study of the *journal intime* in general was Michèle Leleu's *Les Journaux intimes* in 1952.[11] Unfortunately, despite the presence of some insights into individual diarists (particularly Charles Du Bos), this work suffers from its heavy-handed application of the dubious science of *caractérologie*. It considers various diarists in terms of their conformity to normative character types ('nerveux', 'sentimental', 'passionné pré-émotif'), and in doing so it uncritically reproduces a certain stereotype: '[le journal intime] doit [...] nous faire pénétrer dans l'intimité de son auteur qui l'écrit pour lui-même et qui livre ainsi sa personnalité' [the *journal intime* must [...] allow us to enter the private space of its author who writes it for himself and thereby reveals his personality] (5). This is the familiar, persistent myth of the *journal intime*, in which the authentic representation or expression of a diarist's essential personality is guaranteed by the privacy (and presumed absence of 'otherness') of the writing process. Leleu is more lucid, however, in her awareness that her exclusive focus on the published diaries of authors and artists neglects 'la masse énorme des journaux encore inédits' [the enormous mass of still unpublished *journaux intimes*]. The efforts of Philippe Lejeune have since made the latter more accessible (as discussed later), but most critical works after Leleu's are primarily concerned with published *journaux intimes*. While acknowledging that much work could be done on the 'masse énorme' of diary-writing that remains unpublished, I will in fact generally maintain the same focus on published diaries, since I am examining the *journal intime* in its relation to literary history.

A much firmer grounding for study of the *journal intime* was provided by Alain Girard's comprehensive and authoritative work *Le Journal intime* in 1963.[12] The work's broadly sociological approach links the history of the *journal intime* with a far-reaching change in 'la notion de la personne' at the turn of the nineteenth century (vii), and establishes a generic narrative for French diary-writing separate

[10] Franz Kafka, *La Colonie pénitentiaire: nouvelles, suivies d'un Journal intime*, trans. by Jean Starobinski (Paris: Egloff, 1945). Franz Kafka, *Journal intime, suivi de Esquisse d'une autobiographie*, trans. by Pierre Klossowski (Paris: Grasset, 1945). The various critical responses to these publications are discussed in the introduction to Part II.

[11] Michèle Leleu, *Les Journaux intimes* (Paris: PUF, 1952).

[12] Alain Girard, *Le Journal intime* (Paris: PUF, 1963).

from other national traditions (although he acknowledges an influence from Goethe and Byron, 58):

> Les origines du journal intime peuvent être exactement situées dans le temps. Ce nouveau genre d'écrit apparaît à la charnière de deux siècles, à la fin d'un monde et au commencement d'un autre, aux alentours des années 1800, avant l'éclosion romantique. Sa naissance est le résultat d'une rencontre entre les deux courants dominants qui imprègnent la pensée et la sensibilité de l'époque: d'un côté l'exaltation du sentiment, et la vogue des confessions, dans le sillage de Rousseau, de l'autre l'ambition des idéologues de fonder la science de l'homme sur l'observation, en plaçant à l'origine de l'entendement la sensation, à la suite de Locke, Helvétius et Condillac. (ix–x)

> [The origins of the *journal intime* can be precisely situated in time. This new genre of writing appears at the juncture of two centuries, at the end of one world and the beginning of another, around the first decade of the nineteenth century, before the rise of Romanticism. Its birth is the result of a meeting of the two dominant currents shaping the thought and sensibility of the age: on the one hand the elevation of sentiment and the fashion for confessions, under the influence of Rousseau, on the other, the ambition of the ideologues to found the science of man on observation, by placing the senses as the source of understanding, in the wake of Locke, Helvétius and Condillac.]

Girard's historical account of the *journal intime*, once again concerned almost exclusively with famous writers, intellectuals, and artists (vii),[13] argues that it continued to bear the traces of these first influences, and culminated in the landmark of Gide's *Journal 1889–1939* as 'l'exemple le plus significatif et le plus complet de [la] transformation du journal en un genre littéraire' [the most significant and complete example of the transformation of the *journal intime* into a literary genre] (90).

This transformation leads Girard to discuss the perennial question of the diary's status as literature, which here becomes an impasse. For Girard, a 'genre littéraire' must by definition be published (viii), but publication is not in itself sufficient for a diary to be considered as literature, and the *journaux intimes* that diarists wrote without any thought of an eventual publication must be considered as mere 'documents' or 'témoignages' [testimonies] (xxi). Furthermore, he associates literature with the terms 'art', 'ouvrage', and 'œuvre', implying a degree of deliberate linguistic crafting (viii–ix), whereas he assumes the *journal intime* to be an essentially spontaneous creation (here we see the familiar myth once again):

> Si un journal intime cède à quelque convention qu'il soit, n'est-on pas fondé à le récuser tout entier? Il n'est plus ce flot intérieur, jailli de la personne, tel que nous avons décrit pour quelques représentants du genre, mais une construction de leur esprit, pareille à toutes les constructions de l'esprit. / Parler de l'art à propos du journal

---

[13] Girard discusses the following diarists at length: Maine de Biran, Joseph Joubert, Benjamin Constant, Stendhal, Maurice de Guérin, Alfred de Vigny, Eugène Delacroix, and Henri-Frédéric Amiel.

intime serait donc une sorte de non-sens, sauf à renier sa spécificité et ce qui lui confère une valeur propre. (598)

[If a *journal intime* conforms to any convention at all, should we not reject it entirely? It is then no longer that interior stream, springing from the source of one's personhood, as we described it with regard to certain representatives of the genre, but rather a product of the intellect, similar to all other products of the intellect. / To speak of the *journal intime* as art would therefore be a sort of contradiction, unless we were to deny its specificity and the very thing that confers on it its particular value.]

The work concludes with the paradox that 'l'art, ici, consiste dans l'absence de tout art, dans la spontanéité avec laquelle la personne exprime sa vérité' [art, here, consists of the very absence of any art, and in the sponaneity with which the person expresses their truth], and so the diary reveals 'non pas un auteur mais un homme' [not an author, but a man] (599).

Girard's work left an invaluable legacy for criticism on real diary-writing, but also perpetuated certain problems: his historical account of the *journal intime* is excessively isolated both from international influences and from earlier writing in French, while the question of the diary's literary status is impeded by rigid stereotypes of a published, linguistically crafted *genre littéraire* and of the diary as a purely private and spontaneous form of writing. A conference in 1975 on 'Le Journal intime et ses formes littéraires' demonstrated Girard's continuing influence, but some new directions were indicated by Michel Gilot's paper 'Quelques pas vers le journal intime' and the discussion which followed it.[14] He adds to Girard's history of the *journal intime* by pointing to a relationship with earlier forms, including 'mémoires, journaux de voyage, lettres d'amour, feuilles de spectateurs [theatregoers' notes], examens de conscience' (3), and by suggesting that its emergence at the point of a 'crise de la littérature' [crisis in literature] may have imprinted it with a continuing desire to 'faire éclater les cadres traditionnels de la littérature' [explode the traditional structures of literature] (16). He even speculates briefly about a possible influence from fictional works upon real diary-writing (22), referring to Philippe Lejeune's claim in *L'Autobiographie en France* that novels were a major influence on the birth of real autobiographical writing.[15] In the ensuing discussion, a comment by Pierre Reboul also challenged the view that the *journal intime* is defined by its secrecy:

Le journal intime se constitue non pas comme un dialogue de soi avec soi, mais de soi avec l'autre; il y a une présence imaginaire de l'autre à l'intérieur du journal. Il me semble donc que de cette présence imaginaire de l'autre jusqu'à sa publication, il n'y a pas de *hiatus*, mais une sorte de continuité. (21)

[The *journal intime* is constituted not as a dialogue between self and self, but between self and other; there is an imaginary presence of the other within the *journal intime*. It

---

[14] Michel Gilot, 'Quelques pas vers le journal intime', in *Le Journal intime et ses formes littéraires: actes du colloque de septembre 1975 (Grenoble)*, ed. by Victor del Litto (Geneva: Droz, 1978), pp. 1–25.
[15] Lejeune, *L'Autobiographie en France*, pp. 42–3.

therefore seems to me that between this imaginary presence of the other and the text's publication, there is not a hiatus, but a sort of continuity.]

This observation, rather innocuous in appearance, has proven to be extremely useful in subsequent discussions of the diary's literary status, and I shall draw out the implications of this essential 'otherness' of diary-writing (including the *journal intime*).

Béatrice Didier's 1976 work *Le Journal intime* opened a second line of enquiry from that of Girard's historical work, a formal approach founded on 'sociocritique', 'psychanalyse', and 'étude des structures'.[16] Didier changes the focus of criticism from the *intimité* of the diary (whether it refers to the diary's secrecy, or its psychological introspection, or merely differentiates it from the newspaper, 8–9), towards the temporal aspect of the diary denoted by the term *journal* ('le diarisme, la marque du temps, l'au-jour-le-jour' [the diaristic aspect, the marker of time, the texture of day-to-day life], 16). This change in focus does, however, lead to a different historical account of diary-writing in France, stretching back at least to the fifteenth century, attached to a rise in the power of the *petite noblesse* and the *bourgeoisie*, and practised by diarists outside Girard's canon of writers and intellectuals. Didier also proposes a different attitude towards the diary's literary status, challenging its mythic claim to the qualities of spontaneity and authenticity:

Il y a des écrivains qui n'hésitent pas à remanier profondément leur texte, surtout s'ils le destinent à une publication: ils retranchent, ajoutent, améliorent le style. Faut-il le regretter? Le journal est pour nous, essentiellement un texte, beaucoup plus qu'un témoignage biographique. En tant que texte, il nous intéresse à tous ses niveaux, et même si le souci de vérité historique disparaît tout à fait. (20–21)

[There are writers who do not hesitate to make profound changes to their text, especially if they have its publication in view: they cut, add, and improve the style. Is this to be regretted? In our view, the *journal intime* is essentially a text, far more than it is a biographical testimony. As a text, it interests us in every respect, even if the concern for historical truth disappears entirely.]

Whereas Girard insists on the spontaneity and truthfulness of the *journal intime* in revealing the 'homme', Didier allows for its artistic elaboration, and situates it relative to an author's *œuvre* as 'le banc d'essai, le réservoir, le juge, la jauge, etc.' [testing ground, reservoir, judge, gauge] (46). Like Gilot, she suggests that its position at the margins of unequivocally literary works allows it to contest the established 'hiérarchie des genres littéraires' (192–3). Owing to this attitude, she is far more comfortable than Girard in discussing self-consciously literary twentieth-century diarists, such as Paul Léautaud, André Gide, Charles Du Bos, and Julien Green.

One further history of the diary in France, Pierre Pachet's idiosyncratic work *Les Baromètres de l'âme* (1990),[17] nuances many of the claims made in Girard's work. Pachet once again charts the rise of the *journal intime* from the late eighteenth

---

16 Béatrice Didier, *Le Journal intime* (Paris: PUF, 1976), pp. 7–8.
17 Pierre Pachet, *Les Baromètres de l'âme: naissance du journal intime* (Paris: Hatier, 1990).

century, but emphasizes its religious character as 'un écrit dans lequel quelqu'un manifeste un souci quotidien de son âme' [a writing in which someone manifests a daily concern for their soul] (13), and makes a distinction between the attitudes of Catholic and Protestant diarists (34). Surprisingly, he insists even more strongly than Girard that the *journal intime* is essentially private and secret, even going as far as to discount Stendhal, Jules Michelet, and Victor Hugo from his canon of diarists on this criterion. Given his focus on the essential secrecy of the *journal intime*, he ends his historical account at the major 'date charnière' [pivotal date] of 1887–88, when a wave of diary publications made it apparent that an author's diary would now probably come to be published sooner or later (124).[18] This shift towards a more self-conscious, potentially literary use of the *journal intime* is the starting point for my own study, and I shall discuss its significance further in the introduction to Part I.

Like Girard, Pachet's history is one of 'grands auteurs' (12), but he carefully addresses the problems of considering *journaux intimes* in terms of 'l'histoire de la littérature' (9) and as part of an author's *œuvre* (60). First, he presents convincing evidence that diaries were circulated and imitated within social circles from early in the nineteenth century, thereby nuancing Girard's account by which the *journal intime* became a published, deliberately crafted *genre littéraire* only in the twentieth century. Furthermore, Pachet echoes Pierre Reboul's claim that diarists' very use of language already places them in a public space, and constitutes 'une sorte de publication intime que la publication effective, si elle arrive un jour, ne fera que répercuter' [a sort of private publication which an actual publication, if it should occur some day, would only repeat] (49–52). Finally, if it is anachronistic for modern critics to consider early *journaux intimes* as part of the author's *œuvre*, the modern inclination to elevate the *intime* to the level of *littérature* is a consequence of the projects undertaken by these early *intimistes* (60–1).

Besides the historical and formal approaches to diary-writing in France, a third approach has emerged which considers diaries in the broader context of life-writing, particularly inviting comparison of diaries with the neighbouring form of autobiography. Most notably, Philippe Lejeune played an important role in establishing autobiography as an object of literary criticism with his 1975 work *Le Pacte autobiographique*,[19] and later worked extensively on diaries. Some of the

---

[18] Pachet mentions Constant's and Baudelaire's diaries published in 1887, and Stendhal's in 1888, but 1887 also saw the first volumes of diaries by Bashkirtseff and the Goncourt brothers, and the second volume of Amiel's *Fragments d'un journal intime*. More broadly, there was a considerable growth in 'littérature personnelle' at this time, as described here (with derision) by Brunetière: 'Tout le monde sait en effet que, depuis quelque temps, il n'est bruit partout autour de nous que de *Mémoires*, de *Journaux* et de *Correspondances*. On dirait que nos auteurs, après avoir parcouru le monde, n'y ayant rien trouvé de plus intéressant qu'eux-mêmes, n'imaginent pas aussi qu'il y ait rien de plus curieux pour nous.' [Indeed, everyone knows that, for some time now, we have heard talk of nothing but memoirs, *journaux intimes* and correspondence. It seems as if our authors, having searched throughout the world and found nothing as interesting as themselves, imagine that their selves will be of the greatest interest to us too.]; Ferdinand de Brunetière, 'La Littérature personnelle', *La Revue des deux mondes*, 85 (1888), pp. 433–52, p. 434.

[19] Philippe Lejeune, *Le Pacte autobiographique*, rev. edn (first published 1975) (Paris: Seuil, 1996).

consequences of this approach can be seen in *Le Moi des demoiselles*,[20] in which Lejeune extends the field of criticism beyond the diaries of *grands auteurs* to include young women's diaries in the nineteenth century. His interest is in the diaries as texts rather than as a historical *témoignage*, and the work is presented as 'un livre militant, qu'on accorde aux écritures ordinaires l'attention qu'elles méritent' [a work of activism, demanding that we pay the attention that is due to ordinary writing] (11). The question of the literary status of diaries is dismissed rather than addressed, and he refers with irony to associated terms such as 'chef-d'œuvre' and 'génie' (11). His most recent book, *Aux Origines du journal personnel*, traces back the origins of diary-writing in France to the late eighteenth century, several decades earlier than either Girard's or Pachet's historical studies.[21] In practical terms, Lejeune has greatly facilitated the study of unpublished autobiographical writing (including diaries) through his role in the creation of the Association pour l'Autobiographie et le Patrimoine Autobiographique in 1992, which allows researchers access to a large archive of 'écritures ordinaires'.[22]

Lejeune also identifies the unusual position that diaries have come to occupy in the modern field of life-writing, dominated by autobiography, that has emerged in France since the 1970s: whereas autobiography's close relationship with fiction has given rise to the hybrid forms of *autofiction* (to which I shall return), diary-writing maintains a stronger adherence to truthfulness, which can now appear naïve or antiquated. In 'Le Journal comme "antifiction"' (2007),[23] Lejeune even claims that the diaristic practice of writing in response to unfolding, unforeseen experience makes any partial fabrication impossible (this has no bearing on the wholly fictional form of the diary novel), and he attributes suggestions of a degree of fictionality in real diary-writing to 'une mystique académique ou mallarméenne de la littérature' [an academic or Mallarméen mysticism of literature] which conflates fiction with concepts of art and literary value (10). He refers here to Mallarmé's pursuit of an idealized, literary *Livre* [Book], which had a strong influence on subsequent debate around the nature of literature (in particular, Barthes made extensive use of this concept in reference to the literary status of the *journal intime*, as discussed in Chapter 6).[24]

Michel Braud's 2006 work *La Forme des jours* makes a formal study of diaries (still mostly concerned with the *journal intime*) and brings important additions to their history in France, but it also takes a different approach from Lejeune to the question of the diary's literary status in the context of life-writing.[25] Referring

[20] Philippe Lejeune, *Le Moi des demoiselles: enquête sur le journal de jeune fille* (Paris: Seuil, 1993).

[21] Philippe Lejeune, *Aux Origines du journal personnel: France, 1750–1815* (Paris: Honoré Champion, 2016).

[22] The work of the association is described in Philippe Lejeune, 'The Story of a French Life-Writing Archive: "Association pour l'Autobiographie et le Patrimoine Autobiographique"', *Forum: Qualitative Social Research* 12/3 (2011).

[23] Philippe Lejeune, 'Le Journal comme « antifiction »', *Poétique*, 149 (2007), pp. 3–14.

[24] The development of this concept in Mallarmé's writing is presented in Bertrand Marchal, 'Notice' for 'Notes en vue du « Livre »', in Stéphane Mallarmé, *Œuvres complètes*, ed. by Bertrand Marchal, 2 vols (Paris: Gallimard, Bibl. de la Pléiade, 1998), I, pp. 1372–83.

[25] Michel Braud, *La Forme des jours: pour une poétique du journal personnel* (Paris: Seuil, 2006).

to Gérard Genette's definition of *littérarité* [literariness] in *Fiction et diction* (1991),[26] Braud first explores the critical position that all *écriture de soi* should be considered as fiction, and therefore as possessing a *littérarité constitutive* (255–6). However, this limited type of fictionality, 'la mise en discours de l'expérience et non l'affirmation de cette expérience comme réalité extralinguistique' [the transformation of experience into discourse rather than the presentation of this experience as a reality outside of language] (266–7), does not warrant the status of *littérature* according to Genette's scheme. Braud therefore justifies the diary's *littérarité conditionnelle* on the grounds of *diction*, or a deliberate artistic crafting and *fonction esthétique* (close to Girard's concept of a literary *œuvre*) found in the 'construction narrative dont le diariste doit inventer la forme, le ton, le langage' [narrative construction for which the diarist must invent the form, tone, and language] (260). In itself, this conclusion seems to reinforce the common attitude towards the diary as the poor cousin of autobiography, which allows far greater scope for the artistic crafting of its 'construction narrative'. But Braud also follows Didier in claiming an additional literary status for the diary based on the very challenge it poses to the characteristics associated with literature (and with autobiography), such as 'la prééminence de la fiction, le récit clos et structuré comme transcription du temps, et la séparation d'avec le langage ordinaire' [the preeminence of fiction, the complete narrative structured as a transcription of time, and the separation from ordinary language] (269–71).

Two more works should be mentioned, which demonstrate the wealth and diversity of recent treatments of real diary-writing in France. Catherine Rannoux's *Les Fictions du journal littéraire* (2004) is concerned, not with fiction in the general sense of 'nonreferential narrative' (to borrow Dorrit Cohn's definition),[27] but with a Lacanian *Imaginaire* that emerges from the diarists' writing.[28] She bases her analysis on the Bakhtinian principle of dialogism, wherein all use of language has an essential otherness relative to the *sujet de l'énonciation*. Against the background of this *hétérogénéité constitutive* she distinguishes the *hétérogénéité représentée* by which diarists attempt to construct a unique authorial-diaristic voice, by assuming certain voices and distancing themselves from others. Her approach is a sophisticated development of Pierre Reboul's passing mention of the 'présence imaginaire de l'autre à l'intérieur du journal',[29] and shows beyond doubt the public and intertextual nature of these (exclusively twentieth-century) diaries, as opposed to being an essentially private or spontaneous form of writing.

Françoise Simonet-Tenant's *Journal personnel et correspondance* (2009) brings diaries into contact with another area of life-writing, the writing and exchange of letters.[30] She shows that the two forms pose many of the same problems to

[26] Gérard Genette, *Fiction et diction: précédé de Introduction à l'architexte* (Paris: Seuil, 2004).

[27] Dorrit Cohn, *The Distinction of Fiction* (Baltimore: Johns Hopkins University Press, 1999), p. 1.

[28] Catherine Rannoux, *Les Fictions du journal littéraire: Paul Léautaud, Jean Malaquais, Renaud Camus* (Geneva: Droz, 2004), pp. 19–20.

[29] Gilot, 'Quelques pas vers le journal intime', p. 21.

[30] Françoise Simonet-Tenant, *Journal personnel et correspondance (1785–1939) ou les affinités électives* (Louvain-la-Neuve: Academia-Bruylant, 2009).

critical study, and also that they have followed an 'histoire imbriquée' [intertwined history] (traced here, as in Girard's work, up to the landmark of Gide's *Journal 1889–1939*), which is incomplete without due attention to these two 'lieux essentiels d'une petite fabrique de l'intime' [essential domains of a little workshop of the *intime*] (9). In fact, this dual focus on diaries and letters leads to a rare discussion of the relation between fictional and nonfictional forms in the early history of the *journal intime*. In novels around the turn of the nineteenth century the boundaries between diaries and letters became extremely unclear, and Simonet-Tenant suggests that epistolary novels such as Rousseau's *La Nouvelle Éloïse* and Goethe's *Die Leiden des jungen Werthers* (published in French translation in 1776) offered a model for early practitioners of the *journal intime*:

> L'on peut raisonnablement penser que les modèles d'écriture offerts par la fiction, où la lettre délaisse l'événementiel mais se fait confidence et expression de tourments intérieurs, n'ont pas été sans influence sur les premières générations de diaristes. (35)
>
> [One might reasonably suppose that the models of writing offered by fiction, in which letter-writting abandons the description of events to become confession and an expression of interior torments, had some influence on the earliest generations of diarists.]

Like Lejeune, Simonet-Tenant places emphasis on diarists beyond the usual canonical, published, male authors, and in particular shows the broad influence of two largely overlooked 'best-sellers du XIXe siècle', Eugénie de Guérin's *Journal et lettres* (1862) and Mme de Craven's *Le Récit d'une sœur* (1866).

The two principal concerns of these critical works, the history of the *journal intime* in France and the question of the diary's literary status, provide useful points of reference for approaching the relation between real and fictional diary-writing. While the circumstances that gave rise to the *journal intime* as a private writing practice remain enigmatic (and I shall suggest a new perspective on this problem shortly), the development of a published genre of *journaux intimes* by authors, artists, and intellectuals over the last two centuries is more clearly established. The increasing circulation of diaries over the nineteenth century culminated in an abundance of publications around 1887–88 (the starting point of my own study). This inaugurated a period of more self-consciously literary diary-writing, which reached some form of conclusion with Gide's publication in 1939 of his *Journal 1889–1939*: the anthumous publication of a lifelong *journal intime* with an unprecedented claim to being a literary *œuvre*. The subsequent decades are a blind spot in the established historical accounts (which I shall address), until the renewed popularity of the *journal intime* in the 1970s amid the more general rise of life-writing, where diaries nonetheless occupy an anomalous position at odds with the prevalence of *autofiction*.

Discussion of the diary's literary status has been hampered by two persistent myths, that of the *journal intime* as a purely spontaneous and private writing practice (dispelled beyond any doubt by Rannoux), and the 'mystique académique ou mallarméenne de la littérature' stereotyped by Lejeune. But it is also an important question precisely because it is part of the diary's history. Diaries in the nineteenth century were published principally as *témoignages* of an author's life which might be used to illuminate their literary work, following the model of published correspondence (as Simonet-Tenant has demonstrated). Some of the diary publications of the 1880s became more popular than the work for which the diarists were already known (notably those of Amiel, Bashkirtseff, and the Goncourt brothers), and so it became apparent that diaries could possess a *littérarité conditionnelle* of their own, dependent on the perceived qualities of their style or *diction* (in Genette's terms). From this point onwards, more experimental diaries claimed a certain literary status in their very contestation of established concepts of literature. This literary, or rather metaliterary status, is acknowledged by Gilot, Didier, and Braud, but is also underestimated, as it is particularly found in the hitherto neglected relations between real and fictional diaries, and between these diaries and other parts of an author's *œuvre*.

Fictional Diaries

The first general study of fictional diaries was Gerald Prince's article 'The Diary Novel: Notes for the Definition of a Sub-Genre' (1975).[31] His primary concern, which has also preoccupied most studies since, is to find a formal definition for a group of texts making up the class of 'the diary novel', as a sub-genre of fiction ('fiction' here is roughly equated with 'the novel'). He succeeds in identifying the following formal traits present in most diary novels: a 'superficial journal shape' (a text divided into separate, individually dated entries), a first-person narrative, a 'narration intercalée' as described by Gérard Genette (where the act of narration alternates with the action of the events being related),[32] and the absence of an intradiegetic narratee (477). However, as he finds exceptions to each of these rules in works that he considers to be diary novels, he concludes that the sub-genre cannot be defined by formal criteria alone, and instead proposes that its essential feature is 'the theme of writing a diary, and its concomitant themes and motifs' (479). It is typical of much of the criticism to follow that Prince stops short of defining the fictional diary by its relation to the ongoing practice and publication of real diaries, owing to his narrow focus on the diary in the context of the novel.

Valerie Raoul's *The French Fictional Journal* (1980) is, as it claims, 'the first full-length analysis' of the subject (i), although it focuses on works in French.[33] Like Prince, Raoul makes a synchronic study of the genre, leading to the creation of a structural model, followed by a reading of the single work that she sees as the 'archetype', which happens to be Jacques Chardonne's *Eva ou le journal interrompu* (1930). Her model is based on Michał Głowiński's principle of 'formal mimetics: an imitation, by means of a given form, of other forms of literary, paraliterary and

[31] Gerald Prince, 'The Diary Novel: Notes for the Definition of a Sub-Genre', *Neophilologus*, 59/4 (1975), pp. 477–81.

[32] Gérard Genette, *Figures III* (Paris: Seuil, 1972), p. 229.

[33] Valerie Raoul, *The French Fictional Journal: Fictional Narcissism/Narcissistic Fiction* (Toronto: University of Toronto Press, 1980), p. i.

extraliterary discourse'.[34] This provides a framework to approach fictional diaries as a structure of two diegetic levels, an imitation of the *journal intime* framed by the fictional reading pact of the novel. The two diegetic levels each have their own codes, and the interest of this genre lies in the way 'the interference of each of those "codes" in the functioning of the other' is used to explore the writing of diaries and of novels, although her emphasis is on the novel (i). The model is presented as a corrective to a tendency of critics to read diary novels as the thinly veiled diaries of the author, but it also proves to be too rigid for a number of works which are relegated to a final section on 'variants'. This group contains novels with a problematic reading pact or an ambiguous relationship with the author's own diary, including Sainte-Beuve's *Vie, poésies et pensées de Joseph Delorme* (1829), Senancour's *Obermann* (1804), Gide's *Cahiers d'André Walter* (1891), Valery Larbaud's *A.O. Barnabooth* (1913), and Françoise Sagan's *Des Bleus à l'âme* (1972).

Hans Porter Abbott's *Diary Fiction: Writing as Action* (1984) is similarly preoccupied by questions of genre, but with its own distinct approach.[35] Whereas he sees the 'diary novel' as a genre, 'a loose confederation of repeatable elements that accompany the device of the diary', he defines 'diary fiction' as the set to which the genre belongs, which only requires the presence of 'the device of the diary' (15). Of these two, he makes diary fiction the object of his study, and criticizes 'genre study' as paying too much attention to the 'purely abstract existence' of genre 'at the expense of the original and distinctive efforts of particular art' (17). However, his own definition for 'diary fiction' becomes extended so far that it includes works of single-writer epistolary fiction published long before any works generally regarded as diary novels. His broad range of readings also leads to unsatisfactory generalizations about differences between a fatalistic 'European' tradition of diary fiction in opposition to 'the English gift for the moral and practical life' (34).

Lorna Martens's *The Diary Novel* (1985) is the first explicitly historical treatment of the subject, and casts more light on the genre by treating it as a historical phenomenon rather than as a synchronic typological system.[36] She is more aware than earlier critics of the diary novel's multiple points of reference, including different types of real diary-writing (travel diaries, Puritan diaries, ships' logs) and contemporary trends in fictional writing (especially the epistolary novel). She finds that the ongoing history of real diaries has provided 'a continuously present and ever new point of departure' for the diary novel (25), in contrast with Raoul's view that the novels invoke a static 'stereotype of the journal intime'.[37] The temporal and geographical scope of her study, covering two hundred years of diary novels in France, Germany, and Britain, necessarily sacrifices depth for breadth, but provides a useful historical framework for further study. It is in the twentieth century that problems emerge in her history. Given the importance of

---

[34] Michał Głowiński, 'On the First-Person Novel', *New Literary History*, 9/1 (1977), pp. 103–14, p. 106.
[35] Hans Porter Abbott, *Diary Fiction: Writing as Action* (Ithaca: Cornell University Press, 1984).
[36] Lorna Martens, *The Diary Novel* (Cambridge: Cambridge University Press, 1985).
[37] Raoul, *The French Fictional Journal*, p. 95.

real diaries as a continuing model for diary novels, her claim that diary novels after the First World War either 'trade atavistically on the credit of the *journal intime*' or 'use the diary form as device' (189) seems not to square with the fact that more real diaries than ever were being published. She also mentions the existence in the twentieth century of 'works that are neither factual nor fictional, or both, or in some way obscure the distinction between the categories' (31), but fails to explore this phenomenon, partly owing to her adoption of Raoul's narrative model with its rigid separation between real and fictional diaries.

The work of two critics, Jean Rousset and Yasusuke Oura, will demonstrate the relative paucity and isolation of studies within France of fictional diaries. Rousset's *Le Lecteur intime* (1986) is primarily a study of intradiegetic narratees, but leads to a discussion of the *journal intime* as a genre and the origins of the fictional *journal intime*.[38] Unable to account for the emergence of the *journal intime* independently at the hands of several authors before any examples had been published, Rousset finds that 'les choses se passent comme si ces pionniers naissaient de rien' [it is as though these pioneers appeared out of nowhere] (14). He then creates a surprising generic narrative whereby Victor Hugo's *Le Dernier jour d'un condamné* (1829), fortuitously combining the three formal elements of first-person narrative, *narration intercalée*, and an absence of intradiegetic narratee, becomes the origin of both real and fictional *journaux intimes*: 'Voilà énoncés en raccourci les traits propres à ce genre que l'on appellera "journal intime", comme si Hugo, en les faisant expérimenter par son rédacteur imaginaire, définissait à l'avance l'entreprise des diaristes à venir' [Here we find in brief the essential features of this genre that will come to be known as the *journal intime*, as if Hugo, by making his imaginary writer test them out, were defining in advance the project of future diarists] (209). While it is interesting that he considers the influence of fictional forms on real diary-writing, his argument is entirely undermined by the existence of both real and fictional diaries earlier than Hugo's novel.

Yasusuke Oura defended his thesis on French diary novels at Paris VII in 1986, published an article on the role of editorial prefaces in 1987, and set out his general approach to the genre in an article in 1988 (published in Japan).[39] In this last article he comments that only Anglophone researchers had so far treated diary novels as an 'ensemble', naming Prince, Raoul, and Abbott (100), and largely follows their approach. He sees the diary novel as a category within the class of the novel, divided into sub-genres according to their themes (103). He defines the genre by the same three formal traits that are remarked elsewhere (first-person narrative, *narration intercalée*, absence of intradiegetic narratee), but whereas Prince concludes that a formal definition is unsatisfactory, Oura merely remarks that it is difficult to marry diary form with the demands of the novel. Oura's principal contribution is a recognition of the importance of paratext to the

[38] Jean Rousset, *Le Lecteur intime: de Balzac au journal* (Paris: Corti, 1986).

[39] Yasusuke Oura, 'Introduction aux romans journaux français' (unpublished doctoral thesis, Paris VII, 1986). Yasusuke Oura, 'Roman journal et mise en scène « éditoriale »', *Poétique*, 69 (1987), pp. 5–20. Yasusuke Oura, 'Étude sur le roman journal français', pp. 100–17.

diary novel, but he stops short of the implications of his analysis, that this space which mediates between the diegetic levels of real author and fictional diarist is used to problematize the relationship between these two figures. He concludes instead that a mixture of fact and fiction is undesirable (19).

There is a general consensus in these works as to the formal definition and functioning of diary narrative as a novelistic device, and some useful suggestions concerning its history in a French and international novelistic tradition. There is also a common failure, even reluctance, to pursue the relationship of these fictional diaries with real diary-writing. Although several critics acknowledge the existence of this relationship in the guise of the 'theme of writing a diary' (Prince), the novel's formal mimesis of the *journal intime* (Raoul), or reference to the real diary as an 'ever new point of departure' (Martens), it is subsequently dismissed as relating to a fixed 'stereotype of the journal intime'. Nonetheless, the very discomfort of these critics in treating the works that they find inconvenient, the variants to Raoul's model and those that complicate the distinction between fact and fiction, indicates the direction to be followed in my own study. This does not concern a mixture of truth and fiction in the process of composition (which Lejeune considers almost impossible in the diary), but in the paratextual presentation of the works (discussed by Oura), their reading pact (to which I shall return), and their relation to the author's real diaries.

MY OWN APPROACH

The Early History of the *journal intime*

Although my own study takes Pachet's pivotal date of 1887–88 as its starting point, it will be useful to address briefly the emergence of the *journal intime* in France, in order to identify those elements that continue to be relevant to its development in the twentieth century. My aim is not to contest the established criticism on this issue (in fact I draw heavily on works by Girard, Pachet, and Lejeune) but rather to emphasize the fundamental relationship that exists between the *journal intime* and autobiography. In short, the two forms owe their existence to the same set of social, cultural, and intellectual circumstances, yet they are almost diametrically opposed in their initial conception, in a way that frequently brings them into contact throughout their parallel histories.

All the various explanations offered for the emergence of the *journal intime*—a change in 'la notion de la personne' (Girard), religious practices of introspection and confession (Pachet), and the growth of the 'intime' (Simonet-Tenant, Watt)—are also relevant as factors in the emergence of autobiography, which is commonly dated from the publication of Rousseau's *Confessions* in 1782 (for the sake of brevity I shall focus exclusively on nonfictional forms).[40] Furthermore, they can all be seen as manifestations of a broader shift at this time, described by Michel

[40] Jean-Jacques Rousseau, *Les Confessions*, in *Œuvres complètes I: Les Confessions et autres textes autobiographiques*, ed. by Bernard Gagnebin and Marcel Raymond (Paris: Gallimard, Bibl. de

Foucault in *Les Mots et les choses*, which concerns the epistemological foundations of all discourse and knowledge: he considers that the end of the eighteenth century marks the end of the Classical era, characterized by discourses of 'représentation' and 'classifications intemporelles', and the beginning of our own (still continuing) modernity, in which 'une historicité profonde pénètre au cœur des choses, les isole et les définit dans leur cohérence propre' [a profound historicity suffuses the very heart of things, isolates them and defines them with their particular coherence].[41] This new episteme also places 'l'homme' or 'la personne' at the centre of the field of knowledge, giving rise to 'toutes les facilités d'une "anthropologie", entendue comme réflexion générale, mi-positive, mi-philosophique, sur l'homme' [all the facile solutions of an 'anthropology', understood as a general reflection, half-empirical, half-philosophical, on man] (15).

The epistemological shift described by Foucault transcends any given discipline or field of knowledge, but it is noticeable that autobiographical writers from Rousseau onwards, when setting out the terms of their own writing project in 'pactes autobiographiques', frequently use analogies from the natural sciences that were then most authoritative or in vogue.[42] Rousseau's first statement of intent in *Les Confessions* gives some indication of his scientific aspirations ('Je veux donner à mes semblables un homme dans toute la vérité de la nature' [I wish to present a man to my peers in all the truth of nature], 5), but a fuller account of the epistemological basis of his project is provided by the 'préambule du manuscrit de Neuchâtel' (not included in the definitive text):

J'ai remarqué souvent que, même parmi ceux qui se piquent le plus de connoître les hommes, chacun ne connoit guéres que soi, s'il est vrai même que quelqu'un se connoisse; car comment bien déterminer un être par les seuls rapports qui sont en lui-même, et sans le comparer avec rien? Cependant cette connoissance imparfaite qu'on a de soi est le seul moyen qu'on employe à connoître les autres. [...]

Sur ces remarques j'ai résolu de faire faire à mes lecteurs un pas de plus dans la connoissance des hommes, en les tirant s'il est possible de cette règle unique et fautive de juger toujours du cœur d'autrui par le sien; tandis qu'au contraire il faudroit souvent pour connoître le sien même, commencer par lire dans celui d'autrui. Je veux tâcher que pour apprendre à s'apprécier, on puisse avoir du moins une piéce de comparaison; que chacun puisse connoitre soi et un autre, et cet autre ce sera moi.[43]

[I have often remarked that, even among those who pride themselves on their understanding of their fellow men, each person barely knows anyone but himself, if it is even true that one knows oneself; for how can one judge a being only by the relations that exist within it, without comparing it with anything else? Yet this

la Pléiade, 1981), pp. 1–656. Lejeune attributes a foundational importance to *Les Confessions* in *L'Autobiographie en France*, pp. 6, 30.

[41] Michel Foucault, *Les Mots et les choses: une archéologie des sciences humaines* (Paris: Gallimard, 1966), pp. 13–14.

[42] Lejeune provides an anthology of these 'pactes autobiographiques' in *L'Autobiographie en France*, pp. 123–67.

[43] Rousseau, 'Préambule du manuscrit de Neuchâtel', in *Œuvres complètes I*, pp. 1148–9.

imperfect knowledge that each has of himself is the only means that we use to know others. [. . .]

Based on these remarks I have resolved to make my readers take a step further in the knowledge of men, by drawing them away, if possible, from that unique and faulty rule of always judging the heart of others by one's own; whereas often, on the contrary, in order to know oneself one should begin by reading in the heart of others. I wish to attempt to offer at least one item for comparison, to help others learn to understand themselves; so that each might know himself and one other, and this other will be me.]

The project presupposes the existence of a 'moi' or self which is 'la cause interne [. . .] cachée et souvent très compliquée' [the hidden and often very complicated internal cause] of outward acts and appearances (1149). The first challenge is to understand the system governing one's own self, which can then be compared with a second specimen (Rousseau's), in order to extrapolate to a larger understanding of 'l'homme' in general. Rousseau stresses that the self must be understood in its formation over time, by following 'quel enchaînement d'affections secrettes l'a rendu tel' [what chain of secret affections made it the way it is] (1149), and he also insists that it must be grasped in its totality: 'car si je tais quelque chose on ne me connoitra sur rien, tant tout se tient, tant tout est un dans mon caractère, et tant ce bisarre et singulier assemblage a besoin de toutes les circonstances de ma vie pour être bien dévoilé' [for if I pass over anything in silence one will not know me at all, so much is everything related, so much is everything one in my character, and so much does this bizarre and singular assemblage require all the circumstances of my life in order to be properly revealed] (1153).

Rousseau's autobiographical project can therefore be characterized by its totalizing attitude, which remained present in the genre as a utopian ideal, even if these aims could never be realized fully in practice. Another example from the eighteenth century, by Restif de la Bretonne, demonstrates that Rousseau's scientific aims were subsequently recognized and even accentuated further:

[J]e dois anatomiser le cœur humain sur mon sens intime, et sonder les profondeurs du *moi*. Ce ne sont même pas mes *Confessions* que je fais; ce sont *les Ressorts du Cœur humain* que je *dévoile*. [. . .] Je vous donne ici un livre d'histoire naturelle, qui me met au-dessus de Buffon.[44]

[I must dissect the human heart according to my own consciousness, and plumb the depths of the *self*. I am not undertaking my own *Confessions*; I am *revealing* the *Mechanics of the Human Heart*. [. . .] I am presenting you with a book of natural history, which places me above Buffon.]

Rejecting the religious principle of 'confession' (and Rousseau's allusion to the *Confessions* of St Augustine), Bretonne compares his project instead to Georges-Louis Leclerc de Buffon's *Histoire Naturelle* (published 1749–89), a vast and, again, totalizing work of scientific knowledge. An example from the twentieth century, Julien Benda's *La Jeunesse d'un clerc* (1936), shows the persistence of this attitude:

---

[44] Nicolas-Edme Restif de la Bretonne, *Monsieur Nicolas, ou le cœur human dévoilé*, 16 vols (Paris, 1794–97). The passage cited is reproduced in *L'Autobiographie en France*, pp. 131–3 (p. 132).

Je crois que, dans une certaine famille humaine qui traverse toute l'histoire et y aura joué quelque rôle—disons schématiquement les tenants de l'idéalisme absolu—j'aurai été un exemplaire assez complet. C'est le désir d'offrir au psychologue une description un peu poussée de ce spécimen qui m'a fait faire ce livre. C'est un mouvement de savant. Je voudrais verser aux annales de la science de l'Homme une observation bien faite sur un certain type humain.[45]

[I believe that, in a certain human family that runs throughout all of history and has played some role within it—let us call this family, schematically, the proponents of an absolute idealism—I am just about a perfect case. I have been impelled to write this book by the desire to offer the psychologist a slightly exaggerated description of this specimen. It is an exercise in erudition. I would like to deposit in the annals of the science of Man a thorough account of a certain human type.]

The words 'un peu poussé' indicate a degree of irony towards a project which might look increasingly naïve in a post-Freudian era, but it nonetheless presents a continuity with the totalizing aims set out by Rousseau.

In contrast to autobiography's utopian aim of understanding the whole self, the *journal intime* can be characterized as a practice of recording the self in all its variation and instability, and by the renunciation of interpretation and synthesis. Just as for autobiography, the aims of the *journal intime* might never be achieved in absolute terms, while still persisting as an ideal. These epistemological foundations can be identified with the two major influences that Girard finds united in Maine de Biran's *journal intime* (written between 1811 and 1824): first, projects described by Rousseau (but never undertaken by him) for an approach to writing his self that would be far more fragmentary than his autobiographical works, and secondly, the complicated system contrived by Marc-Antoine Jullien for maintaining a meticulous *agenda* and *emploi du temps*.[46]

Biran refers repeatedly in his *journal intime* to a project described by Rousseau in *Les Confessions*, which was to be titled 'La Morale sensitive ou Le Matérialisme du Sage'.[47] According to Biran, 'il est question des variations que les hommes éprouvent dans le cours de leur existence et qui les rendent si souvent dissemblables à eux-mêmes qu'ils semblent se transformer en des hommes différents' [it concerns the variations that men experience in the course of their existence and which often make them so dissimilar to themselves that they seem to be transformed into different men].[48] The self now appears to be endlessly variable and contingent, and also a functioning part of the physical world, as Rousseau suggests:

Le climat, les saisons, les sons, les couleurs, l'obscurité, la lumière, les élémens, les alimens, le bruit, le silence, le mouvement, le repos, tout agit sur notre machine et sur notre ame par consequent, tout nous offre mille prises presque assurées pour gouverner dans leur origine les sentimens dont nous nous laissons dominer.[49]

[Climates, seasons, sounds, colours, darkness, light, the elements, food, noise, silence, motion, rest, all act on our machine and consequently on our soul; all offer us a

---

[45] Julien Benda, *La Jeunesse d'un clerc* (Paris: Gallimard, 1936). Cited in *L'Autobiographie en France*, p. 152.
[46] Girard, *Le Journal intime*, p. 172.   [47] Ibid., pp. 160–1.   [48] Cited in Ibid., p. 160.
[49] Rousseau, *Les Confessions*, p. 409.

thousand almost guaranteed holds for governing in their origin the feelings by which
we let ourselves be dominated.]

We can see adumbrated here a practice of observation of the self, based on the
science of meteorology, with the aim of a heightened degree of self-knowledge, and
therefore self-control. In fact, a more detailed description of the *journal intime* is
given in *Les Rêveries du promeneur solitaire*, which are presented as an 'appendice' to
Les Confessions. In the first *rêverie*, Rousseau finds himself 'seul sur la terre' [alone
on earth] and proposes to examine his self in this unusual state of isolation:

> Ces feuilles ne seront proprement qu'un informe journal de mes rêveries. [...] Je dirai
> ce que j'ai pensé tout comme il m'est venu et avec aussi peu de liaison que les idées de
> la veille en ont d'ordinaire avec celles du lendemain. Mais il en resultera toujours une
> nouvelle connoissance de mon naturel et de mon humeur par celle des sentimens et
> des pensées dont mon esprit fait sa pature journalière dans l'étrange état où je suis. [...]
>
> [...] Je ferai sur moi-même à quelque égard les operations que font les physiciens sur
> l'air pour en connoitre l'état journalier. J'appliquerai le baromettre à mon ame, et ces
> operations bien dirigées et longtems repetées me pourroient fournir des resultats aussi
> surs que les leurs. Mais je n'étens pas jusques-là mon entreprise. Je me contenterai de
> tenir le registre des opérations sans chercher à les reduire en systême.[50]

> [These pages will, properly speaking, be only a shapeless diary of my reveries. [...]
> I will say what I have thought just as it came to me and with as little connection
> as the ideas of the day before ordinarily have with those of the following day. But it
> will always produce a new understanding of my natural temperament and disposition,
> through an understanding of the feelings and thoughts that make up the daily fodder
> of my mind in the strange state that I am in. [...]
>
> [...] I will perform on myself, in a sense, the measurements that natural scientists
> perform on the air in order to know its daily condition. I will apply the barometer
> to my soul, and these measurements, carefully conducted and repeated over a long
> period of time, will be able to provide results as certain as theirs. But I do not extend
> my enterprise that far. I shall be content to keep a record of the measurements without
> seeking to reduce them to a system.]

The *Rêveries* do not, in their end product, resemble a *journal intime*, but Rousseau's
initial aims anticipate not only the practice of keeping a *journal intime*, but also the
contradiction that it entails. The accuracy of his daily observations is guaranteed by
the scientific impersonality with which he records his thoughts, without selection
or interpretation, and without 'les reduire en systême', yet this seems to preclude
the production of a 'nouvelle connoissance de [son] naturel' (unless we posit an
'other' who might interpret these results).

Marc-Antoine Jullien, the other major influence on Biran's *journal intime*, had
little interest in introspection, and demonstrates a very different aspect of the
epistemological shift mentioned earlier. Jullien played an important role in the
revolutionary government between 1793 and 1794, before devoting himself to

---

[50] Jean-Jacques Rousseau, *Les Rêveries du promeneur solitaire*, in *Œuvres complètes I: Les Confessions et autres textes autobiographiques*, pp. 993–1099, p. 1000–1.

the means of educating and controlling a new citizen for a modern, industrial, democratic state.[51] In 1808 he published an *Essai sur la méthode qui a pour objet l'emploi du temps, meilleur moyen d'être heureux*, and from 1813 one could buy notebooks laid out for the purpose of following his scheme (if it is indeed possible). His method requires the maintenance of three diaries: the *Mémorial analytique, ou Journal des faits et observations* is the closest to a *journal intime*, allowing reflection on any subject, together with an indexing system; the *Agenda général, ou Livret pratique d'emploi du temps* includes an account of one's occupations throughout the day, with five columns for additional details of finances, letters sent and received, etc.; the *Biomètre, ou Mémorial horaire*, allows for a summary of the previous fortnight, with its own system of notation and evaluation.

Unlike Rousseau, Jullien is not aiming for a greater understanding of the self or of 'l'homme', but rather he offers a tool for becoming more efficient, productive, and therefore happy, through methods drawn explicitly from the natural sciences. Whereas Rousseau's imagined project of 'La Morale sensitive' renounces any kind of synthesis, Jullien's system involves a meticulous process of notation followed by a second instance of re-evaluation. I shall not dwell on the way in which these two disparate conceptions of diary-writing cohabit in Biran's *journal intime*, since these same elements and their relations will reappear at every stage of diary-writing in the twentieth century, and I shall merely draw two broad points from this brief historical foray: first, that the *journal intime* stands in direct opposition to the totalizing attitude of autobiography, based instead on a fragmentary writing practice, a renunciation of interpretation and synthesis, and a concomitant view of the self as endlessly variable and unstable; secondly, that the various ingredients and aims of the *journal intime* are inherently contradictory. Consequently, we should no more expect to find a pure, fully successful *journal intime* than we would expect to find in *Les Confessions* a complete depiction of the 'bisarre et singulier assemblage' that is Rousseau's self. The *journaux intimes* and autobiographies that have been written over more than two centuries, together with their fictional counterparts, are of interest precisely because they are impure in form, only ever achieving a partial success, and because their authors are spurred on to further reflection and ingenuity by the pursuit of elusive ideals.

Diary-Writing in the (Long) Twentieth Century

This principle of impurity (recalling the 'variants' that do not fit Raoul's model for the fictional diary) has guided my selection of a series of texts for close reading, in order to reveal the historical developments that diary-writing has undergone in France over the twentieth century. They are not necessarily the most widely read texts among published real and fictional diaries, but they all assume the contradictions inherent in the *journal intime*, and in every case a reflection on the very imperfections of the genre has broader implications for the nature of literature or the 'author'.

---

[51] Philippe Lejeune, 'Marc-Antoine Jullien, contrôleur du temps', *Lalies*, 28 (2008), 205–20.

I shall address this history in two parts. The first part covers a period of experimentation with the literary potential of diary-writing from the pivotal date of 1887–88 up to the landmark publication of Gide's *Journal 1889–1939* in 1939 and its reception during the Second World War. The second part follows the course of diary-writing during the decades of impersonal literary formalism after the War, the return of the writing subject to the literary avant-garde in the 1970s, and the rise of life-writing up to the present day. The first period saw many authors make innovative use of diary-writing,[52] but will be explored primarily through the works of Gide, whose life-long exploration of the *journal intime* exerted by far the greatest contemporary and lasting influence. The second period was not dominated by any one diarist, and works by Queneau, Barthes, and Ernaux—all drawing in different ways on models established by Gide—will cast light on the changing nature and role of diary-writing up to the present.

Gide's publications of diary-writing are too numerous to treat comprehensively in this study, but over four chapters I shall examine the most important stages of his experimentation.[53] Gide began writing a diary in 1887 after the discovery of Amiel's *Fragments d'un journal intime*. He incorporated this early diary in his first book-length publication, *Les Cahiers d'André Walter* (1891), presented as the real diaries of a real André Walter, followed by publications of Walter's poetry and travel writing. This creation of an *auteur supposé*, a fully formed author-figure who is only later revealed to be a fabrication, proposed a new, central role for the diary in an author's *œuvre*. The problematic status of Gide/Walter's diaries as simultaneously real and fictional was used to explore an author's desire to transform the (diaristic) contingency of life into the transcendence of art. In 1895 Gide published the manifestly fictional work *Paludes* under his own name. The undecidable status of its narrative as either a diary or some other form, and the mixing of fact and fiction in its complex paratext, combine to make this an extreme example of the 'variants' to Raoul's model. Contrary to Gide's earlier aesthetic, this work used diary-writing in search of a literary *œuvre* that might accommodate the contingency of the author's life. Gide's experiments with fictional diaries culminated in his 1925 novel *Les Faux-monnayeurs*, closely followed in 1926 by *Le Journal des Faux-monnayeurs*, the real diary documenting his composition of the novel. Parts of the real diary are transposed within the novel, attributed to the author-character, Édouard. A structure is created whereby the real diary acts as a supplement to the novel (in the Derridean sense), deconstructing the concept of the literary *œuvre*. The development of these complex structures involving real and fictional diaries prepared the way for Gide's (apparently more straightforward) publication of his real, life-long diary, first as a peripheral component of his *Œuvres complètes*

[52] Non-exhaustively, these include Paul Léautaud, Colette, Valery Larbaud, Charles Du Bos, and Julien Green, without mentioning writers of diaries that were published only after the War.

[53] A brief overview of Gide's fictional diary-writing, including *La Porte étroite* (1909), *La Symphonie pastorale* (1919), and *L'École des femmes* (1929), is provided by David Keypour, 'Le Journal fictif dans l'œuvre d'André Gide', *BAAG*, 82–3 (1989), pp. 217–24. The publication of his nonfictional diary-writing is described in Anton Alblas, *Le 'Journal' de Gide: le chemin qui mène à la Pléiade* (Nantes: Centre d'études gidiennes, 1997).

(1932–39), and then in the single substantial volume of the *Journal 1889–1939*. Yet this work, the first anthumous publication of an author's complete *journal intime* and the first publication of a living author in Gallimard's prestigious Bibliothèque de la Pléiade, made an unprecedented claim for the *journal intime* as a literary *œuvre* in its own right, and became for many readers the most fascinating and representative work of Gide's career.[54]

Queneau's works published under the name of Sally Mara are indicative of the extensive use that authors in this later period made of Gide's innovations in diary-writing, even when he appeared out-dated owing to his classicism, humanism, his aesthetics, and his authorial posture. Sally Mara's 1947 novel *On est toujours trop bon avec les femmes*, the 1950 *Journal intime de Sally Mara*, and her 1962 *Œuvres complètes* (finally attributed to Queneau), constructed an *auteur supposé* in the same manner as Gide's André Walter, but this time playfully exposing the formal processes that make up an *œuvre* centred around a textual author-figure. In the 1970s, when the prevailing theoretical and literary exclusion of the writing subject was challenged by some of the same writers who had been responsible for the so-called 'death of the author', Barthes in particular looked to the example of Gide in order to explore the possibilities of this new, subjective writing, in his ambitious project for a 'Vita Nova' (1977–80). His two principal diaries, the *Journal de deuil* and *Soirées de Paris*, test the practical limits of two utopian ideals of diary-writing: its nature as a fully private and immediate writing practice and its aspiration to be an independent literary *œuvre* respectively. Like Gide's *Journal des Faux-monnayeurs*, Barthes's diaries are placed as components in his imagined novel, entitled *Vita Nova*. From the 1970s up to the present, life-writing of many different sorts has thrived in French writing, yet the position of diary-writing relative to the dominant literary claims of autobiography remains problematic (and in some ways redolent of their relationship in the late-eighteenth century). This is demonstrated by the works of Annie Ernaux, whose diary publications between 1993 and 2011—*journaux extérieurs*, *journaux intimes*, and a *journal d'écriture*—consistently establish diary-writing as a supplement to a number of autobiographical forms. The effect is to question the nature of the *œuvre* and 'author' in a situation where the writer's life is already the subject matter of their principal works.

From this short summary, it is already apparent that a combined approach to real and fictional diary-writing allows several distinct histories to emerge. Most

[54] Both Maurice Blanchot and Barthes addressed the anomalous position of the *Journal 1889–1939* in Gide's *œuvre*. Maurice Blanchot, 'Gide et la littérature de l'expérience', in *La Part du feu* (Paris: Gallimard, 1949), pp. 208–20, p. 208: 'On reconnaît dans le *Journal* l'œuvre qui le [Gide] représente le mieux. Mais pourquoi?' [We recognize in the *Journal* the *œuvre* that best represents Gide. But why?]. Roland Barthes, *La Préparation du roman I et II: cours et séminaires au Collège de France (1978–1979 et 1979–1980)*, ed. by Nathalie Léger (Paris: Seuil, 2003), p. 277: 'Gide, son *Journal*: une grande œuvre, que beaucoup préfèrent au reste de son œuvre [...]. Pourquoi? Difficile à dire, parce que texte très retors' [Gide, his *Journal*: a great *œuvre*, which many prefer to the rest of his work [...]. Why? Hard to say, since it is a very elusive text].

simply, the works discussed in this study test the finite formal possibilities of diary-writing in itself (again, principally those of the *journal intime*). They also gradually explore the complex and practically unlimited structures by which diaries can be integrated in or related to other works. Finally, the chapters that follow chart the history of the diary's changing role in problematizing the literary *œuvre* and the role of the 'author', from a time when fiction was the strongest guarantee of literary status, up to the relative prestige of life-writing in contemporary literary production in France.

SOME CRITICAL CONCEPTS

The 'Other' in the *journal intime*

It is clear by now that there is an inescapable 'otherness' inherent in any practice of diary-writing, and, in particular, it is central to the contradictions of the *journal intime*. The forms of this 'otherness' range from the highly theoretical to the banal. In the most abstract terms, it is a question of the constitutive alterity of language, or its dialogism (as Rannoux terms it, drawing on Bakhtin). The relation between self and 'others' is represented directly in *journaux intimes* when imaginary or real addressees are addressed as 'tu' or 'vous'. In more practical terms, the diary can be shared with other readers (whether or not this was anticipated at the time of writing, or consented to by the diarist), and the variability of these readers' interpretations belies the idea that the *journal intime* contains any fixed meaning or stable inscription of the self. The logical conclusion of this divulging of the secret of the *journal intime* is printed, commercial publication, granting full public access to its supposedly private space, and allowing the text to circulate in an entirely symbolic form, detached from the material form and circumstances of its production. I agree with Pierre Reboul's comment that there is a continuity leading from the 'présence imaginaire de l'autre à l'intérieur du journal' to the diary's publication, and shall attempt to form a coherent approach to this 'otherness', drawing on Jacques Lacan's seminar on Edgar Allan Poe's short story *The Purloined Letter*.[55] I am referring to this text merely for its expediency as one possible model of alterity in language and self-representation, and as such I have no intention of following the extensive theoretical debates that have issued from it.

Lacan's reading of *The Purloined Letter* belongs to a seminar series on Freud's *Beyond the Pleasure Principle* and its discussion of behaviours of 'repetition compulsion', in which patients inescapably re-enact an earlier trauma (possibly in an unrecognizable form) in a way that seems to disregard the 'pleasure principle'. A psychoanalytic approach to the diary might consider the repetitive practice of diary-writing as one such behaviour, since it can be compulsive and ungratifying while bringing little or no self-insight (this experience is parodied in Gide's

---

[55] Jacques Lacan, 'Le Séminaire sur "La Lettre volée"', in *Écrits I* (Paris: Seuil, 1999), pp. 11–61.

Paludes), but my interest is in the broader use that Lacan makes of the concept of repetition compulsion:

> L'enseignement de ce séminaire est fait pour soutenir que ces incidences imaginaires, loin de représenter l'essentiel de notre expérience, n'en livrent que d'inconsistant, sauf à être rapportées à la chaîne symbolique qui les lie et les oriente. (11)

> [The teaching of this seminar maintains that these imaginary incidences, far from representing the essence of our experience, provide only inconsistent traces of it, unless they are placed in relation to the symbolic chain that connects them and orientates them.]

In Lacan's terminology, the *Imaginaire* is concerned with the fiction of a stable, self-identical subject that we call 'I', when in fact the subject is 'excentrique' [ex-centric], constituted from without in the order of the *Symbolique* (concerned with language, social codes, and the 'other').[56] For our purposes, the *Imaginaire* corresponds to the mythic value of the *journal intime* as a form written spontaneously in complete isolation and privacy, providing a truthful manifestation of the diarist's self, whereas the *Symbolique* corresponds to all the forms of the diary's 'otherness' already mentioned.

Poe's tale, the second of his stories featuring the detective Dupin, relates the circulation of a letter whose content is not revealed, but which would incriminate the Queen (to whom it is addressed) if it were to fall into the hands of the King. Lacan demonstrates that the letter (here standing in for the signifier in general, and therefore the order of the *Symbolique*) determines the various attitudes and intersubjective relations of the characters (in the order of the *Imaginaire*). Although it is ostensibly addressed to the Queen, the letter achieves the same effect wherever it is found, and therefore (as Lacan concludes) it 'arrive toujours à destination' [always arrives at its destination] (41). He divides the story into a series of three scenes, in which the same three subject positions arise, but in different characters:

1. In the presence of the King, the Queen receives an incriminating letter. She places it among other documents, where it is effectively hidden from the naïvely realist (or materialist) King, who sees only a collection of papers. A minister arrives, astutely perceives the whole situation, and realizes that the Queen cannot prevent him from nonchalantly taking the letter (substituting another document) in order to blackmail her.

2. The police, working under the Queen's orders, search the home of the minister exhaustively, looking for the missing letter. They have no success, since the Queen/police now possess the naïve realism of the King, and fail to see that the minister has hidden it in plain sight, merely disguised by a change of address. Dupin, brought in by the police, astutely perceives that he can steal the letter from the minister (substituting another in its place).

---

[56] The relation between *Imaginaire* and *Symbolique* in the constitution of the self is set out most clearly (or the least obscurely) in Jacques Lacan, 'Le Stade du miroir comme formateur de la fonction du Je telle qu'elle nous est révélée dans l'expérience psychanalytique', in *Écrits I*, pp. 92–9.

3. The third scene (which is more problematic, and a lot less clear) depicts the
minister in the position of ignorance, Dupin as the new possessor of the
letter (the position formerly occupied by the Queen, then the minister), and
Lacan himself as the astute analyst who perceives the whole situation.

I shall overlook the psychoanalytic significance of the three positions, and
consider instead how they relate to the elements that co-exist and persist in the
journal intime, whether it is kept private, circulated among acquaintances, or
published. The first position, occupied successively by the King, the Queen/police,
and the minister, and characterized by blindness and realism (this does not relate
to Lacan's concept of the *Réel*), corresponds to an attitude identified earlier in the
Introduction from the early history of the *journal intime*: this is the perspective
that considers the self to be a material phenomenon, which can be documented
accurately in all its variability using notations comparable to meteorological
readings, without attempting any interpretation or synthesis. The second position,
occupied in turn by the Queen, the minister, and Dupin, and which Lacan
associates with the *Imaginaire*, corresponds to the view that the *journal intime*
as a whole, when subjected to interpretation and synthesis, constitutes a faithful
portrait of the diarist's self. This is the alluring myth of the *journal intime*, the
illusion of a stable meaning, premised both on the blind materialism of the first
position, and on the supposed secrecy of the diary (which remains oblivious to
the threat posed by the third position). This third position, occupied successively
by the minister, Dupin, and Lacan as the three thieves who perceive the reality
of the situation and so steal away the letter from its apparent owner (again,
this is problematic in Lacan's case), belongs to the order of the *Symbolique* and
corresponds to the 'otherness' present in all *journaux intimes* by virtue of their use
of language. The very secrecy, or *intimité*, of the *journal intime* presupposes this
exterior that would open up the meaning of the text and reveal the diarist's self to
be ex-centric, constituted from without.

Another analogy used by Lacan helps to summarize these three positions:

> Pour faire saisir dans son unité le complexe intersubjectif ainsi décrit, nous lui
> chercherions volontiers patronage dans la technique légendairement attribuée à
> l'autruche pour se mettre à l'abri des dangers; car celle-ci mériterait enfin d'être
> qualifiée de politique, à se repartir ici entre trois partenaires, dont le second se croirait
> revêtu d'invisibilité, du fait que le premier aurait sa tête enfoncée dans le sable,
> cependant qu'il laisserait un troisième lui plumer tranquillement le derrière[.] (15)

> [In order to grasp in its unity the intersubjective complex described here, we would
> willing adopt the model of the technique proverbially attributed to the ostrich for
> protecting itself from danger; for this technique could be considered political, since
> its roles are divided here between three partners: of these, the second believes itself to
> be invisible, because the first has its head buried in the sand, while it actually allows a
> third to pluck a feather calmly from its rear.]

It is important to note that all three positions are present in the diary throughout
the whole of its trajectory from private writing practice to publication. The 'other'
is present from the first, supposedly spontaneous gesture of writing, since the
language of the self is constituted of an endless web of citations that surpasses

one's own knowledge and understanding (or in Lacan's terms, 'l'inconscient, c'est le discours de l'autre' [the unconscious is the discourse of the other], 16). When a *journal intime* is published, all three positions still remain present, actualized by any given reader (since the letter 'arrive toujours à destination'), who is then initiated into the secrecy of the text, and perhaps inevitably succumbs to the same illusion as they form their own reading of, for example, Amiel, Bashkirtseff, or a fictional diarist such as Roquentin in Sartre's *La Nausée*. Herein lies the problem of Lacan's claim to occupy the third, all-seeing position, and this is also the difficulty that I shall face in reading diaries throughout this study.

Lacan's analysis has been keenly contested regarding its implications for psycho-analysis and structuralism, as well as the use it makes of Poe's text. These debates do not concern me, but some of the objections raised by Derrida in his article 'Le Facteur de la vérité' (first published in 1975) have practical implications for my treatment of the *journal intime*.[57] Derrida takes issue with Lacan's treatment of the letter as a 'pur signifiant', which has a 'singulier' relation to its materiality and to space on the grounds that it cannot be split or destroyed, but only displaced in the *ordre symbolique* (454). In fact, the *journal intime* sometimes makes a certain, very relative, claim to being a 'pur signifiant', in that it is concerned with writing the inconsequential 'n'importe quoi' [anything at all] (as Gide puts it) of quotidian existence.[58] Accordingly, its interest may lie more in the fact that it circumscribes a place of secrecy, than in the specific secrets that it contains.[59] Yet Derrida makes the point—perhaps an obvious one—that a letter can always *not* 'arrive à destina-tion', since it can always come apart in its materiality, be destroyed, or dispersed. In practical terms, the *journal intime* is very vulnerable to being lost, destroyed, or reconfigured by an editor who might prefer to gather a selection of *pensées* or other excerpts for publication, thereby undoing the text's former unity. According to Derrida, the signifier can sometimes behave as described by Lacan, but only to the extent that it exists as an 'idéalité (intangibilité d'une identité à soi se déplaçant sans altération)' [ideality (intangibility of a self-identity that can be displaced without alteration)], produced by a process of '*idéalisation*' by which the signifier protects itself from material destruction (475). In this sense, it is only as an *idéalité* that a *journal intime* can be said to persist when published in a printed volume, detached from the original form of its notebooks, cursive script, smudges and blots, whose material absence is compensated for by a codified set of editorial apparatus. Fur-thermore, there cannot be a 'pur signifiant' in an absolute sense, since its *idéalité* is, at least in part, 'déterminée [...] par son contenu de sens, par l'idéalité du message qu'elle "véhicule"' [determined [...] by the meaning it contains, by the ideality of the message that it 'conveys'] (476). In the case of the *journal intime*, the text

[57] Jacques Derrida, 'Le Facteur de la vérité', in *La Carte postale: de Socrate à Freud et au-delà* (Paris: Flammarion, 2014), pp. 421–509.
[58] Anton Alblas, 'Le n'importe quoi, le n'importe comment et le n'importe où: trois dimensions de l'écriture du *Journal* de Gide', in *André Gide et l'écriture de soi: actes du colloque organisé à Paris les 2 et 4 mars 2001 par l'Association des Amis d'André Gide*, ed. by Pierre Masson and Jean Claude (Paris: Presses Universitaires de Lyon, 2002), pp. 153–64, pp. 159–64.
[59] Once again, consider the interest elicited by Gide's *Journal* (1939), despite the fact that it presented very little material that had not already been published in his *Œuvres complètes* (1932–39).

might be characterized as a secret space, but the content of this space must at least be consistent with this *idéalité*, however disappointing its store of secrets might be.

I have so far been concerned with the sorts of otherness that are present in all diaries, but the concept of *idéalisation* is useful for considering the historical development that the *journal intime* has undergone over the specific period that I have chosen to address (from the 1880s up to the present). It would be almost tautological to say that, as soon as the *journal intime* came into being, a process was at work by which a shared, symbolic code was established—shared between the diarist and whatever 'others' might have been present—which recognized this writing project as a distinct kind of activity, producing a transferable (that is, comprehensible by 'others') signifying unity of its own. The process is most clearly visible in the programmatic passages in which diarists discussed the terms of their writing project (comparable to the autobiographical pact identified by Lejeune), but the studies by Girard, Pachet, and Simonet-Tenant relate the gradual dissemination of these codes, initially through the private circulation of documents, and subsequently through the publication of diaries. Throughout the nineteenth century, these codes became both more complex and more prevalent among a public who, for example, could make sense of the rich connotations of the *journal intime* in Sainte-Beuve's *Vie, poésies et pensées de Joseph Delorme* (which does not reproduce the actual text of Delorme's *journal intime*), or indeed were capable of writing their own *journaux intimes*. Pachet regards his pivotal date of 1887–88 as a point when the *journal intime* effectively ceased to exist, having replaced its essential privacy with an openness to publication, but this can instead be considered as a moment when the process of *idéalisation* of the *journal intime* underwent a qualitative change. Henceforth, the *journaux intimes* of writers and artists assumed their inherent 'otherness' from their very conception, at least to some extent (it would be impossible for a diarist to apprehend all forms of 'otherness' in the text), without necessarily losing the experience of privacy and *intimité*. A writer's *journal intime* would now almost inevitably raise questions regarding its own place relative to the same writer's published *œuvre*, the function of the author-figure that it evokes, and potentially, the nature of literature itself. It is therefore this ongoing *idéalisation* of the *journal intime* that is the primary object of this study, rather than its changing forms, style, content, or themes, even though in practice these cannot be entirely separated from its *idéalité*.

Fiction and Reading Pacts

A definition of the 'real' and 'fictional' diary is long overdue in this discussion, and it is now possible to set out an approach that will be sufficiently flexible for the particular texts at hand. It is unsurprising that previous studies of diaries have paid little attention to this issue, since they have focused exclusively on either fictional or nonfictional works, but my own task is more complex than simply accommodating two distinct classes of texts. I have selected works of diary-writing for study precisely on the grounds that they are the sort of 'variants' that do not fit neatly into existing critical models. They are all, in very different ways, impure in their form or conception, embracing the contradictions of their own writing project, and participating in a process of *idéalisation* that calls into question the nature and literary role of the *journal intime*. I shall therefore treat the truth status of diaries as a functional element in the production and interpretation of these texts, which involves a range of different criteria, and allows almost endless permutations. Just as for the definition of the diary itself, the matter is made considerably easier by the fact that the question of a diary's truth status is invariably addressed explicitly in some form of reading pact (established between the diarist and an 'other'), either within the diary or in its published paratexts.

It is only necessary to enumerate some of the different ways in which fictivity has been theorized to realize that it combines several different criteria. For example, in *Fiction et diction* Gérard Genette considers the nature of fiction as a speech act, judging that its 'assertion feinte' is accompanied by an illocutionary act that could be made explicit with a phrase such as 'imaginez que....'.[60] Georges May argues in *L'Autobiographie* that fictivity concerns the degree of resemblance between the life of the author and the *histoire* related by the text (as opposed to the *récit* that is its narrative form), ranging on a spectrum from a novel of complete 'invention' to the narration of 'souvenirs' in the most scrupulous autobiography.[61] Dorrit Cohn's *The Distinction of Fiction* insists on a narrow definition of fiction as 'a literary nonreferential narrative text', in opposition to usages which extend the term to cover all literature or all construction of narrative, but she also closely attaches fiction to particular narrative devices that relate a character's psychological experience in an implausible way (such as interior monologue).[62]

Besides being composed of different criteria (not limited to the examples given earlier), fiction is also a matter of degree rather than an all-or-nothing distinction. From a choice of many historical examples of partial or mixed fictivity, the case of *autofiction* offers the best illustration (although diaries themselves do not lend themselves to this particular hybrid form). The first published use of the term was on the back cover of Serge Doubrovsky's *Fils* (1977), describing the work as a 'fiction d'événements et de faits strictement réels; si l'on veut *autofiction*, d'avoir confié le langage d'une aventure à l'aventure du langage, hors sagesse et hors syntaxe du roman, traditionnel ou nouveau' [fiction of strictly real events and facts; *autofiction*, if you like, in that it entrusts the language of an adventure to an adventure of language, outside the wisdom and syntax of the novel, whether traditional or new].[63] Philippe Gasparini interprets this as the author assuring readers that the events related on the level of *histoire* are 'strictement réels' and that the part of 'fiction' is limited to 'la forme même du récit' [the very form of the narrative], which is manifested here by a 'poétisation de la langue' and a factually untrue narrative framing the narrator-character's truthful recollections.[64] Since the

---

[60] Genette, *Fiction et diction*, p. 133.
[61] Georges May, *L'Autobiographie* (Paris: PUF, 1979), pp. 187–8.
[62] Cohn, *The Distinction of Fiction*, pp. 1–9, 37.
[63] Serge Doubrovsky, *Fils* (Paris: Galilée, 1977).
[64] Philippe Gasparini, *Autofiction: une aventure du langage* (Paris: Seuil, 2008), pp. 17, 27.

term's first appearance, it has been used as a generic label for a broad variety of partial fictions, and in particular Gasparini notes a distinct usage by Philippe Lejeune, Gérard Genette, and Vincent Colonna, to denote texts in which 'le narrateur identifiable à l'auteur s'attribue des aventures manifestement imaginaires' [the narrator, identifiable with the author, attributes to themselves adventures that are manifestly imaginary], and so untrue in the events of their *histoire*.[65]

This passage from the paratext of Doubrovskys's *Fils* is one example of the reading pacts mentioned earlier (in this case, found in the work's paratext). The concept is first described in Lejeune's *L'Autobiographie en France* (1971), where he observes that a common feature of autobiographies is the presence of a passage in which the narrator specifies the terms of their commitment to tell the truth.[66] In *Le Pacte autobiographique* (1975) he addresses the problem that a commitment of this sort could just as easily appear in a novel, attributed to a fictional character, and so he concludes that a claim for the truth status of a work must be authenticated by the nominal identity of the narrator and the author (whose name on the front cover and title page assumes overall responsibility for the work). This author is a problematic figure, 'à cheval sur le hors-texte et le texte' [split between the text and the world outside the text], and for the reader 'l'auteur se définit comme la personne capable de produire ce discours, et il l'imagine donc à partir de ce qu'il produit' [the author is defined as the person capable of producing this discourse, and the reader therefore imagines him based on what he has produced].[67] Other types of reading pact, such as a *pacte romanesque* or a *pacte fantasmatique* (where fictions within an *espace autobiographique* are read as 'des *fantasmes* révélateurs d'un individu' [*phantasies* that reveal an individual], 42), invoke different interpretative codes of fictivity, and are established in different ways, but nonetheless allow a reader to understand the particular truth status of the text.

In practice, the reading pacts of *journaux intimes* are usually more problematic than those found in autobiographies. First, the 'other' or 'others' to whom the diarist makes this commitment is likely to be more ambiguous and complex (this is not to suggest that the *destination* of an autobiography such as Rousseau's *Confessions* is a straightforward matter). Secondly, the nature of the text is often addressed repeatedly, not only in the process of its composition, but also in its treatment by successive editors and publishers. Sometimes this life cycle of a diary is made plain to a reader, which is the case in the various diaries published by Annie Ernaux, but sometimes (more often) it requires scholarly work to untangle its chronology.

The Author-Figure, the *auteur supposé*, and the *œuvre*

An important part of the history of the *journal intime* is the way in which it has been used to reconfigure the concepts of the 'author' and the 'œuvre'. This issue will appear, in very different ways, in every one of the chapters that follow. It is therefore necessary to avoid any fixed definition of these concepts, and to treat them instead as functional elements of discourse (generally speaking, of literary

[65] Ibid., p. 109.   [66] Lejeune, *L'Autobiographie en France*, pp. 17–18.
[67] Lejeune, *Le Pacte autobiographique*, p. 23.

discourse, but this term too poses difficulties), whose operation varies over time and in different contexts. I shall draw on Michel Foucault's 1969 lecture 'Qu'est-ce qu'un auteur?' to distinguish a constructed author-figure, which plays a number of roles in the circulation and interpretation of texts (and in particular, textual *œuvres*), from a writer's material existence.[68] This lecture is itself part of the history of the author-figure, responding to Barthes's influential essay of 1968, 'La Mort de l'auteur',[69] and the inconsistencies of Foucault's approach, revealed in readings by Seán Burke and Adrian Wilson, will be as instructive as his explicit claims.[70] It will also be useful to introduce at this point the concept of the 'auteur supposé', the device by which an invented author-figure is presented to the reader as being a real person.

Foucault begins his enquiry by considering the usage of the author's name (which Lejeune considers central to the reading pact). In comparison with everyday usage, a name such as Homer, Shakespeare, or Stendhal has a number of additional roles:

Il manifeste l'événement d'un certain ensemble de discours, et il se réfère au statut de ce discours à l'intérieur d'une société et à l'intérieur d'une culture. Le nom d'auteur n'est pas situé dans l'état civil des hommes, il n'est pas non plus situé dans la fiction de l'œuvre, il est situé dans la rupture qui instaure un certain groupe de discours et son mode d'être singulier. (826)

[It manifests the event of a certain group of discourse, and relates to the status of this discourse within a society and within a culture. The authorial name does not reside in the civil status of men, nor in the fiction of the *œuvre*, but rather in the breach that establishes a certain group of discourse and its particular mode of existence.]

The first role of these names circulating in the *rupture* between *œuvre* and *état civil* (in practice, they are usually found in paratexts such as title pages and lists of works 'du même auteur') is the *fonction classificatoire*. This function designates a corpus of two or more works as having a particular relation to each other, such as their 'explication réciproque' (826). The second role is the *fonction-auteur*, conferring on some texts (such as poetry, fiction, and philosophy, but not a contract or a letter) a 'mode d'être singulier', which Foucault explores in greater detail. The *fonction-auteur* is historically and culturally contingent, varying over time and applying in different ways to different types of discourse (827–8). It is connected with the legal status of authorship, which allows a writer to collect financial rewards issuing from their intellectual property and to be punished for transgressive publications (827). Most importantly, the *fonction-auteur* involves the construction of a textual author-figure:

[La fonction-auteur] est le résultat d'une opération complexe qui construit un certain être de raison qu'on appelle l'auteur. Sans doute, à cet être de raison, on essaie de

---

68 Michel Foucault, 'Qu'est-ce qu'un auteur?', in *Dits et écrits 1954–1988*, ed. by Daniel Defert and François Ewald, 2 vols (Paris: Gallimard, 2001), I, pp. 817–49.
69 Roland Barthes, 'La Mort de l'auteur', in *OC* ([1968]), III, pp. 40–5.
70 Seán Burke, *The Death and Return of the Author: Criticism and Subjectivity in Barthes, Foucault and Derrida* (Edinburgh: Edinburgh University Press, 1992). Adrian Wilson, 'Foucault on the "Question of the Author": A Critical Exegesis', *Modern Language Review*, 99/2 (2004), pp. 339–63.

donner un statut réaliste: ce serait, dans l'individu, une instance 'profonde', un pouvoir 'créateur', un 'projet', le lieu originaire de l'écriture. Mais en fait, ce qui dans l'individu est désigné comme l'auteur (ou ce qui fait d'un individu un auteur) n'est que la projection, dans des termes toujours plus ou moins psychologisants, du traitement qu'on fait subir aux textes, des rapprochements qu'on opère, des traits qu'on établit comme pertinents, des continuités qu'on admet, ou des exclusions qu'on pratique. (828–9)

[The author function is the result of a complex operation which contructs a certain rational entity that we call the author. Undoubtedly, we try to bestow upon this rational entity an appearance of realism: we evoke, in the individual, a 'profundity', a 'creative' force, a 'project', the original site from which writing springs. But in fact, that which is designated as the author within an individual (or that which makes an individual into an author) is no more than the projection, always in more or less psychological terms, of the treatment that we subject texts to: the way we relate texts to one another, the characteristics that we consider to be important, the continuities we assign, the exclusions that we practice.]

Foucault adds that the author-figure is not created only by the 'traitement qu'on fait subir aux textes', but that texts themselves contain 'un certain nombre de signes qui renvoient à l'auteur' [signs that refer to the author] (830), although these signs cannot be taken to refer directly to the writer or circumstances of composition (as they do in language and texts that lack a *fonction-auteur*).

It should be noted here that the term 'œuvre' covers two usages, distinguished in French by the use of masculine and feminine forms respectively, both of which are implicated in the functioning of the author's name. 'Un œuvre' relates to the corpus of works unified by a particular author's name, and therefore corresponds to the *fonction classificatoire*. 'Une œuvre' refers to the status of an individual, unified work, and corresponds to the *fonction-auteur*, conferring on the work a 'mode d'être singulier'. The nature of the relations within 'un œuvre', and the particular 'mode d'être' of 'une œuvre', are clearly subject to change. These two terms are often conflated, partly owing to the ambiguity introduced when the definite article is used ('l'œuvre'), and in practice the masculine form has largely fallen out of use.

The first problem of Foucault's analysis identified by Adrian Wilson regards the extent to which the author-figure inheres within texts, or alternatively is superimposed upon them by the way they are interpreted (352–3). Secondly, Wilson observes that Foucault treats the text as 'a quasi-natural object, a simple given' (354), and so neglects the process by which the author-figure itself delimits and characterizes a text or *œuvre* (as Foucault initially suggests). Finally, Foucault's emphasis on the author as a function of discourse obscures the fact that it functions by constructing the author-figure as an individual or 'a personal being' (356–60). This is why there is no term equivalent to 'the author-figure' used with any consistency in Foucault's lecture, even though he describes the concept quite precisely as 'un certain être de raison qu'on appelle l'auteur' in the passage cited earlier. The concept of the reading pact helps to address these problems, as its 'signes qui renvoient à l'auteur' simultaneously institute an author-figure as a 'personal being' while delimiting and characterizing the text. Yet the relation of this author-figure to the material existence of the writer remains unclear, and this is one of the questions explored by the experiments of the diaries themselves.

The matter is complicated further by the diaries of *auteurs supposés* in Chapters 1 and 5 of the present study. The *auteur supposé* can strictly be defined as an author-figure who initially appears to be real, but who is eventually revealed to be the artificial creation of another writer (just as we now know that André Walter and Sally Mara were created by Gide and Queneau respectively). Jean-François Jeandillou's 1989 work *Supercheries littéraires* presents an anthology of thirty *auteurs supposés* and uses this corpus to produce a formal typology for the phenomenon.[71] The necessary conditions for the *auteur supposé* guarantee that it functions fully as an author-figure (470–4). First, the name of the author-figure must be present, and its authenticity assured by the claims of the paratext (the real-life *auteur supposant*—Gide or Queneau—must not claim responsibility for the works). Secondly, a substantial piece of work by the *auteur supposé* must be present, and this must be accompanied by a source of biographical information (often provided by a diary, as it is for André Walter and Sally Mara). The *auteur supposé* therefore appears to be a real person claiming responsibility for the works, and whose life or character has a bearing on their interpretation.

Jeandillou also observes that the various strategies employed for authenticating the *auteur supposé* 'participe[nt] moins d'un "faire croire" captieux que d'un "laisser croire" purement ludique' [engage less in outright deception than in a ludic process, allowing readers to believe what they will] (482), suggesting that it is expected that the *supercherie* [hoax] will be uncovered sooner or later. When this happens (as it did for André Walter and Sally Mara), the name of the *auteur supposé* is still retained alongside that of the *auteur supposant*, demonstrating that 'l'auteur imaginaire fait toujours partie intégrante de l'œuvre publiée sous son nom' [the imaginary author always remains an integral part of the *œuvre* published under their name] (475). As will be seen, the complex relationship between the *auteur supposé* (now simultaneously real and fictional) and the *auteur supposant* (the author of the author of the texts), is exploited with very different consequences in the cases of André Walter and Sally Mara.

The Supplement

Throughout this study, diaries will repeatedly be found to exploit their position at the boundaries of a literary *œuvre* (in either of the two senses already mentioned), in order to contest the very nature of the 'author' and the 'œuvre'. A useful critical tool for addressing this marginality of the diary is provided by Derrida's concept of the supplement. The term arises from Derrida's study in *De la Grammatologie* of historical oppositions between the supposedly full presence of *parole* [speech], and *écriture* [writing] as a mere derivative and representation of this presence. More

---

[71] Jean-François Jeandillou, *Supercheries littéraires: la vie et l'œuvre des auteurs supposés* (Paris: Usher, 1989).

specifically, it is discussed in the chapter '"Ce dangereux supplément…"' with reference to Rousseau's 'méfiance sans cesse ranimée à l'égard de la parole dite pleine' [constant distrust with regard to the supposed fullness of speech] (203).[72] This hierarchical binary opposition between *parole* and *écriture* offers an analogy with the opposition between the literary *œuvre*, with its supposed self-sufficiency and presence of the authorial writing subject, and the marginal diary publication as a supplement that reveals and compensates for the deficiencies of the *œuvre*.

Derrida contrasts Rousseau's theory of language with his experience of writing, as it is described in *Les Confessions*. In his theory, Rousseau 'condamne l'écriture comme la destruction de la présence et comme maladie de la parole' [condemns writing as the destruction of presence and the disease of speech] (204), although the *parole* that he values so highly is 'la parole telle qu'elle devrait être' [speech as it should be] (203). In practice, Rousseau recognizes an alienation of the subject in speech itself, 'cette puissance qui, inaugurant la parole disloque le sujet qu'elle construit, l'empêche d'être présent à ses signes' [this force which, while inaugurating speech, dislocates the subject that it constructs, prevents it from being present in its signs], and he rehabilitates writing as 'la restauration, par une certaine absence et par un type d'effacement calculé, de la présence déçue de soi dans la parole' [the restitution, through a certain absence and calculated evasion, of the imperfect presence of speech] (204). Derrida finds that this 'économie des signes' rests on a classical opposition of presence and absence, familiar from his other analyses in the same work:

> L'opération qui substitue l'écriture à la parole remplace aussi la présence par la valeur: au *je suis* ou au *je suis présent* ainsi sacrifié on *préfère* un *ce que* je suis ou *ce que je vaux*. 'Moi présent, on n'aurait jamais su ce que je valais.' Je renonce à ma vie présente, à mon existence actuelle et concrète pour me faire reconnaître dans l'idéalité de la vérité et de la valeur. Schéma bien connu. (205)

> [The operation by which writing is substituted for speech also replaces presence with value: the claim 'I am' or 'I am present' is sacrificed, and *preference* is given to the expression of 'what I am' or 'what I am worth'. 'If I were present, they would never have known what I was worth.' I renounce my present life, my current, physical existence in order to make myself understood in the ideality of truth and value. A familiar pattern.]

However, by studying Rousseau's use of the term 'supplément' in various contexts, Derrida shows that it provides a model for reconciling Rousseau's two conflicting attitudes towards language in theory and practice, whose 'cohabitation est aussi étrange que nécessaire' [cohabitation is as strange as it is necessary]:

> Le supplément s'ajoute, il est un surplus, une plénitude enrichissant une autre plénitude, le *comble* de la présence. […] Cette espèce de la supplémentarité détermine d'une certaine manière toutes les oppositions conceptuelles dans lesquelles Rousseau inscrit la notion de nature en tant qu'elle *devrait* se suffire à elle-même.

---

[72] Jacques Derrida, '« Ce dangereux supplément »', in *De la grammatologie* (Paris: Minuit, 1985), pp. 203–34.

Mais le supplément supplée. Il ne s'ajoute que pour remplacer. Il intervient ou s'insinue *à-la-place-de*; s'il comble, c'est comme on comble un vide. S'il représente et fait image, c'est par le défaut antérieur d'une présence. [...] Quelque part, quelque chose ne peut se remplir *de soi-même*, ne peut s'accomplir qu'en se laissant combler par signe et procuration. Le signe est toujours le supplément de la chose même. (208)

[The supplement adds itself, it is a surplus, a plenitude enriching another plenitude, the very height of presence. [...] This type of supplementarity determines in a certain manner all the conceptual oppositions in which Rousseau inscribes the concept of nature as something that *should* be self-sufficient.

But the supplement also supplements. It adds itself only in order to replace something. It intervenes or insinuates itself *in-the-place-of*; if it fills, it is in the way one fills a void. If is represents and creates an image, it does so owing to the previous failure of a presence. [...] Somewhere, something cannot fill itself *of itself*, cannot be completed without letting itself be filled by a sign and by proxy. The sign is always the supplement of the thing itself.]

The strangeness of this undecidable meaning of the supplement is self-evident, but its necessity is due to its relation to the concept of *différance* (which is beyond the scope of this brief summary). As in 'l'économie de la différance' (206), meaning and presence are deferred indefinitely through an endless chain of 'médiations supplémentaires' [supplementary mediations], which paradoxically produce 'le sens de cela même qu'elles diffèrent: le mirage de la chose même, de la présence immédiate, de la perception originaire' [the meaning of the very thing that they defer: the mirage of the thing itself, of immediate presence, of originary perception] (226).

The equivalent relationship between the *œuvre* and the supplementary diary publication does not function in exactly the same way: here the dominant term (*œuvre*) is associated with an ideal, symbolic presence, while the diary is habitually associated with the supposed spontaneity and presence of *parole* (in Barthes's words, it is a 'parole "writée"' [written form of speech]).[73] In practice, whenever this relation is considered in terms of supplementarity, it will be necessary to consider in what ways the *œuvre* is supposed to 'se remplir *de soi-même*' and the sort of presence it claims for itself, and then how the marginal diary supplements it, both as a 'surplus' and as a substitute revealing the very deficiency that it compensates for. This relationship will function differently again when diaries supplement, for example, the totalizing claims of Gide's novel *Les Faux-monnayeurs* ('une œuvre'), and Ernaux's corpus of autobiographical writings ('un œuvre').

Gender

As mentioned earlier, this study does not set out to examine the question of gender in diary-writing, but it is nonetheless important to acknowledge that gender inevitably plays a role in the writing and self-constructions of all diarists. This issue does not pertain only to Ernaux (as the only female writer discussed at length in

---

73 Roland Barthes, 'Délibération', in *OC* ([1979]), V, pp. 668–81, p. 678.

this study), but the ways in which her work has been treated illustrate some of the broader approaches to gender in criticism on autobiographical writing. Siobhán McIlvanney observes, in her 2001 work *Annie Ernaux: The Return to Origins*, that Ernaux's popularity among Anglophone readers and critics is partly due to her work's resemblance to certain trends in Anglo-American writing:

> In the manner of Christiane Rochefort and Marie Cardinal, Ernaux provides a predominantly 'existential' or materialist analysis of women's social situation, as opposed to the more 'essentialist' or differentialist branch of contemporary French women's writing frequently referred to under the umbrella term of *écriture féminine*, a writing which typically focuses on linguistic or psychoanalytic concerns, on the textual rather than the contextual.[74]

Although Ernaux's works have long been popular with Francophone readers, she was initially neglected in French academic circles, especially in comparison with 'the "holy trinity" of French women writers, Hélène Cixous, Luce Irigaray and Julia Kristeva, and other proponents of differentialist writing' (1–2). The continuing strength of the 'differentialist' tradition in France is demonstrated by the treatment of Ernaux in a work of 2012, Élisabeth Seys's *Ces Femmes qui écrivent: de Madame de Sévigné à Annie Ernaux*.[75] This study starts from 'l'idée d'une distinction entre deux littératures—deux écritures, voire deux lectures—l'une masculine, l'autre féminine' [the idea of a distinction between two literatures—two ways of writing, even two ways of reading—one masculine, the other feminine], and casts Ernaux as the final stage in a series of female writers 'illustrant la conscience de plus en plus aiguë qu'ont les femmes d'elles-mêmes et de l'idée d'une condition féminine' [illustrating the ever increasing consciousness that women have of themselves and of the idea of a feminine condition] (5, 11). In this case, Ernaux has effectively been recuperated as a representative of *écriture féminine*.

Where questions of gender arise, I intend to take account of a shift in critical approaches in Britain and the US that can be dated approximately to 1990, as the year in which Judith Butler published the influential work *Gender Trouble: Feminism and the Subversion of Identity*.[76] From around this time, studies of gender in autobiographical writing developed in directions broadly consistent with Butler's argument that gender and sexuality are performative—that they are produced through the repetition of stylized acts (heavily determined and policed), resulting in socially constructed gender and sexual identities, which are endowed with the ontological status of nature by association with the assumed 'fact' of biological, binary sex. One of the implications of this view is that gender-orientated criticism need not be focused exclusively on women, and even that this focus (typical of the 'differentialist' tradition) can perpetuate normative and

[74] Siobhán McIlvanney, *Annie Ernaux: The Return to Origins* (Liverpool: Liverpool University Press, 2001), p. 1.

[75] Élisabeth Seys, *Ces Femmes qui écrivent: de Madame de Ségivné à Annie Ernaux* (Paris: Ellipses, 2012).

[76] Judith Butler, *Gender Trouble: Feminism and the Subversion of Identity* (New York: Routledge, 1990).

restrictive gender identities. In the same year as the publication of *Gender Trouble*, Lillian Robinson commented that 'some of the most interesting applications of a gender studies approach to biography are those that recognize how problematic maleness and masculinity are in a highly gendered social and intellectual context', and accordingly, a collection from 1991 on *Autobiography and Questions of Gender* includes several essays devoted to male writers.[77] This shift also entailed a recognition of the differences that can exist within an apparently uniform gender identity, arising from the different social and historical circumstances in which gender is 'performed', and the intersection of gender with racial, sexual, and class identities proved to be particularly complex. Françoise Lionnet addressed some of these problems in *Autobiographical Voices: Race, Gender, Self-Portraiture* (1989), and Ernaux's writing itself frequently explores the intersections between gender and class.[78] More broadly, the field of gender studies has made possible new critical approaches to texts, examining the discursive conditions in which the performance of gender takes place. A more recent example of this is the collection of essays from 2004, *Gender and Politics in the Age of Letter-Writing*, which aims to 'uncover new ways of seeing gendered politics in letters'.[79]

Despite these developments in the study of autobiography, relatively little work has been done on gender in diary-writing. An article on this subject by Rebecca Hogan from 1991 can largely be identified with the 'differentialist' approach.[80] Although Hogan is wary of evoking a '"feminine essence" that erases differences among a large and various body of women's texts' (100), she nonetheless makes broad claims about the diary as a 'feminine form' on the grounds that the diary's use of detail, its focus on private and domestic life, and its paratactic structure (without hierarchy or global organization) all conform to established descriptions of *écriture féminine*. More useful information on the role of gender in diary-writing is provided by the historical and sociological approach adopted by Philippe Lejeune (without explicit reference to gender theory). In *Le Moi des demoiselles* (1993), Lejeune's survey of unpublished women's diaries from the nineteenth century casts light on the use of diary-writing in religious, familial, and educational contexts as a form of surveillance and control of women's gender and sexual identities.[81] A brief, published discussion between Lejeune and Ernaux extends these findings into the

[77] Lillian Robinson, 'Foreword' to *Revealing Lives: Autobiography, Biography and Gender*, ed. by Susan Bell and Marilyn Yalom (Albany NY: State University of New York Press, 1990), pp. vii–ix, p. viii. Shirley Neuman (ed.), *Autobiography and Questions of Gender* (London: Cass, 1991).

[78] Françoise Lionnet, *Autobiographical Voices: Race, Gender, Self-Portraiture* (Ithaca: Cornell University Press, 1989). Among many possible examples relating to the intersection between gender and class, see Annie Ernaux, *La Honte* (Paris: Gallimard, 1997).

[79] Máire Cross and Caroline Bland, 'Gender Politics: Breathing New Life into Old Letters', in *Gender and Politics in the Age of Letter-Writing, 1750–2000*, ed. by Caroline Bland and Máire Cross (Aldershot: Ashgate, 2004), pp. 3–14, p. 4.

[80] Rebecca Hogan, 'Engendered Autobiographies: The Diary as a Feminine Form', in *Autobiography and Questions of Gender* ed. by Shirley Neuman (London: Cass, 1991), pp. 95–107.

[81] Philippe Lejeune, *Le Moi des demoiselles: enquête sur le journal de jeune fille*.

twentieth century, albeit in very general terms.[82] Lejeune's research indicates that, even though more women than men write diaries, more diaries by men come to be published, and also that female writers are more likely to consider their diary-writing and their professional writing as 'deux activités autonomes et sans rapport' [two autonomous and unconnected activities] (253).

This same discussion also illustrates the danger of viewing a literary question exclusively through the prism of gender. After discussing his findings regarding the role of gender in diary-writing, Lejeune invites Ernaux to comment on the degree to which her own use of diaries conforms to the pattern that he has observed. This is not an unreasonable question, given that Ernaux's strategy of publishing *journaux intimes* as a complement to her pre-existing autobiographical works avoids the 'publication brute, originale, [l']entrée *directe* dans l'intimité' [raw publication of the original text, *direct* entry into the *intime*] that Lejeune associates with male diarists (Ernaux had not yet published *L'Atelier noir*, her *journal d'écriture*, which is most definitely not 'autonome' with regard to her professional writing). However, Ernaux's account of her own experience of writing, rereading, and publishing these particular texts makes it clear that, if gender is a determining factor in her use of diaries, it is one factor among many (which could be said for all diarists). My own reading of Ernaux's diaries, just as for the other writers under discussion, addresses these works in terms of their handling of certain recurrent problems in diary-writing that persist throughout the twentieth century. This too is only one aspect of these fascinating and varied texts, and it is hoped that the present study will in turn facilitate further interest and critical enquiry from new perspectives.

[82] Philippe Lejeune, 'Un singulier journal au féminin', in *Annie Ernaux: une œuvre de l'entre-deux*, ed. by Fabrice Thumerel (Arras: Artois Presses Université, 2004), pp. 253–8.

PART I

ANDRÉ GIDE'S DIARY-WRITING

INTRODUCTION

The period covered by this first part of my study, leading from the 1880s up to the Second World War, encompasses important publications of both real and fictional diaries by a large number of writers. So why focus on the diary-writing of just one writer, André Gide? In effect, Gide exercised an extraordinary dominance over diary-writing at this time, in his role as innovator, model, and promoter of its possibilities. Although works by several other writers will be touched upon in the chapters that follow, Gide's own works offer the greatest insight into the historical transformations that diary-writing underwent.

It is almost a matter of consensus to place Gide at the head of twentieth-century diary-writing in France, and specialists of Gide's work also agree upon the great importance of diary-writing in his *œuvre*. As Girard comments, 'sans le procédé du journal, et sans le journal, l'œuvre de Gide, sinon sa personnalité même, sont inconcevables' [without diary-writing, and without the *journal intime*, Gide's *œuvre*, and even his very personality, are inconceivable].[1] Yet the general approach taken to Gide's work so far has failed to cast light on his place in the larger historical development of diary-writing over this period. In this respect, Gide's writing has been a victim of its own success: from early in his career, Gide's individual *œuvres* (feminine) were conceived as forming part of a collective *œuvre* (masculine) centred around his own complex author-figure,[2] and even before his life and work were complete it became difficult for readers to avoid treating his corpus as a great, synchronic ensemble of mutually dependent parts, with the *Journal 1889–1939* as its centre of gravity. Indeed, this synchronic (or at least synoptic) approach is often both appropriate and rewarding. For example, Daniel Moutote goes the furthest in reading Gide's *œuvre* with the *Journal* at its centre, producing valuable insights into his work.[3] David Keypour argues convincingly that Gide's

---

[1] Girard, *Le Journal intime*, p. 91.

[2] Several examples are given in Claude Martin, *La Maturité d'André Gide: de 'Paludes' à 'L'Immoraliste' (1895–1902)* (Paris: Klincksieck, 1977), p. 12. Also see Pierre Masson, 'Préface' to André Gide, *Romans et récits*, I, pp. XI–XLVII, pp. XXV–XXVII. Jean Delay finds the earliest reference to this project in a letter from 1893, and he characterizes Gide's total *œuvre* as 'l'un des essais les plus complets qu'ai tenté un homme pour se comprendre et s'expliquer' [one of the most complete attempts that any man has made to understand and explain himself]; Jean Delay, *La Jeunesse d'André Gide*, 2 vols (Paris: Gallimard, 1956–57), I, pp. 11, 28.

[3] Daniel Moutote, *Le Journal de Gide et les problèmes du moi (1889–1925)* (Paris: PUF, 1968).

œuvre is divided between the forms of the *journal intime* and the memoir (more or less synonymous here with autobiography), sometimes even within a single work (such as *La Porte étroite* and *Et nunc manet in te*),[4] whereas Philippe Lejeune considers the *Journal* to play a similar role to the autobiography *Si le grain ne meurt* in establishing Gide's whole *œuvre* as an *espace autobiographique*.[5] Yet these approaches tend to isolate individual works from their immediate context, the circumstances of their publication and reception, and their role in an ongoing process of experimentation. Furthermore, the presence of diary-writing in the fictional works is often treated as a mere novelistic device, or overlooked entirely.[6] As a result, little is yet known about how *Les Cahiers d'André Walter* (1891) or *Paludes* (1895), for example, influenced the writing and publication of diaries long before Gide's whole *œuvre* and *journal intime* appeared in print.

In practical terms, my own method is therefore to follow the course of Gide's diary-writing, through a choice of texts that focuses on the principal stages of his ongoing experimentation in both fictional and nonfictional diary forms, and with an approach that reveals the contemporary and lasting significance of the works in question. In each case I shall examine the precise terms of the texts' reading pact, in light of the allusions and generic conventions familiar to contemporary readers, and with particular attention to the paratexts of first editions (often substantially altered in later editions), before proceeding to a close reading of their use of diary-writing. Early responses to the works in press reviews, letters, diaries, and critical work will also reveal much about their initial impact. This method might appear to run the opposite risk from that of the synoptic approach, in presenting Gide's works as a series of discrete, unrelated events, but on the contrary, the aim is to elucidate the complex interaction between two historical processes: the gradual exploration by Gide and others of diary-writing's literary potential, intimated by the diary publications of the 1880s, and Gide's lifelong construction of his total *œuvre* (by which he was known to diarists in the second half of the twentieth century), dominated by the *Journal* and the figure of an author-diarist.

The texts that I have chosen for close reading manifest a very broad range of uses of diary-writing, which I do not intend to summarize here, but they all conform to a certain recurring pattern in Gide's work. On the one hand, they all aspire in some way to an ideal of the *œuvre* (feminine), which draws on Mallarmé's unattainable ideal of a totalizing 'Livre' [Book], or the 'Livre Somme' [Summation-Book], of which Mallarmé wrote that he was 'persuadé au fond qu'il n'y en a qu'un' [persuaded at heart that there is only one].[7] Pierre Masson notes a particular

---

4 Keypour, 'Le Journal fictif dans l'œuvre d'André Gide', *BAAG*, 82–3 (1989).

5 Philippe Lejeune, 'Gide et l'espace autobiographique', in *Le Pacte autobiographique* (Paris: Seuil, 1996), pp. 165–96.

6 Keypour is one of the few to recognize the diary form in *Paludes*, in 'Le Journal fictif dans l'œuvre d'André Gide'. Clearly, the diary form plays a role in Gide's preference in his fictional writing for narration that is 'systématiquement délégué à un personnage insuffisant ou suspect' [systematically delegated to a flawed or suspect character] (Masson, 'Préface' to André Gide, *Romans et récits*, p. XXIX), and Gide himself referred to this use of the diary in *Les Faux-monnayeurs* as an 'artifice littéraire' (undated manuscript reprinted in *BAAG*, 51 (1981), p. 364).

7 Although Mallarmé pursued the goal of this 'Livre' in practice, Bertrand Marchal concludes that 'le Livre, ici, n'est plus une œuvre, fût-elle la plus grande, mais une limite de la littérature universelle,

similarity between the totalizing aims of *Les Cahiers d'André Walter* and *Les Faux-monnayeurs*: Gide wrote of the former, 'ce n'était point seulement mon premier livre, c'était ma somme' [it was not only my first book, it was my summation] (or in Masson's words, Gide aimed to 'atteindre d'un seul coup à la plénitude de l'art et du bonheur' [attain all at once the full measure of art and happiness]), and with regard to *Les Faux-monnayeurs*, 'il me faut, pour bien écrire ce livre, me persuader que c'est le seul roman et dernier livre que j'écrirai' [to write this book well, I must convince myself that it is the only novel and the last book that I shall write].[8] Each of these *œuvres* functions as a microcosm of Gide's whole, collective *œuvre* (masculine), and demonstrates the place that diary-writing might occupy within it. For example, Gide's creation of André Walter as an *auteur supposé* allows him to experiment with the structure and functioning of this whole life and work (including the role of the author's *journal intime*). Yet these texts are also marked by an almost opposite gesture, by which Gide absents himself as an author-figure, undermines the supposed plenitude of the work, and assigns it a place within the collective *œuvre*, where its shortcomings may be compensated for by its relation to Gide's other works. This gesture can be seen most clearly at the conclusion of *Paludes*, where the success of the author-character's writing project is cast into doubt (and therefore that of Gide's own project too, as will be seen).

As well as conforming to the pattern described above, these very diverse texts can also be seen to address a common, if very broad, problem. This can be roughly equated with the problem that Lacan describes as '[le] rapport de l'homme à la lettre' [the relation between man and the letter], in an article of 1958 in response to Jean Delay's work *La Jeunesse d'André Gide*.[9] Lacan views Gide as being instrumental in a historical development dating back to the invention of the printing press. He argues that the the new phenomenon of an author's *œuvre* of printed works created the category of the 'inédit' [unpublished work] (defined as 'tout ce que l'écrivain n'a pas publié de ce qui le concerne' [everything that the writer did not publish out of the writings that concern him]), which was in a sense the 'négatif' of the *œuvre*, and came to stand in for 'la vie privée de l'écrivain' [the writer's private life] (219). Lacan then attributes to the influence of Sainte-Beuve 'une révolution des valeurs littéraires' in the nineteenth century:

> Ceci, en introduisant dans un marché dont la technique de l'imprimerie depuis quatre siècles réglementait les effets, un nouveau signe de la valeur: que nous appellerons les petits papiers. Le manuscrit que l'imprimé avait refoulé dans la fonction de l'inédit, reparaît comme partie prenante de l'œuvre avec une fonction qui mérite examen. (220–1)

dont tout livre, même génial, ne peut être qu'une lointaine approximation' [The Book, in this case, is no longer an *œuvre*, no matter how great it might be, but rather a limit of universal literature, of which any book, however good, can only be a distant approximation]; Marchal, 'Notice' for 'Notes en vue du « Livre »', p. 1375.

[8] Masson, 'Préface' to André Gide, *Romans et récits*, pp. XXII–XXIII. Masson is citing Gide from *Si le grain ne meurt* and *Le Journal des Faux-monnayeurs*.

[9] Jacques Lacan, 'Jeunesse de Gide ou la lettre et le désir', in *Écrits II* (Paris: Seuil, 1999), pp. 217–42, p. 217.

[He did this by introducing, into an economy that had been determined for four centuries by the printing process, a new sign of value, which we shall call the minor writings. The manuscript that the printed text had relegated to the category of unpublished material now reappears as an active part of the *œuvre*, with a function that warrants examination.]

This revaluation of the 'inédit' can be seen in the *Vie, poésies et pensées de Joseph Delorme* (1829), Sainte-Beuve's own creation of an *auteur supposé*, which was undoubtedly a model for Gide's subsequent creation of André Walter.[10] In this work, the editor claims to have based his biographical account of Delorme on the 'pages mélancoliques' of the latter's *journal intime* (which remains mostly 'inédit'), on the grounds that 'les poésies seules, sans l'histoire des sentiments auxquels elles se rattachent, n'eussent été qu'une énigme à demi comprise' [the poems by themselves, without an account of the sentiments to which they are connected, would have been an enigma, only half-understood].[11] This conception of the 'petits papiers' clearly became untenable at Pachet's pivotal date in the 1880s, as there was no longer any possibility of writers producing these private forms of writing without a thought for their eventual (even if posthumous) publication.

It was in the context of this change in 'valeurs littéraires' that Gide began his own writing career:

> Les petits papiers sont, dès leur issue et toujours plus dans les ficelles qui les empêchent de se perdre, concertés en vue du corps qu'ils doivent constituer sinon dans l'œuvre, disons par rapport à l'œuvre. On peut demander ce qu'un tel dessein laisserait subsister de leur intérêt pour Sainte-Beuve, si c'était bien le naturel qu'il avait en vue. (221)

> [The *petits papiers* are, from their very origin and all the more so when tied up in bundles to keep them from getting lost, organized with a view to the body that they would eventually constitute, if not within the *œuvre*, then at least in relation to the *œuvre*. We might well ask what such as procedure would offer of interest to Sainte-Beuve, if it was indeed the author's natural state that he sought.]

Lacan's article is primarily concerned with texts that remained unpublished in Gide's lifetime, such as 'le Subjectif' (a record of works read) and 'De me ipse et aliis' (a collection of autobiographical notes), which Lacan argues were effectively addressed to Jean Delay as his anticipated 'psychobiographe' [psychobiographer] (222). Nonetheless, two observations by Lacan are just as relevant to the (arguably more complex) question of Gide's publication of diary-writing in his own lifetime. First, the 'petits papiers' could no longer be viewed as a manifestation of 'le naturel' of an author, and their value became dependent instead on their *sincérité* (221). The concept of *sincérité* was to take on considerable importance throughout Gide's career (for example, the very title of *Les Faux-monnayeurs* introduces the novel's exploration of *insincérité*), but it is particularly prominent

---

[10] Charles-Augustin Sainte-Beuve, *Vie, poésies et pensées de Joseph Delorme*, ed. by Gérald Antoine (Paris: Nouvelles Éditions Latines, 1956).

[11] Ibid., p. 2.

as one of the aims of his nonfictional diary-writing.[12] Secondly, it might seem that an interest in Gide's *journal intime* or similar material is redundant, given that his literary *œuvre* is itself an *espace autobiographique* (in the words of Lejeune), containing 'le soliloque de la belle âme Gide' [the soliloquy of Gide's beautiful soul] (in Lacan's words), but Lacan clarifies that the 'petits papiers' do not simply provide additional information on the author's life. He credits Jean Delay with the realization that 'ce n'est pas dans leur contenu, mais dans leur adresse qu'il faut chercher la différence [entre l'œuvre et les] petits papiers' [we must not seek the difference [between the *œuvre* and the] *petits papiers* in their content, but rather in their address], and indicates the particular nature of their 'adresse': 'Jean Delay n'évoque pas en vain ici Montaigne et son mode d'adresse à un autre à venir, de ce privé où il renonce à discerner ce qui sera pour cet autre le signifiant' [with good reason Jean Delay recalls Montaigne here, and his mode of address to an other yet to come regarding his private life, in which he does not attempt to discern what the signifier will be for this other] (222–3). In Chapter 4 I shall discuss Gide's own identification of his *Journal* with Montaigne's *Essais*, but in light of Lacan's comment it will be useful to pose the following question for each of the works of Gide's diary-writing under discussion: how does the 'adresse' of the diary—the relations that are posited between author-figure, text, and reader—relate to the 'adresse' of the individual *œuvre*, and what are the implications of this particular structure for Gide's collective *œuvre* and for the historical development of diary-writing in general?

[12] This is explored in depth in Moutote, *Le Journal de Gide*.

1

Les Cahiers d'André Walter

The importance of *Les Cahiers d'André Walter* (henceforth referred to as *CAW*, 1891) to the history of diary-writing has been obscured by two subsequent attitudes: it has generally either been dismissed from Gide's *œuvre* as a juvenile work, a mere 'témoignage [. . .] sur l'inquiet mysticisme de [sa] jeunesse' [testimony of the anxious mysticism of his youth] (as Gide himself described it in 1926),[1] or assimilated with his later work on the grounds that 'tout Gide est dans André Walter, et André Walter est encore dans le *Journal* de 1939' [all of Gide is in André Walter, and André Walter is still present in the *Journal* of 1939] (in Barthes's words in 1942).[2] The complex relation between Gide's real-life experience and his creation of André Walter, including the use that Gide made of his own diaries in composing *CAW*, is treated in great depth in Jean Delay's *La Jeunesse d'André Gide*,[3] but I intend to address the separate question of the work's significance as a published piece of diary-writing at this point in time. In several respects, *CAW* is a product of a particular moment in literary history. It is heavily influenced by the 'maladie de l'idéal' [disease of idealism] manifested in Amiel's *journal intime* (1884 and 1887),[4] one of the publications which marked Pachet's pivotal date of 1887–88, but it also responds to a contemporary desire to renew the *roman* or literary *œuvre* by contact with other forms of writing. Pierre Masson draws attention to the publication of an 'Enquête sur le roman romanesque' [Enquiry

---

[1] André Gide, *Si le grain ne meurt*, in André Gide, *Souvenirs et voyages*, ed. by Pierre Masson (Paris: Gallimard, Bibl. de la Pléiade, 2001), pp. 79–330, p. 243. Gide repeated this sentiment in the preface to the 1930 edition of *CAW* ('mon excuse est qu'au temps d'André Walter je n'avais pas encore vingt ans' [my excuse is that at the time of André Walter I was less than twenty years old]), when the two early editions were long since unavailable. Despite being included in the first volume (1932) of the 1932–39 *Œuvres complètes*, ed. by Louis Martin-Chauffier, 15 vols (Paris: NRF, 1932–39), it was absent from the 1948 *Récits, roman, soties*, 2 vols (Paris: Gallimard, 1948), and absent again from the 1958 *Romans, récits et soties, œuvres lyriques* (Paris: Gallimard, Bibl. de la Pléiade, 1958). In his 1986 edition of *Les Cahiers et les Poésies d'André Walter*, Claude Martin argues for the work to be reinstated in Gide's *œuvre*, while apologising for its 'gaucheries' (Paris: Gallimard, 1986), p. 26. Happily, it is included in the 2009 Pléiade edition of Gide's *Romans et récits: œuvres lyriques et dramatiques*, and it is to this edition that I shall refer.
[2] Roland Barthes, 'Notes sur André Gide et son « Journal »', in *OC* ([1942]), I, pp. 33–46, p. 37. Barthes's comment could refer either to the author-figure or to *CAW* as a text, but in either case the implication is that Gide's later work consists of a vast elaboration rather than a development over time.
[3] Jean Delay, *La Jeunesse d'André Gide*, 2 vols (Paris: Gallimard, 1956–57). The two parts of Delay's study are titled 'André Gide avant André Walter: 1869–1890' and 'D'André Walter à André Gide: 1890–1895' respectively.
[4] Ibid., I, pp. 328, 533, 557.

into the novelistic novel] in May 1891, just a few months after *CAW* went on sale, which manifests the common attitude that the 'roman romanesque' (referring to Realist and Naturalist novels) was by now moribund, but also contains suggestions, from two authors of interest to Gide, regarding the sort of work that will replace it. Édouard Rod, who had formerly written Naturalist novels but since 1885 had published more experimental works in diary form (also under the influence of Amiel),[5] predicted that 'c'est donc en dehors du roman que se produira [...] l'œuvre marquante des années prochaines' [the major *œuvre* of the coming years will therefore emerge in some form outside the novel], while Edmond de Goncourt declared more specifically that 'la forme la plus parfaite du livre, pour la peinture et le récit de la vie, est le journal, les mémoires' [the most perfect form for the book, for producing a portrait and account of life, is the *journal intime*, or memoirs].[6] Gide's more immediate literary milieu was the Symbolist circle, whose trace is particularly visible in Walter's pursuit of an idealized *œuvre*, identifiable with the Mallarméen concept of the *Livre* (discussed in the introductory chapter to this book).

Arising at this turning point in *fin de siècle* writing, *CAW* can also be seen to contain the seeds of the literary preoccupations of diary-writing throughout the twentieth century, but to appreciate this it is necessary to return to the circumstances of its publication in 1891 and the way it functioned as the work of a fabricated, but plausible, *auteur supposé*. As in many other examples of *auteurs supposés*, the unveiling of Walter's fictional nature is an essential part of the work, and in this case it is inseparably linked to the exploration of the possibilities of the *journal intime* in relation to the literary *œuvre* and author-figure. Fortunately, the press reviews of *Les Cahiers d'André Walter* and *Les Poésies d'André Walter* (1892, similarly attributed to André Walter without any mention of Gide's name) provide valuable information about the way the works were read in the months following their publication, which can inform a new understanding of their use of diary-writing and the device of the *auteur supposé*.

Despite Gide's later claim that 'le succès fut nul' [it had no success at all],[7] *CAW* elicited generally positive responses both in the letters he received from writers to whom he had sent copies (including Mallarmé, Huysmans, and Maeterlinck)[8] and in a large number of press reviews. The latter particularly praised the text's depiction of psychological experience, the portrait of Emmanuèle as an *âme sœur* [sister soul], and the poetic quality of the prose. Aside from these thematic or stylistic concerns, the reviews are particularly useful for demonstrating the different ways in which the text's reading pact was interpreted at the time, which entailed various assumptions about its truth status and the nature of Walter himself. The attitudes of the reviewers can be grouped into the following positions:[9]

---

[5] Édouard Rod, *La Course à la mort* (Paris: L. Frinzine, 1885). Édouard Rod, *Le Sens de la vie* (Paris: Perrin, 1889). Also see Lorna Martens, *The Diary Novel* (Cambridge: Cambridge University Press, 1985), p. 119.

[6] Pierre Masson, 'Préface' to André Gide, *Romans et récits*, I, pp. XI–XLVII, p. XIV.

[7] Gide, *Si le grain ne meurt*, p. 245.

[8] Claude Martin provides a selection of the letters kept by Gide, in his 1986 edition, pp. 306–11.

[9] Examples are drawn from the *dossier de presse* in Claude Martin's 1986 edition, except when stated otherwise.

1. Walter was a real person, is genuinely dead, and *CAW* is the text of his real diary.[10]

2. The above may or may not be true, but the work's truth status is not relevant to the interpretation of the work (for example, as a portrait of a certain type of soul). Reviewers place *CAW* in a context of contemporary authors and literary precedents, including the real diaries of Amiel and the fictional diaries of Sainte-Beuve's Joseph Delorme.[11]

3. Walter is a character created by the real, still living, author, who has attributed to him an autobiographical *confession*. The diary form is artificially created for the purpose of authenticating Walter's existence, and the autobiographical element ends when Walter begins to descend into madness. The strategy of the *supercherie* may be recognized as being significant, and belonging to literary convention.[12]

4. Walter is a fictional character and the diary too is fictional. The work as a whole is a novel. Any relationship between the lives of Walter and of the real author is limited or without interest, and the work is therefore anonymous rather than pseudonymous.[13]

By the time of the publication of *Les Poésies d'André Walter* in a single collection (printed 14 April 1892, with the first reviews appearing the following June), Gide's authorship of *CAW* was well known,[14] yet was still disagreement in the press as to whether his continued attribution of the works to Walter was regrettable, or a meaningful use of a literary convention.

The indications of the paratext, combined with the generic conventions familiar to contemporary readers, made it possible for different reviewers to adopt any one of these four reading pacts, and in each case to produce a coherent interpretation of the diary. The reviewers adopting the first position demonstrate that the circumstances of the diary are essentially believable: that a young André Walter, upon the death of his mother and the marriage of his beloved cousin to another, used diary-writing to mourn his double loss (in the 'cahier blanc' [white notebook]), then to relate the composition of his novel *Allain* (in the 'cahier noir' [black notebook]), until he was interrupted by his own madness and death. Of the reviewers who do not assume Walter to be real, a large part take the *supercherie* [hoax] to be a

---

[10] Georges Pellissier, *Revue encyclopédique*, 1 August 1891; Anonymous, *Revue du Cercle Militaire*, 3 May 1891; Anonymous, 'journal non identifié', 1891, reprinted in *BAAG* 137 (2003), p. 101.

[11] Camille Mauclair, *Revue indépendante*, March 1891; Charles Maurras, *L'Observateur français*, 26 May 1891—Maurras was the first to identity the real author by name, in a note appended to the article; Remy de Gourmont, *Mercure de France*, June 1891.

[12] Henri de Régnier, *La Wallonie*, March-April 1891; Paul Redonnel, *La Plume*, 1 May 1891; Augustin Filon, *La Revue bleue*, 16 May 1891; Émile Verhaeren, *L'Art moderne*, 28 June 1891.

[13] Bernard Lazare, *La Nation*, 7 April 1891; Firmin Roz, *L'Ermitage*, May 1891.

[14] Besides Maurras's mention of the real author's name, *CAW* was listed as a work by André Gide in the contents list of the January–March 1892 issue of *La Wallonie*. This 'dévoil[ement]' [unveiling] was later mentioned in the introductory 'Notice' to *CAW* in the first volume (1932) of Gide's *Œuvres complètes*, p. xvi.

significant part of the work,[15] and make an effort to suspend their disbelief long enough to read *CAW* as a real diary, as in this review by Émile Verhaeren:

> Ces réflexions nous viennent à propos d'un livre non signé, intitulé: *Les Cahiers d'André Walter*. On nous a dit le nom de l'auteur. Nous avons fait notre possible pour l'oublier, si bien qu'à ce moment il nous serait difficile de répondre à une interrogation à ce sujet.[16]

> [These reflections come to mind in relation to a book published without signature, entitled *Les Cahiers d'André Walter*. We have been told the name of the author. We have done our best to forget it, with the result that we would now be hard pressed to answer any question on the matter.]

In this case, an awareness of the *supercherie* frames a feigned belief (or suspension of disbelief) in the reality of the *auteur supposé* himself, just as an awareness of a novelistic reading pact frames a feigned belief in a fictional character.

An understanding of *CAW* as the work of an *auteur supposé* therefore involves a movement from an interpretation based on a belief in the text's explicit claims regarding its truth status, to a broader appreciation of the significance of the *supercherie* itself. My own approach will follow this same progression between readings of the diary as being real and fictional respectively, but will also take account of an intermediate stage between the two: Walter's own philosophy and writing projects are concerned with a transition from the contingent, temporal nature of his real life (associated with the *journal intime* itself), towards transcendence into the necessity and timelessness of a fictional literary *œuvre*. These concerns complement the undecidable nature of the diary's truth status, as both real and fictional, and allow the work as a whole to constitute a broad reflection on the literary potential of diary-writing.

READING *CAW* AS A REAL DIARY

Paratext

Interpreted as a real diary, the *Cahiers* are not only believable, but already constitute an innovative work of diary-writing for this time. A contemporary reader's perception of *CAW* would be determined in the first instance by the paratexts of one of the two early editions. As will be seen, these explicitly specify a nonfictional reading pact, while inscribing the work in a certain tradition and indicating the ways in which it is new and unusual.[17]

---

[15] The term *auteur supposé* was not yet in use, but a letter to Gide from Paul Bourget links Walter to the similar cases of Sainte-Beuve's Joseph Delorme and Balzac's Louis Lambert (letter printed in Claude Martin's edition, pp. 307–8).

[16] André Gide, *Les Cahiers et les Poésies d'André Walter*, ed. by Claude Martin (Paris: Gallimard, 1986), p. 297.

[17] The 2009 Pléiade edition states that the edition published by the Librairie Académique Didier-Perrin went on sale first, on 27 February 1891, followed by the Librairie de l'Art indépendant edition on 25 April. However, Gide claims in *Si le grain ne meurt* that he personally took the Perrin edition,

The term 'anonyme' used by the Pléiade edition to describe both early editions is misleading (1245). It is true in the sense that the name of the man whom we now know to be the real author is entirely absent from the text and paratext, yet to a contemporary reader the front cover and title page of both editions conformed to the convention by which a description of a posthumously published work or document and the name of the real author are grouped together in the title (the phrase 'œuvre posthume' [posthumous work] features on the title page of both editions, and on the front cover of the Perrin edition). The title that most closely resembles *Les Cahiers d'André Walter* is *Les Cahiers de Sainte-Beuve* (1876), but the *Journal de Marie Bashkirtseff* (1887), the *Œuvres complètes de Alfred de Vigny* (1883–85), and *Victor Hugo intime: Mémoires, Correspondances, Documents inédits* (1885) all belong to this same category. In contrast, works which allude to this convention but simultaneously announce their fictionality may use a first name alone (Victorine Monniot, *Le Journal de Marguerite*, 1858) or a generic name (Octave Feuillet, *Le Journal d'une femme*, 1878), in which case there can be no doubt that the full name which appears above or below the title is that of an author rather than an editor.[18]

The largest difference between the two early editions is that the Perrin edition includes a 'Notice' which is absent from the Art indépendant edition. In fact, most of the information provided by the 'Notice' about the origin of the text can be found in the *cahiers* themselves (aside from Walter's family background), and is merely gathered together here in paraphrases or citations. For example, we read in the *cahiers* that Walter bequeathed the manuscript to his friend Pierre C*** (a fabrication like Walter himself, whom we now know to be based on Gide's friend Pierre Louÿs)[19] with the intention that it be published 's['il] devien[t] fou' [if he becomes mad] (102 and 137) and in the hope that it would be of interest to 'ceux qui [...] se désespèrent en croyant qu'ils sont seuls à souffrir' [those who live in despair, believing themselves to be the only ones to suffer] (80 and 137). The 'Notice' supports the illusion of the *supercherie* in several ways. It resembles the prefaces of the posthumous publications of real authors mentioned earlier, it promises the publication of further works from Walter's archives (his poetry and short travel diary were published some time later), and it insists that the *cahiers* are the real diary and notes of the author rather than a carefully crafted work, so that the reader requires the assistance of an editor in interpreting them. Despite the useful function of the 'Notice', its removal from the later, preferred, Art indépendant edition anticipates a pattern observable in later

'dans sa presque totalité' [in its virtual entirety] with the exception of seventy copies destined for the press, to be 'condamn[ée] au pilon' [condemned to be pulped] as soon as the Art indépendant edition was ready (245). We may assume that some copies of each edition were at large, and probably more of the Art indépendant edition than the Perrin edition. I shall therefore give preference to the Art indépendant edition, but discuss both editions where they differ significantly.

[18] Valerie Raoul, *The French Fictional Journal: Fictional Narcissism/Narcissistic Fiction* (Toronto: University of Toronto Press, 1980), pp. 13–15.

[19] Pierre Masson, 'Notice' for *André Walter. Cahiers et Poésies*, in André Gide, *Romans et récits*, I, pp. 1231–44, p. 1239.

publications attributed to *auteurs supposés*, including Larbaud's A.O. Barnabooth and Queneau's Sally Mara: whereas biographical information and strategies of authentication are initially provided by an editor (also fabricated, such as Larbaud's X.M. Tournier de Zamble and Queneau's Michel Presle), the *auteur supposé* is subsequently represented by their *journal intime* without any intermediary. The *auteur supposé* then seems so well established that they need no introduction, and their diary attains a greater independence as a literary work rather than being a document or *témoignage*.

The paratext within the volume continues these claims of authenticity, while making innovations with regard to the publication of a real *journal intime*. The indications of time that begin some diary entries, ranging from a time of day ('minuit', 60) to complete dates ('1er juillet 89', 52), not only identify the text generically as being a form of diary, but also allow a coherent and believable chronology to be reconstructed which locates the events in a specific and very recent historical time.[20] The editor's footnotes (attributable to Pierre C***) provide some few details of Walter's circumstances, such as his learning of his cousin Emmanuèle's death (70), and also information on the nature of the manuscript ('phrases barrées' [sentences crossed out], 74). These editorial interventions reinforce the impression of a real diary (including the ellipses and omissions of a work written without publication immediately in view), but also of a real manuscript on which the printed text is based. A large range of typographic distinctions are used to recreate in print the materiality of this alleged manuscript, including the page layout, various asterisks, horizontal bars and dots for breaking up the text, ellipses of varying length, small capitals, reduced type size for recopied sections, and extensive use of italics. This editorial strategy differs considerably from the relatively uniform typesetting of earlier published diaries such as Amiel's or Bashkirtseff's, let alone publications such as the *Cahiers de Sainte-Beuve* that are closer to being mere collections of *pensées* [thoughts] harvested from the author's notebooks. By comparison, the presentation of *CAW* emphasizes that it possesses its own organic unity founded on Walter's experience of his writing projects, and that an understanding of the chronological and material dimensions of these projects is necessary for the work's interpretation.

A Real Novelistic Diary

The unity indicated by the paratext is manifested in the main text by features more characteristic of a novel than a real diary, such as large-scale structures and

[20] Éric Marty finds that Walter's references to the seasons, particularly spring, are often incongruous with the dates provided, and indicate a resistance in adapting material from Gide's own diaries to their new context in *CAW*. See Éric Marty, 'Gide et sa première fiction: l'attitude créatrice', in *L'Auteur et le manuscrit*, ed. by Michel Contat (Paris: PUF, 1991), pp. 177–97. However, when *CAW* is approached as a real diary, these incongruities (18, 20, 50, 57, and 59) are easily explained by the thematic importance of spring to Walter (related to his conflicted feelings of sexual desire and abhorrence, and also his desire for literary creation), and by his increasing obliviousness to the outside world (which is emphasized in *Les Poésies d'André Walter*: 'Peut-être déjà qu'un printemps / A fui sans que nous l'ayons vu paraître' [Perhaps already one spring / has flown by, without us noticing it appear], 121).

the construction of a coherent narrative of Walter's experience prior to his writing the *cahiers*. Yet when *CAW* is read as a real diary, its unity and self-sufficiency appear consistent with the nature of Walter's writing projects, and in particular with his exploration of the *intime* as a positive value. Rather than challenging a reader's belief in André Walter's reality, these features demonstrate the potential of a published diary to assume some of the novel's independence as an *œuvre*.

The diary's large-scale structures begin with the opening lines of the first entry (the use of verse is not in itself unusual for the *journal intime*), which create a series of expectations for the reader (or prolepses, in narratological terms), in the manner of the introductory proem of a long narrative poem:

> Attends,
> Que ta tristesse soit un peu plus reposée,—pauvre âme que la lutte d'hier a
>   faite si lasse.
>
> Attends.
> Quand les larmes seront pleurées,
> les chers espoirs refleuriront.
> Maintenant tu sommeilles.
>
> Berceuses, escarpolettes, barcarolles,
> Le chant des pleureuses alanguit les chutes. (5)
>
> [Wait,
> Until your sadness has rested a little more,—poor soul, so weary from
>   yesterday's struggle.
>
> Wait.
> When the tears have been shed,
> Cherished hopes will flower anew.
> Now you are sleeping.
>
> Lullabies, swings, barcarolles,
> The song of mourners soothes the descents.]

Something is being postponed ('Attends'), during a period of 'tristesse', 'repos', and 'sommeil', until 'les chers espoirs refleuriront'. The first stage will therefore be predominantly static and retrospective, concerned with 'la lutte d'hier', whereas the following stage will be active and forward-looking ('espoirs'). It is reasonable to associate the two stages with the *cahier blanc* and the *cahier noir* respectively. These expectations are effectively met by the diary that follows. The *cahier blanc* involves a process of mourning, during which Walter relives memories from his time spent with Emmanuèle. At the end of the *cahier blanc* Walter declares, using the same terms as in the proem (a process of analepsis), that the first stage is now complete: 'Te voilà si changée, mon âme! / Tu pleurais tantôt; tu souris maintenant' [You are so changed, my soul! / You were weeping; now you are smiling], and again in the final words of the *cahier*, 'tous les espoirs ont refleuri' [all the hopes have flowered anew] (51). The formal unity of the *cahier blanc* is further reinforced by a number of verbal echoes, such as the cluster of cognates of *pleur* (five instances on pp. 50–1) in the final entry recalling those of the opening lines, and the phrase from p. 6, 'quelque soir, revenant en arrière, je redirai ces mots de deuil' [one evening, looking back, I shall say these words of mourning again], repeated almost exactly on p. 50. The *cahier noir* heralds the second, more active stage with the words, 'étrange:—se mettre enfin à l'œuvre depuis deux ans rêvée' [strange:—finally setting to work on the *œuvre* that I have dreamt of for two years] (52), and relates the composition of Walter's novel *Allain*. His repeated references to the madness of Allain (the novel's eponymous hero) then foreshadow the crisis that eventually brings about Walter's own death and the end of the diary.

These sorts of structures are expected in a novel, where the work's unity is assured by the large-scale composition attributed to an author-figure, but they are incongruous with a real diary, where the diarist's gradual composition (or *narration intercalée*) is affected by the unfolding of contingent events. Yet the structural unity of the *cahiers* is provided by the coherence of the writing projects themselves, in which Walter's role is neither traditionally diaristic nor fully authorial, as he discusses himself early in the *cahier blanc*:

> Sorti toutes les pages écrites qui me rappellent autrefois. Je les veux toutes relire, les ranger, copier, les revivre. J'en écrirai de nouvelles sur des souvenirs anciens.
>
> Je délivrerai ma pensée de ses rêveries antérieures, pour vivre d'une nouvelle vie; quand les souvenirs seront dits, mon âme en sera plus légère; je les arrêterai dans leur fuite: une chose n'est pas tout à fait morte qui n'est pas encore oubliée. Enfin, je ne veux pas m'en aller, sans même détourner la tête, de ce qui m'aura tant charmé durant toute ma jeunesse.—Puis pourquoi chercher après coup les raisons d'une volonté prise, comme pour s'excuser de l'avoir? J'écris parce que j'ai besoin d'écrire—et voilà tout.
>
> Et c'est bien plutôt, avec l'ambition ravivée, l'idée du livre si longtemps rêvé, ALLAIN, qui de nouveau maintenant se réveille. (7–8)

[Have taken out all the written pages that recall the past. I want to reread them all, arrange them, copy them, relive them. I shall write new ones on old memories.

I shall free my thought from its former reveries, in order to live a new life; when the memories have been spoken, my soul will be made lighter; I shall catch them in their flight: a thing is not entirely dead if it is not yet forgotten. And also, I do not want to leave behind, without even looking back, everything that enchanted me throughout all my youth.—But then why should I look for justifications for a decision that has been made, as if to excuse myself for it? I am writing because I need to write—that is all.

And it is above all, with rekindled ambition, the idea of the book so long dreamt of, ALLAIN, that is now awakening.]

Walter isolates himself from society in order to immerse himself in his grief and writing, and so his projects (the recopying, reliving, and retelling of his previous diaries, then the composition of *Allain*) develop organically from his initial situation with little influence from contingent events. However, the development of these open-ended projects is not entirely foreseeable to Walter himself, nor does he fully understand his own motivation for undertaking them. The diary's unity can therefore be attributed to two processes, with two corresponding roles for Walter: first, the logical evolution of a situation that surpasses Walter's understanding (in his more traditionally diaristic role), and secondly, Walter's attempts to comprehend the projects in their totality, by commenting on their progress, referring back to their initial aims, and making predictions for their development (a more authorial role).

These two processes—the diaristic and authorial modes of writing respectively—are also found in Walter's gradual construction of a coherent narrative of his past experience with Emmanuèle. The persistent myth of the *journal intime* creates the expectation that it will be written only for the diarist's self (this misconception was discussed in the introductory chapter) and will be concerned primarily with recent events, therefore resulting in a fragmentary account requiring the provision of supplementary information from an editor, yet Walter creates a self-sufficient account of this earlier period as if he were writing with a general reader in mind. Once again, a plausible explanation is found in the nature of his project and its motivation, which he only partially understands. Walter's apparent intention to relate his memories of Emmanuèle in chronological order actually disguises a different type of narrative, which tends towards an effacement of linear time and causality. A single series of passages provides a useful example (16–17): the first passage moves from a general statement in the imperfect tense ('Ils étaient confiants en nous' [they trusted us]) to a reference to a specific occasion in the perfect tense ('Te souviens-tu de ce beau soir où je suis venu te retrouver [...]?' [Do you remember that fine evening when I came to find you again?]). A recopied diary entry follows, dated from almost two years earlier, which appears to relate in the present tense the occasion mentioned above ('Tout dort autour de nous [...]' [Everything is sleeping around us]). The next passage begins with a participial phrase that seems to pick up the narrative thread of the same particular occasion ('Plus tôt levés que les autres' [Risen earlier than the others]), but continues in the imperfect tense ('nous courions vite au bois' [we would run quickly to the woods]) and speaks of the experience of repeated sunrises. Nothing tells us with any certainty that the three passages refer to the same occasion, and their overall effect is the creation of a timeless, idealized portrait of Walter's existence with Emmanuèle. Walter's motivations for this process are a matter for speculation (Anny Wynchank suggests that he is trying to convince himself that his relationship with Emmanuèle was as he would like it to have been),[21] but his attitude in his diary-writing again approaches that of an author writing for an abstract literary 'other'.

Another unusual feature of the *cahiers* is their unprecedented emphasis on the *intime*. Françoise Simonet-Tenant describes the development of this concept throughout the nineteenth century,[22] which was by this time firmly associated with the privacy and interior focus of the *journal intime*, but Walter elevates it to the level of a worldview:

Pas un événement: la vie toujours intime—et pourtant la vie si violente. Tout s'est joué dans l'âme; il n'en a rien paru. Comment écrire cela? (8–9)

la vie du dehors n'est pas assez violente; de plus âpres frémissements sont dans les enthousiasmes intimes. (17)

---

[21] Anny Wynchank, 'Métamorphoses dans *Les Cahiers d'André Walter*: essai de rétablissement de la chronologie dans *Les Cahiers d'André Walter*', *BAAG*, 63 (1984), pp. 361–73.

[22] Françoise Simonet-Tenant, *Journal personnel et correspondance (1785–1939) ou les affinités électives* (Louvain-la-Neuve: Academia-Bruylant, 2009), pp. 28–35.

[Not a single event: life always *intime*—and yet such violent life. Everything played out in the soul; nothing was visible. How to write that?

the outer life is not violent enough; there are more more passionate tremblings in the fervours of the *intime*.]

Walter believes that the most intense and important experience is *intime*. In practical terms, he prefers his own 'claustration' in Brittany to the literary world of Paris, where 'ils s'excitent, ils s'entraînent—c'est une ruée' [they get excited, they rush about—it's a stampede] (35), and this isolation from contingent events contributes to the diary's unity and the organic development of the writing projects. But his conviction also leads Walter to seek a new way of writing in response to this *intime* experience ('Comment écrire cela?'), which excludes any *événement* that is exterior to the *âme*. In this respect, even when it is considered as a real diary, *CAW* appears as an experimental literary project with broad implications for writing at this time of growth in 'la littérature personnelle' (in the words of Brunetière in 1888).[23]

In summary, the paratext's strategy for authenticating *CAW* involves inscribing the work in the flourishing tradition of posthumous diary publications, and a belief in this authenticity can be sustained throughout a reading of the main text. Yet when *CAW* is compared with these earlier publications, it already appears as an unusual work making radical claims for the possibilities of diary-writing. The editorial presentation of the text, carefully reproducing the chronological and material dimensions of the alleged manuscript, emphasizes the diary's organic unity (rather than being a fragmentary *témoignage* or a collection of *pensées*). This same unity accounts for the apparently novelistic features of the diary: its large-scale structures, its coherent narrative (as if written for a literary 'other', if not for actual readers), and its promotion of the *intime* as a literary value. Walter's own tendency to move from the traditional role of a diarist towards the perspective of an author anticipates the whole work's transition from real diary towards fiction, but before I address this global view of the work as a *supercherie*, it will be useful to examine how Walter himself conceptualizes this transition in his philosophical and aesthetic reflections.

WALTER'S TRANSITION TO FICTION

Walter's experience over the course of the diary (as well as his earlier life) can be viewed as a transition from an initial propensity to inhabit his imagination, which I shall term 'everyday fictivity', towards a theorized literary transformation (in the attempt to write *Allain*), which eventually consumes his life. This transition takes on even greater significance when *CAW* is subsequently considered as the work of an *auteur supposé*, but it is also important to note how types of

---

[23] Ferdinand de Brunetière, 'La Littérature personnelle', *La Revue des deux mondes*, 85 (1888), pp. 433–52.

fictivity are accommodated in the context of a supposedly real diary. Unlike Dorrit Cohn's narrow definition of fiction as referring to 'a literary nonreferential narrative text', Walter's everyday fictivity combines the related concepts (explicitly excluded from her definition) of 'untruth', 'conceptual abstraction', 'l'Imaginaire' in psychoanalytic discourse, and the creation of narrative.[24] This presence of fictivity in a real diary runs counter to Philippe Lejeune's claim that the diary form is essentially resistant to this sort of hybridity, but it is also partly explained by André Walter's own conflation of fiction with literarity, in keeping with a 'mystique [...] mallarméenne de la littérature' [Mallarméen mysticism of literature].[25]

Everyday Fictivity

The most obvious sign of Walter's propensity towards fiction (in the broad sense mentioned earlier) in the time before the beginning of the *cahiers* is that his life is saturated with literature. As a result, the account of his past with Emmanuèle is often an account of their readings together:

> L'âpreté violente de Shakespeare nous laissait brisés d'enthousiasme: la vraie vie n'avait pas de ces enlèvements. (9)
>
> La vie intense, voilà le superbe: je ne changerais la mienne contre aucune, j'y ai vécue plusieurs vies, et la réelle a été la moindre. (12)
>
> Ne pas s'enfermer en sa seule vie, en son seul corps; faire son âme hôtesse de plusieurs. (17)
>
> [Shakespeare's fierce violence left us exhausted with excitement: real life did not offer such raptures.
>
> A life lived intensively, that is what is truly admirable: I would not change my life for any other. Over its course I have lived several lives, and the real one was the least of them.
>
> Not to enclose oneself in only one's own life, one's own body; to make one's soul the host of several others.]

He not only finds greater interest in this sphere of experience than in real life, but also conflates his own identity with others, so that he can '[vivre] plusieurs vies' [live several lives]. This tendency manifests itself in a practical sense in his and Emmanuèle's habit of adopting characters from their reading, such as the following two figures from the gospel of St Luke:

> Je t'appelais alors 'Marthe', parce que *tu t'agitais pour bien des choses.*
>   Mais, le soir, c'était 'Marie' de nouveau; ton âme après les soins du jour redevenait contemplative. (15)
>
> [I called you 'Martha' then, because you were *careful and troubled about many things.*
>   But, in the evening, you became 'Mary' once again; your soul became contemplative again after the cares of the day.]

---

[24] Dorrit Cohn, *The Distinction of Fiction* (Baltimore: Johns Hopkins University Press, 1999), pp. 1–12.
[25] Philippe Lejeune, 'Le Journal comme « antifiction »', *Poétique*, 149 (2007), pp. 3–14, p. 10.

While Walter's initial propensity towards fiction provides a starting point for the more complex fictivity of his writing projects, this readiness to adopt the identities of others specifically anticipates the ambiguous relationship that later comes to exist between André Walter and the character he creates, Allain.

André Walter's immersion in his imagination takes on a new form at the point when he begins writing the *cahier blanc*. The initial description of his writing project moves from repeated references to rest and sleep in the opening lines ('reposée', 'lasse', 'tu sommeilles', 'berceuses', 'alanguit', 5) to a more specific account of a dreamlike state, opposed to waking thought, and in which both the past and the future become more vivid than the present:

> Et puis tu dormiras,—car ne réfléchis pas encore [...].
> Endors le souvenir au gré des rêves. (5)

> On est seul. La pensée se projette comme sur un fond noir; le temps à venir apparaît sur le sombre comme une bande d'espace. Rien ne distrait *de la vision commencée*. On n'est plus qu'elle. (6)

> [And then you will sleep,—do not think just yet [...].
> Let your memory play out in dreams.

> I am alone. Thought projects itself as if onto a dark background; the time still to come appears over the darkness as a ribbon of space. Nothing to distract from *the vision that has begun*. I am no longer anything but this vision.]

This writing process corresponds to the narrative structure described previously, in which the transitions between passages follow a logic other than chronology or causality. It does not, however, resemble the earlier diary entries that Walter recopies, nor the subsequent writing of the *cahier noir*, which is instead associated with a 'réveil' [awakening] (6). The dreamlike state of the *cahier blanc* is therefore an intermediate stage before the more wakeful project that follows (the *cahier noir*, accompanying the composition of *Allain*), as well as being the beginning of Walter's reflections on fiction.

Walter's Philosophy of Fiction

From early in the *cahier blanc* Walter states his desire to 'se faire tel que l'on se veut' [make himself such as he wishes to be] by force of *volonté* (17), a desire which he reformulates throughout the *cahiers*. The challenge which he faces is to enter so fully into his fictional creation that it is transformed into reality:

> Comédien? peut-être...; mais c'est moi-même que je joue. (33)

> Ma mère me disait: 'Tu ne peux pas faire la vie à ton rêve: il faut que tu te fasses à la vie.'
> Et bien! quand on ne peut pas s'y faire, à la vie!... (77)

> [An actor? Perhaps...; but playing the role of myself.

> My mother said to me, 'You cannot make real life fit your dream: you must adapt yourself to real life.'
> But what if we cannot adapt ourselves to it, to this life!...]

The self that he wishes to construct is also conflated with literary fiction by means of certain ambiguous terms, such as in the following biblical quotation:

> *L'Œuvre de chacun sera manifestée* (I Cor., IV, 12.)[26]
>> *L'Œuvre de chacun!*—malheur à moi! (74)
>
> [*Every man's work shall be made manifest* (I Cor. 4.12)
>> *Every man's work!*—woe is me!]

The passage to which he is referring already uses 'œuvre' (in the sense of something that is constructed) as a metaphor for the actions and moral decisions of a person's life, but in its immediate context in *CAW* it also refers to Walter's intended literary *œuvre*, *Allain*. The term 'manifester' is also used in describing his combined moral and aesthetic project, such as in his claim that 'nous vivons pour manifester, point pour vivre.—Fin et moyen: là est la différence' [we live to manifest, not to live.—End and means: that is the difference] (78).

Among the philosophers mentioned by Walter, it is Schopenhauer who is most closely associated with his project to enter into his fictional creations. The following passage leads on from an observation related to Schopenhauer's *Le Monde comme volonté et comme représentation* (first published in French translation in 1886):

> Si j'arrivais à contempler la chimère avec assez de fixité pour que mes yeux éblouis du mirage n'aient plus un seul regard pour les réalités ambiantes, la chimère inventée m'apparaîtrait réelle; et si c'est une image évoquée d'autrefois, j'oublierais que c'est autrefois, je la ferais toute présente, usurpatrice des réalités. (67)
>
> [If I were to succeed in gazing upon the chimera with such concentration that my eyes, dazzled by the mirage, would no longer pay the slightest attention to the reality around me, the imagined chimera would appear real to me; and if it were an image recalled from the past, I would forget that it was from the past, I would make it entirely present, usurping other realities.]

This is no idle speculation, as Walter goes on to extract a practical method from Hippolyte Taine's thesis in *De l'intelligence* (1870) that aesthetic imagination is a form of deliberate hallucination:

> Il suffit que les centres nerveux soient ébranlés; ce ne sont plus seulement les sens qui les ébranlent alors, la perception extérieure,—mais bien l'intime volonté qui, par eux, crée l'image. (89)
>
> [All that is required is that the nervous centres be stimulated; and they are stimulated not only by the senses, by exterior perception,—but also by the interior will, which, through the senses, creates the image.]

He goes on to apply this method, and attempts to maintain a hallucination of the deceased Emmanuèle (90), thereby drawing a step closer to his aim of 'le rêve soumis à la volonté et la vie dans le rêve' [the dream dominated by the will, and life lived in the dream] (77).

---

[26] His citation is actually from I Corinthians 3.13, but there does not appear to be any significance to his error.

However, the final aim of this philosophy of fiction is only gradually elaborated over the course of the *cahier noir*:

> je jette au vent de l'esprit ces pages folles écrites; elles consommeront le chaste désir de nos âmes et chanteront la symphonie de leurs éternelles fiançailles. (52)
>
> Ce qui change, c'est le corps seul: il retourne en poussière—(encore que phénoménalement). La mort n'est pas une conclusion; le roman ne s'arrête pas là,—qui sait seulement s'il s'arrête?... et s'il commence avec la vie?—qui sait seulement s'il commence? (95)
>
> [I cast to the wind of the spirit these mad written pages; they will consummate the chaste desire of our souls and sing the symphony of their eternal betrothal.
>
> It is the body alone that changes: it returns to dust—(and even this only phenomenally). Death is not a conclusion; the novel does not end there,—who knows if it ends at all?... and if it begins with the start of life?—who knows if it begins at all?]

The *cahier noir* begins with the hope that his diaries will allow the consummation of his desire for the timelessness and abstraction of an *œuvre* (here, a symphony). In the second quotation, Walter's sense of his approaching death makes the problem more urgent, but it has also changed its focus: his life is now conceived specifically as a *roman*, and Walter's project for transcendence is implicated in his complex relationship with his own novel, *Allain*, and its eponymous hero.

Walter and Allain

In the later stages of Walter's transition to fiction, the writing of his diary seems to converge with his novel, and he becomes engaged in a 'course à la folie' [race to madness] with Allain (102). He declares a victory in this struggle ('J'ai vaincu [...]. Allain est fou—je ne le suis pas encore' [I have won. Allain has become mad—I am not there yet], 113), but this is cast into doubt, first by his death soon afterwards, and secondly by the decision of Walter's friend and editor, Pierre C***, to publish the *cahiers* instead of *Allain*. Walter's relationship with Allain anticipates Gide's own relation to Walter when the *supercherie* is discovered, but once again Walter should first be considered as a real diarist and author, in order to appreciate how his writing projects differ from Gide's.

Walter's extremely *intime* diary (in the sense discussed earlier) had possessed from the beginning an unusual degree of the unity and self-sufficiency associated with a literary *œuvre*, but now the material circumstances of his writing bring him even closer to the fictional world of *Allain*. He works day and night with the curtains closed and a lamp lit, eating and sleeping only when necessary, in order to create a state in which 'c'est l'heure indifférente; c'est le travail dans l'absolu sans plus de temps ni d'espace' [the time of day is irrelevant; working in the absolute, removed now from time and space] (75). Although the diary's dated entries continue to chart a steady change in Walter's project and state of mind over measurable time, there are even fewer incursions of the outside world in the *cahier noir* than in the *cahier blanc*, and the dates now create an internally consistent chronology rather than an historical one. These changes in Walter's circumstances all help the diary to approach the abstract, rarefied world of *Allain*, which is 'hors du temps et de l'espace' [outside time and space] and in which he has 'redui[t] tout à L'ESSENTIEL' [reduced everything to the ESSENTIAL] (53).

Conversely, this *roman-théorème* with its 'lignes géométriques' (as described by Walter, 53) also bears a surprising resemblance to the *cahiers* in certain respects. In starting the task of composing the novel by writing down 'le plan et [. . .] les principales lignes' (52), Walter certainly shows a greater degree of conscious planning in this work than is entailed in the overall project for the *cahiers*, yet his task also involves a large degree of the unknown:

> Pourtant j'ai laissé les conclusions vagues et flottantes, voulant m'imposer une déduction non prévenue et découvrir peu à peu, au fil de l'évolution patiemment découlée,—d'autant plus ne vois-je pas très bien jusqu'où je pourrai pousser le drame, ni comment l'arrêter, ni pourquoi.
>
> La vérité voudrait, je crois, qu'il n'y ait pas de conclusion: elle doit ressortir du récit même, sans qu'il soit besoin d'une péripétie qui la fasse flagrante. Jamais les choses ne se concluent: c'est l'homme qui tire les conclusions des choses. (52–4)
>
> [Yet I have left the conclusions vague and drifting, as I wish to impose on myself an unforeseeable process of deduction and to discover for myself, little by little, how its evolution will patiently develop.—for this reason I do not have a clear idea how far I will be able to pursue the drama, nor how to stop it, nor why I should do so.
>
> Truth would require, I believe, that there should be no conclusion: it should emerge from the narrative itself, without the need for any peripeteia that would make it stand out. Things never conclude by themselves: it is man who draws conlusions from things.]

Walter's uncertainty of the direction the novel is to take is characteristic of diary-writing, and his 'course à la folie' with Allain (102) suggests that the progress of the *cahier* and the *roman* are very much interdependent. However, his final comment above underlines the broader, programmatic significance of *Allain* as a diaristic novel, just as Walter's novelistic *cahiers* make programmatic claims for the future of diary-writing. In contrast to the dominant contemporary model of Realist or Naturalist novels, in which an authoritative narrator (closely associated with the author-figure of a Zola or a Maupassant) imposes their conclusions, Walter's *Allain* proposes a reading pact more characteristic of a posthumously published diary, where it is the responsibility of the reader to draw whatever conclusions they might find (this recalls the distinct 'adresse' of an author's 'petits papiers', as remarked by Lacan).[27]

This final stage of Walter's writing tends towards a complete convergence of his diary and his novel, which is never fully realized. If it were, it would entail a synthesis of Walter's temporal existence (associated with the *journal intime*) and his desires for literary transcendence in the *roman*, and establish a model for a unification of the author's life and *œuvre* in their (fully literary) *journal intime*.

---

[27] Jacques Lacan, 'Jeunesse de Gide ou la lettre et le désir', in *Écrits II* (Paris: Seuil, 1999), pp. 217–42, p. 222.

As it is, Walter creates an all-or-nothing test of his success, which (for the reader of these *cahiers*) has a foregone conclusion:

S'IL PUBLIE MES CAHIERS—QU'IL GARDE ALLAIN;—L'UN OU L'AUTRE. (102)

[IF HE PUBLISHES MY NOTEBOOKS - LET HIM KEEP ALLAIN;—ONE OR THE OTHER.]

The decision of Pierre C*** to publish the *cahiers* after Walter's madness and death clearly indicates Walter's failure. For having aspired to an aesthetic of excessive purity and necessity, Walter loses both his mind and his life, and could effectively share the epitaph he writes for Allain, 'CI-GÎT ALLAIN QUI DEVINT FOU / PARCE QU'IL CRUT AVOIR UNE ÂME' [HERE LIES ALLAIN, WHO BECAME MAD / BECAUSE HE BELIEVED HE HAD A SOUL] (105). Yet the end of Walter's life and the concomitant failure of his writing projects are also the starting point of his genuine literary transformation, when *CAW* comes to be considered as the fictional work of André Gide.

READING *CAW* AS FICTION

A reader's awareness of the fictionality of *CAW* does not invalidate these first readings or its explicit reading pact as a real posthumous diary, but rather frames them within an additional reading pact that recognizes the implicit convention of the *auteur supposé*. As well as the work's fictionality, it was known soon after its publication that the real author's name was André Gide,[28] although this had a limited bearing on its reception, as Gide was not publicly known for any previous works (I shall therefore avoid making readings based on our subsequently acquired knowledge of Gide). Unlike in the diegetic structure of an openly fictional diary novel, where the diaristic and (dominant) novelistic codes are simultaneously present (as discussed by Valérie Raoul),[29] the unveiling of an *auteur supposé* involves the subsequent transformation of the real diary into fiction. In this particular *supercherie*, Walter's transformation into a fictional author-character is coloured by his own philosophy of fiction, and his complex relationship with Allain takes its place in an even more complex series: André Gide, creator of André Walter, creator of Allain. Walter's development as an *auteur supposé* is eventually brought to an end by the later publication of *Les Poésies d'André Walter*, still attributed to Walter alone, but with an increasing sense of irony which makes it impossible to sustain the requisite suspension of disbelief (as described earlier in the chapter by Émile Verhaeren). With this conclusion, the failure of Walter's over-ambitious writing projects is reconsidered as Gide's partial success, and as just the beginning of his experimentation with diary-writing.

---

28 He was first named in Charles Maurras's review on 26 May 1891 in *L'Observateur français*.
29 Raoul, *The French Fictional Journal*.

Paratext

When the claims of the paratext are reassessed as a function of the *supercherie*, the title continues to allude to posthumous works such as *Les Cahiers de Sainte-Beuve* and the *Journal de Marie Bashkirtseff*, but inscribes the work more directly into a tradition of works by *auteurs supposés*, such as Mérimée's *Théâtre de Clara Gazul* (1825) and Sainte-Beuve's *Vie, poésies et pensées de Joseph Delorme* (1829). Pierre Louÿs, the real-life figure behind André Walter's editor Pierre C***, was soon to join this same tradition with his *Chansons de Bilitis* (1894). The name 'André Walter', now known to be a fabrication, is determined by the necessity of the fictional work: the *nomen* has become *omen*. It is therefore subject to interpretation, particularly in comparison with the name 'André Gide'. While identity between the two figures is suggested by their shared first name, the change of surname suggests several differences between the real author and his creation. For example, it suggests a Germanic side to André Walter (the 'Notice' in the Perrin edition explains his 'teinte métaphysique' [metaphysical tone] by his father's being 'de race saxonne', 137), it alludes to the pious works of Mme André-Walther,[30] and it can even be treated as an elaborate play on the terms *idem* and *alter*.[31]

Gide and Walter

For the majority of readers who knew nothing of Gide apart from his name, the play of same and other between the real author and the *auteur supposé* was the only clue as to why the former succeeded where the latter failed. It might seem a fruitless task to extrapolate from Walter to Gide, as a great range of possible outcomes can be imagined. If we assume the greatest possible resemblance between the two figures, Gide may have had the same experiences as Walter, undertaken the same diary-writing and novelistic projects, but owing to some important difference he completed his novel (*CAW*), which he published in the guise of a real diary under the name of his alter ego, André Walter. At the other extreme, Gide may have experienced nothing resembling Walter's life, he did not keep any diary, and he wrote *CAW* as a work of pure invention, published as a real diary, and attributed to a figure who is completely alien to Gide's own character. We now know from publications of Gide's early diaries that, of these two extremes, the former is closer to the truth. However, it must be possible to interpret the whole work as a *supercherie* without this information, using only the one crucial factor that is common to both these propositions: that the text of *CAW* is, for Walter, a real diary accompanying the composition of a failed novel, whereas for Gide the very same text is itself his successful, or at least successfully completed and published, novel.

---

[30] Alain Goulet, 'Mme André-Walther', *BAAG*, 61 (1984), pp. 107–12.

[31] Anne Chevalier, 'Le même et l'autre dans *Les Cahiers et les Poésies d'André Walter*', *BAAG*, 110–11 (1996), pp. 177–8.

Given this fundamental difference between Gide and Walter, it should be possible to find an explanation for the different outcomes of their writing projects by comparing *CAW* (as Gide's novel) with Walter's 'plan et [...] principales lignes' for the composition of *Allain*:

> UN personnage seulement, et encore un quelconque, ou plutôt son cerveau, n'est que le lieu commun où le drame se livre, le champ clos où les adversaires s'assaillent. Ces adversaires, ce ne sont pas même deux passions rivales—mais deux entités (?) seulement: L'ÂME et la CHAIR;—et leur conflit résultant d'une passion unique, d'un seul désir: *faire l'ange*; découlant comme une déduction nécessaire, comme une conclusion des prémisses une fois posées. (53)

> [ONE character only, and an ordinary one at that, or rather his brain, provides the terrain where the drama takes place, the enclosed field where the adversaries confront one another. These adversaries are not even two rival passions—but only two entities (?): the SOUL and the FLESH;—and their conflict is the result of a single passion, a single desire: *to be as the angels*; then unfolding as a necessary deduction, as an inevitable conclusion from the initial premises.]

In fact, these plans for *Allain* correspond closely to *CAW* itself, which is not surprising given Walter's tendency in the *cahier noir* to make his diaristic and novelistic writing converge. The comparison does not offer a solution to the problem, but it does point towards two distinct lines of enquiry into the nature of *CAW* and of its real author. First, since the convergence of Walter's diary and novel is never complete, it is still possible to infer certain formal differences between *CAW* and *Allain* on the basis of Walter's attempt to 'réduire tout à L'ESSENTIEL' in a novel modelled on the schematic structure and philosophical necessity of Spinoza's *Ethics Demonstrated in Geometrical Order* (53). Secondly, it is possible to compare Walter's diary with Gide's novel, which happen both to be constituted by the text of *CAW*, but where the latter has undergone precisely the transformation into fiction that Walter had contemplated at great length.

The fact that Gide's novel is formally as diaristic as Walter's diary (as they are the same text) may help to explain why Gide succeeds in writing a novel and survives, whereas Walter is led to madness and death through attempting to write *Allain*. Our information concerning the causes of Walter's decline into madness is largely provided by his predictions for Allain:

> Elle [Emmanuèle's counterpart in *Allain*] meurt; *donc* il la possède... Oui, mais Allain vit encore: il demande le surhumain, la chair se vengera. Son âme désirera des communions toujours plus étroites, mais le corps la désolera par l'inquiet désir d'embrasser—et plus son vol sera sublime, et plus la chair l'avilira:
> Avec cela, tous les doutes. L'ennui de la réalité le maintiendra prisonnier dans son rêve: il n'en sortira pas.
> La folie est au bout. (76)

> [She dies; *therefore* he possesses her... Yes, but Allain continues to live: he demands the superhuman, the flesh will takes its revenge. His soul will desire ever closer communions, but the body will afflict it with the anxious desire for an embrace— and the more his soul ascends to sublime heights, the more the flesh will drag it down:

And then come all the doubts. His distaste for reality will keep him prisoner in his dream: he will not escape from it.
At the end, madness.]

Despite his prescience regarding the consequences of Allain's desire (both sexual and aesthetic) for an ideal that is incompatible with his condition, Walter shares these desires by attempting to transpose his own experience from the diary into the form of an abstract and sublime *œuvre* ('Et là, tout le roman impossible' [and therein, the whole impossible novel], 54). He therefore becomes engaged in a 'course à la folie' with Allain (102), to which he eventually succumbs. Yet Gide has survived his own 'course à la folie' with Walter precisely because his novel (*CAW*) does not undertake a similar attempt at an impossible ideal. Gide's writing project succeeds in the convergence of the diary and the novel, not by aiming at an ideal *œuvre* characterized by necessity and coherence, but by accommodating in the novel the contingency and relative formlessness of a real diary, and allowing the reader to 'tire[r] les conclusions des choses' [draw the conclusions from things] (54).

However, this focus on the form of *CAW* neglects the significance of the text's transformation from Walter's real diary to Gide's fictional novel. It may not be that Gide succeeds where Walter fails, but rather that Walter's desire to transpose his experience into fiction is accomplished by an ontological change in the text brought about by the altered perspective of the reader. Walter anticipates this important role of readers by the series of intradiegetic readers and addressees he evokes. At the beginning of the *cahier blanc* it is Walter's own *âme* that is addressed as *tu* ('maintenant tu sommeilles', 5). A few entries into the *cahier* Emmanuèle is addressed as *tu* for the first time (9), which continues for most of the diary. This form of address is consistent with the therapeutic effects of Walter's writing in the *cahier blanc* (which he does not fully understand), but in the *cahier noir* he reflects further on the role of a reader (or more broadly, a detached spectator):

Nous-mêmes, quand nous ne sommes pas seulement spectateurs, devenons d'involontaires acteurs d'une pièce dont nous ne savons pas le sens. Nous ignorons la seconde signification de nos actes; leur portée dans l'immatériel nous échappe; ils ne s'arrêtent pas où nous croyons. (78)

On sacrifie toute chose une à une; par amour d'un devoir, on peut mutiler son bonheur; on devient vertueux, sublime; on consent que très peu le sachent,—que toi seule, fût-ce que toi morte,—encore l'on s'en passe; c'est le sacrifice absolu de soi-même... mais que Dieu demeure au moins, dernier refuge, après que tout le reste a sombré—et que Dieu vous voie et bénisse l'effort; sinon, c'est le néant de toute sa vie (86)

[We ourselves, when we are not mere spectators, involuntarily become actors in a play whose meaning we do not understand. We fail to grasp the further meaning of our acts; their significance on a more abstract plane escapes us; they do not end where we think they do.

We sacrifice everything, one at a time; for the love of duty, we may ruin our happiness; becoming virtuous, sublime, we accept that very few should know it,—that only you should know it, even though you are dead,—even this we can give up; a complete

self-sacrifice... but may God at least remain, a last refuge, after everything else has
gone—and may God see you and bless your struggle; otherwise, a whole life is as
nothing.]

As he develops his plans and theories, Walter comes to desire the position of
the spectator, or other, who can grasp the 'seconde signification' of his acts,
on the condition of remaining separated by a diegetic boundary. Finally, this
spectator becomes assimilated with God, and Walter realizes that 'le sacrifice
absolu de soi-même' is necessary for his apotheosis in an *œuvre posthume*. This
second line of enquiry leads to the unexpected conclusion that Walter achieves his
desired transformation by sacrificing his life and identity to attain the extradiegetic
authorial posture of Gide himself. Alternatively, or in more banal terms, Gide was
once Walter, or at least shared in his experience and desires, but has now killed off
this past self, and so can recreate him with an ironic distance.

Les Poésies d'André Walter: The End of an *auteur supposé*

However ironically we might interpret André Walter's words when reading *CAW*
in the knowledge that it is a work of fiction, this irony is never commanded by an
imposing authorial voice and remains, as it were, at the reader's discretion.[32] The
publication of *Les Poésies d'André Walter* in 1892 continued from *CAW* the strategy
of presenting the text as the work of a real André Walter, despite the fact that the
identity of the real author had long since been publicly revealed. However, an
authorial voice other than Walter's becomes gradually more palpable throughout
Les Poésies d'André Walter, which threatens the continued functioning of the *auteur
supposé*, and eventually brings the whole *supercherie* to some form of conclusion.

The first poem begins, 'Il n'y a pas eu de printemps cette année, ma chère'
[There has been no spring this year, my dear] (121), drawing attention to Walter's
obliviousness to the seasons as a consequence of his introversion. It is possible to
view this from two perspectives, that of Walter's autobiographical poetic voice, and
the ironic, extradiegetic perspective of Gide, who is increasingly impatient with his
creation. The latter perspective becomes increasingly obtrusive. The twelfth line
reinforces the impression of impatience ('Ces in-folio, ça va devenir monotone'
[All these tomes, this will become monotonous], 121) and the first line of the final
poem continues the language of monotony and frustration: 'La plaine monotone
encore, marécageuse et sans chemins' [The monotonous plain again, marshy and
without paths] (134).

The closing words of the collection mark the end of Walter's career as an *auteur
supposé*:

> Tu m'as dit:
> 'Je crois que nous vivons dans le rêve d'un autre
> Et que c'est pour cela que nous sommes si soumis.'
> Ça ne peut pas durer toujours comme ça.

---

[32] This situation was altered with the 1930 edition of *CAW*, the first to be accompanied by André
Gide's name as author, and in which the authorial voice is inescapably present.

Je crois que ce que nous aurions de mieux à faire
Ce serait de nous rendormir. (134–5)

[You said to me:
'I believe that we live in the dream of another
And that is why we are so submissive.'
It cannot always go on like that.

I believe that the best thing for us to do
Would be to go back to sleep.]

The *auteur supposé* himself is becoming conscious of his artificiality as 'le rêve d'un autre', and the voice of the real author makes itself unavoidably felt. The strategy of the *auteur supposé* 'ne peut pas durer toujours', and its gradual unveiling comes to an end as the illusion can no longer be maintained. This final stage of the *auteur supposé* provides a conclusion without invalidating or eclipsing the earlier developments. A reader's interpretations of *CAW* as Walter's real diary and as Gide's novel still remain, but now framed by an ironic perspective of Walter as an author-character or alter ego who has served his purpose. The *auteur supposé* project as a whole has demonstrated the importance and potential of diary-writing, indicated the desires and problems that accompany it, and provided some partial solutions, but the ironic tone of its ending establishes the (now familiar) Gidean attitude of an author ready to *passer outre* [move on, go beyond], and to pursue the problems of diary-writing by other means.

CAW AND THE DESIRE FOR A DIARISTIC *ŒUVRE*

CAW belongs to a long line of works, attributed to *auteurs supposés*, that have been excluded from or marginalized in the real author's literary *œuvre*, yet the publishing strategy of the *auteur supposé* is central to the significance of *CAW* as a piece of diary-writing. This chapter has demonstrated the principal stages of a reading of *CAW* that recognizes the functioning of this literary convention. The strange, partly independent co-existence of these interpretations (unlike in an explicitly fictional diary novel, where there is a clear and simultaneous hierarchy of the diegetic levels) makes possible the various aspects of its legacy. The striking innovations of *CAW* as a real diary—an editorial presentation that emphasizes its material and chronological unity, which is due to the diarist's complete investment in an *intime* and partly literary writing project—remain in force even after it is known that André Walter is a fabrication. Walter's reflections on his writing projects continue to open up new possibilities for diary-writing's literary potential and the combined role of the diarist and author-figure, even after his idealistic zeal and resultant failure come to be viewed from the ironic perspective of the real author, André Gide. This complexity of the *auteur supposé* in exploring the relation of the *journal intime* with the literary *œuvre* and author-figure is itself part of the legacy of *CAW*, whose influence can be seen in later *auteurs supposés* such as Larbaud's A.O. Barnabooth and Queneau's Sally Mara. As for the work's relation to Gide's later diary-writing, there is some truth in each of the two general attitudes that emerged long after its publication. It is an overstatement to say that 'tout Gide est dans André Walter' [all of Gide is in André Walter],[33] but *CAW* does establish the desire for a union of the author's life and *œuvre* in the *journal intime*, which persists in much of Gide's writing up to and beyond the *Journal 1889–1939*. And although it cannot be dismissed as a juvenile work, *CAW* eventually leads to an ironic recognition by Gide that this writing project, with its over-ambitious, totalizing claims, is just the first step in a long and varied process of experimentation with diary-writing.

[33] Barthes, 'Notes sur André Gide et son « Journal »', p. 37.

2

Paludes

Whereas *CAW* has been neglected, the importance of *Paludes* as a work of diary-writing has been overlooked owing to the work's very success. *Paludes* has proved to be, if not the most widely read of Gide's works, the one that is most capable of reinventing itself, becoming once again startling, unsettling, and exceedingly funny to new generations of readers. Following its publication in 1895, it was retrospectively positioned in 1914 as the inaugural work in a series of *soties* (with the publication of *Les Caves du Vatican*),[1] appreciated by exponents of the *nouveau roman*,[2] discussed in Barthes's *La Préparation du roman*,[3] and was the subject of a book-length paean by Bertrand Poirot-Delpech in 2001.[4] In effect, critics have adopted the various perspectives of these key moments in its reception, addressing, for example, its satire of the Symbolist milieu,[5] its irony as a specimen of the *sotie*,[6] the narrator's tendency to detach writing from its referent,[7] its structure of *mise en abyme*,[8] the philosophical question of contingency,[9] and its circularity,[10] but rarely has its status as diary-writing even been acknowledged, let alone explored. Yet *Paludes* constitutes a second stage in Gide's experimentation with published diary-writing, in some respects continuing from *CAW* (both works possess a complex and undecidable reading pact, and create oppositions between the diary and the literary *œuvre*), and in other ways providing its polar opposite: an explicitly fictional work that pursues a desire for the contingency of the diary, in the hope that this will be the means of achieving freedom and action in writing.

---

[1] The list of 'ouvrages du même auteur' presents *Paludes* as the first *sotie* (Gide adopted this generic term from a form of satirical play, common in the fifteenth and sixteenth centuries), followed by *Le Prométhée mal enchaîné* and *Les Caves du Vatican*; André Gide, *Les Caves du Vatican: sotie par l'auteur de Paludes*, 2 vols (Paris: NRF, 1914).

[2] Nathalie Sarraute considered it to be one of 'les œuvres les plus importantes de notre temps' [the most important *œuvres* of our time]; Nathalie Sarraute, *L'Ère du soupçon: essais sur le roman* (Paris: Gallimard, 1956), p. 62.

[3] Roland Barthes, *La Préparation du roman I et II: cours et séminaires au Collège de France (1978–1979 et 1979–1980)*, ed. by Nathalie Léger (Paris: Seuil, 2003), pp. 204, 232, 291, 348.

[4] Bertrand Poirot-Delpech, « *J'écris Paludes* » (Paris: Gallimard, 2001).

[5] Wolfgang Holdheim, *Theory and Practice of the Novel: A Study on André Gide* (Geneva: Droz, 1968), p. 171.

[6] Christian Angelet, 'Ambiguïté du discours dans *Paludes*', in *André Gide 3: Gide et la fonction de la littérature*, ed. by Claude Martin (Paris: Revue des lettres modernes, 1972), pp. 85–96.

[7] David Walker, 'L'Écriture et le réel dans les fictions d'André Gide', in *Romans, réalités, réalismes*, ed. by Jean Bessière (Paris: PUF, 1989), pp. 121–36.

[8] Pascal Dethurens, 'L'Ironi(qu)e mise en abyme dans *Paludes*', BAAG, 96 (1992), pp. 411–24.

[9] Alain Goulet, 'De la Contingence et de la rhétorique dans *Paludes*', BAAG, 54 (1982), pp. 191–206.

[10] Pierre Albouy, '*Paludes* et le mythe de l'écrivain', *Cahiers André Gide*, 3 (1972), pp. 241–51.

Although Gide's writing of his own *journal intime* was considerably advanced by 1895, for contemporary readers of the first edition of *Paludes* Gide was the author of *CAW* and *Les Poésies d'André Walter* (for which he had now publicly assumed responsibility), and of the three *traités* [fictional treatises], *Le Traité du Narcisse* (1892), *Le Voyage d'Urien* (1893), and *La Tentative amoureuse* (1893). In order to assess the significance of *Paludes* in the trajectory of Gide's experimentation with diary-writing and in the history of diary-writing more broadly, it is necessary to consider the unusual paratext of this first edition, which situates the work within Gide's *œuvre* (attaching it more strongly with the *traités* than with *CAW*), identifies the philosophical problem of contingency as a theme, and establishes a strange new type of reading pact with an indeterminate relationship between diaristic and novelistic generic codes. This indeterminacy in the paratext contributes to the work's *saugrenu* [absurd, ridiculous, uncanny] sense of humour, and continues in the narrative structure of the main text, which is irresolvably unstable in two respects: first, in its status as either a fictional *journal intime* or some other narrative form, and secondly, in the relationship between the main text and the literary *œuvre* undertaken by the narrator (also entitled *Paludes*).[11] The narrator's *journal intime* and *agenda* also play an important role in the work's pursuit of the philosophical problem of contingency announced in the paratext. I shall examine the role of diary-writing in *Paludes* from these three perspectives in turn, the paratextual, the narratological, and the philosophical, although they are intimately related in the work's overall strategy of experimentation.[12]

PARATEXT: GIDE THE 'BIBLIOCLASTE'

The *saugrenu* structures of *Paludes* begin even before a reader arrives at the main text, in a manipulation of paratext that is Gide's greatest claim to belong to the class of authors described by Vincent Colonna as 'biblioclastes, des écrivains qui creusent la structure du livre, troublent ses contraintes linéaires, énonciatives, paratextuelles, typographiques' [biblioclasts, those writers who hollow out the structure of the book, who disrupt its linear constraints, its enunciative, paratextual and typographic conventions].[13] The paratext also provides a large quantity of information about the nature of the text and how it is to be read, both through

---

[11] To avoid confusion, I follow other critics in referring to Gide's text and the narrator's projected work as *Paludes I* and *Paludes II* respectively.

[12] In the following discussion, the edition of *Paludes* to which I mainly refer, and from which quotations are taken, is the first (Paris: Librairie de l'Art indépendant, 1895) (page references will be given in parentheses in the text). Gide made considerable changes to the text and paratext in the 1920 NRF edition, and in the edition prepared for the first volume (1932) of his 1932–39 *Œuvres complètes*, most notably removing the subtitle and the table of contents, yet most of the effects of the paratext described here remained in force, as will become apparent. It would have been convenient to refer to the 2009 Pléiade edition of *Paludes*, in *Romans et récits*, I, pp. 257–326, but this edition, based on the 1932 edition in the *Œuvres complètes*, does not provide complete information on textual variants, and, moreover, its presentation of the very paratext whose importance I am undertaking to demonstrate is partial.

[13] Vincent Colonna, *Autofiction et autres mythomanies littéraires* (Paris: Tristram, 2004), p. 133.

Table 2.1. Elements of paratext in Gide's principal works up to *Paludes*
Information pertains to the paratext of the first edition, excluding any prior publication in literary journals or by private circulation. The original formatting has been retained.

Title	Subtitle	Epigraph	Dedication
Les Cahiers d'André Walter (1891)	—	—	—
Les Poésies d'André Walter (1892)	*L'ITINÉRAIRE SYMBOLIQUE*	—	—
Le Traité du Narcisse (1892)	*(THÉORIE DU SYMBOLE)*	[only added from second edition, 1899:] *Nuper me in littore vidi.* / VIRGILE.	*À mon ami* PAUL VALÉRY
Le Voyage d'Urien (1893)	Voyage sur l'Océan pathétique	*Dic quibus in terris...* / VIRGILE	*à Henri de Regnier.* [*sic*]
La Tentative amoureuse (1893)	*Le Traité du vain Désir* [given only as a running head]	Le désir est comme une flamme brillante [...]	[the main text is followed by:] *Notes de la Tentative Amoureuse.* / À ALBERT MOCKEL
Paludes (1895)	*(Traité de la Contingence)*	*Dic cur hic.* / (L'autre École.)	Pour mon Ami EUGÈNE ROUART / j'écrivis cette satire de quoi?

allusions to other works in Gide's *œuvre* and through unique paratextual features. In the following discussion it will be useful to refer to table 2.1, which presents a summary of the paratext as presented in the first edition of each of Gide's principal works up to *Paludes*.

Situating *Paludes* in Gide's *œuvre*

The title *Paludes* recalls the marshy setting of *Les Poésies d'André Walter* (particularly poems XVII and XX),[14] but the paratext generally associates *Paludes* more closely with the three works immediately preceding it, by means of a series of verbal echoes in their titles, subtitles, epigraphs, and dedications (the various anomalies to this pattern, apparent in table 2.1, show that this was an emergent strategy which Gide reinforced in later editions). The subtitle of *Paludes*, *Traité de la Contingence*, inscribes the work in the series of *traités* beginning with *Le Traité du Narcisse*, and suggests that its particular theme of 'la Contingence' is to be addressed in a similarly allegorical fashion to the ideas treated in these earlier works. The epigraph to *Paludes*, 'Dic cur hic', echoes that to *Le Voyage d'Urien*, 'Dic quibus in terris...', but whereas the latter is a quotation from Vergil, that of *Paludes* is taken from

---

[14] André Gide, *Les Poésies d'André Walter*, pp. 132–3, 134–5.

Leibniz, which reinforces the importance of contingency as a theme and, more specifically, as an ethical problem.[15]

The attribution of the epigraph to 'L'autre École' suggests that this particular subject marks a departure from the *école* with which Gide had been associated, that of a Symbolist aesthetic preoccupied with the necessity that is discussed in *Le Traité du Narcisse* (but also in *CAW*, in which the necessity of Spinoza's philosophy is preferred to the contingency of Leibniz, 59). The dedication to Eugène Rouart is largely a pretext for the ludic description of *Paludes* as 'cette satire de quoi?' [this satire of what?].[16] This generic description followed by an indirect question and grammatically unconventional question mark tells us that it is a satire, but perhaps not as we know it.

Diary-Writing

No part of the paratext mentioned so far relates directly to diary-writing. Although a spate of works by Gide in diary form followed the initial publication of *Paludes*,[17] and the 'Préface pour une seconde édition de "Paludes"' (1895) links the work closely with *Les Nourritures terrestres* and its travel diaries in North Africa,[18] the only preceding work of diary-writing was *CAW*, which is less strongly alluded to than the *traités*.[19] However, both the table of contents and the chapter headings

---

[15] 'Dic quibus in terris' refers to Vergil's *Eclogues*, 3.104 and 3.106. Leibniz glosses the expression 'dic cur hic' in Chapter 21, 'De la puissance et de la liberté', of the *Nouveaux essais sur l'entendement humain*: 'Et pour cela il est bon de s'accoustumer à se recueillir de temps en temps, et à s'elever au dessus du tumulte présent des impressions, à sortir pour ainsi dire de la place où l'on est; à se dire: *dic cur hic, respice finem, Où en sommes nous?* à propos ou *venons au propos, venons au fait*' [And to this end it is good to accustom oneself to gather one's thoughts from time to time, and to raise oneself above the present tumult of impressions, to step outside, as it were, of the place where one stands; and to say: *dic cur hic, respice finem, Where have we come to? To the point* or *let us come to the point, to the matter at hand*]; in Gottfried Wilhelm Leibniz, *Sämtliche Schriften und Briefe* (Berlin: Akademie-Verlag, 1962–), Reihe 6: *Philosophische Schriften*, VI: *Nouveaux essais* (1990), pp. 168–212, p. 196. See also the discussion of Gide's Latin epigraphs and titles in Jean Deprun, 'Gide, Leibniz et le Pseudo-Virgile', in *Lettres et réalités: mélanges de littérature générale et de critique romanesque offerts au professeur Henri Coulet par ses amis* (Aix-en-Provence: Université de Provence, 1988), pp. 29–38, pp. 30–32.

[16] Rouart's own reputation probably did not have a great significance for contemporary readers, as his work *Vengeance de moines* was published only privately in 1892, and David Walker's preface to Rouart's *La Villa sans maître* (1898) demonstrates that even Gide was unaware of the earlier work; Eugène Rouart, *La Villa sans maître*, preface by David Walker (Paris: Mercure de France, 2007), p. 11.

[17] 'Réflexions sur quelques points de morale chrétienne' (1896), 'Notes de voyages: Tunis et Sahara' (1897), *Réflexions sur quelques points de littérature et de morale* (1897), *Feuilles de route, 1895–1896* (1897).

[18] '—mais que le lecteur patient veuille bien ne regarder tout ce livre que comme une préface à celui qu'il sera bientôt heureux de lire sous ce titre: LES NOURRITURES TERRESTRES.—"Un vilain titre", dit Angèle.—"Tant pis", repartis-je.' [but may the patient reader please consider this whole book as merely a preface to the one that he will soon happily read, under the title: LES NOURRITURES TERRESTRES. 'An awful title,' said Angèle.—'Too bad,' I replied.]; André Gide, 'Préface pour une seconde édition de "Paludes"', *Mercure de France*, 16 (November 1895), pp. 199–204, p. 201. It was later reprinted under the title 'Postface pour la nouvelle édition de *Paludes* et pour annoncer *Les Nourritures terrestres*', in André Gide, *Le Voyage d'Urien, suivi de Paludes* (Paris: Mercure de France, 1897), pp. 273–86.

[19] When Henry Maubel discusses *Paludes* as a 'journal' in a contemporary press review, he immediately compares it with *CAW*; Henry Maubel, 'Notes en marge de *Paludes*', *Le Coq Rouge*, 3 (June 1895), pp. 97–9, reprinted in *BAAG* 54 (1982), pp. 212–15, pp. 212–13.

in the first edition contain elements inviting the reader to interpret the text as a diary.[20] At the beginning of Chapters 2 to 6 the indication of the day is printed in the format conventional at the time for a published *journal intime* (smaller type size, right-aligned, and followed by a full stop), while roman numerals from I to VI take the place of chapter titles. This page layout suggests that the text follows the model of the diary novel described by Valerie Raoul, in which the conventions of the diary are subordinated to those of the novel (in this case through the implicit hierarchy of typographical elements).[21] Conversely, the table of contents sets out the chapters and their contents in the following format:

Neither the days of the week nor the thematic title headings have a clear precedence, as the former lead sequentially while the latter are given more weight typographically (in small capitals). These two elements connote the diaristic and novelistic aspects of the narrative respectively, and their ambivalence in this part of the paratext announces a generic indeterminacy that continues throughout the main text.[22]

Indeterminacy in the Paratext

Two further aspects of the paratext prepare for the indeterminacies of the main text. The first is the insistence on moving the responsibility or authority of interpretation from the author to the reader. This process begins in the (untitled) preface:

> Et cela surtout m'y intéresse que j'y ai mis sans le savoir,—cette part d'inconscient, et que je voudrais appeler la part de Dieu.—Un livre est toujours une collaboration, et tant plus le livre vaut-il, que plus la part du scribe y est petite, que plus l'accueil de Dieu sera grand.—Attendons de partout la révélation des choses;—du public, la révélation de nos œuvres. ([vii])

> [And that part interests me above all, that I put there without knowing it,—this part issuing from the unconscious, and which I would like to call God's share.—A book is always a collaboration, and the greater the book's value, the smaller the part of the scribe will be, and the greater the space made available for God's share.—Let us expect

---

[20] These features have been obscured by the formatting of the text in the new Pléiade edition, in which Pierre Masson presents the days of the week and the thematic chapter headings ('Hubert', 'Angèle', 'Le Banquet', etc.) as 'titre' and 'sous-titre' respectively. As a result, the days of the week are no longer formatted as they would be in a *journal intime*. See Gide, *Romans et récits*, I, p. 1301, n. *a*.

[21] Valerie Raoul, *The French Fictional Journal: Fictional Narcissism/Narcissistic Fiction* (Toronto: University of Toronto Press, 1980), pp. 24–5.

[22] It should be noted that the strategy of superimposing two inconsistent series of section headings was to be pursued by Gide in *Le Prométhée mal enchaîné* (1899), and can also be observed in Roland Barthes's *Le Plaisir du texte* (1973) (the fragments that make up the work are untitled in the main text, but a 'Table' at the end of the book reveals the titles by which they are arranged alphabetically) and in the paratextual presentation of the photographs in *Roland Barthes par Roland Barthes* (1975); see, respectively, Roland Barthes, *Œuvres complètes*, IV, pp. 217–64 and pp. 575–771 (photographs, pp. 579–622).

the revelation of things to come from all around;—and from the public, the revelation of our *œuvres*.]

The reading pact proposed here involves a 'collaboration' between reader and author (demoted to a *scribe*), and the public is responsible for the 'révélation' of the *œuvre*. The effect is reinforced by two other parts of the paratext. First, the typographical proximity of the question posed to the reader by the dedication (unconventionally placed immediately above the preface)—'J'écrivis cette satire de quoi?'—suggests that this is precisely one of the instances in which the reader's participation is required. The second is the 'Table des phrases les plus remarquables de Paludes' [List of the most remarkable phrases of Paludes], which lists two phrases selected by the author from the main text, followed by a footnote that states: 'pour respecter l'idiosyncrasie de chacun, nous laissons à chaque lecteur le soin de remplir cette feuille' [in order to respect the idiosyncracy of each person, we leave the reader with the task of completing this page] (102).[23]

My final point about the paratext does not concern its specific components but rather its sheer abundance. If the front matter in the first edition is extensive but not exceptional in nature (half-title with epigraph, second half-title with subtitle, *justification du tirage* [printing information], title page, 'du même auteur', dedication and preface, contents page, fourth statement of the title, and finally a second statement of the epigraph), the items of end matter are more unusual: an 'Envoi', an 'Alternative' (followed by the word 'FIN'), and the 'Table des phrases les plus remarquables de Paludes'. The overall effect of this accumulation of paratextual items is to destabilize the unity of the text by complicating the division between diegetic levels. Rather than a binary opposition between the authorial and editorial responsibility of a concise paratext framing a distinct and fictional main text (attributable, in a first-person narrative, to a homodiegetic narrator), the frames are multiplied, and for several of them the attribution of responsibility remains ambiguous. The separation of the paratext and main text is undermined by echoes between the two, such as the phrase 'j'écrivis' [I wrote] and the repeated statement of the title 'Paludes' (which is shared by the narrator's own intended work). In the last three items of paratext there is a gradual move from the position of the narrator to that of Gide as author, but in each case the attribution remains ambiguous. Of the three, the 'Envoi', citing Matthew 11.17, offers the most confusion:

> Nous vous avons joué de la flûte
> Vous ne nous avez pas écouté.
>
> Nous avons chanté
> Vous n'avez pas dansé (99)
>
> [I played the flute for you
> You did not listen to us.
>
> We sang for you
> You did not dance]

---

[23] This second paratextual feature is also characteristic of Gide's recurrent gesture (discussed above in the introduction to Part I) of absenting himself as an author-figure from his literary work, undermining its self-sufficiency as an *œuvre*, and resisting a sense of conclusion.

Who is this figure, or figures, whose gospel has been ignored—the author of *Paludes I* or of *Paludes II*? To what is the 'Alternative' an alternative—the whole of *Paludes I*, or its ending, or the choices made by the narrator? Whatever the attribution of the 'Table des phrases les plus remarquables de Paludes', it is precisely at this point that responsibility for interpretation of the text is transferred to the reader.

In summary, the paratext of *Paludes* initially associates the text with the extremely artificial fictional worlds and specific philosophical problems of the *traités* while also announcing a break with the author's earlier works by means of a new type of satire. Like *CAW*, it capitalizes on an undecidable diegetic structure and reading pact, but with very different effects: *Paludes* lays claim to both novelistic and diaristic codes (in the table of contents and chapter headings) while leaving their relationship ambiguous, and it confuses boundaries between the paratext and main text, between the author and narrator, and between the roles of the author and the reader.[24]

INDETERMINACIES OF THE MAIN NARRATIVE

The main text continues not only the paratext's indeterminacies but also its profusion of disparate elements. The narrator is at the centre of a complex circulation of texts and writing situations that cluster around the two most salient narrative instances—that of the main narrative of *Paludes I* and that of the narrator's literary work, *Paludes II*—thereby multiplying and confusing their boundaries. For example, *Paludes II* is accompanied by a series of notes, drafts, summaries, and explanations. I shall limit my enquiry to the two principal narrative instances, and more specifically to the ambiguous status of the main narrative as diary-writing (in this case as a *journal intime*) and its relationship with *Paludes II*. The single exception I make is to discuss the narrator's *agenda*, another daily writing practice that is structured by the chronology of its composition and which closely borders the writing of the main diary narrative.

An Ambiguous Diary Narrative

The ambiguity in the status of the main narrative is not between a real or fictional diary (as it is in *CAW*), but rather between fictional diary-writing or some other

[24] The principal change brought about by Gide's later revisions of the text is to remove its association with the *traités*, especially by the removal of the subtitle. At the time of the 1920 edition, *Paludes* had already been repositioned in Gide's *œuvre* as the first of his *soties* (the word 'traité' does not, in any case, appear in this edition's list of 'ouvrages du même auteur'), whereas the 1932–39 *Œuvres complètes* tend to expunge generic categories in order to emphasize the biographical development of Gide's work. Nonetheless, the question of contingency remains in the main text and in the epigraph's allusion to Leibniz; the dedication continues to define the work ambiguously as a 'satire de quoi?'; the various arrangements of the chapter headings and days of the week still equivocate between novelistic and diaristic codes; and the crucial 'Envoi', 'Alternative', and 'Table des phrases...' are retained in all editions.

(equally fictional) form of narrative. This situation is also to be distinguished from the altogether more conventional opposition, described by Valerie Raoul, between the codes governing the intradiegetic communicative situation of the diary and the extradiegetic situation of the novel respectively.[25] It is difficult to describe with clarity a process of obfuscation that essentially resists any resolution, but my approach will be to assess those features that reinforce the impression of the narrative as being diary-writing, then the features that propose a form of writing that positively excludes the diary, and finally those moments that simultaneously and ambiguously point to different forms of writing.

As mentioned earlier, the first chapter does not begin with an indication of the day, but by this point the contents page has established that each of the six chapters corresponds to a day of the week, and the day is printed at the start of Chapters 2 to 6, typeset as if in a published diary. The first two sentences of the work begin 'vers cinq heures' [around five o'clock] and 'à six heures' [at six o'clock] respectively (1), and subsequent events in the chapter occur at 'huit heures' (3), and 'neuf heures' (9). The chapter finishes with the words 'Et puis je me couchai, ayant achevé ma journée' [And then I went to bed, having completed my day] (9). These features do not resemble a real diary, but signify diary-writing in a fictional context, parodying the meticulous inscription of trivial events. On several occasions the nature of the narrative as diary-writing is foregrounded by the mention of the practicalities of writing, such as when the narrator struggles to remember exactly what he said during the day (85). Finally, whenever *Paludes II* is presented as a diary narrative—the first excerpt is entitled 'JOURNAL DE TITYRE / ou / PALUDES' (5)—the reader, by a structure of *mise en abyme*, is invited to project this characteristic on to *Paludes I*.

The many ways in which the narrative is implausible as a real diary do not necessarily conflict with its nature as fictional and satirical diary-writing; rather, it is those features that positively contradict the fiction of diary-writing or announce a different type of narrative that account for its indeterminacy. Returning to the opening of the text, it is worth examining the first sentence, while remembering that the diaristic indication of the day is absent from the first chapter alone: 'Vers cinq heures le temps fraîchit; je fermai mes fenêtres et je me remis à écrire' [Around five o'clock the weather turned cold; I closed my windows and started to write again] (1). The omission of the day and the postponement of the first person and the situation of writing to the second half of the sentence all contribute to a delay in the recognition of the narrative as diary-writing. Instead, it briefly appears to be a third-person narrative beginning, novelistically, *in medias res*. The writing of the diary is also sometimes manifestly impossible. For example, the account of the events of the Friday continues through the night and into the morning of the narrator's departure on his 'petit voyage' [little trip] (30), at which point he declares 'hâtons-nous' [let us make haste] (83), and the following chapter (or diary entry) begins. There are also occasions when the text is so unlike a diary as to constitute

[25] Raoul, *The French Fictional Journal*, p. 20.

a different type of narrative entirely, such as the long sequence of speeches at Angèle's salon (42–61),[26] which becomes a pastiche of Plato's *Symposium* (one of the allusions of the chapter's title, 'Le Banquet'), and the account of the narrator's waking and sleeping thoughts, which is an early example of the interior monologue (65–8).

Finally, certain elements in the narrative point simultaneously to both diaristic and other types of writing. The particular choice of the days Tuesday to Sunday as a structuring device across the six chapters suggests the quotidian nature of the diary, but also contradicts it by denoting an internally consistent but ahistorical time frame (unlike dated diary entries, which are situated in historical time). It pointedly begins mid-week, mid-*cahier*, and even mid-entry, thereby effacing the materiality and structural unity of the diary itself, which are given great prominence in *CAW* (and indeed in most fictional diaries). Furthermore, when the narrator describes his practice of diary-writing most directly, on the occasion of his 'petit voyage', he foregrounds the writing situation but also contradicts our understanding of the diary narrative up to that point. He shows a passage of his diary entry to Angèle, which is then the basis for their conversation, but confusingly this conversation too is transcribed in the same diary entry. He not only restricts his comments to the day's 'moments poétiques' (84), but even makes untrue claims on the grounds that they 'rend[ent] excellemment l'impression de [leur] voyage' [provide an excellent portrait of the impression of their trip] (86). In contradiction to the strict truthfulness that Philippe Lejeune considers essential to the diary,[27] on this occasion the narrator applies to his diary-writing the same principle that he sets out with regard to the (fictional) *Paludes II*: 'arrang[er] les faits de façon à les rendre plus conformes à la vérité que dans la réalité' [to arrange the facts in such a way as to make them more consistent with the truth than they are in reality] (7).

The Narrator's *agenda*

The narrator's *agenda* further confuses the status of the main narrative (which for convenience I shall refer to as the narrator's *journal intime*). Unlike the *journal intime*, the *agenda* is explicitly introduced and explained on its first appearance (11). In the *agenda* the narrator writes a week in advance what he intends to do on a given day, so that he has time to forget what he has written. When the day arrives, his plans, up to a point, guide his actions. He writes on the facing page of the *agenda* what he has actually done, then he subtracts the second column from the first to arrive at 'le déficit', or 'ce qu['il] aurai[t] dû faire' [what he should have done] (11). Here the *agenda* approaches another diary-writing practice, that of the *livre de comptes* [accounts book], as well as the complex diary-writing system

---

[26] This section was considerably reduced after the 1895 and 1897 editions, by the removal of the speeches of the characters Baldakin and Stanislas. These speeches are reproduced in the section 'En marge de *Paludes*', in *Romans et récits*, I, pp. 319–22.

[27] Philippe Lejeune, 'Le Journal comme « antifiction »', *Poétique*, 149 (2007), pp. 3–14.

established by Marc-Antoine Jullien (discussed in the introductory chapter). He also occasionally falsifies the record of his initial intentions so as to reduce his apparent 'déficit':

> Sur l'agenda, sitôt levé je pus lire: tâcher de se lever à six heures. Il était huit heures, je pris ma plume; je biffai; j'écrivis au lieu: Se lever à onze heures.—Et je me recouchai, sans lire le reste. (69)
>
> [In the *agenda*, as soon as I got up, I read: try to get up at six o'clock. It was eight o'clock, I picked up my pen; I crossed it out; I wrote in its place: Get up at eleven o'clock.—I went back to bed, without reading the rest.]

The *agenda* destabilizes the main narrative's status as diary-writing by its prominence (the narrator's *journal intime* is never so explicitly identified or described as the *agenda*) but also by its proximity. It incorporates a daily record of the narrator's life and parodies several aspects of diary-writing, such as the application of book-keeping habits to the morality of one's everyday behaviour, and a capacity for self-deception. As a consequence, it can be considered a close counterpart to the *journal intime*, and a part of the narrator's diary-writing more generally.

Between *Paludes I* and *Paludes II*

The opposition between *Paludes I* and *Paludes II* is a focal point for the work's enquiry (as a *traité*) into questions relating to the diary and the literary *œuvre*, and to the philosophical problem of contingency, and once again this relationship is governed by the *saugrenu* indeterminacy introduced by the paratext. The contradictory indications regarding its nature can be divided into those that are ambiguous (not merely vague but positively depicting an ambiguous relationship), those that establish a structure of *mise en abyme*, and those that suggest a consubstantiality of the two texts (not mere analogy but identity).

The first mention of *Paludes II* foregrounds the ambiguity of its relationship with *Paludes I*, in a conversation between Hubert and the narrator:

> IL DIT: 'Tiens! tu travailles?'
> JE RÉPONDIS: 'J'écris Paludes.'
>   —'Qu'est-ce que c'est?'—'Un livre.'
>   — 'Pour moi?'—'Non.'
>   — 'Trop savant?. . .'—'Ennuyeux.'
>   — 'Pourquoi l'écrire alors?'—'Sinon qui l'écrirait?'
>   — 'Encore des confessions?'—'Presque pas.'
>   — 'Quoi donc?'—'Assieds-toi.' (1)
>
> [HE SAID: 'Oh! Are you working?'
> I REPLIED: 'I'm writing Paludes.'
>   — 'What is it?'—'A book.'
>   — 'For me?'—'No.'
>   — 'Too learned?. . .'—'Too boring.'
>   — 'Then why write it?'—'Otherwise, who would write it?'
>   — 'Yet more confessions?'—'Not exactly.'
>   — 'Then what?'—'Sit down.']

As the narrator is never given a name, which could either sign or refute an autobiographical pact (following Lejeune's definition in *Le Pacte autobiographique*),[28] the statement 'j'écris Paludes' could be attributed to the author writing *Paludes I* or to an intradiegetic narrator composing a metadiegetic *Paludes II* (metadiegetic in Gérard Genette's sense of a 'récit au second degré' [narrative in the second degree] relative to the main narrative).[29] The narrator's responses are also provocatively elusive. 'Paludes' is not distinguished typographically to indicate its status as an *œuvre* (for example, by italics or small capitals, as for André Walter's work, 'ALLAIN'), but rather it is defined only vaguely as a 'livre', and the final response, 'Assieds-toi', suggests that we are not about to be given satisfying answers any time soon. Indeed, the mystification continues every time the narrator declares 'j'écris Paludes'.

In contrast to this ambiguity, some features positively suggest a relationship of *mise en abyme* between *Paludes I* and *Paludes II*. More specifically, this relationship entails a situation in which the (intradiegetic) narrator of *Paludes I* is in the process of writing the (metadiegetic) *Paludes II*, which offers the reader an analogy with *Paludes I*. The analogy is explained intradiegetically by the narrator's project of converting his experience as related in his diary-writing (in the narrative of *Paludes I*) into a literary form (in *Paludes II*). While this terminology of diegesis offers precision, an example will provide greater clarity. In the following extract the narrator gives a summary of *Paludes II* to Hubert:

> 'Je raconte:—Le premier jour, il constate qu'il s[e] contente [de son champ], et songe à qu'y faire? Le second jour, un volier passant, il tue au matin quatre macreuses ou sarcelles et vers le soir en mange deux qu'il a fait cuire sur un maigre feu de broussailles. Le troisième jour, il se distrait à se construire une hutte de grands roseaux. Le quatrième jour, il mange les deux dernières macreuses. Le cinquième jour, il défait sa hutte et s'ingénie pour une maison plus savante. Le sixième jour...'
> —'Assez! dit Hubert.' (2)

> ['I narrate:—On the first day, he remarks that he is content with his field, and wonders what to do with it? On the second day, as a group of birds pass over, he kills four scoter or teal and towards the evening he eats two of them, which he cooks on a small brush fire. On the third day, he enjoys himself and builds a hut out of large reeds. On the fourth day he eats the two remaining scoter. On the fifth day, he takes down his hut and devises a more sophisticated house. On the sixth day...'
> —'Enough!', said Hubert.]

The six days of *Paludes II* and the lack of finality both match the structure of *Paludes I*, which also ends with an ellipsis. Starting from this parallel between the two texts, the reader is invited to draw further comparisons and to explain them as metaphors created by the narrator's literary project. The same is true of many other accounts that the narrator gives of *Paludes II*, such as the more concise summary: 'c'est l'histoire des animaux vivant dans les cavernes ténébreuses, et qui perdent la

---

[28] Philippe Lejeune, *Le Pacte autobiographique*, rev. edn (first published 1975) (Paris: Seuil, 1996).
[29] Gérard Genette, *Figures III* (Paris: Seuil, 1972), pp. 241–3.

vue à force de ne pas s'en servir' [it is the story of animals living in dark caverns, and who lose the ability of sight from lack of use] (47).

In complete contradiction to this relationship of *mise en abyme*, certain features of the text suggest a relationship of what I shall term 'consubstantiality', in the sense (used by the Early Church Fathers to describe the Holy Trinity) of being separate in nature while sharing the same being or substance. This means that, over the course of the text, the narrator is simultaneously writing his diary and *Paludes II*, which happen to be exactly the same text. Or, in other words, *Paludes I* is intradiegetically the narrator's diary and extradiegetically the narrator's literary work, *Paludes II*; and whenever the narrator says 'j'écris Paludes', he is referring both to *Paludes I* and to *Paludes II*. Pierre Albouy remarks on this effect brought about by the repeated exchange in which a friend suggests to the narrator 'tu devrais mettre cela dans Paludes' [you should put that in Paludes], to which he replies that 'ça y est déjà' [it is already in there] (for example, on p. 37), for the precise reason that the phrase that his friend is remarking upon has just occurred in *Paludes I*.[30] Although the narrator's repeated accounts of *Paludes II* often suggest a structure of *mise en abyme*, some are also, conversely, capable of supporting the hypothesis of consubstantiality, such as his claim at Angèle's salon that 'en ce moment, Paludes c'est l'histoire du salon d'Angèle' [at this moment, Paludes is the story of Angèle's salon] (45). This description of *Paludes II* resembles only the immediate circumstances of the narrator and the present moment of the narrative, rather than the whole of *Paludes I*.

CONTINGENCY IN THE DIARY AND THE *ŒUVRE*

Of all the theoretical problems discussed by the characters of *Paludes*, it is the issue of contingency (fundamentally associated with the *journal intime* in both *CAW* and *Paludes*) that is mentioned by the paratext, that is at the root of the narrator's practical problems, and that is integrated in the text's structural indeterminacies.[31] I shall set out the narrator's expression and practical experience of his philosophical problems, before discussing his attempts to overcome them through diary-writing and through writing *Paludes II* (however these two might be related). It should be remembered throughout this discussion that the narrator is neither entirely the victim of the extradiegetic author-figure's irony nor entirely his mouthpiece pitched against the conflicting voices of the other characters. His experience of the philosophical questions at stake in the work must be placed in the context of the 'satire de quoi?' and its indeterminate narrative structure.

---

[30] Pierre Albouy, *Paludes et le mythe de l'écrivain*, p. 244.
[31] For a broader treatment of the philosophical issues of *Paludes* see Reidar Due, '*Paludes* and the Subversion of the Moral Subject', *Orbis Litterarum*, 57 (2002), pp. 259–74.

The Narrator's Philosophical Problems in his Everyday Life

The narrator frequently expresses and reformulates the philosophical problems of his everyday life, such as in this conversation with his friend Roland:

> 'Quelle existence intolérable! La supportez-vous, cher ami?'
> —'Assez bien, me dit-il—mais intolérable pourquoi?'
> —'Il suffit qu'elle puisse être différente et qu'elle ne le soit pas. Tous nos actes sont si connus qu'un suppléant pourrait les faire et répétant nos mots d'hier former nos phrases de demain.' (33)

> ['What an intolerable existence! Can you bear it, dear friend?'
> —'Well enough, he said—but why intolerable?'
> —'It is enough just that it could be different and that it isn't. All our acts are so familiar that a substitute could carry them out and, by repeating our words from yesterday, provide our sentences for tomorrow.']

Their immediate manifestation is the repetitive, predictable nature of the characters' acts and words. Yet it is an intimation of the contingency of reality, of different possibilities, that makes his current stagnation so 'intolérable'. He is resolved to commit an 'acte libre' (43) and to encourage his friends to share in his revolt against necessity and stagnation, but with little success. His practical attempts to escape from routine are comically futile and often lead to further repetition, such as in these phrases from the start of the Thursday and Friday: 'au lieu de mon bol de lait, pour varier, je pris un peu de tisane' [In place of my bowl of milk, for a change, I had a little tisane] (31), 'je pris au lieu de lait, pour varier, un peu de tisane' [I had, in place of milk, for a change, a little tisane] (69). His greatest practical attempt to escape from his routines is the trip he makes with Angèle in search of 'l'imprévu' [the unforeseen] (34), but this too results in failure, as he admits to her the following morning (88). As for his influence on others, Hubert and Roland embark on a far more ambitious trip, to Biskra, but they deny that this is a consequence of the narrator's influence, pointing out that 'tu ne peux donner aux autres que ce que tu as' [you can only give to others what you already possess] (96).

A Possible Response: Diary-Writing

The narrator, who prefers to write '*Tityre sourit*' [*Tityre smiled*] than to smile in reality (23), is more concerned with exercising his freedom in writing than in action, and trying to liberate others by this means from the stagnation of necessity. Among the various forms of the *journal intime*, the narrator attempts to take advantage of its capacity to express the contingency of existence that otherwise eludes him:

> —Quelle arrogance dans le *choix*! Regardons tout avec une égale insistance [...].
> Regardons! Regardons!—Que vois-je?
> Trois marchands de légumes passent.
> —Un omnibus déjà.
> —Un portier balaie devant sa porte.
> [...]

Les kiosques reçoivent les journaux; des messieurs pressés les achètent.—On pose les tables d'un café......
Mon Dieu! [...] voici que de nouveau je sanglote... c'est nerveux, je crois;—cela me prend à chaque énumération. [...]—La vie—la vie des autres!—cela, la vie?—voir la vie! Ce que c'est pourtant que de vivre!!... Et qu'est-ce qu'on en pourrait dire d'autre? Exclamations. (83)

[What arrogance in *selection*! Let us pay an equal attention to everything [...]. Look! Look!—What can I see?
Three greengrocers walk by.
—An omnibus, already.
—A doorman sweeps in front of his doorway.
[...]
The kiosks take delivery of the papers; busy gentlemen come to buy them.—People are setting the tables at a café......
My God! [...] there I go sobbing again... it's nervous, I think;—this happens to me with every enumeration. [...]—Life—the life of others!—Is this life?—behold, life! But what a thing it is to live!!... And what else could one say about it? Exclamations.]

At the other extreme from the 'arrang[ement des] faits' in his account of the trip with Angèle, this comprehensive 'énumération' drives him to a nervous crisis and the discovery of the limits of his diary-writing, as his account degenerates into questions, ellipses, exclamations, and (marking another failure in his project) repetition.

Unlike the retrospective narrative of the *journal intime*, the *agenda* is an attempt to achieve a freedom of action and to experience the contingency of reality by means of the complex writing project described earlier (in this respect too its aims are similar to the elaborate diary-writing system of Marc-Antoine Jullien). This system is designed to ensure that the narrator's actions are not determined by the conditions in which he finds himself, but instead by decisions that he has, supposedly freely, made himself: 'on est sûr, les ayant résolues d'avance et sans gêne de ne point dépendre chaque matin de l'atmosphère' [one is certain, having resolved upon them in advance and at leisure, that one does not depend on the atmospheric conditions each morning] (11). He expresses no concern that he does not in practice consider these resolutions to be binding, nor that they might be influenced by the 'atmosphère' at the time when they were initially conceived. The *agenda* is also a means of confronting the 'imprévu':

si je n'eusse pas marqué pour ce matin ce que j'eusse dû faire, j'aurais pu l'oublier, et cela m'eut [*sic*] empêché de me réjouir de ne l'avoir point fait. C'est toujours là le charme qu'a pour moi ce que j'appelai si joliment *l'imprévu négatif.* (71–2, emphasis original)

[if I had not written down for this morning what I was supposed to have done, I might have forgotten it, and that would have taken away from me the pleasure of not having done it. That is the charm that I always find in what I call, so prettily, the *negative unforeseen*.]

The system makes the 'imprévu' measurable, writeable, and not only derisory but also 'négatif'. In contrast to the failure of the *journal intime*, this appears to be a minuscule success.

A Possible Response: The *œuvre*, or *Paludes II*

The composition of *Paludes II* is also described from the very beginning in terms related to the narrator's philosophical problems:

—'Pourquoi l'écrire alors?'—'Sinon qui l'écrirait?' (1)

—'Pourquoi écrivez-vous?' reprit-elle après un silence.

—'Moi?—je ne sais pas,—probablement que c'est pour agir.' (5)

'Ne pourrons-nous jamais poser rien hors du temps?—que nous ne soyons pas obligé de refaire. —Quelque œuvre enfin qui n'ait plus besoin de nous pour durer.' (89)

[— 'Then why write it?'—'Otherwise, who would write it?'

—'Why do you write?', she asked, after a silence.

—'Me?—I don't know,—probably in order to act.'

'Will we never be able to place something outside of time?—that we would not be compelled to repeat. —Some *œuvre* at last that would no longer have any need of us to endure.']

He hopes, through writing *Paludes II*, to 'agir' and 'poser [quelque chose] hors du temps', as an escape from necessity and repetition. His writing is frequently presented as offering him salvation from the condition that he ascribes to others, with the repeated phrase 'moi, cela m'ést égal parce que j'écris Paludes' [that's no matter to me because I'm writing Paludes] (for example, on p. 8). He also seems to be uncomfortably aware of contradictions in his writing project. It is supposed to constitute an act that does not belong to a series of repetitions, but *Paludes II* is followed by the similar project of 'POLDERS', which continues on from the earlier work without contradicting it (98). Furthermore, his justification for writing *Paludes II*, 'sinon qui l'écrirait?', suggests that the composition of the work is itself a necessity.

These conflicts continue in a discussion of the work that arises from the narrator reading aloud the notes for *Paludes II* to Angèle:

—*Attentes mornes du poisson; insuffisance des amorces, multiplication des lignes (symbole)—par nécessité il ne peut rien prendre.*

—'Pourquoi ça?'

—'Pour la vérité du symbole.'

—'Mais enfin s'il prenait quelque chose?'

—'Alors ce serait un autre symbole et une autre vérité.' (7)

mais comprends donc qu'ici c'est bordé de talus comme ailleurs; nos routes sont forcées, nos travaux de même. (37)

[—*The dreary wait for fish to bite; insufficiency of the bait, multiplication of fishing lines (symbol)—out of necessity he cannot catch anything.*

—'Why is that?'

—'For the truth of the symbol.'

—'But then what if he caught something?'

—'Then it would be another symbol and another truth.'

but understand that we are surrounded by embankments here just as elsewhere; our paths are forced, our labours too.]

The necessity of the literary work appears to limit the narrator's freedom in composing *Paludes II*. Two means of escape are envisaged. First, *Paludes II* could be different on the intradiegetic level: Tityre could catch a fish, in which case this would become a new *symbole* rendered necessary by a different *vérité*. Secondly, his insistence that 'la généralisation, c'est au lecteur, au critique de la faire' [it is for the reader or critic to make generalizations] (47) implies that different interpretations (interpreting the *vérités* of the *symboles*) are possible on the extradiegetic level (consistent with the claims of the paratext). Considered in the light of a structure of *mise en abyme*, this appears rather prosaic: in composing *Paludes II* the narrator struggles to exercise freedom in the face of necessity, but he can imagine *Paludes II* being different, expressing different *vérités* from among his experiences in the *journal intime*, and he wishes those around him to arrive at their own interpretations of the work. The dynamics of necessity and contingency are more striking when *Paludes I* and *Paludes II* are considered as being consubstantial. It then follows logically that *Paludes II* could be different intradiegetically, to the precise extent that it is possible for the narrator to exercise freedom and choose between different possibilities in his diary-writing, and that *Paludes II* could be different extradiegetically, to the precise extent that *Paludes I* is generically and structurally indeterminate and subject to the interpretation of the reader rather than of the author.

The narrator's efforts to excite discontent and action in others are directed above all towards Angèle, as he attempts to make her aware of her own unhappiness and induce her to cry. On two occasions she becomes only 'colorée' (62, 86), but her eventual tears coincide with the completion of *Paludes II*:

> 'Auriez-vous donc un peu compris mon angoisse? En votre sourire aurai-je mis peut-être enfin quelque amertume?—Eh! quoi! vous pleurez maintenant.—C'est bien! Je suis heureux! J'agis!—Je m'en vais terminer Paludes!'
>
> Angèle pleurait, pleurait et ses longs cheveux se défirent. (95–96)

> 'Have you, then, come to understand a little of my anguish? Have I perhaps finally succeeded in bringing some bitterness to your smile?—What's this! You're weeping now.—It's good! I'm happy! I'm committing an act!—I'm off to finish writing Paludes!'
>
> Angèle wept, wept, and her long hair fell loose.]

This response is brought about by dictating to Angèle a passage from *Paludes II*, which is consistent with the structure of *mise en abyme*. Yet on other occasions the narrator's attempts to excite Angèle's discontent take the form of spoken dialogue (62) and a reading of the *journal intime* (86), which can be explained only by the structure of consubstantiality: from this perspective everything that occurs in *Paludes I* also belongs to *Paludes II*, and whatever means have brought about Angèle's unhappiness and the narrator's joy simultaneously constitute the success and resolution of *Paludes II*.

However, this success is called into doubt one last time by the laments of the 'Envoi' (ambiguously attributable to either Gide or the narrator):

> Nous avons chanté
> Vous n'avez pas dansé
>
> [...]

Nous avons bâti sur le sable
Des cathédrales périssables. (99–100)

[We sang
You did not dance
[...]
We built upon the sand
Fragile cathedrals.]

It now appears that the work (*Paludes II*, and perhaps *Paludes I*) has not succeeded in provoking a response, and that it is not the *œuvre* 'hors du temps' (89) that he (the narrator, and perhaps Gide) had desired.

PALUDES AS THE OTHER POLE OF GIDE'S DIARY-WRITING

It is difficult to arrive at a firm conclusion concerning such a profoundly ironic work, in which neither the narrator's perspective nor the author-figure's is ever stable or fully endorsed, but beyond its nihilistic humour and its satire of contemporary artistic stagnation, *Paludes* is also the second stage of Gide's exploration of diary-writing's literary potential. In some respects *Paludes* continues from *CAW* without contradicting it (like the narrator's project, POLDERS, continuing from *Paludes II*). Both works promote the idea of diary-writing being part of an author's writing process and published work, while establishing a series of related oppositions between the diary and literature, reality and art, nonfiction and fiction, contingency and necessity. Furthermore, both works foreground the role of paratext in establishing reading pacts that determine (or leave indeterminate) the ontological status of the whole text. This does not necessarily involve a straightforward choice between fiction, nonfiction, or other conventional categories, but can be a creative process with unlimited permutations. Yet the paratext of *Paludes* associates it more closely with the *traités* than with *CAW*, and like the other *traités* it uses a manifestly fictional situation to examine certain philosophical and aesthetic questions. This use of the *journal intime* to explore the possibilities of writing for action, free will, or an *acte libre*, has a clear legacy in diary novels including Jean-Paul Sartre's *La Nausée* (1938) and Michel Butor's *L'Emploi du temps* (1956). This aspect of *Paludes* is also, in a sense, diametrically opposed to *CAW*: whereas the earlier work envisaged the transformation of diaristic experience into the necessity of an ideal literary *œuvre*, *Paludes* values the contingency of diary-writing and seeks a new kind of author-figure and *œuvre* that can accommodate it. Gide's later experiments with diary-writing all operate somewhere between these two poles established early in his career by *CAW* and *Paludes*.

3

Le Journal des Faux-monnayeurs

Thirty years after the publication of *Paludes*, in a radically changed literary landscape (to which I shall return), Gide published two works that once again used diary-writing to call into question the very nature of the *œuvre* and the author-figure: *Les Faux-monnayeurs* (henceforth referred to as *FM*, 1925) and *Le Journal des Faux-monnayeurs* (*JFM*, 1926).[1] Even when considered separately, both *FM* and *JFM* occupy an important place in the development of Gide's diary-writing. As his only *roman*,[2] *FM* is not only Gide's most ambitious work of fiction but also the culmination of his experimentation with fictional diaries.[3] *JFM* is Gide's first work to use the term 'journal' in its title (as remarked by David Walker),[4] and this book publication of a whole, self-contained, nonfictional diary (together with that of *Numquid et tu?...* in the same year)[5] heralds the large-scale publication of Gide's *journal intime* in the *Œuvres complètes* (1932–39) and then in the Pléiade *Journal 1889–1939* (1939).[6] Yet the greatest significance of these works for diary-writing lies in the unusual relationship between them, which can best be described using the Derridean concept of the supplement (discussed in the introductory

---

[1] André Gide, *Les Faux-monnayeurs* and *Le Journal des Faux-monnayeurs* in *Romans et récits*, II, pp. 173–517 and 519–82 respectively. References in parentheses in the text pertain to this edition of *JFM*, except where indicated otherwise.

[2] Gide refers to *FM* as his 'premier roman' in the work's dedication to Roger Martin du Gard, present from the publication of the first instalment in the *NRF*, 138 (March 1925), pp. 260–308, and in the first edition (Paris: NRF, 1925). Pierre Masson remarks that Gide's reticence to define his fictional works as *romans* dates back to the beginning of his career and 'la période de crise qui affectait alors le roman, genre discrédité aux yeux des symbolistes' [the period of crisis that the novel was undergoing at that time, a genre which was discredited in the eyes of the Symbolists]; Pierre Masson, 'Préface' to André Gide, *Romans et récits*, I, pp. XI–XLVII, pp. XII–XIV.

[3] Besides the use of a fictional author-diarist's *journal intime* in *CAW* and *Paludes*, a diary narrative is used in *La Porte étroite* (1909) and *La Symphonie pastorale* (1919), and once again in *L'École des femmes* (1929).

[4] David Walker, 'Notice' for *Le Journal des Faux-monnayeurs*, in André Gide, *Romans et récits*, II, pp. 1248–54, pp. 1248–9.

[5] André Gide, *Numquid et tu?...* (Paris: Éditions de la Pléiade, 1926). This diary was written in 1916–19, and circulated in a private publication in 1922 before its commercial publication in 1926, the first work in the Pléiade series 'Écrits intimes', edited by Charles Du Bos.

[6] This initial appearance of *JFM* as the integral publication of a unified diary text can now be qualified in light of the 2009 Pléiade edition. *JFM* is indeed closely based on the two *cahiers* that Gide devoted to this writing project, but David Walker's notes (1254–9) detail the points where minor revisions were made, and the list of 'Éléments du journal manuscrit non retenus par Gide' [Elements of the journal manuscript that were not kept in the text by Gide] (569–79) reproduces the fifteen passages that Gide excluded from the published text (and one more, excluded from the 1927 edition onwards). These passages are devoted above all to reflection on individual characters or parts of the novel, rather than contributing to the two major themes of the diary that I identify later.

chapter). Initially, *FM* claimed for itself a certain self-sufficiency as a literary *œuvre*, including an account of the very transformation of lived experience into an artistic form (described in the *journal intime* of the author-character Édouard), but the publication shortly afterwards of *JFM* supplemented the earlier work, both as a 'plénitude enrichissant une autre plénitude', and as an addition that reveals the 'comble' or shortcomings for which it compensates.[7] This relationship builds on the various structures in *CAW* and *Paludes* that place diary-writing in opposition to, or at the margins of, the literary *œuvre*. In doing so, it points towards a more diaristic concept of literature, and a greater possibility for real diaries to be published and read as literary works.

The two works have been approached in various ways, but rarely taking full account of the relationship between them. Most straightforwardly, *JFM* can be used as a valuable documentary source concerning Gide's composition of *FM*, such as in David Walker's study of the manuscript of the diary.[8] This approach does not necessarily limit *JFM* to a documentary role subordinate to the novel (as the principal *œuvre*), whereas David Keypour's largely immanent reading of *FM* positively discredits the project of *JFM*, on the grounds that a true account of the creative process can be found only in the literary work itself.[9] Conversely, Catharine Savage successfully demonstrates that *JFM* can be read as an 'œuvre autonome', although her justification for this—that its first-person narrative, thematic coherence, and structural unity make it fiction, and therefore literature—is a misrepresentation of the work's reading pact.[10] The most sophisticated treatment of the relationship between *FM* and *JFM* is Daniel Moutote's interpretation of the two works as 'la seule tentative pour réaliser complètement la mise "en abyme" définie en 1893 dans le *Journal*' [the only attempt to realize in its entirety the device of 'mise en abyme' defined in 1893 in the *Journal*].[11] However, the intertext with this particular passage from Gide's *journal intime*, written over thirty years earlier and unpublished until 1932, is not directly relevant to the historical question of the works' significance at the time of their publication in 1925–26, and furthermore, Moutote's commitment to a model of *mise en abyme* leads to a critical impasse.[12]

[7] Jacques Derrida, '« Ce dangereux supplément »', in *De la grammatologie* (Paris: Minuit, 1985), pp. 203–34, p. 208.

[8] David Walker, 'En relisant le *Journal des Faux-monnayeurs*', in *André Gide et l'écriture de soi: actes du colloque organisé à Paris le 2 et 3 mars 2001 par l'Association des Amis d'André Gide*, ed. by Pierre Masson and Jean Claude (Lyon: Presses universitaires de Lyon, 2002), pp. 89–101.

[9] David Keypour, *André Gide: écriture et réversibilité dans 'Les Faux-monnayeurs'* (Montreal: Presses de l'Université de Montréal, 1980), p. 217. In this passage, Keypour is drawing on Maurice Blanchot, 'Le Journal intime et le récit', in *Le Livre à venir* (Paris: Gallimard, 1959), pp. 224–30.

[10] Catharine Savage, 'Le Journal des Faux-monnayeurs: œuvre accessoire ou œuvre autonome', *BAAG*, 88 (1990), pp. 535–44.

[11] Daniel Moutote, *Réflexions sur 'Les Faux-monnayeurs'* (Paris: Champion, 1990). The undated diary entry in which Gide discusses the concept of *mise en abyme* is from September 1893, in the *Journal 1889–1939*, pp. 40–2. It was first published in the first volume (1932) of the *Œuvres complètes* (1932–39), pp. 510–13.

[12] This complex structural problem can be summarized as follows: Moutote views *JFM* as the equivalent of a painting's depiction of a mirror that reflects the artist and his or her studio (here, Gide and his 'cabinet de travail', 88), despite the fact that it is not contained within *FM* itself. He then equates *JFM* and *FM* respectively with the 'deux foyers' [two centres] of the work described by Gide:

Just as for *CAW* and *Paludes*, an understanding of the new use of diary-writing in *FM* and *JFM* requires careful attention to the works' context and paratext at the time of publication. This will reveal that, whereas *FM* first appeared as a self-sufficient literary work (despite the shortcomings recognized by contemporary reviewers), *JFM* was presented shortly afterwards as a coherent work in its own right, which also formed a larger, combined structure together with the *roman*. My own study will therefore focus on the way *JFM* establishes its complex relation to *FM*. The structural coherence of the diary is underpinned by long, programmatic entries at the beginning and end of each of the two *cahiers*, which identify two major themes of the diary-writing project: a reflection on this diary's function in the composition of *FM*, and deliberation about its place in a complex opposition between life and art (involving both works). The development of these two themes over the course of the diary gradually elaborates the structure of supplementarity that joins *JFM* with *FM*, and thereby proposes a more open, diaristic form of literary *œuvre* (as discussed earlier, this pertains both to the indivual literary *œuvre* and to the author-figure's collective *œuvre*).

CONTEXTS AND PARATEXTS

Contexts

It is beyond the scope of this study to summarize the vast intellectual and artistic changes (not to mention social and political ones) that took place in the thirty years between the publication of *Paludes* in 1895 and *FM* in 1925, but the most important context for the latter work, and for diary-writing in general at this time, was the literary milieu centred around the *Nouvelle Revue Française*. From its first published issue in 1909, the *NRF* rapidly came to occupy the 'middle ground of French intellectual life', and its coterie of writers (Gide foremost among them) became 'the leading representatives of the French radical-republican intellectual tradition', while remaining receptive to new generations of artists and thinkers.[13] For Gide's role in this milieu, I shall refer to the account provided by Lina Morino's 1939 work *La Nouvelle Revue Française dans l'histoire des lettres*.[14] Although the founding members of the journal had no intention of creating a literary school or manifesto, there was a common sentiment that the era of literary Symbolism had passed, and that there was a pressing need to resuscitate the theatre and the *roman* (25–6). *FM* and *JFM* are marked both by the preoccupations of this early period of the journal's history (these concerns are apparent in the continuities from

---

'd'une part, l'événement, le fait, la donnée extérieure; d'autre part, l'effort même du romancier pour faire un livre avec cela' [on the one hand, the event, the fact, the exterior datum; on the other, the very effort of the novelist to make a book out of that material] (*JFM*, 537). These 'deux foyers' can be seen within each of the two works, but the structure cannot be applied to the two works together, as *FM* does not contain 'l'effort même du romancier' to treat the reality that is depicted in *JFM*.

13 Martyn Cornick, *The "Nouvelle Revue Française" Under Jean Paulhan, 1925–1940* (Amsterdam: Rodopi, 1995), pp. 1–2.

14 Lina Morino, *La Nouvelle Revue Française dans l'histoire des lettres* (Paris: Gallimard, 1939).

Gide's work on *Les Caves du Vatican*)[15] and by a new set of literary concerns that arose from (in Morino's words) 'l'inquiétude d'après-guerre sur ce qu'on a appelé le nouveau mal de siècle' [the anxiety of the post-War period regarding the so-called new disease of the century] (133–4). The period immediately following the First World War saw a proliferation of artistic groupings and manifestos, but Morino considers that these tended towards placing the highest value on psychological experience and introspection:

> Ces tendances si diverses en apparence des surréalistes, des 'aventuriers', des 'évadés, des 'enfants terribles' se réduisent toutes en définitives au sentiment profond qu'il *n'y a rien à fonder sur la réalité extérieure*. De là, la certitude que la seule réalité perceptible c'est le moi: dissolution par conséquent de l'individu dans l'analyse. [...] L'introspection [...] fut pour eux une véritable nécessité. Elle a été la recherche ardente d'une salut. (134)

> [These trends, so varied in their appearance, of the Surrealists, 'explorers', fugitives, 'enfants terribles', all ultimately amount to the same deep conviction that *nothing can be built upon exterior reality*. From this point, the certainty that the only reality that can be perceived is the self: resulting in a dissolution of the individual in analysis. [...] For them, introspection [...] was a veritable necessity. It was the passionate search for some sort of salvation.]

In the *NRF* itself a debate concerning fundamental literary values arose in 1924, centred around Marcel Arland's article 'Sur un nouveau mal du siècle', in which he espouses 'l'absolue sincérité' (*sincérité* is of course one of the central themes of *FM*), and Jacques Rivière's response to Arland in the article 'La Crise du concept de littérature'.[16] The high value attached to introspection at this time is notably visible in the work of Charles Du Bos (also attached to the same milieu), who had kept a diary since 1908, but was encouraged by Gide to see in this writing project '[son] œuvre essentielle', and published his first 'extraits d'un journal' in 1928.[17] Du Bos had promoted an interest in the *intimité* of authors by means of his critical writing, some of which was published in a single volume in 1922 under the title *Approximations*.[18] From 1926 he oversaw a series of publications of diaries and related forms in the collection 'Écrits intimes', published by the Éditions de la Pléiade, beginning with Gide's *Numquid et tu? ...* and followed in 1927 by René Boylesve's mostly diaristic *Feuilles tombées* (published the year after Boylesve's death).[19]

---

[15] Alain Goulet summarizes the development of 'la question du roman' in Gide's long gestation of *Les Caves du Vatican*, although at the point of publication in 1914 this work is labelled a 'sotie' and Gide's 'roman' still remains to be written; Alain Goulet, 'Notice' for *Les Caves du Vatican*, in André Gide, *Romans et récits*, I, pp. 1463–83, p. 1465. André Gide, *Les Caves du Vatican: sotie par l'auteur de Paludes*, 2 vols (Paris: NRF, 1914).

[16] Marcel Arland, 'Sur un nouveau mal de siècle', *NRF*, 125 (February 1924), pp. 149–58, p. 155. Jacques Rivière, 'La Crise du concept de littérature', *NRF*, 125 (February 1924), pp. 159–70.

[17] Michèle Leleu, 'Une « Météorologie intime »: le « Journal » de Charles Du Bos', *Cahiers de l'Association des études françaises*, 17 (1965), pp. 133–50, pp. 141–42. Charles Du Bos, *Extraits d'un journal, 1908–1928* (Paris: Éditions de la Pléiade, 1928).

[18] Charles Du Bos, *Approximations* (Paris: Plon, 1922) The collection includes studies of Amiel, 'la vie de Baudelaire', '"le milieu intérieur" chez Flaubert', and Gide's *La Symphonie pastorale*.

[19] René Boylesve, *Feuilles tombées* (Paris: Éditions de la Pléiade, 1927).

If *FM* was 'le roman-somme qu'[attendait le public]' [the total-novel that the public expected] at this moment in 1925 (142), it was also another step in Gide's ongoing use of diaries in varied forms, since he remained the greatest exponent of the literary possibilities of diary-writing.[20] *La Porte étroite* and *La Symphonie pastorale* had continued to use diary-writing to explore some major themes of Gide's work, such as authenticity, self-knowledge, and the very process of writing (although the diarists in these works are not author-characters). Gide's publications of real diaries in literary journals and individual volumes generally consisted of either travel writing, or diaries devoted to reflecting on literary or aesthetic matters.[21] These publications are not presented as extracts from a single, life-long *journal intime*, but as either the spontaneous thought of the author at a specified time and (often) place, or as a *cahier* which shows the author's continuing thought on a specific subject.

One further work of Gide's diary-writing from this period has been overlooked, partly because its constituent parts have more recently been dispersed in separate collections. *Amyntas* (1906, and published in a new edition in 1925) groups together four texts which had been printed separately, and yet which form a unified whole.[22] 'Mopsus', the first of the four, is attached to the fictional world of the *traités* by its mythological and Vergilian characters, and its lyrical mode recalls the travel diaries in *Les Nourritures terrestres* (1897). The first entry begins with an indication of the place, El Kantara, typeset in the conventional format for the dating of a diary (right-aligned, in reduced type size, ending in a full stop), but there are no dates to place the entries in real, historical time. 'Mopsus' is also distinguished from the other three texts by being printed in italics. In contrast, the other texts are presented as real diaries by their titles (more prosaic descriptions of their content), by the historical dates of their diary entries, and by their less lyrical style. In the context of this collection, the real and fictional diaries function together to treat the same themes in different ways, and the preface to the last of the four texts, 'Le Renoncement au voyage', explicitly addresses the literary merits of diary-writing and the issue of its publication.

In summary, by the time of the publication of *FM* in 1925, a number of roles for diary-writing were well established in Gide's own published *œuvre*: first, the use of fictional diaries as a metaliterary device for exploring writing itself, or as a support for several of the themes which reappear in *FM* (including the thematization of reality and fiction); secondly, the use of real diaries devoted either to a specific journey or to a specific literary or theoretical problem; and finally, the combination of real and fictional diaries within a single signifying structure.

---

[20] A thorough survey of Gide's publication of diaries over the period in question is provided in Anton Alblas, *Le 'Journal' de Gide: le chemin qui mène à la Pléiade* (Nantes: Centre d'études gidiennes, 1997).

[21] Early examples from Gide's *œuvre* of these two types of diary-writing respectively are *Feuilles de route (1895–1896)* (Brussels: N. Vandersypen, 1897), and *Réflexions sur quelques points de littérature et de morale* (Paris: Mercure de France, 1897).

[22] André Gide, *Amyntas* (Paris: Mercure de France, 1906). In Gide's lifetime it was published in new editions in 1925, 1928, 1933 (in the 1932–39 *Œuvres complètes*, III, pp. 3–11), and 1937. In the new Pléiade editions, 'Mopsus' is included in *Romans et récits*, I, pp. 1199–203, and the remaining parts of *Amyntas* ('Feuilles de route', 'De Biskra à Touggourt', and 'Le Renoncement au voyage') are integrated into the text of the *Journal 1887–1925*.

The Publication and Paratexts of *FM* and *JFM*

It will prove useful to summarize the chronology of the first publications of *FM* and *JFM*, the paratextual indications of their genre or reading pact, and their presentation of diary-writing, even though some of these details might initially appear trivial.

FM was printed in five issues of the *NRF* between March and August 1925, continuing up to the end of the second part of the novel. The main text is preceded on the page by no more than the title and the dedication, which identifies the work as Gide's 'premier roman'.[23] A large number of chapters have their own epigraph, present in all editions, which offer literary parallels to the characters and situations at hand. The second instalment contains the first excerpt from Édouard's *journal*, typeset as follows:

JOURNAL D'ÉDOUARD

18 Octobre.—Laura ne semble pas se douter [...][24]

Surprisingly, the dates of the diary entries in the later instalments are typeset differently, in the conventional format for real diaries (right-aligned, in reduced type size, followed by a full stop).

The first edition of *FM* was printed on 28 November 1925, but it was not put on sale until February 1926.[25] However, the press reviews begin in early February, so copies of the novel must have been circulated to the press in advance of this. Compared with the publication in the *NRF*, the book publication places greater emphasis on the work's specificity as a *roman*. Besides the inclusion of the dedication, the title is followed by the word 'ROMAN' on the cover and title page, and the list of 'œuvres du même auteur' classes Gide's other works under different generic headings, such as 'récit', 'sotie', and 'divers' [miscellaneous].[26] The presentation of Édouard's *journal* is also different in the book publication, and consistently appears as follows:

JOURNAL D'ÉDOUARD

« 18 Octobre.—Laura ne semble pas se douter [...] »[27]

The date never appears in the format conventional for real diaries, and every paragraph of the *journal* is surrounded by *guillemets*. Although this *journal* is one of the principal forms of narrative in *FM* alongside the heterodiegetic narrator,[28] its presentation positions it as just one voice among the many documents (such as letters) and characters (such as Vincent's discourses on scientific subjects) that make up this extremely polyphonic novel. The overall effect is to increase the separation between Édouard and Gide in the diegetic framework, and to prompt

---

[23] *NRF* 138 (March 1925), p. 260.   [24] *NRF* 140 (May 1925), p. 906.

[25] Alain Goulet, 'Note sur le texte' for *Les Faux-monnayeurs*, in *Romans et récits*, II, pp. 1220–3, p. 1222.

[26] This list includes all the works mentioned previously in my discussion of the context for *FM* and *JFM*. *CAW* and *Amyntas* are classed under 'divers'.

[27] André Gide, *Les Faux-monnayeurs* (Paris: NRF, 1925), p. 91.

[28] Thirteen of the forty-three chapter titles listed in the table of contents begin with or include a reference to the 'Journal d'Édouard'.

the reader to view this author-character with ironic distance rather than as a spokesman of the real author.

JFM was published in the *NRF* in August and September 1926. Just as for the journal publication of *FM*, the only paratextual information is the title ('JOURNAL DES FAUX-MONNAYEURS', without a definite article), and the dedication, which is present in all later editions: 'J'offre ces cahiers d'exercices et d'études à mon ami / JACQUES DE LACRETELLE / et à ceux que les questions de métier intéressent' [I offer these notebooks of exercises and studies to my friend / JACQUES DE LACRETELLE / and to those who find interest in matters of technique].[29] The dates of diary entries in this publication are typeset in the conventional manner for a real diary.[30]

The first edition of *JFM* in book form was printed on 30 October 1926 and the first press reviews appeared in November.[31] In this edition the title was changed to *Le Journal des Faux-monnayeurs*, with a definite article, suggesting that the existence of this diary is in some way expected by the reader. This expectation might be based on the assumption that all novelists now keep a diaristic account of the process of writing (which would in itself be a major development in the history of diary-writing), or it might imply that *FM* had suggested the existence of this diary (by analogy between Édouard and Gide) and had even anticipated its publication. However, all subsequent editions revert to the original title, *Journal des Faux-monnayeurs*. The other major change from the journal publication was the addition of several items as an 'appendice', providing further documentary material relating to Gide's composition of the novel.[32]

One further point remains concerning the significance of Jacques de Lacretelle's name in the dedication. This establishes a strong connection between *JFM* and a work published by Lacretelle in late 1926, *Colère: suivi d'un journal*.[33] *Colère* is something between an essay and a *récit* with an ambiguous truth status, while the *journal* is the (ostensibly real) diary of the author's composition of this text. The closing words of the diary provide the most illuminating comments on the nature of the work as a whole:

> Je crois qu'un bon moyen est d'écrire de temps à autre des récits sur soi-même et de les publier comme s'il s'agissait de récits romanesques. Ainsi on prendra l'habitude de transcrire des choses vues et des sentiments éprouvés. Les petits bonshommes imaginaires se promèneront tout naturellement dans l'esprit avec les vivants. Ce jeu

[29] *NRF* 155 (August 1925), p. 129.

[30] One small exception is that the full stop is omitted over the first six pages (out of forty-four), which appears to be an error, corrected in all subsequent editions.

[31] André Gide, *Le Journal des Faux-monnayeurs* (Paris: Éos, 1926).

[32] The 'appendice' contains two newspaper articles relating to the *faits divers* that Gide used in the composition of *FM*, a letter from a reader of the novel, some 'Extraits d'un premier projet' (described by the subheading as 'Pages du journal de Lafcadio'), and a passage entitled 'Identification du démon'.

[33] Jacques de Lacretelle, *Colère: suivi d'un journal* (La Haye: Le Bon Plaisir, 1926). The contents of this work were republished shortly afterwards in *Aparté* (Paris: NRF, 1927), together with a third text entitled 'Dix jours à Ermenonville', which is a response to Rousseau's seminal work of *intimisme*, *Les Rêveries du promeneur solitaire*.

mixte ne saurait être mauvais. On y gagnera ceci, de mettre plus de vie dans son art et peut-être plus d'art dans sa vie.[34]

[I believe that a good method is to write narratives about oneself from time to time, and to publish them as if they were novelistic narratives. In this way we get the habit of transcribing the things we have seen and the feelings we have experienced. In one's mind, little imaginary fellows will quite naturally walk side by side with real living people. This combination cannot be a bad thing. The advantage is that one puts more life into one's art, and perhaps more art into one's life.]

By publishing *Colère* and the *journal* in the same volume, Lacretelle presents the spectacle of this transcription from reality to fiction, or at least to the *romanesque*, of 'choses vues' and 'sentiments éprouvés'. It raises a similar issue to *FM* and *JFM* concerning the relationship between art and life (the final sentence evokes Oscar Wilde's approach to this question),[35] and furthermore, it describes the phenomenon (also found in *JFM*, as observed by Catharine Savage)[36] whereby real and imaginary characters co-exist in a shared space.

Even from this summary of the works' early publication history and paratexts, it is possible to draw some preliminary conclusions regarding the relationship between *FM* and *JFM*. The commonly cited dates for their publication are 1925 and 1927 respectively, which gives the impression of a two-year interval between their appearances in the public sphere, but in fact the interval is considerably smaller. After only partial publication in the *NRF*, *FM* entered circulation in book form in February 1926. The entirety of the diary of *JFM* was printed in the *NRF* in August and September of the same year, and the first reviews appeared in November. This proximity between the publication of *FM* and *JFM*, together with the allusion to Lacretelle's *Colère* and the addition of the definite article to the title *Le Journal des Faux-monnayeurs*, allow the two works to be considered as a combined project with a unified signifying structure.

Contemporary Reviews

The contemporary reviews of *FM* and *JFM* confirm this pattern, whereby the former work initially appeared to stand alone, however imperfectly, then the latter joined it to form a new form of composite *œuvre*.[37] In the reviews of *FM* before the publication of *JFM*, common topics include a condemnation of the work on moral grounds (with regard to its portrayal of homosexuality), its specificity as

---

[34] Lacretelle, *Aparté*, pp. 139–40.

[35] Gide, in his 1902 homage to Oscar Wilde, considered that his life and work should be approached with the following claim of Wilde's in mind: 'J'ai mis tout mon génie dans ma vie; je n'ai mis que mon talent dans mes œuvres' [I have put all my genius into my life; I have put only my talent into my works]; André Gide, 'Oscar Wilde', in *Essais critiques*, ed. by Pierre Masson (Paris: Gallimard, Bibl. de la Pléiade, 1999), pp. 836–54, p. 837.

[36] Savage, 'Œuvre accessoire ou œuvre autonome', pp. 539–40.

[37] A large number of reviews are collected in the *dossiers de presse* in BAAG. An index of the articles on *FM* is provided in BAAG 135/136 (2002), pp. 382–90.

Gide's only *roman*, and the relationship between Édouard's *journal* and the rest of the novel (which is assimilated with the opposition between *vie* and *art*). It does not occur to reviewers that a further work is needed to make sense of *FM*, but its shortcomings lead to a certain dissatisfaction. Most reviewers consider Édouard to be a spokesman for Gide without any irony, which allows Édouard to be conflated with both the author and the narrator. This leads to a dissatisfaction with the work's opposition between *vie* and *art* (more specifically, it is lacking in *vie*):

> La réalité qui arrive à Édouard sous des traits purs nous parvient à nous comme une réalité déformée. Il nous paraît inutile que le personnage principal ou l'auteur s'applique encore à l'interpréter, puisque déjà il le fit.[38]

> [The reality that Édouard experiences in a pure form comes to us as a reality that is already deformed. It seems futile for the principal character or the author to set about interpreting it, since he has already done it.]

Since Édouard is simultaneously situated at the centre of the work's many threads and conflated with Gide himself, he cannot remain a living character fully integrated in his environment, nor can he provide the sort of reality that is present in the real diary of *JFM*. It is therefore unconvincing to see Édouard transform this 'réalité déformée' into literary art.

However, the publication of *JFM* brings about a considerable change in attitudes towards *FM*:

> Le roman les *Faux-Monnayeurs* et sa critique de genèse par M. André Gide lui-même: le *Journal des faux-monnayeurs*, forment deux œuvres à ce point inséparables qu'elles n'en constituent plus, à vrai dire, qu'une seule aujourd'hui, la plus importante du grand écrivain et l'une des plus révélatrices sur sa personnalité si complexe et d'apparence si fuyante.[39]

> [The novel *Les Faux-monnayeurs* and the account of its genesis by André Gide himself—the *Journal des Faux-monnayeurs*—form two works that are so inseparable that they have now come to constitute just a single *œuvre*, the most important one that the great writer has produced and one of the most revealing of his personality, which is so complex and so elusive.]

The possibility of viewing *FM* and *JFM* as parts of a single *œuvre* partly resolves the problem described earlier, by creating a distinction between Édouard and his diary on the one hand, and 'M. André Gide lui-même' and *JFM* on the other. This composite *œuvre* containing real and fictional diary-writing is centred around the 'personnalité' of the 'grand écrivain' (even more than *FM* alone had been). In this respect, *JFM* seems to take on the role that Philippe Lejeune attributes to *Si le grain ne meurt*, that of opening an *espace autobiographique* (or here, a diaristic space) in Gide's fictional writing.

---

[38] Robert Marin, review of André Gide, *Les Faux-monnayeurs*, *Sélection*, 5/2 (1925–26), pp. 156–8, reprinted in *BAAG*, 65 (1985), pp. 122–4, pp. 123–4.

[39] F[rédéric] L[efèvre], '*Le Journal des Faux-monnayeurs* par André Gide', *Les Nouvelles littéraires*, 13 November 1926, p. 3.

THE DIARY-WRITING PROJECT IN *JFM*

Given that *JFM* (rather than *FM*) is responsible for constructing the complex relationship between the two works, this relationship is best understood by considering the particular nature of the diary-writing project in *JFM*. Like *CAW*, *Paludes*, Édouard's *journal* in *FM*, and Lacretelle's 'Journal de Colère', *JFM* is an author's diary accompanying a literary project, and several aspects of the text assure its unity and specificity in this regard. The diary entries vary considerably in their frequency, but the occasional long intervals between them are commented on to indicate that there is a continuity from the first entry to the very last, in spite of the apparent interruption ('Resté nombre de mois sans rien écrire dans ce cahier; mais je n'ai guère arrêté de penser au roman' [Passed several months without writing anything in this notebook; but I have scarcely stopped thinking about the novel], 529). The title connects *JFM* strongly with *FM*, but certain comments distinguish this diary from other supports for the author's writing ('J'inscris sur une feuille à part les premiers et informes linéaments de l'intrigue' [I am noting on a separate page the first, vague outlines of the plot], 522), and the period of its composition—beginning some time after Gide began work on the novel and continuing briefly after its completion—suggests that it has a function beyond a merely documentary or instrumental role for *FM*.

JFM begins with certain aims for the diary-writing project, which are evaluated and modified over time, and these reassessments of the project are structured above all by the diary's two *cahiers* (just as they are in *CAW*). One might expect a diarist to continue directly from writing in one *cahier* to the next, but in *JFM* there is in fact a sizeable overlap between the two (as shown in table 3.1). The implication of this unusual structure is that the change from one *cahier* to the other is determined by a change in the writing project itself, and that in the period from August to December 1921 Gide wrote in whichever of the two *cahiers* better served his immediate purpose. The distinct character of each of the two *cahiers* is addressed in their first and last entries (all made up of a series of discontinuous but related notes), and these four long, programmatic entries cast light on the changing terms of the diary-writing project.

The first *cahier* opens with a reflection on the means of narrating the novel, but this soon appears to be just one aspect of a larger problem (at this early stage

Table 3.1. The chronological overlap between the two *cahiers* of *JFM*

Last three entries of first *cahier*	First three entries of second *cahier*
22 juillet [1921].	
	Colpach, août 1921.
Cuverville, 25 novembre 1921.	
	28 novembre 1921.
Cuverville, 7 décembre [1921].	
	Pontigny, 20 août 1922.

Gide envisaged placing Lafcadio, a character from *Les Caves du Vatican*, in the new novel):

> J'hésite depuis deux jours si je ne ferai pas Lafcadio raconter mon roman. Ce serait un récit d'événements qu'il découvrirait peu à peu et auxquels il prendrait part en curieux, en oisif et en pervertisseur. Je ne suis pas assuré que cela me retiendrait d'aborder certains sujets, d'entrer dans certains milieux, de mouvoir certains personnages... Aussi bien est-ce une folie sans doute de grouper dans un seul roman tout ce que me présente et m'enseigne la vie. Si touffu que je souhaite ce livre, je ne puis songer à tout y faire entrer. Et c'est pourtant ce désir qui m'embarrasse encore. Je suis comme un musicien qui cherche à juxtaposer et imbriquer, à la manière de César Franck, un motif d'andante et un motif d'allegro.
>
> Je crois qu'il y a matière à deux livres et je commence ce carnet pour tâcher d'en démêler les éléments de tonalités trop différentes. (521)
>
> [I have been deliberating for two days whether to make Lafcadio the narrator of my novel. It would be a narrative of events that he would discover gradually, and which he would participate in through curiosity, idleness, and perversion. I am concerned that this would prevent me from approaching certain subjects, entering certain milieux, moving about certain characters... But then surely it is madness to group in a single novel everything that life offers and teaches me. However cram-full I wish this book to be, I cannot expect to put everything in it. And yet it is this very desire that still confounds me. I am like a musician attempting to juxtapose and combine, in the manner of César Franck, an andante motif and an allegro motif.
>
> I believe there is enough material for two books and I am starting this notebook to try to separate the elements of tonality that are too different from one another.]

The first explicit statement of the diary's purpose is to sort among the excess of material at the author's disposal (from *la vie*), and adapt it to the formal constraints of the *roman* (the metaphor from music reinforces this concern for artistic form). However, the diversity of types of writing in the various notes that make up the first entry suggests that the diary's function is both broader than this and more of a subject for experimentation. Following the initial deliberation regarding the novel's narrative form, the entry later proposes different possible plots (consistent with the stated intention of the diary), makes general claims about novelistic practice ('Il n'est pas bon d'*opposer* un personnage à un autre' [It is not good to place one character *in opposition* to another], 522), and resolutions for his own writing ('Ne jamais exposer d'*idées* qu'en fonction des tempéraments et des caractères' [Never present *ideas* except as a function of temperaments and characters], 522), and relates his own experience of writing while insisting on its particularity ('Je dis: "on" mais après tout, je ne sais si d'autres éprouvent cela' [I say 'we', but after all, I do not know whether others experience that], 523).

These various aims for the diary are pursued throughout the first *cahier*, but its last entry reports a hiatus in the process of writing:

> À présent me voici arrêté. Me repenchant sur le travail d'hier, il me paraît que je fais fausse route; le dialogue avec Édouard, en particulier (si réussi qu'il puisse être), entraîne le lecteur et m'entraîne moi-même dans une région d'où je ne vais pas pouvoir redescendre vers la vie. Ou bien alors il faudrait précisément que je fasse peser l'ironie

du récit sur ces mots: 'Vers la vie'—laissant entendre et faisant comprendre qu'il peut y avoir tout autant de vie dans la région de la pensée, et tout autant d'angoisse, de passion, de souffrance... (535–6)

[I now find myself ground to a halt. Looking back over yesterday's work, it seems to me that I am following the wrong path; the conversation with Édouard in particular (however successful it might be) leads the reader and myself to a region from which I will not be able to get back down to life. Or perhaps I should precisely bring the irony of the narrative to bear on these words: 'down to life'—suggesting and allowing the reader to understand that there can be just as much life in the domain of thought, and just as much anguish, passion, suffering...]

The *cahier* comes to an end when it has developed the project as far as it can without a fundamental reassessment of its terms, specifically regarding the opposition between *la vie* on the one hand and art (or here, *la pensée*) on the other. Yet the two *cahiers* overlap chronologically at this point, and even as the first *cahier* is being concluded, the second *cahier* elaborates the renewed terms of the diary-writing project.

The second *cahier* begins much like the first, at least formally, with a paragraph that explicitly discusses the project's new direction, followed by a series of notes demonstrating the means at its disposal:

Peut-être l'extrême difficulté que j'éprouve à faire progresser mon livre n'est-elle que l'effet naturel d'un vice initial. Par instants, je me persuade que l'idée même du livre est absurde, et j'en viens à ne plus comprendre du tout ce que je veux. Il n'y a pas, à proprement parler, un seul centre à ce livre, autour de quoi viennent converger mes efforts; c'est autour de deux foyers, à la manière des ellipses, que ces efforts se polarisent. D'une part, l'événement, le fait, la donnée extérieure; d'autre part, l'effort même du romancier pour faire un livre avec cela. Et c'est là le sujet principal, le centre nouveau qui désaxe le récit et l'entraîne vers l'imaginatif. Somme toute, ce cahier où j'écris l'histoire même du livre, je le vois versé tout entier dans mon livre, en formant l'intérêt principal, pour la majeure irritation du lecteur. (537)

[Perhaps the extreme difficulty that I have in making progress with my book is the natural consequence of an initial fault. From time to time, I am convinced that the very idea of the book is absurd, and I get to the point where I no longer understand at all what I want. There is not, strictly speaking, a single centre to the book, around which my efforts would converge; but these efforts are drawn towards two centres, in the manner of an ellipse. On the one hand, the event, the fact, the exterior datum; on the other, the very effort of the novelist to make a book out of that material. And that is the principal subject, the new centre that unbalances the narrative and draws it towards the realm of imagination. In conclusion, this notebook in which I am writing the very story of the book, I now imagine placing it in its entirety in my book, forming its principal interest, to the great irritation of the reader.]

The movement between reality and fiction is now the organizing principle of the whole project, centred around the figure of a *romancier*, and with an important role for this very diary. The notes that follow this first paragraph cover a wide range of topics, some explicitly discussing matters pertaining to the novel, others recounting an anecdote, giving a character portrait, or discussing a literary milieu, but together they provide a full spectrum of modes of writing from ostensible truth to avowed fiction, with many ambiguous shades in between. This is to be the field of experimentation in the second *cahier*.

The final entry of the second *cahier* consists of a reflection on the division of *FM* into parts, a brief statement of the novel's completion, and a discussion of some comments from Gide's friend Roger Martin du Gard. This last item offers a suggestion of the place of *JFM* in the whole project (in editions of *JFM* from 1927 onwards these sentences are the last in the *cahier*, as Gide cut the three paragraphs that follow after them):[40]

> Martin du Gard me communique cette citation de Thibaudet:
> 'Il est rare qu'un auteur qui s'expose dans un roman, fasse de lui un individu ressemblant, je veux dire vivant... Le romancier authentique crée ses personnages avec les directions infinies de sa vie possible; le romancier factice les crée avec la ligne de sa vie réelle. Le génie du roman fait vivre le possible; il ne fait pas revivre le réel.'
> Et cela me paraît si vrai que je songe à épingler ces phrases, en guise de préface, en tête des *Faux-monnayeurs* [...].
> Mais, tout considéré, mieux vaut laisser le lecteur penser ce qu'il veut—fût-ce contre moi. (557–8)

> [Martin du Gard sends me this quotation from [Albert] Thibaudet:
> 'It is rare for an author, who reveals himself in a novel, to create from himself an individual that is true to life, by which I mean living... The true novelist creates his characters out of the infinite directions of his possible life; the false novelist creates them out of the single trace of his real life. The genuis of the novel brings the possible to life; it does not restore life to the real.'
> And this seems to me so true that I imagine pinning these sentences, as a preface, at the head of my *Faux-monnayeurs* [...].
> But, all things considered, it is better to let the reader think whatever he will—even if it is against me.]

Gide's final decision is to leave the reader of *FM* relatively free of paratextual guidance, yet this epigraph 'en guise de préface' is, at least hypothetically, reinstated by the publication of this passage in *JFM*. It relates to the relationship between reality and fiction in the composition of the novel, but not in the way that we might expect. It is rhetorically surprising that, in the citation chosen by Gide for the epigraph, the two oppositions regarding the *romancier* and the *roman* respectively both lead from the positive to the negative. Rather than making a general statement about good novelistic practice (which would end on the more positive proposition), he is suggesting a structure which encompasses both *FM* and *JFM*: the 'romancier authentique', one M. Gide, demonstrates in his diary (*JFM*) and in his completed novel (*FM*) the right way to create fictional characters, whereas the 'romancier factice', Édouard, demonstrates the wrong way in his own

---

[40] The paragraphs that were cut from 1927 onwards are found in the list of 'Élements du manuscrit non retenus par Gide', p. 579. This cut has the effect of adding further emphasis to the lines cited here.

diary and in his failure to produce a novel; a reader should therefore seek the *possible* in *FM* rather than the 'réel' (for which, we should look to *JFM*).

All of these moments of reassessment at the beginning and end of the two *cahiers* broadly address two aspects of the diary-writing project, which are also the criteria distinguishing the *cahiers* from each other: the question of this diary's function in the composition of *FM*, and the relationship between reality and fiction in the writing project as a whole. These programmatic entries are made possible by the unity and coherence of the diary-writing project, but the fact remains that, as in most diaries, the writing progresses in fits and starts, in fragments, and in the passage of time, and largely transcends the comprehension and control of the diarist. I shall therefore follow the development of these two dominant themes over the course of the diary, before considering the overall relationship that *JFM* establishes with *FM*, and the significance of this particular use of diary-writing.

TWO THEMES OF *JFM*

The Function of the Diary

Over the initial period of relatively frequent diary entries in the first *cahier*,[41] four distinct functions of the diary emerge, whose development over time is interrelated. The first function to become apparent is an instrumental role in working on the technical problems of the composition of the *roman*. This includes the initial attempt to 'démêler les éléments de tonalités trop différentes' (521) [separate the elements of tonality that are too different from one another] by considering and discounting different possible plots, but it also covers a wide range of deliberations over the whole length of *JFM*. It specifically excludes the 'brouillons' or 'avant-textes' [drafts] for the *roman* ('j'inscris sur une feuille à part les premiers et informes linéaments de l'intrigue' [I am noting on a separate page the first, vague outlines of the plot], 522), and it promotes a certain conception of the author-figure that is opposed to a reliance on 'inspiration':

> J'attends trop de l'inspiration; elle doit être le résultat de la recherche; et je consens que la solution d'un problème apparaisse dans une illumination subite; mais ce n'est qu'après qu'on l'a longuement étudié. (524)

> [I expect too much from inspiration; it should be the result of searching; and I accept that the solution to a problem may appear in a sudden illumination; but only after one has worked at it for a long time.]

JFM is the site of the author's labour and 'recherche', and in this respect it corresponds to the 'études' mentioned in the dedication.

---

[41] There are thirteen entries between 17 June 1919 and 16 August 1919, whereas the following twelve entries of the first *cahier* lead up to 7 December 1921.

The second function is the diary's role in recording the experience of writing, which is introduced by example in the first entry rather than being addressed explicitly:

Il arrive toujours un moment, et qui précède d'assez près celui de l'exécution, où le sujet semble se dépouiller de tout attrait, de tout charme, de toute atmosphère; même il se vide de toute signification, au point que, désépris de lui, l'on maudit cette sorte de pacte secret par quoi l'on a partie liée, et qui fait que l'on ne peut plus sans reniement s'en dédire. N'importe! On voudrait lâcher la partie. . .
Je dis: 'on' mais après tout, je ne sais si d'autres éprouvent cela. (522–3)

[There always comes a moment, which precedes very closely the moment of execution, when the subject seems to lose all appeal, all charm, all atmosphere; it even empties itself of meaning, to the extent that, becoming disenchanted with it, we curse this sort of secret pact that binds us together, and which means that we cannot extricate ourselves without renouncing. All the same, we would like to escape this pact. . .
I say 'we', but after all, I do not know whether others experience that.]

This function too continues for the length of the diary, and a large number of entries comment on the rhythm of the project's progress, and social encounters that either pertain to or distract from the author's work. It also complements the instrumental role of the diary, by creating a documentary record of the author's intellectual labour.

A single passage in the long first entry simultaneously introduces the third and fourth functions of the diary: the formulation of aphoristic statements concerning the *roman* as a genre, and the transfer of material from the diary to within *FM* itself:

Ne jamais exposer *d'idées* qu'en fonction des tempéraments et des caractères. Il faudrait du reste faire exprimer cela par un de mes personnages (le romancier): 'Persuade-toi que les opinions n'existent pas en dehors des individus. Ce qu'il y a d'irritant avec la plupart d'entre eux, c'est que ces opinions dont ils font profession, ils les croient librement acceptées, ou choisies, tandis qu'elles leur sont aussi fatales, aussi prescrites, que la couleur de leurs cheveux ou que l'odeur de leur haleine. . .' (522)

[Never present *ideas* except as a function of temperaments and characters. Besides, I should make one of the characters say that (the novelist): 'Be assured that opinions do not exist outside of individuals. What is irritating among most of them is that these opinions that they profess, they believe that they have accepted them freely, or chosen them, whereas they are just as much determined, just as irrevocably given to them, as the colour of their hair or the smell of their breath. . .']

The third function adds another element to the author-figure manifested in the diary, as a source of gnomic wisdom concerning the genre of the *roman*. The fourth function is so far quite straightforward: the author wishes both to employ the aphorism in the composition of the novel, and to make it available to the reader as a tool for the novel's interpretation. There is not yet a clear parallel established between *FM* and a novel at a metadiegetic level (a *mise en abyme* in its simplest sense),[42] and although the aphorism is attributed to a character provisionally called 'le romancier' (who will become Édouard), this character will apply it to people on his own diegetic level rather than to characters of his own creation. However, it is significant that the very transfer of material from *JFM* to *FM* is rehearsed in the diary itself, and it is through these successive 'exercices' that the transfer becomes gradually more complex.

The second half of the first *cahier* provides further examples of each of the four functions described earlier (deliberation of technical problems, a record of writing, formulating aphorisms, and exercising the transfer of material from this diary to *FM*). However, the development of this last function has far-reaching consequences for the others:

> Je ne dois noter ici que les remarques d'ordre général sur l'établissement, la composition et la raison d'être du roman. Il faut que ce carnet devienne en quelque sorte 'le cahier d'Édouard'. Par ailleurs, j'inscris sur les fiches ce qui peut servir: menus matériaux, répliques, fragments de dialogues, et surtout ce qui peut m'aider à dessiner les personnages. (531)

> [I must note here only remarks of a general nature on the construction, composition, and raison d'être of the novel. This notebook must become in some way 'Édouard's notebook'. Besides, I write on loose pages the things that might be useful: small pieces of material, lines of speech, fragments of dialogue, and especially things that will help me sketch out the characters.]

The connection between these three sentences is not immediately obvious: the diary must be limited to certain types of writing (first sentence), because of the new conception of the use of the diary in the novel (second sentence), and besides, this is already being done by relegating to 'fiches' those materials that could be summarized as 'brouillons' (third sentence). It remains vague how the diary is to become 'le cahier d'Édouard', but it follows logically from this passage that it is to be presented to the reader in its entirety, intradiegetically, ostensibly referring to a projected novel of Édouard's but evidently inviting analogy with Gide's novel. If it were not being reproduced in its entirety it would not matter if it contained fragmentary material that would be out of place in the intradiegetic 'cahier d'Édouard'. Although the diary is explicitly restating its limitations, it is also broadening its fourth function, the transfer of diaristic material into the novel, to cover all of the others, both henceforth and retrospectively, so that the whole process and experience of the novel's production can be reproduced within it.

The second *cahier* is distinguished by a fundamentally different approach to the diary's fourth function (the use of material from the diary in *FM*), which is addressed at the beginning of the first entry (cited earlier). This conception of the diary's function is now more specific about using the diary 'tout entier', but it also

---

[42] In practice, a structure recognized as a *mise en abyme* is rarely this simple, as is demonstrated throughout the study by Lucien Dällenbach, *Le Récit spéculaire: essai sur la mise en abyme* (Paris: Seuil, 1977).

speaks in more general terms about 'le romancier' (instead of 'Édouard') and 'le livre' (instead of 'le roman'). In fact, the term 'livre' appears six times in the first paragraph ('roman' is excluded, while 'récit' appears once), as if insisting that the work 'n['est] pas assimilable à rien d'autre' [cannot be assimilated with anything else] (528). While this passage retreats from the earlier model in which the diary was to become the 'cahier d'Édouard', it reinforces that the diary is to be 'l'intérêt principal' of the project's end product, which may be something other, or larger, than the 'roman' alone. In this respect, the nondescript term 'livre' evokes the far more ambitious aims of the Mallarméen *Livre*.

The possible use of this diary in *FM* (or in the less clearly defined *livre*) is further complicated by the recognition of a fifth function, that of adapting material from the writer's real life to the fictional world of the novel. On 22 April 1921, in the first *cahier*, Gide had suggested that his experience of meeting a 'jeune vagabond' [young vagabond] at a train station could provide the model for the first encounter between Édouard and Lafcadio (532). In hindsight, this appears to be an early example of 'l'événement, le fait, la donnée extérieure [et] l'effort même du romancier pour faire un livre avec cela' (537), of which the second *cahier* provides many more examples.[43] However, once this fifth function becomes explicit, it is also apparent that it is incompatible with the earlier model for re-using the diary as the 'cahier d'Édouard', since Gide's effort to transform his real experience into the fiction of *FM* cannot be the same as Édouard's efforts to transform this same fiction (or reality, as it appears to him) into a metadiegetic fiction. This contradiction lies behind the vagueness in the opening of the second *cahier*, but already a possible solution presents itself: it is possible to imagine the *livre* as a composite work similar to Lacretelle's *Aparté*, consisting of the diary and the *récit*, which could in turn contain the 'cahier d'Édouard' as a modified form of the diary. This *livre* did not in fact come to pass as a single published volume, but the model of a composite work is suggested once again by the final entry's discussion of a possible epigraph with relevance to both *FM* and *JFM* (discussed earlier), just as the overall structure of Lacretelle's *Colère* and 'Journal de *Colère*' is addressed in that diary's closing words.

This account of the diary's various functions demonstrates that the diarist's initial intentions for an instrumental, documentary, and gnomic role for *JFM* are gradually subsumed in a project to transfer these diaristic traces of the novelist's work into the *roman* itself. This same project is later cast into doubt by the additional function of adapting real, lived experience into fiction, although a structure of a composite *livre*, including both the real diary and *FM*, is suggested in its place. It is already apparent that the opposition constructed in the diary between reality and fiction—the second major theme identified at the beginning and end of the two *cahiers*—has important consequences for the relation of *JFM* to *FM*. It will therefore be useful to consider in greater detail the devices and theoretical reflections involved in this opposition.

[43] There is a notable predilection for 'la donnée extérieure' that is observed on trains, including the varied incidents and real-life characters described on pp. 539–40, 547, and 549–50.

Reality and Fiction

The devices used in *JFM* for instilling elements of reality in the writing of the *roman* are diverse, and increase in sophistication over the course of the diary. In the most general terms, the passage of time and real life has a welcome disrupting effect on the composition of *FM*, expressed using a metaphor of ventilating the enclosed space of the novel: even the long intervals in the author's work 'aèrent le sujet et le pénètrent de vie réelle' [air out the subject and instil it with real life] (524), and this 'aération' helps to dispel a 'parfum livresque' [bookish odour] (529). The diary also contains discussion of the *faits divers* that are used to avoid an '*à priori*' construction of a logically coherent narrative (525).[44]

The most elaborate and extensively used device of this sort is the diarist's creation of fictional characters drawing on his own experience, a process which has been described at length by David Walker and Catharine Savage.[45] Walker remarks that Gide begins by discharging his views on the novel on to Édouard (who begins life as 'le romancier', 522), then distances himself from his creation ('Il me faut me reculer et l'écarter de moi pour bien le voir' [I must step back and separate him from myself to see him properly], 544), and only once Édouard has been 'dompté et apprivoisé' [subdued and tamed] does Gide go on to develop the other characters of the novel.[46] The diarist discusses this part of the writing process explicitly, using a metaphor of carving the characters from his own flesh (551), or commenting more abstractly that 'cet effort de projeter au-dehors une création intérieure, d'objectiver le sujet (avant d'avoir à assujettir l'objet) est proprement exténuant' [this effort to project an interior creation on the outside, to objectivize the subject (before having to make a new subject of this object) is thoroughly exhausting] (528). As Savage observes, this creation of fictional characters involves modes of writing that confuse or eliminate the diegetic boundaries between the author-diarist and his creations:[47]

> À mesure que G. s'enfonce dans la dévotion, il perd le sens de la vérité. (537)
>
> D'opinion propre, somme toute, Valentin n'en avait pas. (538)
>
> M. dit de Lucien qu'il est 'tout pénétré par sa façade'. (538)
>
> Bernard a pris pour maxime [...] (542)
>
> [As G. immerses himself in piety, he loses the meaning of truth.
>
> All things considered, Valentin did not have his own opinion.
>
> M. says of Lucien that he is 'entirely saturated by his façade'.
>
> Bernard took as his motto [...]]

These excerpts move freely between tenses characteristic of the *journal intime* (the present and the perfect) and the more novelistic imperfect tense, and they all begin

---

[44] Two newspaper articles pertaining to these cases are reprinted in the *appendice*, pp. 559–60.
[45] Walker, 'Notice' for *Journal des Faux-monnayeurs*. Savage, 'Œuvre accessoire ou œuvre autonome'.
[46] Walker, 'Notice' for *Journal des Faux-monnayeurs*, p. 1251.
[47] Savage, 'Œuvre accessoire ou œuvre autonome', pp. 539–40.

a paragraph, fragment, or entry without any other introduction to determine its context or truth status. These ambiguous statements, and many others, smooth the transition from the diarist's own experience to the lives of his characters, and allow the latter to gain in solidity and independence by cohabiting with real people (including the diarist) in the world of the diary.

When the diary is read as part of a composite structure consisting of both *JFM* and *FM* (resembling Lacretelle's *Aparté*), these processes of creating fiction from real experience invite comparison with Édouard's analogous attempts in his own *journal*, and especially with the short excerpt of his novel that he gives to Georges to read (*FM*, 442–4). Without an extensive analysis of this passage, it is safe to say that Édouard's fiction fails because it is both excessively artificial (as Georges comments with regard to his own obvious avatar, 'Eudolfe est un nom ridicule' [Eudolfe is a ridiculous name]; *FM*, 444) and excessively dependent on the reality on which it is based, so that the characters have no independent life of their own. Taken together, the works depict the 'romancier factice [qui] crée [ses personnages] avec la ligne unique de sa vie réelle' (Édouard in *FM*) and the 'romancier authentique' (Gide in *JFM*) creating fiction with 'les directions infinies de sa vie possible' (*JFM*, 557). In this respect, the publication of *JFM* seems to complete the composite structure, or *livre*, of which *FM* provides just the first component, incomplete and unsatisfactory on its own terms.

However, a more complex relationship between the works is suggested by the way in which *JFM* constructs an opposition between reality and fiction, or rather subverts it, as can be seen in the following passages:

> Je fus amené, tout en l'écrivant [*Si le grain ne meurt*], à penser que l'intimité, la pénétration, l'investigation psychologique peut, à certains égards, être poussée plus avant dans le 'roman' que même dans les 'confessions'. (529)

> le dialogue avec Édouard, en particulier (si réussi qu'il puisse être), entraîne le lecteur et m'entraîne moi-même dans une région d'où je ne vais pas pouvoir redescendre vers la vie. Ou bien alors, il faudrait précisément que je fasse peser l'ironie du récit sur ces mots: 'Vers la vie'—laissant entendre et faisant comprendre qu'il peut y avoir tout autant de vie dans la région de la pensée, et tout autant d'angoisse, de passion, de souffrance... (535–6)

> Les plus douteux égarements de la chair m'ont laissé l'âme plus tranquille que la moindre incorrection de mon esprit (537)

> [I came to the point, while writing *Si le grain ne meurt*, of thinking that *intimité*, introspection, psychological investigation can, in some respects, be taken to greater lengths in the 'novel' even than in 'confessions'.

> [this passage translated above]

> The most questionable sins of the flesh left my soul more calm than did the slightest fault of the spirit.]

The first passage refers to a discussion of reality and fiction in *Si le grain ne meurt*, but which is transformed by the present context: the comment in *Si le grain ne meurt* that 'peut-être approche-t-on de plus près la vérité dans le roman [que dans l'autobiographie]' [perhaps we get closer to the truth in the novel [than in autobiography]] suggests that this autobiography might have borrowed something from the genre of the *roman*, but in *JFM* it expresses a desire that *FM* should possess qualities more often associated with ostensibly truthful writing, and should perhaps borrow something of the diary's *intimité*.[48] The second and third citations above are similarly associated with a desire to reconcile the fiction of the projected novel with some aspects of reality. This is achieved rhetorically by a slippage of terms towards an opposition between *vie* and *pensée*, or *chair* and *esprit*, but they are nonetheless reformulations of the fundamental opposition between the reality of the diary and the fiction of the *roman*. They do not express a simple preference for the latter term in each opposition (fiction, *pensée*, *esprit*), but they recuperate these terms by recognizing that they possess some of the very qualities that are conventionally associated with their opposite term (reality, *vie*, *chair*).

This unstable relationship between diaristic reality and novelistic fiction contributes to a conception of a more open form of literary *œuvre*, which contrasts with the supposed self-sufficiency of *FM*, and also with the model by which *JFM* and *FM* together form a complete, composite *œuvre*:

Pourquoi, dès l'instant que j'accepte qu'il ne soit assimilable à rien d'autre (et il me plaît ainsi), pourquoi tant chercher une motivation, une suite, le groupement autour d'une intrigue centrale? Ne puis-je trouver le moyen, avec la forme que j'adopte, de faire indirectement la critique de tout cela [?] (528)

Ne pas établir la suite de mon roman dans le prolongement des lignes déjà tracées; voilà la difficulté. Un surgissement perpétuel; chaque nouveau chapitre doit poser un nouveau problème, être une ouverture, une direction, une impulsion, une jetée en avant—de l'esprit du lecteur. (551)

[Why, once I have accepted that it cannot be assimilated with anything else (and that it is how I like it), why search so persistently for a motivation, a continuity, a way of grouping everything around a central intrigue? Can I not find the means, with the form that I am adopting, to make an indirect critique of all that[?]

Not to establish the continuity of my novel in the prolongation of the lines that have already been traced; that is the difficulty. A perpetual rising up; each new chapter must present a new problem, must be an opening, a direction, an impetus, a leap forward—on the part of the mind of the reader.]

By integrating contingent reality into the fiction of the novel, the author-diarist replaces the 'groupement autour d'une intrigue centrale' and the 'prolongement des lignes déjà tracées' (which give an impression of necessity and simple causality) with a 'surgissement perpétuel'. This is manifested in *FM* by an unpredictable change of direction at the start of each chapter. The 'ouverture' of this *œuvre* also resists any perfect resolution or conclusion:

Celui-ci s'achèvera brusquement, non point par épuisement du sujet, qui doit donner l'impression de l'inépuisable, mais au contraire, par son élargissement et par une sorte d'évasion de son contour. Il ne doit pas se boucler, mais s'éparpiller, se défaire... (556)

[It will end abruptly, not from the subject's being exhausted, since it must give the impression of being inexhaustible, but, on the contrary, through the opening up of

---

[48] André Gide, *Si le grain ne meurt*, p. 267.

the subject and a sort of escape from its established contours. It must not wrap itself up neatly, but be dispersed, undone...]

FM itself ends with a passage from Édouard's *journal* that anticipates yet another new 'surgissement' ('je suis bien curieux de connaître Caloub' [I am very curious to get to know Caloub], 466), but also the publication of *JFM* alongside *FM* can be seen to enlarge or unravel the novel rather than completing a neatly tied 'boucle'.

This concept of a more open literary *œuvre*, with its constant 'jetée en avant—de l'esprit du lecteur' (551), also entails an important role and a large degree of interpretative freedom for the reader (even more so than in *CAW* and *Paludes*):

> Puis, mon livre achevé, je tire la barre, et laisse au lecteur le soin de l'opération; addition, soustraction, peu importe: j'estime que ce n'est pas à moi de le faire. Tant pis pour le lecteur paresseux: j'en veux d'autres. (557; see also 546, 558)

> [Then, having completed my book, I draw a line under it, and leave the task of the calculation to the reader: addition, subtraction, no matter: I consider that it is not my place to do it. Too bad for the lazy reader: I want better ones.]

The transfer of responsibility to the reader is facilitated within *FM* by the figure of the narrator, whose poor understanding of the characters and plot provides a pastiche of the conflated author-figure and omniscient narrator associated with the nineteenth-century Realist novel. The reader, faced with this 'auteur imprévoyant' [author without foresight] (*FM*, 337), is immeasurably 'plus perspicace' [more perceptive] and 'découvre dans les personnages maintes choses, et dans le cours du récit maintes vérités, malgré l'auteur et pour ainsi dire à son insu' [discovers in the characters many things, and in the course of the narrative many truths, despite the author and, as it were, behind his back] (546). More fundamentally, an author-figure is evoked by *FM* and *JFM* (responsible for the 'exercices' and 'études' of *JFM*, and its gnomic wisdom concerning the *roman*) who is in a position to view both Édouard and the dysfunctional narrator with irony. But he too relinquishes to the reader the role of interpreting characters and events that owe their independence to their origins in reality (particularly those characters, events and *faits divers* that Gide developed into fiction in *JFM* itself). Finally, the very relation of *JFM* to *FM* assures the interpretative freedom of the reader: owing to its undecidable status as either the completion of a composite *œuvre* or the open-ended 'élargissement' of an ongoing project, *JFM* allows any number of coherent readings (including the various approaches of critics discussed earlier) without allowing any finalized, exclusive interpretation.

THE DIARY AS SUPPLEMENT

The importance of *JFM* and *FM* independently as works of diary-writing, real and fictional respectively, should not be underestimated, but their greatest significance for Gide's experimentation with diaries—and so for the history of diary-writing more broadly—lies in the complex relationship between them. Both *CAW* and *Paludes* made use of diary-writing's ambiguous status at the boundaries of the literary, but the publication of *JFM* very soon after that of *FM* developed the implications of this marginal status to a much greater degree, in a structure that can accurately be described using the Derridean concept of the supplement. In short, the addition of a supplement to a work (or other structure) that is already supposedly complete has two distinct meanings, whose 'cohabitation est aussi étrange que nécessaire' [cohabitation is as strange as it is necessary]: it simultaneously forms an even more complete structure ('une plénitude enrichissant une autre plénitude' [a plenitude enriching another plenitude]), and compensates for the very lack that it reveals in the earlier work ('il ne s'ajoute que pour remplacer' [it adds itself only in order to replace something]), thereby opening up an 'enchaînement infini [de suppléments]' [endless chain of supplements].[49]

The account given above of the way *JFM* gradually constructs its relation to *FM*, through reflections on its own function as a diary and on an opposition between reality and fiction, reveals the dynamics of supplementarity in the case of these two publications. The paratextual description of *FM* as Gide's only *roman*, and the discussion of this genre by Édouard and other characters, make a strong claim for the work's self-sufficiency as a literary *œuvre*, notwithstanding the dissatisfaction expressed by contemporary reviewers. The diarist's initial intentions for *JFM* create a role for it as a separate work in its own right, incidental to *FM*, portraying an author-figure at work in his 'exercices' and 'études'. From the very beginning of *JFM* there is also a deliberation concerning the use of this diary in the literary project itself, which gradually takes shape as a composite structure that includes both *JFM* and *FM*, more complete and self-sufficient than *FM* alone (as observed in the review by Frédéric Lefèvre). This combined *œuvre* offers the most coherent model for comparing Gide's and Édouard's respective projects, and their literary response to the reality of their lives, yet it also co-exists with a different, more open conception of the literary *œuvre*: since the publication of *JFM* revealed the insufficiencies of *FM*, even this more complete, supplemented *œuvre* also seems open to an indefinite series of supplements, in which a reader's interpretation is always possible but never finalized or comprehensive.

This relationship of supplementarity develops significantly from the two contrasting approaches to diary-writing in *CAW* and *Paludes*—the desire for a totalizing diary-*œuvre* and an appreciation of the diary's contingency respectively. While both these earlier works construct oppositions between the diary and the literary *œuvre*, the supplementary role of *JFM* with respect to *FM* allows the diary to draw closer to assuming a literary status in its own right (paradoxically, it does so by embracing the very marginality of the diary), and also to envisage an *œuvre* that is more open to the contingency and incoherence that the diary easily accommodates. This composite structure is an important step towards the culmination of Gide's diary-writing in the *Journal 1889–1939*, which makes unprecedented claims for the *journal intime* as a unified literary work with the capacity to enlarge and unravel its own coherence as an *œuvre*.

---

[49] Derrida, '« Ce dangereux supplément »', pp. 208, 226.

4

The *Journal 1889–1939*

Gide's *Journal 1889–1939* published in 1939 is justly recognized as the culmination of his diary-writing,[1] and as a landmark in the emergence of the *journal
intime* as a literary genre,[2] yet its place in the history of diary-writing remains
poorly understood for two reasons.[3] Most critical work on the *Journal* treats the
(somewhat virtual) totality of Gide's lifelong *journal intime* as a document running
parallel to his whole *œuvre*, and does not address the significance of this particular
publication late in his career.[4] Meanwhile, the legacy of Gide's *Journal* in the latter
part of the twentieth century has been obscured by the tendency of subsequent
authors (especially those in the literary avant-garde) to downplay the influence
exerted on them by such a canonical, institutionalized author-figure from the
previous generation.[5] Ironically, this failure to examine the historical role of the

---

[1] David Keypour cites both Alain Girard and Daniel Moutote in support of this position; David
Keypour, 'Le Journal fictif dans l'œuvre d'André Gide', *BAAG*, 82–3 (1989), pp. 217–24, p. 217.
[2] Alain Girard, *Le Journal intime* (Paris: PUF, 1963), p. 90.
[3] André Gide, *Journal 1889–1939* (Paris: Gallimard, Bibl. de la Pléiade, 1939), henceforth
referred to as the *Journal*. The new Pléiade edition in two volumes is also an invaluable source of
information on Gide's lifelong *journal intime*, and reveals the considerable extent of editing and
selection that lies behind the apparently integral publications in Gide's lifetime. Citations from the
Journal will be followed by a page reference for the first edition and then, whenever possible, to the
corresponding volume and page in the new Pléiade edition. André Gide, *Journal 1887–1925*, ed.
by Éric Marty (Paris: Gallimard, Bibl. de la Pléiade, 1996). André Gide, *Journal 1926–1950*, ed. by
Martine Sagaert (Paris: Gallimard, Bibl. de la Pléiade, 1997).
[4] In *Le Journal de Gide et les problèmes du moi (1889–1925)* (Paris: PUF, 1968), Daniel Moutote
begins from the position that 'toute l'œuvre d'André Gide se présente dans une relation essentielle avec
la personne de son auteur' [all André Gide's *œuvre* is presented in an essential relation to the person
of its author] (XIII). This produces '[une] vision de soi [qu']il faut [. . .] expliquer en sa constitution
progressive par les documents contemporains de chacun de ses moments, et d'abord par le journal,
qui la prépare et finalement la constitue' [a vision of the self which must be explained in its progressive
constitution by means of the documents that accompany each of its moments, and first of all by the
journal, which shapes it and finally constitutes it]. Éric Marty's *L'Écriture du jour: le 'Journal' d'André
Gide* (Paris: Seuil, 1985) examines the *Journal* for its realization of the capacity of diary-writing to
attain a 'présence-à-soi[,] présence ou sentiment de présence de l'événement et celui de l'écriture'
[presence *of self*, presence or perceived presence of the event, and of the event of writing itself] (12),
drawing on a study by Maurice Blanchot, 'Gide et la littérature de l'expérience', in *La Part du feu*
(Paris: Gallimard, 1949), pp. 208–20.
[5] Alain Goulet's survey of Gide's influence on writers in 1975 includes several examples of
this attitude, including that of Julien Gracq: 'il me semble que c'est la génération immédiatement
précédente qui a surtout été intéressée par Gide. Pour ma part, je ne le rouvre guère souvent' [it seems
to me that it was especially the generation immediately before my own that was interested in Gide.
For my own part, I only rarely read him]; Alain Goulet, 'Une Enquête sur l'influence de Gide en
1975', in *Actualités d'André Gide: actes du colloque international organisé au Palais Neptune de Toulon
et à la Villa Noailles à Hyères les 10, 11 et 12 mars 2011*, ed. by Martine Sagaert and Peter Schnyder
(Paris: Honoré Champion, 2012), pp. 106–30, p. 115.

Journal is partly the result of its very success in presenting a real *journal intime* as a literary *œuvre*, and in establishing a diaristic author-figure as the organizing principle of Gide's works throughout his career. Nonetheless, my own study of the *Journal* will demonstrate that its historical importance lies not only in its consolidation of Gide's earlier experiments in real and fictional diary-writing, but also in the possibilities it opens for later writers.

Like all Gide's works discussed in the previous chapters, the *Journal* belongs to two broad contexts: first, the ongoing development of Gide's own literary career (especially his use of diary-writing), and secondly, the intellectual and cultural context at the moment of publication in 1939. These two contexts are of course closely related, but at this point when Gide had become so dominant in literary life, there appears to have been a particularly strong influence from the former to the latter, or as Anton Alblas describes it, Gide's ongoing diary publications contributed to 'le développement d'un environnement propice à l'éclosion du *Journal 1889– 1939*' [the development of an environment conducive to the emergence of the *Journal 1889–1939*].[6] Lina Morino, writing in 1939 (but before the publication of the *Journal*) about the history of the *Nouvelle Revue Française*, concludes with an account of contemporary literary culture, at least as it was viewed from this particular milieu. She describes here the public expectation for the posture of a *romancier*, but it could equally be applied to the role of a writer in general:

> On exige de lui qu'il soit homme d'abord, auteur ensuite; mais foncièrement un homme qui dit vrai; qu'il se confie à son œuvre, qu'il s'y découvre autant qu'il s'y explique. Car, il faut, quoi qu'on fasse, passer par l'étude de l'individu, qui est la seule donnée concrète.[7]

> [They demand that he should be a man first of all, and an author second; but essentially a man who speaks the truth; that he should confide in his *œuvre*, and explore himself there just as much as he explains himself. For, whatever one does, it is necessary to proceed by the study of the individual, which is the only solid basis for knowledge.]

This is far removed from an earlier form of interest in the writer as an 'homme', the interest that led Sainte-Beuve to look to a writer's unpublished *petits papiers* in search of the *naturel* which might explain their literary *œuvre*.[8] Instead, it reflects the Gidean principle of *sincérité*, by which an author's published *œuvre* itself manifests the writer's personal process of exploration or experimentation.[9]

---

[6] Anton Alblas, *Le 'Journal' de Gide: le chemin qui mène à la Pléiade* (Nantes: Centre d'études gidiennes, 1997), p. 67.

[7] Lina Morino, *La Nouvelle Revue Française dans l'histoire des lettres* (Paris: Gallimard, 1939), p. 185.

[8] This attitude was discussed in the introduction to Part I, with reference to Jacques Lacan, 'Jeunesse de Gide ou la lettre et le désir', in *Écrits II* (Paris: Seuil, 1999), pp. 217–42.

[9] This principle is perhaps best expressed by Blanchot (in a discussion of Gide's *Journal*) as 'le souci de faire servir la littérature à une expérience véritable: expérience de soi-même, expérience de ses pensées' [the concern for making literature provide a genuine experience: an experience of oneself, and of one's thoughts]; Blanchot, 'Gide et la littérature de l'expérience', p. 210. First printed in 1947 in *L'Arche*.

Whereas Marcel Arland's espousal of *sincérité* on behalf of a new generation in 1924 was keenly contested (see Chapter 3), it now appears to have become the status quo. By this time, several writers of Gide's close acquaintance had begun publishing their respective *journaux intimes* in instalments—Charles Du Bos (from 1931), Denis de Rougemont (from 1937), and Julien Green (from 1938)[10]—but the wider significance of the value of *sincérité* in literature is demonstrated by an autobiographical work published in 1939, Michel Leiris's *L'Âge d'homme*. The following passage is taken from the book's 'prière d'insérer', written by Leiris in 1939:

> Entre tant de romans autobiographiques, journaux intimes, souvenirs, confessions, qui connaissent depuis quelques années une vogue si extraordinaire (comme si, de l'œuvre littéraire, on négligeait ce qui est *création* pour ne plus l'envisager que sous l'angle de l'*expression* et regarder, plutôt que l'objet fabriqué, l'homme qui se cache— ou se montre—derrière), *L'Âge d'homme* vient donc se proposer, sans que son auteur veuille se prévaloir d'autre chose que d'avoir tenté de parler de lui-même avec le maximum de lucidité et de sincérité.[11]

> [Among so many autobiographical novels, *journaux intimes*, recollections, confessions, which have known such an extraordinary popularity in the last few years (as if we have come to neglect the part of *creation* in a literary *œuvre*, and consider it only as a form of *expression*, and to see, rather than the object that has been made, the man who hides—or shows himself—behind it), *L'Âge d'homme* now shows itself, without the author wishing to boast of having done anything more than to speak about himself with the highest degree of lucidity and sincerity.]

Leiris's assessment of the contemporary literary scene in 1939 echoes Brunetière's comments on the proliferation of 'la littérature personnelle' in 1888,[12] but now these forms (both fictional and nonfictional) are involved in a more complex dynamic of authorial revelation and evasion, owing to the writer's experience of self-discovery in the course of the writing process.

As for the development of diary-writing in Gide's own works, the most important publications after *JFM* were the individual volumes of real diaries (to which I shall return) and the inclusion of large parts of Gide's lifelong *journal intime* in the fifteen volumes of his *Œuvres complètes* (1932–39, henceforth referred to as the *OC*).[13] In fact, one peculiarity of the *Journal* is that its publication made such an impact even though most of its contents had already appeared in print in one or both of these two formats. A study of the *Journal* must therefore take place against the background of these earlier publications, and especially the *OC*, since this constituted another important attempt to organize Gide's whole *œuvre* around a diaristic author-figure. I shall pay particular attention to the paratext of

---

[10] Charles Du Bos, *Extraits d'un journal, 1908–1928* (Paris: Éditions de la Pléiade, 1928). More regular instalments of Du Bos's *journal* were published from 1946. Denis de Rougemont, *Journal d'un intellectuel en chômage* (Paris: Albin Michel, 1937). Julien Green, *Journal: 1928–1934* (Paris: Plon, 1938).

[11] Michel Leiris, *L'Âge d'homme*, in *L'Âge d'homme, précédé de L'Afrique fantôme*, ed. by Denis Hollier (Paris: Gallimard, Bibl. de la Pléiade, 2014), pp. 751–942, pp. 755–6.

[12] Ferdinand de Brunetière, 'La Littérature personnelle', *La Revue des deux mondes*, 85 (1888), pp. 433–52, p. 434.

[13] André Gide, *Œuvres complètes*, ed. by Louis Martin-Chauffier, 15 vols (Paris: NRF, 1932–39).

the *Journal* and the unusual circumstances of its publication, which distinguished it from the earlier editions: it was not only the first publication of a living author's (apparently) complete *journal intime* as a substantial independent work, but also the first publication of a living author in the prestigious Bibliothèque de la Pléiade, previously devoted to deceased, canonical authors. Gide's commentary on Montaigne's *Essais* in *Les Pages immortelles de Montaigne*, published in 1939, also had important implications for the *Journal*, and can effectively be considered as a part of its paratext (or more specifically, its epitext).[14] The paratext and format of the *Journal*, as well as certain entries that take on a programmatic role in this new edition, make unprecedented claims for this diary as a new type of literary *œuvre*, drawing on all Gide's previous experimentation in diary-writing.

One further peculiarity of the *Journal* is the way in which, after an initial recognition of its importance, its legacy was soon lost from view, eclipsed by the events of the Second World War. Although the *Journal* was printed in May 1939, it only went on sale in September,[15] after the outbreak of hostilities in Europe (the German invasion of Poland began on the 1st and France formally declared war on Germany on the 3rd). As Leiris later wrote of the even greater neglect of *L'Âge d'homme*, 'le livre sorti en 1939 a été emporté par la guerre' [the book that came out in 1939 was swept away by the War].[16] Yet I shall argue that the *Journal*, in addition to its acknowledged importance in Gide's *œuvre*, had a secret legacy by which it exerted an influence long after Gide had fallen from favour. Like *JFM* before it, the *Journal* remains open to supplement and interpretation, and so in the final part of this chapter I shall demonstrate its continuity in the work of two writers, Jean-Paul Sartre and Roland Barthes, who came to dominate two successive generations of the literary avant-garde which otherwise seemed alien to Gide's influence. For different reasons, Sartre and Barthes found themselves with considerable leisure time to spend with the *Journal*, the former having been called up for military service, the latter in a sanatorium being treated for tuberculosis. In very different ways, Sartre's *Carnets de la drôle de guerre: septembre 1939—mars 1940* and Barthes's 'Notes sur André Gide et son "Journal"' (1942) engage deeply with the *Journal* in order to question these writers' own broad literary aims and their roles as *auteurs*.[17] An understanding of this circuitous route through which Gide's influence passed will prove useful in following the developments in diary-writing later in the twentieth century.

---

[14] André Gide, *Les Pages immortelles de Montaigne: choisies et expliquées par André Gide* (Paris: Corrêa, 1939). In Gérard Genette's terminology, the epitext is the part of the paratext that lies outside the object of the printed book (in opposition to the peritext), such as interviews in which an author discusses a published text; Gérard Genette, *Seuils* (Paris: Seuil, 1987), pp. 10–11.

[15] Éric Marty, 'Notice', in André Gide, *Journal 1887–1925*, pp. 1297–321, p. 1317.

[16] From an interview with Madeleine Gobeil in 1966, cited in Denis Hollier, 'Notice' for *L'âge d'homme*, in Michel Leiris, *L'Âge d'homme, précédé de l'Afrique fantôme*, pp. 1212–38, p. 1236.

[17] Jean-Paul Sartre, *Les Carnets de la drôle de guerre: septembre 1939–mars 1940*, in *Les Mots et autres écrits autobiographiques*, ed. by Jean-François Louette (Paris: Gallimard, Bibl. de la Pléiade, 2010), pp. 143–679. Roland Barthes, 'Notes sur André Gide et son « Journal »', in *OC* ([1942]), I, pp. 33–46. First printed in *Existences* (journal of 'Les Étudiants au sanatorium'), 27 (July 1942), and reprinted in an issue of *Le Magazine littéraire* devoted to Barthes, 97 (February 1975), pp. 24–8.

THE *JOURNAL INTIME* IN GIDE'S *ŒUVRES COMPLÈTES*

After *JFM*, Gide's publication of diary-writing became more frequent, but can appear surprisingly conventional compared with his earlier works.[18] However, Anton Alblas identifies the first publication of the 'Pages de journal' in the *NRF* (1932) as a turning point, marking the beginning of Gide's attitude towards his principal *journal intime* (as opposed to a travel diary, or a diary devoted to a specific topic) as 'un moyen légitime de "produire"' [a legitimate means of 'production'].[19] The publications in the 'Pages de journal' series assume that there is interest and literary value in Gide's *journal intime* and its portrayal of this 'Jean-Jacques [Rousseau] moderne' (in the words of Robert Brasillach),[20] and the later instalments demonstrate that Gide is prepared to publish material even from the very recent past.[21] Nonetheless, the fifteen volumes of Gide's *Œuvres complètes* (1932–39), incorporating the majority of the *journal intime* written between 1889 and 1932, constitute his most abundant publication of diary-writing over this period. Moreover, the paratextual presentation of the *journal intime* in these volumes addresses the question of the diary's relation to Gide's other works, and leads to the first clear conception of Gide's total *œuvre* as a unified whole centred around a diaristic author-figure.

Gide's earlier attempts to create order and unity in his *œuvre* include the successive regroupings of his works by genre, and the collections of *Morceaux choisis* and *Pages choisies* published in 1921,[22] but the introduction to the first volume of the *OC* describes its new form and more ambitious aims:

> L'édition des œuvres de Gide, dont nous commençons la publication, n'est pas une édition critique. Il ne s'agit ici que de donner, dans leur ordre chronologique, les livres, les poèmes, les cahiers et les feuillets qui composent l'œuvre d'André Gide, dans un texte correct, et accompagnés seulement de notices documentaires.
>
> Il nous a paru que cette entreprise devait être tentée du vivant de l'auteur, avant que sa production fût arrêtée.
>
> Une figure légendaire de Gide tend à se former, qui ne ressemble pas à son image véritable et menace d'effacer celui-ci. On connaît la résistance de ces masques de

---

[18] *L'École des femmes* (1929) is a conventional diary novel, in that it conforms to Valerie Raoul's model (see introductory chapter). Gide's publications of real diaries after *JFM*, such as *Voyage au Congo* (1927) and *Le Retour du Tchad* (1928), play an important role in presenting his new intellectual and political interests, but are not formally innovative or unusual in their use of the diary itself.

[19] Anton Alblas, *Le 'Journal' de Gide: le chemin qui mène à la Pléiade* (Nantes: Centre d'études gidiennes, 1997), p. 42. In the present discussion I am indebted to Alblas's meticulous study of Gide's composition, editing, and publication of material from his *journal intime* throughout his career.

[20] Robert Brasillach, 'André Gide, *Pages de journal (1929–1932)*', *BAAG*, 74–5 (1987), pp. 53–8, p. 55. First printed in *L'Action française*, July 1934.

[21] The 'Pages de journal' were printed sporadically in the *NRF* following the first instalment in June 1932 (985–1004), which featured diary entries from 1929. Three book publications followed: *Pages de journal (1929–1932)* (Paris: Gallimard, 1934), *Nouvelles pages de journal (1932–1935)* (Paris: Gallimard, 1936), and *Pages de journal: 1939–1942* (New York: Pantheon Books, 1944).

[22] André Gide, *Morceaux choisis* (Paris: NRF, 1921). André Gide, *Pages choisies* (Paris: Crès, 1921).

fantaisie, peu à peu composés, faits de pièces et de morceaux qui permettent le jeu et auxquels leur mobilité prête une apparence véridique et un semblant de vie.[23]

[The edition of Gide's *œuvres*, which we are here undertaking to publish, is not a critical edition. Our concern is only to provide, in their chronological order, the books, poems, notebooks and loose pages that make up André Gide's *œuvre*, in an accurate text, and accompanied only by documentary information.

We considered that this project should be attempted in the author's lifetime, before his literary production had come to an end.

A legendary figure of Gide is being formed, which does not resemble his true image and threatens to obscure it. We know how persistent these fabricated masks can be, constituted over time, made up of pieces and scraps that allow it to operate and whose mobility lends to it an appearance of truth and the semblance of life.]

The *OC* will replace the fallacious 'figure légendaire' of Gide with his 'image véritable', by means of an emphasis on the continuities of his life and career. This is achieved through a chronological arrangement of his works, which effaces their generic divisions. For example, the typesetting of the table of contents presents the main texts uniformly and ignores generic or hierarchical differences between texts such as *traités* and the *journal* (while distingushing between these main texts and new, paratextual material in the 'introduction' and 'notices'):

TABLE DES MATIÈRES
DU TOME I

A composite image is formed more literally by the single photograph of Gide at the beginning of every one of the fifteen volumes, each contemporary with the works contained in that volume. Altogether, these fifteen photographs provide an impression of a chronological sweep in Gide's career, attached to the physical

---

[23] Gide, *OC*, I, pp. IX–X. These paratextual notes were, as David Walker describes them, 'rédigés par Louis Martin-Chauffier, mais suggérés ou même parfois dictés par Gide, au fur et à mesure de l'élaboration des *Œuvres complètes*' [written by Louis Martin-Chauffier, but suggested or even sometimes dictated by Gide, as the work on the *Œuvres complètes* progressed]; David Walker, 'Notice' for *Le Journal des Faux-monnayeurs*, in André Gide, *Romans et récits*, II, pp. 1248–54, p. 1249.

presence and appearance of the author himself. The *journal* too, together with the other works, is present in the service of this 'image véritable'.

The role of the *journal* relative to the other contents of the *OC* remains ambiguously situated between two different positions throughout the fifteen volumes. In the statement of the project cited earlier, the *cahiers* and *feuillets* of the *journal* are presented as an integral part of 'l'œuvre d'André Gide' alongside his 'livres' and 'poèmes'. Soon afterwards, the presence of the *journal* is explained by stating that 'mieux que tout commentaire, [il] servira à éclairer l'œuvre, en montrant les raisons profondes qui ont poussé l'auteur à écrire chacun de ses ouvrages' [better than any commentary, it will serve to illuminate the *œuvre*, showing the fundamental reasons that pushed the author to write each of his works].[24] Here it is neither *œuvre* nor *ouvrage*, and is relegated to the role of documentary evidence for the elucidation of the unequivocally literary works. The paratextual 'notices' which run throughout the *OC* vary between these two conceptions of the *journal*:

> On verra par le *Journal* publié dans ce tome [...] les circonstances dans lesquelles l'auteur interrompit la *Porte Étroite* pour écrire d'un seul jet l'*Enfant Prodigue*.[25]
>
> C'est [...] un moment où la lassitude, le doute et l'inquiétude spirituelle rendent au journal, devenu refuge et seule expression, un accent intime qu'il avait en grande partie perdu.[26]
>
> [We can see in the *Journal* published in this volume [...] the circumstances in which the author interrupted work on *La Porte étroite* to write *L'Enfant Prodigue* in a single burst.
>
> It is a moment when fatigue, doubt and spiritual anxiety lend to the *journal*, which had become his refuge and sole means of expression, a note of the *intime* that it had largely lost.]

The former citation presents the *journal* in a plainly documentary role, while the latter is indistinguishable from the paratext's general approach in discussing the 'livres' and 'poèmes'.

There is a similar ambiguity as to whether the *journal* in the *OC* is an integral and coherent text in its own right. It is initially stated that 'une très grande partie du journal' [a very large part of the *Journal*] will be printed (but not the whole of it),[27] yet the division of the *journal* by *cahiers*, numbered from one to thirty-eight, reinforces the material unity of the *journal* and implies that the manuscripts are reproduced in their entirety. The paratext mentions and explains some specific exemptions, such as the diaries covering Gide's time at the Foyer franco-belge and the suppressions relating to his conjugal situation, but this too suggests that the publication of the *journal* is otherwise integral. However, the paratext sometimes undermines the coherence of the *journal* by emphasizing that its composition was interrupted over several periods (particularly a period of ten years from 1892 to 1902) and that its boundaries with other works are complex

---

[24] Gide, *OC*, I, p. X. [25] Ibid., V, p. VII.
[26] Ibid., VII, p. XII. [27] Ibid., I, p. X.

and confused. It is separated from the *feuillets*, the *Feuilles de route (1895–1896)*, and the *Réflexions sur quelques points de littérature et de morale* by a relatively subtle difference in attitude,[28] while the 'notices' discuss at length the editorial decisions taken when material is shared between the diary and other works (such as for *CAW* and *Les Nourritures terrestres*), or when Gide's diary-writing practice has been divided between the *journal* proper and separate works such as *Numquid et tu?...* and *JFM*.

In summary, the following points should be kept in mind regarding the *journal* in the *OC*, as the most important context for the publication of the *Journal 1889– 1939*: it is presented as an almost integral publication of a diary-writing project running throughout Gide's career, but which is significantly interrupted, dispersed, and poorly defined in relation to his other works. Although the *journal* takes up a substantial part of the *OC*, its role is never clearly determined as either a documentary source for the elucidation and contextualization of the literary works, or a literary work in its own right. Yet this very ambiguity in the relationship of the *journal* with the other works plays a role in the project of the *OC* to create an essentially diaristic 'image véritable' of the author, presented as a long chronological sweep that a reader can follow 'en sa constitution progressive'.[29]

THE *JOURNAL 1889–1939*

The unprecedented claims of the *Journal* to constitute a literary *œuvre* in its own right, and its ensuing critical success, are mainly attributable to the new paratext and form given to material that had largely been published earlier in the *OC* and in the 'Pages de journal'. In assessing the work's paratext, I shall begin by considering the significance of Gide's almost contemporary publication of *Les Pages immortelles de Montaigne* as an epitext to the *Journal*, in which he identifies his own diary-writing project with Montaigne's *Essais*. The peritext and form of the *Journal*, as a single volume published in Gallimard's Bibliothèque de la Pléiade series, have considerable significance in themselves (discussed by the majority of contemporary reviewers), but also give a new prominence and programmatic significance to certain diary entries. As a whole, the publication is not just an assertion of the literary potential of the *journal intime*, but a subtle reflection on the implications of a diaristic *œuvre* and author-figure.

Les Pages immortelles de Montaigne

The content of *Les Pages immortelles de Montaigne* (henceforth referred to as *PIM*) is in large parts reproduced from Gide's 1929 *Essai sur Montaigne*,[30] but

[28] These other texts are 'des fragments de journal, mais, dans les deux sens du mot, plus "détachés" que des notes régulièrement prises' [fragments of a *journal*, but, in both sense of the word, more 'detached' than notes that are taken with regularity]; Ibid., II, p. XIII.

[29] This is effectively the approach taken by Daniel Moutote, although he refers to the text of the *Journal 1889–1939*; Moutote, *Le Journal de Gide*, p. XIII.

[30] André Gide, *Essai sur Montaigne* (Paris: Éditions de la Pléiade, 1929).

the circumstances, format, and modifications of the later work invite the reader to consider its observations about Montaigne's *Essais* to apply directly to Gide's *Journal* as well. Gide was already closely associated with Montaigne owing to his earlier critical writings and to the manifest similarities of his diary-writing with the *Essais*,[31] and Barthes in his 'Notes sur André Gide et son "Journal"' draws a connection between *PIM* and the *Journal* in particular:

> Ce n'est jamais sans raison que Gide écrit une œuvre critique. Sa préface à des 'morceaux choisis' de Montaigne, le choix même des textes, nous apprend autant sur Gide que sur Montaigne.[32]

> [Gide never wrote a work of criticism without a reason. His preface to the 'morceaux choisis' of Montaigne, the very choice of texts, teaches us as much about Gide as it does about Montaigne.]

The relationship between Gide and Montaigne in *PIM* is heavily determined by its inclusion in the 'Pages immortelles' series published by the Éditions Corrêa, even though the standard paratextual presentation of this series was not of Gide's own creation. Most of the works in the series have a frontispiece and title page as shown in figure 4.1 (p. 115). In each of the four works depicted, the title page gives the greatest typographic weight to the name of the author whose work is being discussed (Voltaire, Rousseau etc.) and of the author undertaking this discussion (André Maurois, Romain Rolland etc.), although the names of the latter are in slightly smaller type, and the presence of their first names distinguishes these living authors from the deceased, canonical ones. Yet the closely cropped photographs of the frontispieces (excluding the frame from the portrait of Montaigne, for example) obscure the distinction between the living and the dead, and while the modern authors are positioned lower, they have also been depicted in such a way as to bring out certain physical likenesses, such as Voltaire's and Maurois's long nose, and Montaigne's and Gide's mostly bald scalp. The overall effect is to suggest that each of these works is an engagement between two authors of comparable literary stature (although deference is paid by the living author to the deceased one), more motivated by strong sympathies than by a critical attitude, and in which the canonical author and his work is in some sense brought to life.

The opening words of Gide's text help to establish an analogy between Montaigne's *Essais* and his own *Journal* which persists throughout the work:

> Montaigne est l'auteur d'un seul livre: *les Essais*. Mais dans ce livre unique, écrit sans composition préétablie, sans méthode, au hasard des événements et des lectures, il prétend se donner à nous tout entier.

> [Montaigne is the author of a single book: *les Essais*. But in this unique book, written without any pre-established composition, without method, following the vagaries of events or readings, he claims to present himself to us in his entirety.]

---

[31] See, for example, Percy Mansell Jones, *French Introspectives: From Montaigne to André Gide* (Cambridge: Cambridge University Press, 1937).

[32] Barthes, 'Notes sur André Gide et son « Journal »', p. 35.

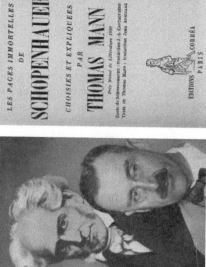

Figure 4.1. The 'Pages immortelles' series of the Éditions Corrêa

The frontispiece and title page of four works in the 'Pages immortelles' series. The photographs and the format of the title page suggest in each case an engagement between two authors with strong sympathies, and of comparable literary status.

This method (or lack of method) of *écriture* describes the *Journal* as accurately as it does the *Essais*. Yet besides these similarities in the composition of the *Essais* and the *Journal*, the two works also have in common a certain paradox: Gide effectively applies himself in *PIM* to explain how an author can use a fragmentary and contingent mode of writing to 'se donner à nous tout entier', and thereby to produce his or her 'livre unique'. Since neither Montaigne nor Gide can accurately be described as 'l'auteur d'un seul livre' in a literal sense, the term 'livre unique' must be taken in the specific, more abstract sense that their total *œuvre* is characterized by this general writing project and the author-figure that emerges from it. In Gide's case, this evokes another form of the Mallarméen idealized *Livre*.

Gide gives numerous examples of how the enormously varied reflections of the *Essais* serve an essentially self-reflexive project. While Montaigne does not escape the contemporary convention of excessive (in Gide's view) recourse to citation of classical authors, he does show an unusual capacity to appropriate them, or in his own words (cited by Gide), ' "Que nous sert-il d'avoir la panse pleine de viandes", dit-il, "si elle ne se digère, si elle ne se transforme en nous, si elle ne nous augmente et fortifie?" ' [What use is it to have our belly full of meat, if it is not digested, if it is not transformed within us, if it does not improve or strengthen us?].[33] René-Gustave Nobécourt, in his review of the *Journal*, remarks on Gide's similar tendency to use his discussion of other works and authors to 'préciser quel *écrivain* lui-même il veut être' [specify what sort of *writer* he wants to be].[34] Above all, Gide values Montaigne's inconstancy in the face of convention and received wisdom. By confronting '[les] croyances établies, [les] conformismes' [established beliefs, conformist attitudes] with 'un esprit toujours en éveil, à la fois très souple et tendu, joueur, amusé de tout, souriant' [a mind that is always alert, both flexible and taut, playful, amused and good humoured towards everything], Montaigne manages to remove the mask of the 'figure conventionelle de l'humanité' [conventional figure of humanity] to reveal 'l'essentiel', the 'être réel'.[35] As a consequence, the author-figure that emerges from the *Essais* is an elusive figure, always in motion, rather than a static portrait:

> 'Je ne peints pas l'estre, je peints le passage'. (Les Allemands diraient: le Werden). Car Montaigne reste préoccupé du perpétuel écoulement de toutes choses, et, par ces mots, indique la non-stabilité de la personnalité humaine, qui *n'est* jamais, mais ne prend conscience d'elle-même que dans un insaisissable devenir.[36]

> ['I do not paint the being, I paint the movement'. (The Germans would say the 'Werden'). For Montaigne remains preoccupied with the perpetual flow of all things, and, through these words, indicates the non-stability of the human personality, which never *exists* in one moment, but becomes aware of itself only in an intangible process of becoming.]

---

[33] Gide, *PIM*, p. 10.
[34] René-Gustave Nobécourt, 'Le *Journal* d'André Gide', *BAAG*, 59 (1983), pp. 407–22, p. 414. First printed in *Journal de Rouen*, 15 and 22 August 1939.
[35] Gide, *PIM*, pp. 10–11.   [36] Ibid., pp. 17–18.

Once again, this 'passage' or 'Werden' is as much a part of the *Journal* as it is of the *Essais*, and Gide indirectly claims that the *Journal* reveals his own 'être réel' in the process of its 'insaisissable devenir'.

The complex relationship between the particular 'être réel' of Montaigne and the general 'être réel' of the human condition is central to the nature of the *Essais* as a literary *œuvre*:

> Même il en vient à penser que la peinture qu'il présente de lui pourrait bien devenir d'intérêt particulier; et c'est en raison de cette vérité profonde que nous prenons autant d'intérêt à sa peinture; car 'chaque homme porte la forme entière de l'humaine condition' (Livre III, chap. 2). Il y a plus: Montaigne est convaincu que 'l'être véritable est le commencement d'une grande vertu' (Livre II, chap. 18), comme dirait Pindare; et ces mots admirables, que Montaigne emprunte à Plutarque (qui lui-même les tient de Pindare) je les fais miens; je voudrais les inscrire en tête des *Essais*, car c'est là surtout et partout l'important enseignement que j'y puise.[37]

> [He even comes to think that the portrait that he presents of himself could be of a particular interest; and it is due to this fundamental truth that we take so much interest in his portrait; for 'each man carries within him the whole form of the human condition' (Book III, chapter 2). And there is more: Montaigne is convinced that 'true being is the beginning of a great virtue' (Book II, chapter 18), as Pindar would say; and these laudable words, which Montaigne borrows from Plutarch (who himself takes them from Pindar), I would make them my own; I would like to inscribe them at the head of the *Essais*, for that is, above all and throughout, the major lesson that I draw from them.]

Gide presents the *Essais* (and, implicitly, the *Journal*) in terms of a humanistic model of the literary *œuvre*, which depicts the common human condition by means of particular human experience. He also valorizes *vérité* within this model (in the *Journal* this becomes the problem of *sincérité*), and inscribes it in a prestigious literary heritage that includes Pindar, Plutarch, Montaigne, and himself. Yet Gide is also aware of a danger in associating the value of the work with 'l'extraordinaire personnalité de l'auteur',[38] that this canonical author-figure and his 'livre unique' might be made safe and inert by the very respect that is paid to him. His response is to insist here, as in his earlier works of diary-writing, that it is the role of the reader to find elements of the work which were unknown to the author, citing Montaigne that 'un suffisant lecteur descouvre souvent es escrits d'autruy des perfections autres que celles que l'auteur y a mises et apperceües, et y preste des sens et des visages plus riches' [a competent reader often discovers in the writings of others perfections other than those that the author put there and was aware of, and bestows them with richer meanings and appearances].[39] Accordingly, Gide aims in *PIM* to bring new life to this canonical author,[40] and in the *Journal* he continues in the same literary tradition as the *Essais*.

---

[37] Ibid., pp. 15–16.   [38] Ibid., p. 10.

[39] Ibid., pp. 12–13. This citation from Montaigne closely resembles Gide's phrase from the preface to *Paludes*: 'Et cela surtout m'y intéresse que j'y ai mis sans le savoir' [And that part interests me above all, that I put there without knowing it]; André Gide, *Paludes* (Paris: Librairie de l'Art indépendant, 1895), p. vii.

[40] Gide, *PIM*, p. 44.

The most important implications of *PIM* for the *Journal*, when considered as an epitext to this work, can be summarized as follows: the fragmentary, contingent writing of the *Journal* both gives rise to a complete portrait of an author-figure, and produces his 'livre unique', in the narrow sense that the author's whole *œuvre* is determined by this portrait. Yet this author-figure is not stable or coherent, and its *être réel* can only be perceived in its movement or 'insaisissable devenir'. Finally, The *vérité* or *sincérité* of this author-figure is the basis for the value of the *Journal* as a literary *œuvre* in a humanist literary tradition, which remains open to future readers and writers.

Paratext and Form of the *Journal*

The only preface to the *Journal* is a 'note de l'éditeur', far shorter than the 'notices' provided by the *OC*, and which concisely draws attention to the principal features of the new format of this publication, as if their significance were self-evident. It begins by mentioning the very features that are most remarked upon by contemporary reviewers:

> Nous sommes heureux de publier pour la première fois dans la *Bibliothèque de la Pléiade* l'œuvre d'un écrivain contemporain: le *Journal* d'André Gide, qui, commencé en 1889, s'étend aujourd'hui sur une période de cinquante ans. (9)

> [It is with pleasure that we publish for the first time the *œuvre* of a contemporary author in the *Bibliothèque de la Pléiade*: the *Journal* of André Gide, which, begun in 1889, today extends over a period of fifty years.]

This touches on three new aspects of the *Journal*: the entry of a living author into the Bibliothèque de la Pléiade, the status of the *Journal* as an *œuvre* (and, implicitly, its presence in a single volume without any other works), and the period of time which it covers. In effect, every new aspect of the form of the *Journal* reinforces and qualifies this deceptively simple editorial claim of the text's status as an *œuvre*, and I shall consider the implications of each of these features in turn.

It is difficult to over-estimate the esteem in which the Bibliothèque de la Pléiade had come to be held since the publication of its first volume, the works of Baudelaire, in 1931.[41] Gide's inclusion in this series is not simply an honour similar to admission into the Académie française, and while this was the beginning of the publication of living authors in the Pléiade, it also presented Gide as belonging to a group of canonical authors who constitute 'le plus résistant et le plus élégant de ce qui a été écrit en français depuis six ou sept siècles' [the most durable and elegant work that has been published in French over the last six or

---

[41] Nobécourt comments in his review that 'il n'[en] est plus nécessaire de signaler la prodigieuse réussite technique et littéraire (son succès près du public cultivé, ami des beaux livres et de grandes œuvres, nous en dispense)' [it is no longer necessary to mention its huge success, both technical and literary (its popularity with the public of good taste, lovers of fine books and great works, spares us this task)]; Nobécourt, 'Le *Journal* d'André Gide', p. 408.

seven centuries].[42] It is a 'consécration' which makes Gide into 'l'un des *maîtres du vingtième siècle et son Journal son enseignement majeur*' [one of the *masters of the twentieth century, and his Journal* contains his major teaching].[43] The fact that the *Journal* alone out of all Gide's works is chosen for inclusion in the Pléiade makes a claim for it to be Gide's 'livre unique', in the narrow sense suggested in *PIM*, and indeed reviewers variously describe it as the organizing centre of Gide's corpus ('son centre de gravité et son principe d'unité tout à la fois' [both its centre of gravity and its unifying principle]),[44] and as the greatest collection of his 'enseignement' ('dirons-nous qu'il contient le meilleur, le plus vrai de sa vie?' [should we say that it contains that which is best, and most true from his life?]).[45]

Besides its inclusion in the Bibliothèque de la Pléiade, it is above all the formal unity of the *Journal* that invites readers to interpret it as an *œuvre* in a way which was not possible in the earlier publications. The particular choice of dates, and the duration of the *Journal*, have a great significance in this regard. It is claimed that the diary printed here coincides chronologically with the whole diary-writing project, which was 'commencé en 1889' (whereas the *OC* mentions that the manuscripts extend back earlier than this to *cahiers* which were used in the composition of *CAW*, v. I, p. XXII, and these earlier diaries are now included in the new Pléiade edition) and continues right up to 'aujourd'hui' (the final entry, dated 26 January 1939, is as recent as could practically be expected). Its range of fifty years is not only a substantial and round figure, but more importantly it precisely covers Gide's career from his twentieth year, in which he began work on *CAW*, up to the completion of his threescore years and ten (his seventieth birthday was the following November) and the publication of the final volume of the *OC*. The emphasis of the 'note de l'éditeur' on the continuity of the diary over this long period also contrasts with the frequent mentions in the *OC* of interruptions in its composition. The effect of these editorial choices is that the *Journal* appears to be the first integral publication of this diary-writing project, which lends its own inherent unity to the work, and occupies a privileged position in relation to the author-figure and his whole literary career. It has only recently become apparent, in light of the far more complete Pléiade editions published in 1996 and 1997, just how much this appearance of an integral publication is an artifice produced by Gide's selection of the material at his disposal.

Just as the *Journal* replaces the interrupted chronology of the diary in the *OC* with a greater continuity, it also appears more unified and independent in its relationships with Gide's other works of diary-writing:

Nous avons reversé dans le cours du *Journal* certaines suites (*La Mort de Charles-Louis Philippe, le Voyage en Andorre, la Marche Turque*) que l'auteur en avait extraites pour

---

[42] Franz Hellens, 'Le *Journal* d'André Gide', *BAAG*, 59 (1983), pp. 422–5, pp. 422–3. First printed in *Le Soir*, 2 February 1940.

[43] Nobécourt, 'Le *Journal* d'André Gide', p. 408.

[44] Claude-Edmonde Magny, 'Le *Journal* de Gide à la Pléiade', *BAAG*, 139 (2003), pp. 389–92, p. 389. First printed in *Esprit*, February 1940, pp. 306–10.

[45] Nobécourt, 'Le *Journal* d'André Gide', p. 408.

les publier en revue d'abord, puis dans divers volumes: *Prétextes, Nouveaux Prétextes, Incidences*; d'autres enfin, firent l'objet de publications séparées: *Feuilles de Route, Numquid et tu...?* etc.

Nous avons intercalé dans le *Journal*, en fin d'années, à l'époque approximative à laquelle ils furent écrits, des *Feuillets* restés épars et non datés par l'auteur. (9)

[We have poured back into the main course of the *Journal* certain sections (*La Mort de Charles-Louis Philippe, le Voyage en Andorre, la Marche Turque*) which the author had removed in order to publish them, first in journals, then in various volumes: *Prétextes, Nouveaux Prétextes, Incidences*; others again provided the material for separate publications: *Feuilles de Route, Numquid et tu...?* etc.

He have placed within the *Journal*, at the end of each year, in the approximate period when they were written, some *Feuillets* [loose pages] that remained separate and undated by the author.]

Whereas the paratext of the *OC* explains the editorial decisions taken when material is shared between the *journal* and works such as *CAW* and *Les Nourritures terrestres*, this issue is now passed over in silence, and the *Journal* consequently appears less dispersed in its boundaries with Gide's other works. Furthermore, the separate and destabilizing presence of works such as *Feuilles de Route* in the *OC* is replaced by a striking metaphor of the *Journal* as a river, from which the author previously drew water to fill separate vessels (which provided a certain external and artificial unity in addition to the partial, inherent unity of these *suites*), and to which these individual works are now returned. These extracts belong to the greater unity of the river, which corresponds to the unity of the overall diary-writing project. The *feuillets* too are more fully incorporated in the unity of the *Journal* than they were in the *OC*.

The two remaining features of the *Journal* mentioned by the 'note de l'éditeur' are less obvious in their implications: the change from a division by *cahiers* in the *OC* (which 'restait assez arbitraire', 9) to a division by year, and the greater presence of full names instead of initials, which are also listed in the newly created index. Whereas the prominence of the *cahiers* in the *OC* contributes to the impression of an integral publication, it also creates internal divisions. Contrary to the claim of the 'note de l'éditeur', it is the division by years which is arbitrary and, for that very reason, allows a greater continuity in the *Journal* over its fifty-year span. The restoration of full names and the presence of the index increase the impression of a complete and even critical edition, but they also propose new ways of reading the *Journal*. These editorial choices suggest that part of the interest of the *Journal* is its depiction of a literary milieu peopled by well-known figures. The index allows a reader to follow the appearances of these individual characters (and the authors, artists, and their works that Gide discusses), rather than pursuing signifying structures which involve the totality of the *Journal*.

Each of these aspects of the *Journal*—its publication as a single volume in the Bibliothèque de la Pléiade, the dates and continuity of its fifty-year span, its apparent independence and coherence relative to Gide's other works, and even its depiction of the literary milieu in which Gide lived and worked—in some way supports the paratextual claim of its status as a literary *œuvre*. Overall, this is achieved by an emphasis on its formal unity, and more fundamentally, on its apparently integral presentation of a diary-writing project that possesses a unity of its own, much like that of Gide's earlier individual diary works such as *CAW* or *JFM* (*Paludes*, however, does not appear to contain the narrator's *journal intime* in its entirety). Just as in these earlier works, the *Journal* begins (or rather, appears to begin) with some broad aims for the diary-writing project, periodically reflects on its progress, and ends with some concluding comments (or comments that positively resist closure). The new form of the *Journal* therefore gives greater prominence to these passages, most of which had appeared in previous publications, but which now take on a programmatic significance and cast further light on the specific nature of the *Journal* as a literary *œuvre*.

Programmatic Passages

There are many isolated passages in the *Journal* that comment on this diary as a whole and the ways in which it might eventually be read,[46] but a number of entries stand out by constituting a coherent series of reflections stemming from an initial formulation of the diary-writing project. The distinctive nature of these passages is also borne out by the fact that contemporary reviews and subsequent criticism have consistently cited and discussed them, while pointing out that certain sentiments are repeated in the *Journal*, as if spontaneously and without 'composition préétablie'.

The most structurally prominent passages in the *Journal* are the first and last entries. Although the same entry is found at the beginning of the *journal intime* in the *OC* and in the *Journal*, the former presents it as an arbitrary starting point determined by editorial decisions, whereas in the *Journal* it appears to be the absolute beginning of the diary-writing project:

Avec Pierre. Nous montons au sixième d'une maison de la rue Monsieur-le-Prince, en quête d'un local où se puisse tenir le cénacle. [...]

Et nous rêvons tous deux la vie d'étudiant pauvre dans une telle chambre, avec la seule fortune qui assure le travail libre. Et à ses pieds, devant sa table, Paris. Et s'enfermer là, avec le rêve de son œuvre, et n'en sortir qu'avec elle achevée.

Ce cri de Rastignac qui domine la Ville, des hauteurs du Père Lachaise: 'Et maintenant, à nous deux!' (Autumn 1889, 13 / I, 103)

[With Pierre. We climb up to the sixth floor of a building on the rue Monsieur-le-Prince, in search of a location where we can hold our cenacle. [...]

And we both dream of living the life of a poor student in just such a room, having only enough money to allow us to work unimpeded. And at one's feet, before one's table, Paris. And to shut oneself away there, with the dream of one's *œuvre*, and only to emerge once it is complete.

This cry of Rastignac's that dominates the City, from the heights of Père Lachaise: 'And now, it's between you and me!']

---

[46] For one example among many: 'peut-être ce carnet m'aidera-t-il à empêcher la mésinterprétation de mes œuvres que, si souvent, je vois mal comprises' [perhaps this notebook will help to prevent the misinterpretation of my works, which I so often see being poorly understood], 1 February 1931, 1028/II, 252.

The diarist assumes the ambition of the young Rastignac at the end of *Le Père Goriot*, and sets himself the goal of producing an *œuvre* that will guarantee his success as a great author (surrounded by a *cénacle*, just as Mallarmé was at this time). In its present context, the fifty years of the *Journal* can be seen as the long path towards the eventual realization of this goal in the 'consécration' of Gide by his entry into the Bibliothèque de la Pléiade. Furthermore, beyond the young Gide's immediate concern at this time for writing *CAW* (itself an early attempt to create the whole life and *œuvre* of an author, or at least of an *auteur supposé*), the *Journal* can be seen as the fulfilment of this imagined *œuvre*, in its role as a 'livre unique' unifying a body of work around an author-figure. The path towards this goal is as much made up of the everyday (diaristic) details of friends and *cénacles* as it is of solitary intellectual labour. The diarist's decision to associate himself with a fictional character establishes a certain attitude towards the diary itself, developed in greater detail in the passages which follow, but which generally conceives of his life and his literary expression as being intimately related to each other in a way which effaces boundaries between reality and fiction.

The final entry of the *Journal* cannot claim the same importance as the first, since there is no apparent reason for Gide to stop writing the diary altogether at this point, yet it does provide some degree of finality to the project undertaken fifty years earlier:

> Avant de quitter Paris, j'ai pu achever de revoir les épreuves de mon *Journal*. À le relire, il me paraît que les suppressions systématiques (du moins jusqu'à mon deuil) de tous les passages relatifs à Em., l'ont pour ainsi dire *aveuglé*. Les quelques allusions au drame secret de ma vie y deviennent incompréhensibles, par l'absence de ce qui les éclairerait; incompréhensible ou inadmissible, l'image de ce moi mutilé que j'y livre, qui n'offre plus, à la place ardente du cœur, qu'un trou.
>
> [...] Rien ne me rappelle à Paris avant mai. Me voici libre, comme je ne l'ai jamais été; libre effroyablement, vais-je savoir encore 'tenter de vivre'?... (26 January 1939, 1331–32 / II, 639–40)

> [Before leaving Paris, I have been able to look over the proofs of my *Journal*. As I reread them, it seems to me that the systematic suppressions (at least up to my bereavement) of all the passages relating to Em. [Madeleine] have, as it were, left it *blind*. As a result, the few allusions to the secret drama of my life become incomprehensible, through the absence of the very thing that would make sense of them; incomprehensible too, or inadmissible, the image of this mutilated self that I present, which no longer offers anything but a void in the place of a passionate heart.
>
> [...] Nothing calls me back to Paris before May. Now I am free, more than I have ever been before; terrifyingly free, will I still be able to 'try to live'?...]

Whereas the paratext of the *OC* mentions the omission from the printed *journal intime* of material pertaining to Em. (the name used by Gide to refer to his wife, Madeleine Gide), this information is presented at the very end of the *Journal* in a comment that simultaneously concludes the diary and opens it up to a further supplement (in the manner of *FM* and *JFM*). The diarist's appraisal of the *Journal* could be expressed as follows: it is consistent with the initial project that the *Journal* should be concerned with the development of the *auteur* rather than the private life of the *homme*, but it now appears that the two cannot be separated without mutilating one or the other, and although the present work possesses a certain unity as the anthumous summation of a literary career, it is to be complemented (or supplemented) by the posthumous divulgation of the 'drame secret' (in what was to become *Et nunc manet in te*).[47] The closing words of the *Journal* show a similar mixture of finality and continuity. By this point, Gide's literary and diary-writing projects have arrived at some sort of completion with the publication of the *OC* and the *Journal*, and even his 'drame secret' has largely come to an end (Em. had died in 1938), yet he now finds that he has a greater opportunity than ever before for the 'travail libre' imagined in the first diary entry, and the final question mark and ellipsis indicate the continuing challenge of this 'disponibilité'.

One of the most commonly cited passages, three years and a mere sixteen pages into the *Journal*, develops the idea introduced in the first entry that there is a close relationship between the diarist's literary projects and his own life:

> La vie d'un homme est son image. À l'heure de mourir, nous nous refléterons dans le passé, et, penchés sur le miroir de nos actes, nos âmes reconnaîtront *ce que nous sommes*. Toute notre vie s'emploie à tracer de nous-mêmes un ineffaçable portrait. [...] On raconte sa vie et l'on se ment; mais notre vie ne mentira pas; elle racontera notre âme, qui se présentera devant Dieu dans sa posture habituelle.
>
> On peut dire alors ceci, que j'entrevois, comme une sincérité renversée (de l'artiste):
>
> Il doit, non pas raconter sa vie telle qu'il l'a vécue, mais la vivre telle qu'il la racontera. Autrement dit: que le portrait de lui, que sera sa vie, s'identifie au portrait idéal qu'il souhaite; et, plus simplement: qu'il soit tel qu'il se veut. (3 January 1892, 29 / I, 149)

> [A man's life is his image. At the moment of death, we will reflect on the past, and, leaning over the mirror of our acts, our souls will recognize *what we are*. All our life traces an indelible portrait of us. [...] When we tell of our life, we lie; but our life will not lie; it will tell of our soul, which will be presented before God in the posture that has become habitual to it.
>
> We can therefore say this, which I envisage as a reversed sincerity (of the artist):
>
> He must not recount his life as he has lived it, but live his life as he would recount it. In other words, the portrait that his life will constitute should be identified with the ideal portrait that he would wish for; and, more simply, he should be such as he would want to be.]

This discussion has been related to a variety of topics in Gide's *œuvre*,[48] but it has a particular relevance to the *Journal* itself. Still near the start of his literary career, the diarist imagines his future self looking back on his life, which constitutes an *image*. When one discusses one's life directly (such as in autobiography) one cannot avoid self-flattery and deceit. His solution is to reverse the terms of this *sincérité* so that

---

[47] André Gide, *Et nunc manet in te* (Paris: Ides et calendes, 1951).
[48] For example, David Keypour uses it to consider Gide's relationship with the fictional characters he creates; David Keypour, *André Gide: écriture et réversibilité dans 'Les Faux-monnayeurs'* (Montreal: Presses de l'Université de Montréal, 1980), p. 228.

he is not attempting to record truthfully what his life has been, but to live his life as if he were composing his 'portrait idéal'. The means of this 'sincérité renversée (de l'artiste)' is the diary-writing project, which becomes the 'miroir de [ses] actes' and the 'ineffaçable portrait' created by his 'traces'. This is a reformulation of the initial project to produce a combined *œuvre* and author-figure, which continues to be addressed in later entries, but two of its implications for the *Journal* are already evident: rather than a narrative of Gide's life, his writing of the diary is a series of acts (an idea explored earlier in *Paludes*) that leaves a trace of his life, and which already presumes a reader to interpret it (here conceived as *Dieu*, just as it is in *CAW*).

However, the *Journal* repeatedly addresses a conflict between this aim for *sincérité* and the presence of a reader:

> Le désir de bien écrire ces pages de journal leur ôte tout mérite même de sincérité. Elles ne signifient plus rien, n'étant jamais assez bien écrites pour avoir un mérite littéraire; enfin, toutes escomptent une gloire, une célébrité future qui leur donnera de l'intérêt. Cela est profondément méprisable. (August 1893, 39/I, 168)

> Si ces carnets viennent au jour, plus tard, combien n'en rebuteront-ils pas, encore... Mais combien j'aime celui qui, malgré eux, à travers eux, voudra demeurer mon ami. (7 February 1916, 537/I, 926)

> La fâcheuse habitude que j'ai prise ces temps derniers de publier dans la *N.R.F.* quantité de pages de ce journal (par impatience un peu et parce que je n'écrivais plus rien d'autre) m'a lentement détaché de lui comme d'un ami indiscret, à qui l'on ne peut rien confier qu'aussitôt il ne le redise. Combien plus abondante ma confidence, si elle eût su rester posthume. Et encore, écrivant ceci, je l'imagine imprimé déjà et suppute la désapprobation du lecteur. (16 May 1936, 1251/II, 521)

> [The desire to write well in these diary pages takes away all their value of sincerity. They no longer have any meaning, since they are never sufficiently well written to have a literary value; ultimately, they are all written in anticipation of some glory, a future celebrity that will give them their interest. That is deeply contemptible.

> If these notebooks should come to be published, at some later point, how many will be disgusted by them, again... But how I love that reader who, despite them, because of them, will still wish to remain my friend.

> The unfortunate habit that I have adopted lately of publishing in the *N.R.F.* a large number of pages from this *journal* (partly out of impatience and because I was no longer writing anything else) has gradually distanced me from it, as if from an indiscreet friend, to whom one cannot entrust any information without him immediately passing it on. How much more candid I might have been, if it could have remained unpublished until after my death. And even as I write this, I imagine it already printed, and anticipate the disapproval of the reader.]

The diarist, anticipating the 'désapprobation' of a reader, feels a temptation to adopt an authorial role in composing the *Journal*, for example, to 'bien écrire' and to create a more flattering portrait by limiting his 'confidence'. But these impulses are at odds with the *sincérité* which is not just desired on moral grounds, but is central to the type of 'mérite littéraire' that the *Journal* is to possess. As a result, the writing of the diary involves a struggle to remain ignorant or forgetful of the total *œuvre* that the diary will become, and to avoid an authorial posture while gradually producing the image of an author-figure. This struggle is a constant feature of the *Journal* ('Va-t-il falloir encore et jusqu'à la fin recommencer cet effort lamentable?' [Will I always, and to the very end, have to begin again this awful effort?], 572/I, 967), and the 'insaisissable devenir' described in *PIM* here takes the form of Gide's attempts to 'exiger de [soi] davantage' [demand more from himself] (696/I, 1131), to '[se] ressaisir' [put himself back together] (782/I, 1245), and to '[se] débattre' [struggle inwardly] (934/II, 143). The fifty years of this 'effort lamentable' make up a portrait of the author-figure over his literary career, yet at the end of this period Gide finds himself once again having to 'recommencer' and 'tenter de vivre', and in the open-ended, diaristic *œuvre* of the *Journal* it remains for the reader to judge and interpret his *sincérité*.

The *Journal* as an *œuvre*

In light of these comments on the paratext of the *Journal*, its form, and its most salient programmatic passages, it will be useful to summarize the way in which this publication presents itself as a literary *œuvre*. This is the image that we must keep in mind—rather than the virtual totality of Gide's *journal intime* presented by the new Pléiade edition—when considering how it was received and continued in the work of Sartre and Barthes.

The analogy that Gide establishes in *PIM* between Montaigne's *Essais* and his own *Journal* presents the latter as being a text written contingently ('au hasard des événements') and without an authorial concern for the unity of the eventual work ('sans composition préétablie'). Also by analogy with the *Essais*, the *Journal* attains the status of an *œuvre* by constituting the 'livre unique' and portrait of an author-figure (who shares some of the features of a deceased, canonical author), and by inscribing itself in a humanistic tradition that valorizes *vérité* and asserts that the universalities of the human condition are to be found in the particularity of an individual. Both the inclusion of the *Journal* in the Pléiade and the dates of its fifty-year span reinforce the presentation of Gide as a canonical author and of the *Journal* itself as being, to borrow Alblas's term, 'pré-posthume'.[49] The new features of its format and paratext (particularly compared with the *journal intime* in the *OC*) contribute to its unity, independence, and self-sufficiency as an *œuvre*, and its appearance as the integral publication of a diary-writing project that extends over Gide's whole career. This apparently integral publication gives a much greater significance to certain programmatic entries, which reflect on the diary's aims and gradual development. The very first entry begins the project with the intention of recording the diarist's progress in his literary career towards becoming a *grand auteur*, in such a way that the resultant author-figure is a part of the literary project, just as one might create a fictional character. Subsequent entries show that this process involves a mode of writing as action, whose trace creates the

---

[49] Alblas, *Le 'Journal' de Gide*, p. 68.

image of the author-figure over time. The diarist's acts of writing can generally be characterized as a struggle to maintain *sincérité* (analogous with the literary *vérité* discussed in *PIM*), by avoiding self-flattery and the temptation to anticipate (and thereby falsify) the totality of the *œuvre* which will be presented to the reader.

The reading pact entailed by this conception of the *Journal* as an *œuvre* may be described as follows: a reader of the *Journal* can seek the *image* that emerges from the totality of its fragmentary, contingent diary entries, in the diarist's 'insaisissable devenir', and in his struggle for sincere self-realization. This *image* is inseparably connected to the author-figure and his life-long literary project, and so can be approached as his 'livre unique', which may be of interest from a humanistic perspective, and which harbours new readings and possibilities, unanticipated by the author, for future generations.

A HIDDEN LEGACY: READINGS BY SARTRE AND BARTHES

Despite the initial critical success of the *Journal* in 1939, the popularity of Gide's works substantially waned after the Second World War. Very broadly speaking, the literary avant-garde in France was dominated first by existentialism then by structuralism, each of them resistant in their own way to what Gide had become, a canonical, institutionalized *grand écrivain* representing an earlier generation. Yet by strange, almost clandestine means, the *Journal* continued to exert an influence on later diary-writing, life-writing, and indeed on the literary field more generally. The transmission of this hidden legacy can be observed in two texts by writers associated with existentialism and structuralism respectively: Sartre's *Carnets de la drôle de guerre* and Barthes's 'Notes sur André Gide et son "Journal"' (although Barthes had not yet entered the structuralist phase of his work). Both these texts are fragmentary, often contradictory engagements with the *Journal*, in which the authors negotiate their own positions relative to Gide and reflect on problems that are to be fundamental to their subsequent works (although Sartre had already published several philosophical works and, perhaps the most famous of French diary novels, *La Nausée*, in 1938). The later authors sometimes use Gide as a straw man in opposition to their own ideas, but they more often pursue and prolong structures that—consistent with the nature of Gide's diaristic *œuvre*—remained open-ended in the *Journal*.

Sartre's *Carnets de la drôle de guerre*

Sartre wrote this diary over only seven months, but prolifically (it covers fourteen *carnets*, of which unfortunately only six have survived), and since its publication it has been attributed great importance as containing the seeds of Sartre's later philosophical thought[50] and as the beginning of his various life-writing projects,

---

[50] For example, in Arlette Elkaïm-Sartre's preface to the first edition (Paris: Gallimard, 1983), p. 9.

following his reading of Michel Leiris's *L'Âge d'homme*.[51] His duties during his brief mobilization, until his capture and detention as a prisoner of war, left him large amounts of time in which to read and write. Gide's *Journal* is probably the most abundantly commented work, and plays a particularly important role in Sartre's reflections in the first and third *carnets* on his own diary-writing project (and presumably in the lost second *carnet* as well). His relationship with the *Journal* develops over three phases: first he identifies with Gide as an intellectual companion, then emphasizes or even exaggerates the differences between Gide's diary-writing project and his own, before entering a complex dialogue with the *Journal*. This dialogue touches on a number of Sartre's most pressing intellectual concerns, but particularly develops the problem of his role as an *écrivain* and his relationship with his literary work.[52]

Just four days into his own diary, Sartre introduces his reading of the *Journal* as follows:

> Commencé le journal de Gide. À partir d'août 14. Lecture réconfortante en somme. [...] Je sens *ses* jours de guerre avec *mes* jours de guerre. [...] Peu à peu le commerce avec un esprit de 'ma partie' me redonne une sorte de légèreté intellectuelle que j'ai perdue tout net depuis le 1er septembre. (18 September 1939, 156)

> [Began Gide's *journal*. Started from August 1914. Comforting reading, overall. [...] I experience *his* days of war alongside *my* days of war. [...] Gradually the contact with a mind of 'my type' gives me back a sort of intellectual liveliness which I had completely lost since 1 September.]

Rather than reading from the beginning of the *Journal*, Sartre establishes a parallel between his own war diary and Gide's, which makes it both a source of comfort and a model for his own diary-writing at this time. He repeatedly cites Gide's comments regarding his situation in the First World War in order to make the same point about his own situation, or even cites without further comment, allowing Gide to speak for him directly (for example, 'Gide, 1er juin 1918: "Je pense parfois, avec horreur, que la victoire que nos cœurs souhaitent à la France, c'est celle du passé sur l'avenir"' [Gide, 1 June 2018: 'Sometimes I think, with horror, that the victory that are hearts long for, for France, is a victory of the past over the future], 160). The *Journal* is also a model for the future publication of his own diary:

> Naïvement séduit par l'épaisseur du journal de Gide. Je voudrais que mon 'journal de guerre' fût aussi épais. Car, naturellement, j'envisage de publier. (189)

> [Naïvely impressed by the thickness of Gide's *journal*. I would like my 'war diary' to be just as thick. Because, of course, I expect to publish it.]

The *Journal*, a large published volume devoted to the diary alone, is an object of desire for Sartre, but already this is expressed with some irony (he recognizes the *naïveté* of his desire), suggesting that he will have to develop his own distinct role as an author and diarist.

[51] Jean-François Louette, preface to Sartre, *Les Mots et autres écrits autobiographiques*, p. XXXI.
[52] During this discussion, page references in parentheses in the main text pertain to Jean-Paul Sartre, *Les Carnets de la drôle de guerre: septembre 1939–mars 1940*, in *Les Mots et autres écrits autobiographiques*, ed. by Jean-François Louette (Paris: Gallimard, Bibl. de la Pléiade, 2010), pp. 143–679.

From this initial attitude of identification with Gide, Sartre increasingly makes observations of the *Journal* that establish differences with his own diary-writing. He finds in the *Journal* 'complaisances' [self-indulgences] which he tries to extinguish in himself (22 September, 164), 'le bien écrire', which he opposes to his own style marked by 'je ne sais quoi d'épais et de germanique' [some dense and Germanic quality] (182), and a humanism which he finds 'curieux' but to which he does not subscribe (306). The oppositions between the two diaries progress to more complex comparisons, such as the long discussion (including numerous citations) that follows his remark that he was 'frappé hier, en feuilletant à nouveau le journal de Gide, de son aspect *religieux*' [struck yesterday, leafing once again through Gide's *journal*, by its *religious* aspect] (349–51). This aspect of the *Journal* is seen to determine its role as 'une humble tâche quotidienne' [a humble daily task], and as 'un livre de comptes moraux, avec une page pour le crédit, une page pour le débit' [a moral account book, with a page for credit, a page for debit] in the service of an 'examen de conscience protestant' [Protestant examination of conscience] (much like the satirical *agenda* in *Paludes*), as 'un livre de *relectures* et de méditations à propos de ces relectures' [a book of *rereadings* and reflections on these rereadings], in which every note is an '*acte* de prière, *acte* de confession, *acte* de méditation' [*act* of prayer, *act* of confession, *act* of reflection]. In contrast, Sartre's own diary is supposedly 'païen et orgueilleux' [pagan and arrogant], 'un témoignage médiocre et par là même *général*' [a testimony that is mediocre, and therefore *general*], and also made up of 'enregistrements' [recordings] of past thoughts and feelings written 'froidement et afin de progresser' [dispassionately and in order to move beyond them], which are therefore not acts in the same sense as Gide's.

Despite Sartre's insightful reading of the *Journal*, these comparisons with his own diary are often contradictory and unconvincing. For example, it is not evident why his 'témoignage médiocre' should be more 'général' than Gide's 'humble tâche quotidienne', and this same passage reads very much as an 'acte' of 'méditation' on his 'relectures' rather than a dispassionate record of earlier reflections. Yet this same entry leads him to a more sophisticated dialogue with the *Journal*, beyond either identification or opposition, when he resolves to 'confronter la formation morale de Gide et la [sienne]' [compare Gide's moral education with his own] (351). This process does not consist of direct observations of the *Journal* so much as an attempt to formulate, apparently for the first time (364), his fundamental attitudes towards his general projects as an *écrivain* and for his life, with reference to the structures that he finds in the *Journal*, in an autobiographical account that extends over several long diary entries.

After recounting his experience of losing what little religious faith he had at the age of twelve, he asserts that 'le problème moral qui [l]'a préoccupé jusqu'ici, c'est en somme celui des rapports de l'art et de la vie' [the moral problem that has preoccupied him until now is essentially that of the relations between art and life] (354). Among the biographical details and successive philosophical preoccupations mentioned in this account, the overriding theme is his desire for the 'vie d'un grand écrivain' (355), which closely resembles both the initial writing project and the final result of the *Journal*. This desired *vie* is imagined as being united by 'une [*sic*] "œuvre", c'est-à-dire une série d'ouvrages reliés les uns aux autres par des thèmes communs et reflétant tous [sa] personnalité' [an *œuvre*, that is, a series of works connected to one another by their common themes and all reflecting his personality], undertaken as a project to 'se surmonter soi-même' [overcome oneself], and as 'un canevas à remplir avec, déjà, une foule d'indications faufilées, qu'il faut ensuite broder' [a tapestry to be filled in, which already has a number of lines basted, which must then be stitched in full], and which offers a 'salut par l'art' [salvation through art] from the essential nullity of life (360–3). Yet this desire is presented as an 'illusion biographique, qui consiste à croire qu'une vie vécue peut ressembler à une vie racontée' [biographical illusion, which involves believing that a life lived can resemble a life narrated] (363), which had already been denounced in *La Nausée* by Roquentin's realization that life cannot be experienced as an *aventure*.

Sartre does not arrive at any alternative to this 'illusion biographique', but he aims (with little hope of success) to resist his desire through an effort to achieve an ideal of *authenticité*:

> Vis-à-vis de Gauguin, Van Gogh et Rimbaud j'ai un net complexe d'infériorité parce qu'ils ont su se perdre. Gauguin par son exil, Van Gogh par sa folie et Rimbaud, plus qu'eux tous, parce qu'il a su renoncer même à écrire. Je pense de plus en plus que, pour atteindre l'authenticité, il faut que quelque chose craque. C'est en somme la leçon que Gide a tirée de Dostoïevski et c'est ce que je montrerai dans le second livre de mon roman. Mais je me suis préservé contre les craquements. Je suis ligoté à mon désir d'écrire. (307)

> [With regard to Gauguin, Van Gogh and Rimbaud I have a clear inferiority complex because they were able to lose themselves. Gauguin by means of his exile, Van Gogh through his madness, and Rimbaud, most of all, because he was able to renounce writing itself. I think more and more that, to attain authenticity, something has to break. That is essentially the lesson that Gide drew from Dostoyevsky and it is what I shall demonstrate in the second part of my novel. But I have protected myself against anything breaking. I am bound up in my desire to write.]

Just as Gide had inscribed himself in a humanist literary tradition in *PIM*, Sartre here traces a lineage from Dostoevsky, to Gide and then to himself, of writers who have aimed for *authenticité* by renouncing their 'désir d'écrire'. In Gide's *Journal*, this *authenticité* corresponds to the struggle for *sincérité*, and the accompanying need to avoid 'le bien écrire' and be forgetful of one's eventual *œuvre* and author-figure. Although Sartre did not write any more diaries or publish these *carnets* in his lifetime, his pursuit of *authenticité* had broad implications in his critical, philosophical, fictional, and dramatic writing (this extends far beyond the scope of the present study), and particularly in the renunciation of his 'illusion biographique' and of his belief in a 'salut par l'art' in the autobiographical work *Les Mots* (1964).[53] This concern for *authenticité* in one's role as an *écrivain* is undoubtedly the most important aspect of Sartre's inheritance from Gide's

---

[53] Jean-Paul Sartre, *Les Mots* (Paris: Gallimard, 1964).

Journal, but it also demonstrates the hidden nature of this legacy, as Éric Marty has suggested that Sartre refrained from publishing any critical work on the *Journal* in his lifetime precisely because of its 'influence déterminante sur lui' [determining influence on him].[54]

Barthes's 'Notes sur André Gide et son "Journal" '

Barthes too remained taciturn regarding his influence from Gide following his first engagement with the *Journal* in his 'Notes sur André Gide et son "Journal"' (1942), but unlike Sartre he acknowledged his debt to Gide much later in his career, notably in his 1975 work *Roland Barthes par Roland Barthes*,[55] and even embarked on experimental diary-writing projects of his own. These diaries themselves occupy an important place in the history of diary-writing, which I shall discuss in Chapter 6, but Barthes's early reflections on the *Journal* demonstrate different aspects of its legacy from those that are manifested in Sartre's *Carnets*. Barthes's readings focus on the nature of the *Journal* as an *œuvre*, and indicate a way for him to pursue this same problem in his own practice of a fragmentary form of writing (which is characteristic of many of Barthes's later works).[56]

Barthes is particularly interested in the figure of Gide that emerges from the *Journal*, as 'homme' (33), 'personnalité' (33), 'image' (36), and 'œuvre' (41). He finds a humanist model for this combined *homme* and *œuvre* in Montaigne, as he is described by Gide in *PIM*. For Barthes, Gide and Montaigne form one of 'ces duos qui s'engagent, de siècle à siècle, entre écrivains de même classe' [these pairs of writers of the same class, who engage with one another, each from their own centuries] (35). Gide's 'menus aveux' [little confessions] make him 'l'homme par excellence, comme le fut Montaigne' [the quintessential man, as Montaigne was too], and the *Journal* has the same essential reflexivity as the *Essais*: 'bien que le trait de Gide soit toujours d'une grande acuité, il n'a de valeur que par sa force de réflexion, de retour sur Gide lui-même' [although Gide's writing always has a greaty acuity, all its value lies in its reflexivity, looking back on Gide himself] (34). He also inscribes the *Journal* in a series of works by Protestant authors, although Gide does not follow the model of earlier *confessions*:

> Rousseau, Amiel, Gide nous ont donné trois grandes œuvres confidentes. [...] Toutefois le *Journal* de Gide contient une nuance propre; il est plus souvent écrit comme un dialogue que comme un monologue. C'est moins une confession que le récit d'une âme qui se cherche, se répond, s'entretient avec elle-même (à la façon des *Soliloques* de Saint Augustin). (34)

---

54 Éric Marty, 'Notice' in Gide, *Journal 1887–1925*, p. 1321.

55 For example, 'Gide est ma langue originelle, mon *Ursuppe*, ma soupe littéraire' [Gide is my first language, my primordial soup, my literary soup]; Roland Barthes, *Roland Barthes par Roland Barthes*, in *OC* ([1975]), IV, pp. 575–771, p. 677.

56 During this discussion, page references in parentheses in the main text pertain to Roland Barthes, 'Notes sur André Gide et son « Journal »', in *OC* ([1942]), I, pp. 33–46.

[Rousseau, Amiel, and Gide have given us three great works of confession. [...]
However, Gide's *Journal* has its own distinct nature; it is more often written as a
dialogue than as a monologue. It is less a confession than it is the account of a soul
in search of itself, answering itself, conversing with itself (in the manner of Saint
Augustine's *Soliloquies*).]

This 'âme qui se cherche' resembles the impression given by the *Journal* of an
active process of moral struggle (for *sincérité*), from which the author's portrait
will emerge. Yet although Barthes treats the *Journal* as an *œuvre* (feminine) on the
grounds of the humanistic generality of 'l'homme par excellence', he also views
it in a relationship with the broader *œuvre* (masculine) of Gide's corpus of works.
Commenting on the often-cited passage of the *Journal* concerning the 'rétroaction
du sujet sur lui-même' [reverse action of the subject on himself] (*Journal*, 40–1/1,
170–2), he opposes the *œuvre* as 'Gide tel qu'il devrait (voudrait) être' [Gide as
he should be (would like to be)] to the *Journal* as 'Gide tel qu'il est, ou plus
exactement: tel que l'ont fait Édouard, Michel et Lafcadio' [Gide as he is, or more
precisely: as Édouard, Michel and Lafcadio made him] (42), and he even doubts
that 'le *Journal* ait grand intérêt, si au préalable, la lecture n'a pas éveillé de curiosité
sur l'homme' [the *Journal* has any interest, if a reading of his work has not already
excited our curiosity about the man] (33).

   This uncertainty as to the *Journal's* independence relative to Gide's other works
is partly explained by contradictions that arise when Barthes directly addresses its
status as an *œuvre*:

   Il ne faut donc point croire que le *Journal* s'oppose à l'œuvre, et ne soit pas lui-
   même une œuvre d'art. Il y a des phrases qui sont mi-chemin entre la confession et
   la création; elles ne demandent qu'à être insérées dans un roman et sont déjà moins
   sincères (ou plutôt: leur sincérité compte moins qu'autre chose, qui est le plaisir qu'on
   prend à les lire). Je dirai volontiers ceci: ce n'est pas le *Journal d'Édouard* qui ressemble
   au *Journal* de Gide; au contraire, bien des propos du *Journal* ont déjà l'autonomie
   du *Journal d'Édouard*. Ils ne sont plus tout à fait Gide; ils commencent d'être hors de
   lui, en route vers quelque œuvre incertaine où ils ont envie de prendre place, qu'ils
   appellent. (34–5)

[We should therefore not imagine that the *Journal* is distinct from the *œuvre*, and
that it is not an artistic *œuvre* in its own right. There are sentences that are half way
between confession and creation; they could easily be inserted into a novel and are
already less sincere (or rather: their sincerity is less important than something else,
which is the pleasure that we have in reading them). I would gladly say this: it is not
the *Journal d'Édouard* that resembles Gide's *Journal*; on the contrary, many passages
of the *Journal* already have the autonomy of the *Journal d'Édouard*. They are no longer
entirely Gide; they are on their way towards some uncertain *œuvre* where they long to
be, which they call into being.]

From initially asserting that the *Journal* is an independent *œuvre*, it soon appears to
be half way between, on the one hand, 'confession' valued according to its *sincérité*,
and on the other hand, 'création' valued according to the 'plaisir' it gives a reader,
and the capacity of the *roman* and fiction to be autonomous with respect to the
author. Of these two concepts of the *œuvre*, the former seems closer to Gide's own

programmatic statements in the *Journal*, but Barthes implicitly favours the latter. In other fragments he associates it with an atemporal quality of the *Journal* (such that 'tout Gide est dans André Walter, et André Walter est encore dans le *Journal* de 1939' [all of Gide is in André Walter, and André Walter is still present in the *Journal* of 1939], 37), and with Gide's readiness to relinquish authorial control and experience the 'plaisir' of a reader (like Pygmalion, falling in love with his own *œuvre*, 41). The last phrase of the passage cited above reduces the *Journal* again to being merely 'en route' to the *œuvre*, but some new type of *œuvre* which it announces and for which it indicates the direction to follow.

The way in which Barthes himself sets out on this route to a new sort of *œuvre* is indicated by the very form of this text, emphasized by the first fragment, which serves as a preface:

> Retenu par la crainte d'enclore Gide dans un système dont je savais ne pouvoir être jamais satisfait, je cherchais en vain quel lien donner à ces notes. Réflexion faite, il vaut mieux les donner telles quelles, et ne pas chercher à masquer leur discontinu. L'incohérence me paraît préférable à l'ordre qui déforme. (33)

> [Held back by the fear of enclosing Gide in a system that I knew could never be satisfactory, I looked in vain for an organizing theme for these notes. Upon reflection, it is better to present them just as they are, without seeking to disguise their discontinuity. Incoherence seems to me to be preferable to an order that would deform.]

The ambiguity in Barthes's reasoning can be expressed by the following question: what is it that an imposed 'ordre' would 'déformer'? The more obvious answer is that it would misrepresent the *Journal* itself, and Barthes thereby echoes other readers (and Gide's attitude towards Montaigne) who find that it resists synthesis or reduction to a 'système'. But an 'ordre' would also obscure Barthes's own work in producing these notes, which might be 'incohérentes' but which possess a significance that surpasses the author's immediate understanding and is to be presented to the reader for interpretation. Barthes is therefore adopting the posture of Gide in the *Journal* by writing and publishing in the form of fragments (albeit undated ones, and therefore with an ahistorical, purely internal temporality). Barthes used fragmentary forms of writing in many different ways throughout his career, but it will suffice to note that, in a sense, he resolves the problem of the status of the *Journal* as an independent *œuvre*, by forming his own works in the image of the *Journal* but without the counterweight of the rest of Gide's *œuvre*. Barthes's later work thereby fulfils one of the potentialities that he finds in the *Journal*, which he describes much later in *Roland Barthes par Roland Barthes* as 'l'écrivain tel qu'on peut le voir dans son journal intime, [. . .] *l'écrivain moins son œuvre*, forme suprême du sacré: la marque et le vide' [the writer as we can see him in his *journal intime*, *the writer without his œuvre*, the epitome of the sacred: the mark and the void].[57]

---

57 Barthes, *RB par RB*, p. 656.

THE *JOURNAL 1889–1939* IN THE HISTORY OF DIARY-WRITING

Although the importance of the *Journal* has long been recognized, both as a part of Gide's work and as a remarkable example of a published *journal intime*, this recognition has not led to a clear understanding of its role in the history of diary-writing. By addressing the circumstances and form of its publication in 1939, especially against the background of the publication of the *OC*, I have demonstrated how the *Journal* constitutes a new, diaristic type of *œuvre*, envisaged in Gide's work from as early as *CAW* in 1889, drawing on his experiments in diary-writing from throughout his career, and which opens up new possibilities for subsequent readers and writers. *CAW* can be seen in hindsight as a dry run (by means of the *auteur supposé*) of this construction of a combined author and *œuvre*, but which leads to André Walter being consumed by his desire to attain the totalizing perspective of a godlike reader and a complete transformation into his artistic ideal (whereas Gide continues, at the end of the *Journal*, to 'tenter de vivre'). *Paludes*, pursuing these problems in its peculiar satirical way, posits a mode of writing that is a free and contingent act, and therefore allows the reader a freedom of interpretation. *JFM* develops this concept of a more open text by embracing the marginal and supplementary role of the diary, and anticipates the even more complex supplementarity of the *Journal*—an addition to Gide's existing corpus, but forming a more unified whole, and inviting further supplements both by Gide himself and by later writers.[58] The *Journal* builds on all these elements and, perhaps most of all, on the way in which a large number of Gide's earlier diary-writing projects possessed a coherence and unity of their own.

As for the (partly hidden) legacy of the *Journal*, its literary claims provided an important model for the subsequent publication of real *journaux intimes* (to which I shall return), but it is a mistake to regard it as completing the transition of the *journal intime* to a fully literary genre (as Girard does).[59] It can even be viewed as a strange anti-*œuvre*, questioning and reinventing the author-figure and the literary *œuvre* itself. Sartre's and Barthes's respective engagements with the text show how its conception of the author-figure and literary *œuvre* contributed to an ongoing reflection on these problems (this contribution has so far been undervalued), and the chapters in the second part of this study will examine how writers pursued the agenda of Gide's diary-writing, in radically different circumstances, but still drawing on his experimentation in all its diversity.

---

[58] This supplementary role could be attributed to Gide's *Pages de journal: 1939–1942* (1944), the posthumously published *Et nunc manet in te* (1951), and even his attempt to 'raconter [sa] vie' in a fictional form in *Thésée* (1946); André Gide, *Thésée*, in *Romans et récits* ([1946]), II, pp. 983–1028, p. 987.

[59] Girard, *Le Journal intime*, p. 90.

PART II

DIARY-WRITING AFTER GIDE

INTRODUCTION

Whereas diary-writing in the first part of the twentieth century was dominated by Gide's gradual experimentation with the form of published diaries, culminating in his *Journal*, the second half of the century (or the period from the Second World War to the present) was not dominated by any one diarist, except perhaps by the spectre of Gide himself. Gide's wide range of diary-writing provided inescapable points of reference for the diarists who wrote and published after him, even when they wished to distance themselves from the form of author-*œuvre* associated with the *Journal*. Diary-writing over this period is characterized instead by substantial changes in attitudes towards the author-figure, and towards the relationship between a writer's life and his or her literary work. The authors discussed in the following chapters (Queneau, Barthes, and Ernaux) have been chosen because, in very different ways, they cast light on these changes. Far from constituting a canon of modern diarists,[1] these are authors for whom diary-writing occupies a problematic and marginal place in their *œuvre*, and also has a problematic relation to its Gidean models.

In the years after the War, diary-writing occupied a complex, even contradictory position in French writing. On the one hand, there was a resurgence of interest in diaries among the reading public, as testified by Michèle Leleu in 1952:

> L'un des traits de ce temps est peut-être l'intérêt croissant que porte un public très vaste à toute une catégorie d'écrits, bien différents parfois de ton, de nature ou de portée, et qui lui sont présentés sous la dénomination générale de *Journaux intimes*.[2]

> [One of the characteristics of this period is perhaps the growing interest that a very large public is taking in a broad category of writings, sometimes very varied in tone, nature, or subject matter, and which are offered up under the general term *journaux intimes*.]

The works that sustained this interest included both lifelong diaries (following the example of Gide's *Journal*) and partial diary publications covering several years

---

[1] See n. 8, p. 3 for references to several bibliographies of real diaries.
[2] Michèle Leleu, *Les Journaux intimes* (Paris: PUF, 1952), p. 3.

(on the model of Gide's 'Pages de journal'). These were produced almost entirely by writers of an older generation born no later than 1900, such as Julien Green, Charles-Ferdinand Ramuz, Henry de Montherlant, Julien Benda, Paul Léautaud, and Valery Larbaud.[3] One exception was Claude Mauriac, belonging to a later generation (he was born in 1914), but whose diary-writing was nonetheless influenced by his personal association with Gide.[4] The most important posthumous diary publication in this period was undoubtedly that of Franz Kafka in 1945.[5] Kafka's popularity in France increased suddenly at this time, for a number of reasons,[6] but it was undoubtedly enhanced by the publication of his *journal intime*, which seemed to illuminate (if not resolve) the 'énigme' of his fictional works.[7] Critics treated this diary text, not as an *œuvre* in its own right, nor as a mere document concerning Kafka's life, but as an extension of his literary writing, working from the perspective that 'les romans comme le journal sont le témoignage de cette tension personnelle entre le monde et le moi' [both the novels and the *journal intime* are the testimony of this personal tension between the world and the self].[8]

On the other hand, diary-writing was largely neglected at this same time by the literary avant-garde. If Sartre's conception of the *écrivain engagé* expressed in *Qu'est-ce que la littérature* (1948) was at odds with the individualism of Gide's *Journal* (he evidently relinquished his desire to publish his own *Carnets de la drôle de guerre* in his lifetime),[9] the diary was even more discredited by the subsequent rise of structuralist theory, with its critique of the psychological and writing subject.[10] In the field of fictional writing, the *nouveau roman* (initially associated with phenomenology, then later with structuralism) promoted a literary formalism while rejecting introspection or the depiction of psychologically

---

[3] In each case the author's first major publication of a real diary is given: Green, *Journal: 1928–1934*; Charles-Ferdinand Ramuz, *Journal 1896–1942* (Paris: Grasset, 1945); Henry de Montherlant, *Carnets XXIX à XXXV: du 19 février 1935 au 11 janvier 1939* (Paris: La Table ronde, 1947); Julien Benda, *Les Cahiers d'un clerc (1936–1949)* (Paris: Emile-Paul Frères, 1949); Paul Léautaud, *Journal littéraire I: 1893–1906* (Paris: Mercure de France, 1954); Valery Larbaud, *Journal inédit I: 1912–1920* (= *Œuvres complètes* IX) (Paris: Gallimard, 1954).

[4] Claude Mauriac, *Conversations avec André Gide: extraits d'un journal* (Paris: Michel, 1951). Mauriac took the more unusual approach of publishing thematically reordered excerpts from his diaries in the 'Temps immobile' series, beginning in 1970 with *Une amitié contrariée* (Paris: Grasset, 1970).

[5] Franz Kafka, *La Colonie pénitentiaire: nouvelles, suivies d'un Journal intime*, trans. by Jean Starobinski (Paris: Egloff, 1945). Franz Kafka, *Journal intime, suivi de Esquisse d'une autobiographie*, trans. by Pierre Klossowski (Paris: Grasset, 1945). Franz Kafka, *Journal: texte intégral, 1910–1923*, trans. by Marthe Robert (Paris: Grasset, 1954).

[6] Marthe Robert, *Kafka* (Paris: Gallimard, 1960), p. 43.

[7] Maurice Blanchot, 'La Lecture de Kafka', in *La Part du feu* (Paris: Gallimard, 1949), pp. 9–19, p. 13. First printed in *L'Arche*, 11 (November 1945), pp. 107–16.

[8] Alain Girard, 'Kafka et le problème du journal intime', *Critique*, 1 (1946), pp. 21–32, p. 28.

[9] Jean-Paul Sartre, *Qu'est-ce que la littérature?* (Paris: Gallimard, 1948).

[10] The influence of structuralism grew in France after the publication of Claude Lévi-Strauss, *Les Structures élémentaires de la parenté* (Paris: PUF, 1949), and the public dispute between Barthes and Raymond Picard following the former's *Sur Racine* (Paris: Seuil, 1963) marked a general shift away from academic author-centred literary criticism.

coherent characters.[11] Barthes's assessment of the situation in 1966 was that the *journal intime* had become 'impossible' because 'la littérature contemporaine, du moins par son avant-garde, [tenait] pour acquise la vérité des expériences de la dépersonnalisation' [contemporary literature, or at least its avant-garde, took for granted the truth of its experiments with depersonalization].[12] Yet this rejection, or suspicion, of the *journal intime* by the literary avant-garde was never absolute. In the 1938 novel *La Nausée*, Sartre had demonstrated the capacity of the diary form, not for conveying psychological depth, but for depicting the experience of existential anguish.[13] Michel Butor, a central figure of the *nouveau roman*, showed with his 1956 novel *L'Emploi du temps* that a fictional *journal intime* could itself produce a labyrinthine textual world, a 'laboratoire du récit' [laboratory of narrative] in which we can 'étudier de quelle façon la réalité nous apparaît ou peut nous apparaître' [study how reality appears to us, or how it can appear to us].[14] And theorists and novelists alike associated the work of Kafka with their own modernity, including his newly translated *journal intime*.[15]

Queneau, who will be discussed in Chapter 5, bridges these two generations, and seems to encompass within his own work their conflicting attitudes towards the *journal intime*. He was already established in his literary career by the start of the War, and had been writing a diary since 1914 (published posthumously),[16] but his idiosyncratic literary formalism and his foundation of OuLiPo in 1960 were consistent with the direction of the later avant-garde. From this perspective, his publication of works attributed to the *auteur supposé* Sally Mara between 1947 and 1962—a novel, *journal intime*, and volume of *œuvres complètes*—appears as a playful formalist exploration of the type of diaristic author-figure that many of the newer generation had simply dismissed.

In the mid-1970s this exclusion of the subject began to be challenged more directly in theory and in literary practice, leading to the publication of a growing number of diaries and autobiographical works.[17] In the following years, many of the same writers who had participated in the earlier 'dépersonnalisation' of literature, such as Sarraute, Robbe-Grillet, and Derrida, now explored the forms

---

[11] Two important works that established the aesthetics of this formalism were Nathalie Sarraute's 1956 collection *L'Ère du soupçon: essais sur le roman*, and Alain Robbe-Grillet, *Pour un nouveau roman* (Paris: Gallimard, 1963).

[12] Roland Barthes, 'Alain Girard: « Le Journal intime »', in *OC* ([1966]), II, pp. 806–10, p. 809.

[13] Jean-Paul Sartre, *La Nausée* (Paris: Gallimard, 1938).

[14] Michel Butor, *L'Emploi du temps* (Paris: Minuit, 1956). Michel Butor, 'Le Roman comme recherche', in *Essais sur le roman* (Paris: Minuit, 1964), pp. 7–14, p. 9; first printed in *Les Cahiers du sud*, 334 (April 1956).

[15] For example, Blanchot began his 1949 collection of essays *La Part du feu* with two texts on Kafka ('La Lecture de Kafka' and 'Kafka et la littérature'), and the first text in Sarraute's *L'Ère du soupçon* is entitled 'De Dostoïevski à Kafka'.

[16] Raymond Queneau, *Journal 1939–1940: suivi de Philosophes et voyous* (Paris: Gallimard, 1986). Raymond Queneau, *Journaux 1914–1965*, ed. by Anne Isabelle Queneau (Paris: Gallimard, 1996).

[17] 1975 appears to be a turning point, with the publication of Barthes's *Roland Barthes par Roland Barthes*, Georges Perec's *W ou le souvenir d'enfance* (Paris: Denoël, 1975), and Philippe Lejeune's study of the genre in *Le Pacte autobiographique*. The parallels with the growth in *littérature personnelle* in the 1880s are discussed in Chapter 6.

of subjective writing that they could adopt without entirely abandoning the values of their previous works.[18] Barthes himself, having earlier famously declared 'La Mort de l'auteur' (1968), now returned to his early influence from Gide, and within the broad project of his 'Vita Nova' (which encompassed most of his work from 1977 until his death in 1980) he tested the limits of the literary potential of diary-writing at this time (notably in the diaries published posthumously under the titles *Journal de deuil* and *Soirées de Paris*, which are discussed in Chapter 6).

From this point up to the present day, a wide range of subjective forms of writing have proliferated in France, broadly referred to in English as the field of life-writing. Diary-writing has shared in this success. A significant number of authors undertook a regular publication of their *journal intime*, often with very little delay, including Gabriel Matzneff (from 1976), Charles Juliet (1978), Claude Roy (1983), Renaud Camus (1987), André Blanchard (1989), and Marc-Édouard Nabe (1991).[19] At the time of writing, the publications of Matzneff, Juliet, and Camus are still continuing, and for some of these authors the *journal intime* was, or remains, the principal area of their literary production (particularly Juliet and Camus).[20] Yet the prestige of these publications is undoubtedly inferior to that of other forms of life-writing, and diaries across this period assume greatest importance when they belong to a larger project with broadly autobiographical aims, such as that of Hervé Guibert.[21] Diary-writing has therefore retained its marginal status, no longer subordinate to the constitutively literary forms of poetry or the novel, but instead to the new literary pretensions of autobiography. This role of diary-writing, implicated in new concepts of literature and authorship quite unlike the Gidean author-*œuvre*, will be examined in the final chapter of this study with reference to Ernaux's gradual construction of an *œuvre* (both commercially successful and highly self-reflexive) that employs a wide range of forms and writing practices in order to 'Écrire la vie'.[22]

[18] Nathalie Sarraute, *Enfance* (Paris: Gallimard, 1983). Alain Robbe-Grillet, *Le Miroir qui revient* (Paris: Minuit, 1984). Jacques Derrida, *La Carte postale: de Socrate à Freud et au-delà* (Paris: Flammarion, 1980).

[19] Gabriel Matzneff, *Cette Camisole de flammes: 1953–1962* (Paris: La Table ronde, 1976). Charles Juliet, *Journal: 1957–1964* (Paris: Hachette, 1978). Claude Roy, *Permis de séjour: 1977–1982* (Paris: Gallimard, 1983). Renaud Camus, *Journal romain: 1985–1986* (Paris: POL, 1987). André Blanchard, *Entre Chien et loup: carnets, avril–septembre 1987* (Paris: Le Dilettante, 1989). Marc-Édouard Nabe, *Nabe's dream: juin 1983—février 1985* (Monaco: Rocher, 1991).

[20] It should be noted that some of the interest in these publications may derive from the notoriety of their authors: Renaud's association with far-right politics, Nabe's provocative political statements, and Matzneff's self-professed 'pédérastie'; Gabriel Matzneff, *Les Moins de seize ans: suivi de Les Passions schismatiques* (Paris: Scheer, 2005), pp. 28–9 (first printed in 1974).

[21] Jean-Pierre Boulé cites an interview with Guibert from 1992 in which the latter claims that his *journal intime* is the generative centre of his writing, or 'la colonne vertébrale, la chose essentielle' [the backbone, the essential substance]; Jean-Pierre Boulé, *Hervé Guibert: Voices of the Self*, trans. by John Fletcher (Liverpool: Liverpool University Press, 1999), p. 4.

[22] *Écrire la vie* (Paris: Gallimard, 2011) is the title given to her volume of *œuvres complètes*.

5

Raymond Queneau's *Œuvres complètes de Sally Mara*

Queneau's work provides a unique insight into the legacy of Gide's diary-writing during the post-War years, partly because it forms a bridge between the two groups, or generations, who held such different attitudes towards the *journal intime* at this time. Born in 1903, Queneau was a near contemporary of the prolific diarist Julien Green (1900–1998), and wrote his own *journaux intimes* intermittently from 1914 over long periods of his life.[1] His decision to give the title of 'Le Journal d'un jeune homme païvre' to his diary written between 1920 and 1927, alluding to Octave Feuillet's 1858 diary novel *Le Roman d'un jeune homme pauvre*, indicates that he had at least considered the literary potential of this diary.[2] Like Sartre—another near contemporary (born 1905) and part of a shared *germanopratin* milieu (centred in Saint-Germain-des-Prés)—Queneau wrote a particularly extensive diary during the period of the 'drôle de guerre', soon after the publication of Gide's *Journal*.[3] And yet—again like Sartre—he refrained from publishing any of his real *journaux intimes* in his lifetime, although he anticipated a posthumous publication.[4] Queneau was already established as an author before the War by his fictional works and critical writing, but his idiosyncratic literary formalism anticipated the later development of the *nouveau roman* by a new generation of writers. After the War, his continuing experimentation with formal apparatus and constraints in writing (leading to the founding of OuLiPo in 1960) was consistent with the interests of a literary avant-garde influenced by phenomenological, existentialist, and later structuralist ideas, which treated the psychological and

---

[1] Raymond Queneau, *Journal 1939–1940: suivi de Philosophes et voyous* (Paris: Gallimard, 1986). Raymond Queneau, *Journaux 1914–1965*, ed. by Anne Isabelle Queneau (Paris: Gallimard, 1996).

[2] 'Le Journal d'un jeune homme païvre' is included in Queneau's *Journaux 1914–1965*, Ibid., pp. 63–149. The diaeresis in the word 'païvre' has no basis in etymology, but forms a link with the following lines of Queneau's autobiographical poem *Chêne et chien* published in 1937: 'Hélas quel païvre jeune homme / Plus tard je suis devenu' [Alas, what a poor young man / I would later become]; Raymond Queneau, *Chêne et chien*, in Raymond Queneau, *Romans I (Œuvres complètes II)*, ed. by Henri Godard (Paris: Gallimard, Bibl. de la Pléiade, 2002), pp. 3–36, p. 20.

[3] As well as reading Gide's *Journal* in July 1939, he also read Julien Green's *Journal II: 1935–1939* (Paris: Plon, 1939) and Eugène Dabit's *Journal intime: 1928–1936* (Paris: Gallimard, 1939) in the same month; Queneau, *Journaux 1914–1965*, pp. 524–5. His attitude towards Gide was ambivalent, however, and he wrote in his *journal* on 14 August that he felt ill at ease when asked by Jean Paulhan to write an article in homage to Gide; *Journaux 1914–1965*, p. 366.

[4] Queneau, *Journaux 1914–1965*, p. 6.

writing subject with suspicion.[5] Yet, as I discussed in the introduction to Part II, this suspicion did not necessarily translate into a complete rejection of diary-writing, and Queneau himself produced an elaborate exploration of the diaristic author-figure in the series of publications attributed to the *auteur supposé* Sally Mara: the mock epic novel *On est toujours trop bon avec les femmes* (1947) parodies James Joyce and the American hard-boiled thriller, but the addition of Sally Mara's *Journal intime* (1950) constitutes her as an author-figure in a way that draws heavily on Gide, and the *Œuvres complètes de Sally Mara* (1962) conclude an irreverent and sophisticated reflection on the formal apparatus of the author-figure, while suggesting that it cannot be completely reduced to a textual *fonction-auteur* (to borrow Foucault's term).[6]

The relative critical neglect of these works is due to the commonly expressed conviction that their use of a pseudonym and their erotic content indicate that they were written merely to 'toucher un chèque' [pick up a cheque], and that 'on peut avoir scrupule, en effet, à considérer ces œuvres au même titre que les autres' [one might have some qualms about considering these works in the same manner as the others].[7] But there is another reason why the works' importance for the history of diary-writing has been overlooked even by the studies which have taken place, focusing on subjects as diverse as the intertextual relationships with James Joyce's *Ulysses*[8] and the erotic novel,[9] various aspects of their linguistic creativity,[10] and even including Evert van der Starre's synchronic reading of the *Œuvres complètes de Sally Mara* as a *mise en abyme* modelled on the structure of *Les Faux-monnayeurs*.[11] These studies have ignored the way in which the strategy of the *auteur supposé* developed and was unveiled over the course of the successive publications, in

---

[5] Queneau's experimental formalism is most clearly manifested in his *Exercices de style* (Paris: Gallimard, 1947) and *Cent mille milliards de poèmes* (Paris: Gallimard, 1963).

[6] References for these texts are to Raymond Queneau, *Les Œuvres complètes de Sally Mara* (Paris: Gallimard, 1979) (henceforth referred to as *OCSM*), comprising (in order) the *Journal intime* (*JI*), *On est toujours trop bon avec les femmes* (*OETTBALF*, the abbreviation used by Sally Mara herself, 8), and *Sally plus intime* (*SPI*). References to these works are given in the main text in parentheses.

[7] Spoken by François Caradec and Claude Debon respectively in discussion following Evert van der Starre's conference paper 'Sally Mara romancière? Exercices de style?', later published in *Raymond Queneau romancier: actes du 1er colloque international Raymond Queneau, Verviers, 27–30 août 1982*, 2 vols (= *Temps mêlés: documents Queneau*, 150 + 17–19, 20–1) (Verviers: Temps mêlés, 1983), II, pp. 85–107 (104–5); reprinted, without the discussion, in Evert van der Starre, 'Sally Mara romancière? Exercices de style?', in *Au ras du texte: douze études sur la littérature française de l'après-guerre* (Amsterdam: Rodopi, 2000), pp. 9–28. Subsequent references are to the latter publication. For an account of the reception of the Sally Mara works see Jean-Yves Pouilloux, 'Notice' for *Les Œuvres complètes de Sally Mara*, in Raymond Queneau, *Romans II (Œuvres complètes III)*, ed. by Henri Godard (Paris: Gallimard, Bibl. de la Pléiade, 2006), pp. 1719–37, pp. 1719–20, and Marie-Noëlle Campana, *Queneau pudique, Queneau coquin* (Limoges: Presses universitaires de Limoges, 2007), pp. 53–4.

[8] André Topia, 'Sally Mara ou le sexe a-t-il une âme', in *Études sur Les Œuvres complètes de ~~Raymond Queneau~~ Sally Mara*, ed. by Evert van der Starre (Groningen: Institut de langues romanes, 1984), pp. 1–21.

[9] Campana, *Queneau pudique, Queneau coquin*, pp. 137–55.

[10] Wiecher Zwanenburg, 'Aux Frontières de la formation des mots', in *Études sur Les Œuvres complètes de ~~Raymond Queneau~~ Sally Mara*, pp. 35–56; Q.I.M. Mok, 'L'Art de faire des fautes', in ibid., pp. 57–73.

[11] van der Starre, 'Sally Mara romancière?'.

the same manner as Gide's André Walter and Larbaud's A.O. Barnabooth, but also drawing on the comically unstable diegetic framework of *Paludes*, and the construction of an author-*œuvre* in Gide's own *Journal* and *Œuvres complètes*.[12] An understanding of this process reveals the shifting positions of the works' three signatories (Sally Mara, Raymond Queneau, and the fictional translator and editor Michel Presle), which can be understood most clearly using the narratological concept of metalepsis (the transgression of boundaries between diegetic levels, to which I shall return), and in which the textual apparatus of authorial power, authority, and presence are laid bare.

An appraisal of Queneau's treatment of diary-writing and the author-figure in these works first requires an account of his attitude towards the author-figure in his critical writing (particularly in an introduction written for a translation of Faulkner's *Mosquitoes*, in which he alludes to *OETTBALF*), and a clarification of the useful concepts of the *auteur supposé* and metalepsis. It will then be possible to consider the form and circumstances of the three works in turn, the way in which the three principal author-figures develop and enter into conflict, and the implications of their drama played out in the wings of the texts.

CONTEXT AND CONCEPTS FOR READING SALLY MARA

Queneau and the Author-Figure

Queneau was generally more discreet than Gide in using biographical material in the composition of his works. His earliest novels can be seen in hindsight to draw on his own experience, and the works *Les Derniers jours* (1936), *Odile* (1937), and *Chêne et chien* (a 'roman en vers' [verse novel], 1937) go as far as to 'établiss[er] avec l'autobiographie un système de relations complexe et volontairement déroutant, mais prégnant' [establish with autobiography a system of relations that is complex and deliberately disconcerting, but also significant], but from this point onwards the traces of his existence in his written work are far more difficult to identify.[13] Nonetheless, an author-figure is strongly felt as a continuity throughout Queneau's works, manifested by a distinctive idiolect (including phonetic spellings, such as 'asteure' for 'à cette heure'), an interest in technical areas of language and knowledge (which he exercised in his directorship of the Encyclopédie de la Pléiade from 1954), and a recognisably *pataphysique* sense of humour (characteristic of the 'Collège de 'Pataphysique', a literary group which later gave rise to OuLiPo). Queneau's interest in the phenomenon of the

---

[12] Queneau read Gide's work extensively and repeatedly, as documented in Florence Guéhéniau, *Queneau analphabète: répertoire alphabètique de ses lectures de 1917 à 1976*, 2 vols (Brussels: F. Guéhéniau, 1992), but in his own diary (published posthumously) he is interested above all in Gide's real life and character, and records a large number of irreverent personal observations under the heading of 'Gideana'; Queneau, *Journaux 1914–1965*, pp. 621–7.

[13] Henri Godard, 'Préface' to Raymond Queneau, *Romans I (Œuvres complètes II)*, ed. by Henri Godard (Paris: Gallimard, Bibl. de la Pléiade, 2002), pp. IX–LVIII, pp. XXVIII–XXX.

author-figure is shown by his repeated use of author characters in his fictions,[14] and there are also certain consistencies in his attitude towards the author-figure in the essays published together in 1950 in a volume entitled *Bâtons, chiffres et lettres*.[15] In the essay 'Technique du roman' (first published in 1937), Queneau relates the strictly mathematical approach he used in writing his first novel, *Le Chiendent* (1933):

> En ce temps-là, je voyais dans 13 un nombre bénéfique parce qu'il niait le bonheur; quant à 7, je le prenais, et puis le prend[s] encore, comme image numérique de moi-même, puisque mon nom et mes deux prénoms se composent chacun de sept lettres et que je suis né un 21 (3 × 7). Bien qu'en apparence non-autobiographique, la forme de ce roman en était donc fixée par ces motifs tout égocentriques: elle exprimait ainsi ce que le contenu croyait déguiser.[16]

> [At that time, I considered the number 13 as being beneficial because it is opposed to happiness; as for 7, I took it then, and still take it, as a numerical image of myself, since my surname and my first two names all consist of seven letters, and because I was born on the 21st of the month (3 × 7). Although it appears non-autobiographical, the form of this novel was determined by these entirely egocentric factors: in this way it expressed that which the content itself seemed to disguise.]

Although he later claims, 'je me suis dégagé de cette arithmomanie tout en conservant ce souci de structure' [I freed myself from this arithmomania while keeping the concern for structure],[17] this novel establishes a pattern of placing an elusive authorial presence in the text ('comme on dit dans mon pays, c'est de l'identification, sans en être, tout en étant' [as we say in my country, it is a case of identification, only not, but it still is]),[18] an *image* like that created by Gide in his *Œuvres complètes* and *Journal*, but which may be formal or 'numérique' rather than belonging to the 'contenu'. This game of disguise and disclosure also presumes that readers are curious about the author, and will pursue him or her in their reading of the text.

Queneau displays this same curiosity with regard to Faulkner in his introduction to a French translation of *Mosquitoes*, a text which suggests by means of several allusions to *OETTBALF* (published one year earlier without any mention of Queneau's name) that it has a direct relevance to the Sally Mara project.[19] He begins by asking, 'où donc les romanciers vont-ils prendre ce qu'ils nous

---

[14] Evert van der Starre lists the following fictional authors in Queneau's works: 'Pierre Le Grand (*Le Chiendent*), "Queneau" (*Les Enfants du limon*), [...] l'anonyme à la machine (*Zazie*), enfin Hubert Lubert et ses confrères (*Le vol d'Icare*)' [Pierre Le Grand (*Le Chiendent*), 'Queneau' (*Les Enfants du limon*), [...] the anonymous character with a typewriter (*Zazie*), and finally Hubert Lubert and his fellow writers (*Le vol d'Icare*)]; Evert van der Starre, *Curiosités de Raymond Queneau: de « l'Encyclopédie des Sciences inexactes » aux jeux de la création romanesque* (Geneva: Droz, 2006), p. 81.

[15] Raymond Queneau, *Bâtons, chiffres et lettres* (Paris: Gallimard, 1950).

[16] Raymond Queneau, 'Technique du roman', in *Bâtons, chiffres et lettres* ([1937]), pp. 22–7, p. 24.

[17] Raymond Queneau, *Entretiens avec Georges Charbonnier* (Paris: Gallimard, 1962), p. 56.

[18] Queneau, 'Technique du roman', p. 24.

[19] Raymond Queneau, Introduction to William Faulkner, *Moustiques* (Paris: Minuit, 1947), pp. 7–14; reprinted as Raymond Queneau, '*Moustiques* de William Faulkner', in *Bâtons, chiffres et lettres* (1950), pp. 77–84. Subsequent references are to this edition, except when indicated otherwise.

racontent' [where do novelists go to find the things they tell us],[20] and also comically repeats the apparently trivial question, 'si Faulkner fit jamais une croisière sur un quelconque *Nausikaa* invité par une quelconque Mrs. Maurier' [whether Faulkner ever made a trip on a boat like the Nausikaa, invited by someone like Mrs. Maurier] (as happens in Faulkner's novel).[21] Here Queneau himself is in the position of a reader seeking in a text something of its author's life, or conversely wondering how the author used his lived experience to produce a work of fiction. But this is not the state of affairs that Queneau has in mind for his own authorial practice, and his interest lies more particularly in Faulkner's trajectory as an artist from writing *Mosquitoes* (1927), in which 'il éprouve le besoin de s'exprimer directement' [he feels the need to express himself directly], to publishing *The Sound and the Fury* (1929), after which 'les origines privées de ces œuvres devenaient de plus en plus obscures' [the 'private' origins of these works became increasingly obscure], which makes him a true 'romancier' in Queneau's eyes.[22]

In itself, this reflects the development in Queneau's work from the authorial presence of *Le Chiendent* to the relative authorial absence of his later novels, and also casts light on Sally Mara's own trajectory from the direct disclosure of the *JI* to the fictional transpositions of her novel *OETTBALF*. Yet Queneau's allusion to Sally Mara's novel in this very article, buried in the middle of a circuitous sentence (which describes, moreover, a form of metalepsis), suggests that it has a more direct application to the Sally Mara works:

> tout comme Charlie Chaplin apparaît incidemment dans *A woman of Paris* sous les aspects d'un portefaix, Faulkner fait coucou au détour d'une conversation [...]. Et il a des porte-parole, des masques, on dit pour lui ce qu'il veut dire, le roman lui-même tourne autour du thème: 'on est toujours trop bon avec les femmes', et il est difficile de ne pas croire que l'auteur y croit lui-même, bien que l'"inventeur" de cette théorie dans *Mosquitoes* soit lamentablement ridicule (c'est le Mécène).[23]
>
> [just as Charlie Chaplin appears briefly in *A Woman of Paris* in the guise of a porter, Faulkner pops up in the course of a conversation [...]. And he has spokesmen, masks, people speak on his behalf, the novel itself revolves around the theme 'we always treat women too well', and it is hard to avoid thinking that the author himself believes it, even though the 'inventor' of this theory in *Mosquitoes* is pitifully ridiculous (the patron of the arts).]

Another allusion occurs in the comment that, 'on ne saurait jamais prévoir ce que peut écrire un individu; qu'on le connaisse depuis ikse [*sic*] années, et c'est toujours surprenant' [one can never foresee what an individual might write; even when one has known them for eks number of years, it is still a surprise], which is a

[20] Queneau, '*Moustiques* de William Faulkner', p. 77.
[21] Ibid., pp. 78, 81, 82, 84.   [22] Ibid., p. 81.
[23] Queneau, Introduction to William Faulkner, *Mosquitoes*, p. 12. In *Bâtons, chiffres et lettres* the allusion is strengthened by the use of a capital letter for 'On', by italicizing the title, and by referring to it in the index under 'Mara (Sally). / *On est toujours trop bon avec les femmes*' (82).

near-quotation of Michel Presle in the preface to *OETTBALF*.[24] The significance of these allusions to Sally Mara is left open to interpretation, but we can at least say that it concerns the author's disguises and identification with the text, the nature of the author's act of literary creation, and the process by which the literary work is distanced from its 'origines "privées"'.

One final reflection from this article with relevance to the Sally Mara project is an assertion of the importance to a work of the author's signature attached to it:

> L'écrivain, même crêvé, est-il un tel néant que l'œuvre puisse s'inscrire dans la 'culture' humaine sans sa signification originelle d'œuvre DE quelqu'un? Alors ce quelqu'un est quelqu'un. Une littérature commence dans une civilisation lorsque le quelqu'un en question signe Homère, par exemple. On ne peut plus dès lors considérer cette signature uniquement comme quelques lettres assemblées, un mot ultra-particulier, un nom propre à l'abandon, perdu, plus utilisable, sans renoncer à toute curiosité humaine.[25]

> [Is the writer, even a dead one, so immaterial that the work can be inscribed in human 'culture' without its original significance as being the work *of* someone? Well then, this someone is someone. A civilization's literature begins when the someone in question signs his name as Homer, for example. From that moment we can no longer consider that signature as merely a few letters strung together, an ultra-particular word, a proper noun cast adrift, lost, no longer usable, without renouncing all human curiosity.]

Given the importance of this comment with reference to a work that constantly plays on the significance of its three signatories (Michel Presle, Sally Mara and Raymond Queneau), it is perhaps appropriate that Queneau chose the name 'Homère' as an example, an author whose very existence is surrounded by legend, and is discussed by the characters of the *JI* (104).

Sally Mara as an *auteur supposé*

The concept of the *auteur supposé* has already been discussed in relation to Gide's creation of André Walter, but it will be useful to recall the definition of the concept, and identify its particular features in the case of Sally Mara. I shall continue to use the definition set out in Jean-François Jeandillou's *Supercheries littéraires* (1989), which includes Sally Mara in its anthology of thirty *auteurs supposés*.[26]

Essentially, Jeandillou's definition requires that the *auteur supposé* be convincingly presented by paratextual material as the real author of the work or works in question.[27] Accordingly, the real author, or *auteur supposant*, must not claim

---

[24] Queneau, '*Moustiques* de William Faulkner', p. 8. Michel Presle writes, 'on ne sait jamais ce que les gens ont "derrière" la tête. On peut connaître quelqu'un depuis vingt ans, s'il écrit, il sera toujours une surprise' [one never knows what people have 'inside' their heads. One can know someone for twenty years, but if he should write something, it will always be a surprise] (*OCSM*, 8).

[25] Queneau, '*Moustiques de William Faulkner*', p. 83.

[26] Jean-François Jeandillou, *Supercheries littéraires: la vie et l'œuvre des auteurs supposés* (Paris: Usher, 1989).

[27] This notably differs from Jean-Benoît Puech's definition and practice, for whom the formal apparatus are sufficient without a genuine attempt to deceive, and who has publicly acknowledged

authorial responsibility, which excludes *auteurs fictifs* such as Gide's Édouard and Queneau's Hubert Lubert in *Le Vol d'Icare*, but also cases in which the fictionality of the *auteur prétendu* is revealed only by the presence of the real author's name on the cover, such as John Shade and Charles Kinbote in Nabokov's *Pale Fire*.[28] A substantial part of the *auteur supposé*'s work must be present, which avoids confusion with the *référence factice*.[29] Finally, the *auteur supposé* must possess some sort of biography constituting him or her as a separate individual from the *auteur supposant*, which excludes pseudonyms, whether or not the name of the real author is actually known.[30] From as early as Sainte-Beuve's *Vie, poésies et pensées de Joseph Delorme* (1829), the *journal intime* has played an important role in fabricating and authenticating this separate authorial existence.

Several of the more general family resemblances between *auteur supposés* are particularly relevant to the Sally Mara works. Jeandillou's anthology contains a large number of male *auteurs supposants* creating female *auteurs supposés*, including (besides Queneau's Sally Mara) Mérimée's Clara Gazul, Pierre Louÿs's Bilitis, and Apollinaire's Louise Lalanne. There are also several cases in which the work has supposedly been translated into French from another language, including the works of Bilitis, Yves Gandon's Tsing Pann Yang, and Boris Vian's Vernon Sullivan (this is also true of *OETTBALF*, supposedly translated from Irish). It is reasonable to suppose that gender, culture, and language are all convenient criteria for the *auteur supposant* to make the *auteur supposé* 'other' with regard to him- or herself, and each of these is used to great effect in the Sally Mara novels (whereas André Walter shows a closer resemblance to his *auteur supposant*, André Gide). Jeandillou also acknowledges that the historical reality of his examples does not always conform strictly to his definition, particularly with regard to how convincing the *supercherie* [hoax] may be in each case, and observes that often 'la stratégie adoptée participe moins d'un "faire croire" captieux que d'un "laisser croire" purement ludique' [the strategy adopted is less that of a specious 'deception' than that of a purely ludic 'misdirection'].[31] Rather than seeing this 'laisser croire' as contradicting the requirement that the *auteur supposé* be presented as a real author, I would supplement Jeandillou's definition with the suggestion that the process involves a gradual, controlled, and indeed 'ludique' public disclosure of the artificial nature of the *auteur supposé* over time, which, for Sally Mara as for André Walter, plays an important role in the project as a whole.

Finally, it is worth noting a particular correspondence between the Sally Mara project and another *auteur supposé* project, made up of the works of Valery Larbaud's A.O. Barnabooth (read by Queneau in 1922, 1944, and 1976).[32]

---

his authorship of the works attributed to Benjamin Jordane since his first use of this name in his doctoral thesis; Jean-Benoît Puech, 'L'Auteur supposé: typologie romanesque' (unpublished doctoral thesis, EHESS, 1982). Also see Jean-Benoît Puech, *Du Vivant de l'auteur* (Seyssel: Champ Vallon, 1990), pp. 53–4.

[28] Jeandillou, *Supercheries littéraires*, pp. 470–1.   [29] Ibid., p. 473.
[30] Ibid., pp. 477–8.   [31] Ibid., pp. 474, 482.
[32] Guéhéniau, *Queneau analphabète*, II, p. 1722. Valery Larbaud, *Poèmes d'un riche amateur: ou Œuvres françaises de M. Barnabooth, précédées d'une introduction biographique*, published without

In both cases a work of prose fiction (and also poems, in Barnabooth's case) was initially published under the name of the *auteur supposé*, together with biographical information provided by a fictional editor (X.M. Tournier de Zamble and Michel Presle respectively). These works were followed by the *journaux intimes* and *œuvres complètes* of the *auteurs supposés*, by which they became far more substantial author-figures, while claiming for themselves the former authority of their editors. In each case their publications were eventually accompanied by the name of the real author, yet both Larbaud and Queneau continued to equivocate, however unconvincingly, about their responsibility for the works, thereby continuing indefinitely the 'ludique' public disclosure of their respective *auteurs supposés*.[33] These close parallels reinforce the importance of the development of the *auteur supposé* over time (particularly the addition of a *journal intime* to a previously published literary work), and suggest that the changing relations between Sally Mara, Michel Presle, and Raymond Queneau are central to the project's exploration of the diaristic author-figure.

Metalepsis

The interactions of the texts' three signatories in the diegetic framework (including Sally Mara's gradual assertion of her authority as a diaristic author-figure) can best be understood using the concept of metalepsis, which can be found to exist in these works in an exceedingly wide variety of forms and at every level of their structure. It is therefore necessary, not only to define metalepsis as it has been used by other critics, but also to find a flexible model for my own purposes, which can be adapted to these different circumstances.

The modern use of the term metalepsis begins in Gérard Genette's 1972 publication *Figures III*, in which he adopts the ancient rhetorical concept of 'la *métalepse de l'auteur*, [...] qui consiste à feindre que le poète "opère lui-même les effets qu'il chante", comme lorsqu'on dit que Virgile "fait mourir" Didon au chant IV de l'*Énéide*' [*authorial metalepsis*, [...] which involves the pretence that the poet himself 'brings about the effects of which he sings', as when Virgil 'makes Dido die' in Book IV of the *Aeneid*].[34] The concept has since been considerably extended, applied to many different forms of representation, and subjected to various taxonomies, as demonstrated by the works issuing from a conference on 'La Métalepse, aujourd'hui' in 2002.[35] I shall merely draw attention to certain distinctions that have been made between its different forms, which will elucidate its nature in the Sally Mara works.

mention of Larbaud's name (Paris: Léon Vanier, 1908). Valery Larbaud, *A. O. Barnabooth, ses Œuvres complètes: c'est-à-dire un conte, ses poésies et son journal intime* (Paris: NRF, 1913).

[33] Jeandillou, *Supercheries littéraires*, p. 277. Pouilloux, 'Notice' for *Les Œuvres complètes de Sally Mara*, p. 1722.

[34] Gérard Genette, *Figures III* (Paris: Seuil, 1972), p. 244.

[35] *Métalepses: entorses au pacte de la représentation*, ed. by John Pier and Jean-Marie Schaeffer (Paris: EHESS, 2005). The conference also gave rise to Gérard Genette, *Métalepse: de la figure à la fiction* (Paris: Seuil, 2004).

The first such distinction can be demonstrated by two often repeated and discussed examples from *Figures III*. When the narrator of Diderot's *Jacques le fataliste* asks the reader, 'qu'est-ce qui m'empêcherait de *marier* le Maître et de le *faire cocu*?' [what is there to stop me from *making* the Master *marry*, and *making him a cuckold*?], he disturbs the convention whereby a narrator relates the events of the story as if they had actually happened. Conversely, when a character in Julio Cortázar's 'Continuidad de los parques' is murdered by a character in the novel he is reading, the expectation that the events of a novel are imaginary and immaterial is overturned.[36] Several critics have described these two types respectively as *métalepse d'énonciation* (*in verbis*) and *métalepse d'énoncé* (*in corpore*),[37] or *métalepse rhétorique* and *métalepse ontologique*.[38] Both types are to be found in the Sally Mara works, although in practice the difference between them is often more complex than the examples given here.

Another important distinction, made by Genette, regards the direction of the transgression of diegetic situations. Most examples of metalepsis involve the intrusion of one diegetic level into its respective metadiegetic level, generally an internally framed narrative, but occasionally the movement is in the opposite direction, which Genette terms *antimétalepse*. He discusses this in the context of Woody Allen's short story 'The Kugelmass Episode',[39] in which a university professor enters the world of *Madame Bovary* and brings Emma Bovary back with him to twentieth-century Manhattan.[40] The example is somewhat flawed as it is still the higher diegetic level that instigates the transgression, but this *antimétalepse* is nonetheless an important element of the Sally Mara works as well (which might have provided Genette with a better example).

It is also necessary to clarify the difference between metalepsis and *mise en abyme* (since van der Starre has used the latter concept to analyse the *OCSM*), a subject which has already attracted discussion and caused confusion.[41] As Marie-Laure Ryan remarks, whereas metalepsis creates 'des brèches dans la structure de l'édifice narratif' [breaches in the structure of the narrative construct], *mise en abyme* merely adds a metadiegetic layer 'sans permettre à ces images de déborder de leur cadre' [without allowing these images to go beyond their respective frames].[42] The diegetic framework then invites the reader (sometimes very unambiguously, as in the case of *Les Faux-monnayeurs*) to draw an analogy between the metadiegetic level and another diegetic level. The confusion between the two devices may be due to the fact that they can produce similar consequences (including a self-reflexive

---

[36] Genette, *Figures III*, pp. 244 (emphases original).
[37] Klaus Meyer-Minnemann, 'Un procédé narratif qui "produit un effet de bizarrerie": la métalepse littéraire', in *Métalepses*, pp. 133–50, pp. 143–6.
[38] Marie-Laure Ryan, 'Logique culturelle de la métalepse', in *Métalepses*, pp. 201–23, pp. 207–8.
[39] Woody Allen, 'The Kugelmass Episode', in Woody Allen, *Complete Prose* (New York: Picador, 1980), pp. 345–60.
[40] Genette, *Métalepse*, p. 27.
[41] Vincent Colonna, *Autofiction et autres mythomanies littéraires* (Paris: Tristram, 2004), p. 131. Dorrit Cohn, 'Métalepse et mise en abyme', in *Métalepses*, pp. 121–30, pp. 125–30.
[42] Ryan, 'Logique culturelle de la métalepse', p. 208.

function, disorientation, and comic effects), and both usually involve relatively complex diegetic frameworks. As a result, one is likely to find both devices in the same work (which is the case for the Sally Mara works).

These distinctions all help to demonstrate the diverse possibilities of metalepsis, and will inform my own flexible approach: for each case of metalepsis I shall examine the initial terms of the 'pacte représentationnel' that determines the diegetic structure[43] (and I shall include in this not only straightforward narrative but also translation, citation, and the position of authoritative editorial commentary granted to paratext), the way in which these terms are violated, and the consequences of the violation for the texts' signatories.

SALLY MARA'S DEVELOPMENT AS A DIARISTIC AUTHOR-FIGURE

The ground is now prepared for an analysis of the three Sally Mara publications as an *auteur supposé* project, in which the roles of the three signatories in the diegetic structure (Sally Mara, Michel Presle, and Raymond Queneau) develop and interact over time by various processes of metalepsis. Although the project eventually arrives at a formalist treatment of the diaristic author-figure and *œuvre* that had been established by Gide's diary-writing, it is necessary to consider the works in turn, beginning with the 1947 publication of *OETTBALF*. At this point, before the publication of her *Journal intime* or *Œuvres complètes*, Sally Mara occupied a precarious position as the *auteur supposé* of an erotic *roman noir*.

On est toujours trop bon avec les femmes

It was against the background of Boris Vian's successful *J'irai cracher sur vos tombes* (1946) that Jean d'Halluin commissioned Queneau to write *On est toujours trop bon avec les femmes* for the same publishing house, Éditions du Scorpion.[44] Vian's novel was published under the pseudonym of Vernon Sullivan, with the claim that Vian was merely its French translator. The pseudonym both served as a protection against censorship and offered the exoticism of an American work, at a time when the American novel and cinema exerted a strong influence on French fictional writing.[45] *OETTBALF* claims for itself the sex, violence, and exoticism of this genre, and was originally sold under the marketing slogan 'Inédit dans la chaste

---

[43] John Pier and Jean-Marie Schaeffer, 'Introduction: la métalepse aujourd'hui', *Métalepses*, pp. 7–15, p. 12.

[44] Vernon Sullivan [i.e. Boris Vian], *J'Irai cracher sur vos tombes, traduit de l'américain par Boris Vian* (Paris: Scorpion, 1946). Pouilloux, 'Notice' for *Les Œuvres complètes de Sally Mara*, p. 1719.

[45] See the contemporary study by Claude-Edmonde Magny, *L'Âge du roman américain* (Paris: Seuil, 1948), and the recent article by Didier Alexandre, 'Les Écrivains français et le roman américain 1943–1951: histoire d'un désamour?', *Romanic Review*, 100 (2009), pp. 81–92.

Irlande' [Unpublished in chaste Ireland].[46] Yet Queneau's *supercherie* already went further than Vian's at this stage, in that he invented not only an author but also the fictional translator and editor Michel Presle, who gives some scant biographical details about Sally Mara in a preface (including the claim that she had died in Cork in 1943, 8). The original publication also announces the intention to publish another work by Sally Mara (in a notice under the heading 'à paraître' [still to be published]),[47] not another novel but her (supposedly real) *Journal intime*, which is also to be translated by Michel Presle. Queneau's own name is entirely absent from this initial publication.

The status of Michel Presle in the 1947 publication of *OETTBALF* depends heavily on the extent to which readers detect the *supercherie*. An initial clue to his fictionality is the similarity of his name to the well-known contemporary actress Micheline Presle,[48] a connection which, through a (characteristically *quenellien*) reversal of gender, anticipates some of the subsequent relations between the three signatories. Secondly, although the artificiality of the world of *OETTBALF* (the literary nature of the names borrowed from *Ulysses*, for example) in itself poses no threat to the claims made by its paratext (that Sally Mara is a real author who genuinely wrote a novel in Irish that a real Michel Presle has translated into French), certain processes of metalepsis undermine these claims.

One such process involves the text's claims regarding the stages of translation it has undergone. On the grounds that Michel Presle's French translation of Sally Mara's novel in Irish is a reinterpretation and retelling of her original work, the two versions may be viewed as two different diegetic levels, each with its own logical conventions. To confuse matters further, the dialogue in Sally Mara's Irish version is notionally translated from conversations that the characters would have conducted in English. The transgression of the boundaries between these diegetic levels is demonstrated by a passage that plays heavily (and comically) on the complications of translation:

> Ni français ni anglais, mais assez voisin du breton, [l'esprit irlandais] procède par 'intuition'. Caffrey ne pouvant ouvrir la lourde eut donc l'*ankou* [footnote: Celticisme pour 'intuition'. (N.d.T.)] que quelqu'un se trouvait là, enfermé! Cette *anschauung* [footnote: Germanisme pour 'ankou'. (N.d.T.)] lui boucla immédiatement les tripes. Essuyant la sueur qui lui dégoulinait encore de la tronche, il oublia ses troubles égocentriques et, découvrant son devoir *d'un seul coup d'un seul*, [footnote: Gallicisme pour 'anschauung'. (N.d.T.)] il résolut de rendre compte à Mac Cormack de la découverte qu'il venait de faire. (222)

> [Neither French nor English, but rather close to Breton, [the Irish spirit] proceeds by 'intuition'. As Caffrey could not open the door, he had the *ankou* [footnote: Celticism for 'intuition'. (translator's note)] that someone was in there, locked in! This *anschauung* [footnote: Germanism for 'ankou'. (translator's note)] suddenly gave him a tight feeling in his gut. Wiping the sweat that was still streaming from his

---

[46] Pouilloux, 'Notice' for *Les Œuvres complètes de Sally Mara*, p. 1738. [47] Ibid., p. 1725.
[48] Queneau himself acknowledged this etymology of the name in 1967 in an 'hommage' to the actress (reprinted in Queneau, *Romans II (Œuvres complètes III)*, p. 1505).

face, he forgot his egocentric troubles and, recalling his duty *d'un seul coup d'un seul,*
[footnote: Gallicism for 'anschauung'. (translator's note)] he resolved to report back
to Mac Cormack about the discovery he had just made.]

If we try to imagine the supposed source text for Michel Presle's translation, we
might infer that an Irish equivalent of 'intuition' had been used for the first term
(although the meaning of the translator's quotation marks is not clear). But if the
word 'ankou' had been used in the Irish source text for the second term in the
sequence, it would not make sense for this to be described as a 'celticisme', as
Presle claims. It would make sense, however, in the context of the diegetic level of
Michel Presle's French translation, where the word 'intuition' is followed by a word
of Celtic origin (although the term 'ankou' actually refers to a figure from Breton
mythology). It is not necessary to pursue the illogicalities of this passage further,
but only to observe that they carry out a general strategy of obfuscating the issue of
translation, and making it possible to surmise that the work was originally written
in French and not translated from Irish at all.

A further effect of metalepsis is provided by the fact that in several ways the
novel appears characteristic of the *germanopratin* culture of Jean d'Halluin and
Jean-Paul Sartre. For example, Gertie's comment, 'si le roi d'Angleterre était un
con, tout serait permis!' [if the King of England were an idiot, anything would
be allowed!] (249) echoes the claim in Dostoevsky's *The Brothers Karamazov* that
'si Dieu n'existait pas, tout serait permis' [if God did not exist, anything would
be allowed] (in its French translation), but it also recalls the discussion of this
same phrase in Sartre's *L'Existentialisme est un humanisme*, published in 1946.[49]
The metaleptic process here is more straightforward than in the previous example:
the diegetic framework depends on the fact that *OETTBALF* could, plausibly,
have been written by Sally Mara before she died in 1943, but in practice the
literary conventions and concerns of Michel Presle's diegetic level are applied to
that of Sally Mara. A reader may conclude from this that Michel Presle is the real
author of *OETTBALF* (perhaps under a pseudonym) and that his invention of the
character of Sally Mara is analogous with Boris Vian's claim to be the translator of
J'irai cracher sur vos tombes. In this context, the details that Michel Presle provides
of Sally Mara's life and death ('morte très simplement et très obscurément d'une
maladie quelconque en 1943' [she died simply and in obscurity from some sort of
disease in 1943], 8) seem to belong to his intention to create an author-character
who is inert, condemned to the past, and under his control. His expectation to
remain in control of Sally Mara's publications is also manifested in the paratext,
which announces that he is to be the translator of her *Journal intime*.

Although Sally Mara's position in the diegetic framework is kept in check by
the authority of Michel Presle's preface and numerous footnotes (often provided
with little motivation except to make his presence felt), she already demonstrates
an ability to participate in the same processes of metalepsis and manipulation of
paratext. When the revolutionary insurgent Caffrey observes, 'on en apprend des

49 Ibid., p. 1744, n. 10.

mots nouveaux aujourd'hui. On voit qu'on est dans le pays de James Joyce' [we're learning new words today. It's clear that we're in the land of James Joyce] (242), Sally Mara comments in a footnote: 'Il y a là un léger anachronisme, mais Caffrey, étant analphabète, ne pouvait savoir en 1916 qu'*Ulysse* n'avait pas encore paru. (N. de l'A.)' [There is a slight anachronism, but Caffrey, being illiterate, could not know in 1916 that *Ulysses* had not yet been published (author's note).] The fictional world that Caffrey inhabits, created and controlled by Sally Mara from a higher diegetic level, does not allow him to be acquainted with the works of Joyce, and yet this framework is disturbed by applying the logic of Sally Mara's diegetic level (where the knowledge of when Joyce's works were published determines whether Caffrey can refer to them) to Caffrey's diegetic level (he is unaware that they have not been published, and so he can refer to them). A transgression of the same nature occurs when Sally Mara allows the character John Mac Cormack to refer to a comment that was made 'quelques pages plus haut' [a few pages above] (in his words, 301). These relatively anodyne metalepses undertaken by Sally Mara draw attention to the analogous metaleptic practices of Michel Presle and also foreshadow her own subsequent (antimetaleptic) rebellion from his control.

There is already cause to speak of an author at a higher diegetic level than Michel Presle at this point, to the precise extent that the *supercherie* is suspected by the reader. All the elements of the text that manifest the presence of Michel Presle—his name on the title page, the preface, his footnotes, the processes of metalepsis that suggest the artificiality of Sally Mara—make him into an author-figure. Even if Michel Presle were the author's real name, it would be necessary to distinguish 'la personne et sa vie réelle' from 'le personnage et sa vie représentée' [the character and his life as it is represented].[50] This might be true for any text, but the relationship between the two is foregrounded here by the artificial nature of Michel Presle's character. The biographical details provided by his preface offer no means of verification (his acquaintance, the poet Padraic Baoghal, who he implies is well known, does not exist), and his redundant comment that Cork is a 'ville assez agréable' [fairly pleasant city], paradoxically, shows its artificiality by providing an *effet de réel*.[51] The concept of the 'pseudonym' as a way of describing the relationship of this author with Michel Presle appears hopelessly vague, as it does not address the nature or degree of identification between the two. Do they share some biographical details, character traits, the same attitude towards the novel at hand? Is the real author also to be identified with Sally Mara, or is she further distanced from him by her lower diegetic level (at two removes)? A question mark hangs over the real author at this point, but he or she nonetheless occupies a position at the top of the diegetic framework.

Sally Mara's precarious status in *OETTBALF*—as the author of a single work of fiction, and continually under the paratextual control of Michel Presle—

---

[50] Jean-Benoît Puech, 'Présentation', in *L'Auteur comme œuvre: l'auteur, ses masques, son personnage, sa légende. Colloque des 25 et 26 avril 1997, Université d'Orléans*, ed. by Nathalie Lavialle and Jean-Benoît Puech (Orléans: Presses universitaires d'Orléans, 2000), pp. 9–12, p. 10.

[51] Roland Barthes, 'L'Effet de réel', in *OC* ([1968]), II, pp. 25–32.

is radically changed by the publication of her *Journal intime*, which not only constitutes a more substantial author-*œuvre* in the manner of Gide's *Journal*, but also resembles André Walter's progress towards assuming an authorial role in his own *Cahiers*.

The *Journal intime*

The *Journal intime* announced in 1947 was published in 1950, again with Jean d'Halluin's Éditions du Scorpion, but, instead of being translated into French by Michel Presle (as expected), it is supposedly written in French by the narrator/diarist Sally Mara. Notices from the publisher accompanying this edition announce another work to come, '*Sally plus intime* (dont, au moment de mettre sous presse, nous apprenons que l'on vient de retrouver le manuscrit)' [*Sally plus intime* (at the moment of going to press, we have learnt that the manuscript for this work has just been found)],[52] thereby reinforcing the impression of an author with a continuous supply of new works (although she is still presumed to be dead). Michel Presle is no longer a writer of paratext in this work, but a character in the same world as Sally Mara. As for Queneau, his name appears just once, in a footnote that mentions him (truthfully) as the French translator of Maurice O'Sullivan's *Twenty Years A-Growing* (118).

The relative lack of paratextual material (there is no preface and only two footnotes, both signed 'MP') reduces Michel Presle's capacity to maintain control over Sally Mara by these means. This reduction in his authority is exacerbated by the fact that the claim from the paratext of *OETTBALF* that Michel Presle would be the translator of the *JI* turns out to be false. Furthermore, although his preface to *OETTBALF* presents him as having known Sally Mara personally, it is emphasized far more in the *JI* that he inhabits the same physical world as she does, and that this world is eminently artificial (for example, Sally Mara happens to run the hundred metres in the same time as Jesse Owens did at the 1936 Olympics).[53] Michel Presle therefore seems to be relegated to the same diegetic level as Sally Mara, where they are both presided over by the presumed real author of the work.

However, Michel Presle's role is very different from that of any other character in the work. His departure from Dublin is the stimulus for Sally Mara's 'double résolution' (18) to begin keeping her *journal intime* in French and to write a novel in Irish. He is also the source of her knowledge of French (just as Padraic Baoghal, poet and 'lubrique paltoquet' [lecherous know-it-all], 70, teaches her the Irish language which she uses to write *OETTBALF*), and notably he is responsible for teaching her a language that is sexually charged but of which she does not understand the connotations: ' "Foutre, me disait-il, est un des plus beaux mots de la langue française." Il signifie: jeter, mais avec plus de vigourosité' ['*Foutre*,' he told me, 'is one of the most beautiful words in the French language.' It means to throw, but with more vigorosity] (17). This partial understanding gives rise

---

[52] Pouilloux, 'Notice' for *Les Œuvres complètes de Sally Mara*, p. 1738.
[53] Queneau, *Romans II (Œuvres complètes III)*, p. 1740, n. 4.

to the many unintentional (from Sally Mara's perspective) double entendres and neologisms which provide much of the work's humour and which have already been the subject of several studies.[54] He is absent for most of the duration of the *JI*, and his involvement (sporadically sending her perfume, a magazine, bottles of pastis, and eventually returning and mentioning Joyce to her) is almost always unmotivated by the causality of Sally Mara's own world, a *deus ex machina*. He therefore transcends the boundary between the diegetic level of the author and that of Sally Mara, and represents in a material way the control that an author wields over a lower diegetic level. The significance of his acts may be summarized as follows: he leaves his character with a certain language to be explored, understood, and mastered; he occasionally supplies her with additional objects or texts, but what she does with them is out of his control; he also takes a sexual interest in his character, which remains unconsummated (186); finally, his control of the character wanes and she ends the work of her own accord.

Sally Mara's antimetaleptic rebellion begins to take shape over the course of this work, partly by means of the very processes which lower Michel Presle's status in the diegetic framework. Instead of writing her diary in English and allowing a translator to reinterpret it, she usurps this higher diegetic level by being not only a character in the Anglophone world of the *JI* but also its narrator and French translator. It is common, of course, for novels narrated in the first person, and especially diary novels, to foreground the dual role of narrator and actor, but this union of two diegetic levels creates a tension from the beginning of the *JI*, which is exploited to comic effect. For example, the situation of her translating English dialogue into French, which is sometimes presented in a manner that respects its logic, is also often subverted. She claims not to understand a limerick which Joël has recited (in English) and which she reproduces (in French):

> Michael l'épicier n'est pas le seul à dire
> Que le melon pour l'homme est un divin plaisir
> Et qu'un jeune garçon vous met en allégresse
> Quant à la femme? Bonne à continuer l'espèce. (45)

> [Michael the grocer is not the only one to say
> That the melon is a divine pleasure for a man
> And that a young man can turn you on.
> As for women? Good for carrying on the species.]

Despite claiming not to understand the limerick, she is able to produce a French translation in alexandrine rhyming couplets that conveys the sexual meaning of the supposed original. This creates a logical contradiction between the diegetic level on which she is an actor and that of narration/translation.

Amid this confusion in the diegetic structure, there is a steady transition in Sally Mara's diegetic status that is inseparable from her sexual and linguistic

---

[54] Zwanenburg, 'Aux Frontières de la formation des mots'. Mok, 'L'Art de faire des fautes'. Ronald Landheer, 'Queneau et la rhétorique du sous-entendu', in *Études sur Les Œuvres complètes de ~~Raymond Queneau~~ Sally Mara*, pp. 74–104.

education. Early in the *JI*, every occasion when her double entendres and errors in the use of French create a humorous effect of which she is unaware, such as in the phrase 'ces pages destinées à la seule postériorité' [these pages destined only for posteriority] (23), requires the control and consciousness of a higher diegetic level. However, after the revelations brought about by witnessing the 'noces' [wedding] of the goats at the end of the first section (91), she comes to understand 'environ un sur cinq' [about one in five] of Joël's limericks (104). She steadily becomes more sexually experienced and confident, even treating Mève 'impérativement' [forcefully] during their brief liaison (125). Her errors take on the form of a deliberate use of humour, generally making use of her new-found sexual knowledge, and the closing words of the novel complete her transition:

> Alors Barnabé m'a crié:
> —Sally, tiens bon la rampe!
> J'ai avancé la main dans l'obscurité, mais je n'ai trouvé qu'un cordage humide et froid.
> Je compris alors que ma vie conjugale venait de commencer. (187)
>
> [Then Barnabé cried out to me:
> —Sally, hold onto the rail!
> I reached out my hand in the darkness, but all I found was a cold, damp bit of rope.
> I understood then that my married life had just begun.]

With this move from the perfect tense of diaristic *discours* to the *passé simple* of novelistic *histoire*,[55] she simultaneously realizes that her marriage is to be sexually unsatisfying and becomes conscious of the significance of the 'rampe' motif (the phrase '[tenez/tiens] bon la rampe' occurs at the beginning and end, and accompanies certain important events in Sally's journey, thereby structuring the narrative in a manner more characteristic of a novel than a diary). Although this entails her becoming aware of her fictional status in the *JI*, by the same act she elevates herself to the higher diegetic level of the author, just as André Walter strives (at the expense of his life) to assume an artistic, authorial role in writing *Les Cahiers d'André Walter*.

Her new role as novelist, together with the final word 'commencer' (alluding to the circularity of *Finnegans Wake*), leads the reader back to *OETTBALF* (supposedly written by Sally Mara after the *JI*), which now assumes a new significance as a *mise en abyme* relative to the *JI*. As van der Starre has discussed this relationship between the two works at length, I shall only briefly repeat some of his observations. Besides many other similarities between the novels, the journey of the heroine Gertie through *OETTBALF* closely resembles that of Sally Mara in the *JI*, with certain notable exceptions: Gertie is more free from moral restrictions owing to the exceptional circumstances of the Republican revolt, and, instead of Sally Mara's long and difficult exploration of sexuality, Gertie takes only twenty-four hours to achieve a knowledge and experience that is even more comprehensive and encyclopedic (in the manner of the Marquis de Sade, or indeed of Queneau, director of the Encyclopédie de la Pléiade from 1954).[56] Sally Mara's creation of

---

[55] Émile Benveniste, *Problèmes de linguistique générale* (Paris: Gallimard, 1966), pp. 238–44.
[56] van der Starre, 'Sally Mara romancière?', p. 14.

Gertie and of the world of *OETTBALF* is therefore a concentrated sublimation of her desires that are thwarted at the end of the *JI*. However, we must avoid a simple and direct identification of Sally Mara with Gertie, as the various 'complexes' (37) of the *JI* are spread schematically among the insurgents of *OETTBALF*, of which van der Starre provides a catalogue, including 'nécrophilie', 'homosexualité + hétérosexualité latente' and 'amour platonique' [Platonic love].[57]

The author-figure at the top of the diegetic framework of the 1947 publication has a considerably increased presence in the 1950 publication, as the irony of Sally Mara's use of French and the text's novelistic structure require the conscious control of a higher diegetic level (at least until Sally Mara finally assumes this control for herself), a role that Michel Presle can no longer fill. Even without knowing the author's name, the reader can project on to this figure the aspects of authorship experienced by Sally Mara (partial autobiography, sublimation of desire) and by Michel Presle (partial control, experimentation, sexual interest). In light of Sally Mara's fragmented identification with the characters in her own novel (both male and female), it is not surprising to see more than one counterpart to the author, and we might also look for a degree of identification with the novel's other creative characters, such as the poet Padraic Baoghal, and Joël with his 'épopée fantastique' [fantastical epic] (163).

While the publication of the *JI* constitutes Sally Mara as a more substantial author-figure, and even a combined author-*œuvre* in the manner of Gide's *Journal*, it also introduces the central paradox of her existence: that the formal devices that establish her as an author-figure simultaneously limit her to a fictional, textual existence in her *journal intime* and at the margins of her literary work. This paradox is pursued to its extreme in the single volume of her *Œuvres complètes*, which literally forms her work into a 'livre unique' (to a greater extent than Gide's *Œuvres complètes* or *Journal*), and in which she directly confronts her *auteur supposant*, Raymond Queneau.

Les Œuvres complètes de Sally Mara

Queneau's name appeared explicitly as author for the first time on the cover of the 1962 publication of the *Œuvres complètes de Sally Mara*, relegating Sally Mara's name to the title. This edition demonstrates the importance of paratext to the interplay of the three signatories, as it brings about considerable changes in their positions in the diegetic framework, even though the eleven pages of *Sally plus intime* constitute the only substantial new work. Besides this, the volume includes a contents page, a bibliography (with only one, unpublished but apparently real, entry),[58] and a new preface, signed by Sally Mara. The two previous works, *OETTBALF* and the *JI*, are printed in the order in which Sally Mara allegedly wrote them rather than the order in which they were actually published (just as Gide's *Œuvres complètes* emphasize above all the continuity of the author's life and career). Paratextual convention makes this format and title page (with one author too

---

[57] Ibid., p. 18.   [58] Pouilloux, 'Notice' for *Les Œuvres complètes de Sally Mara*, pp. 1730–1.

many) into a parody of the edition of *œuvres complètes* and its claim to represent
the complete creative life of a writer. The volume adds even greater depth to the
character of Sally Mara while affirming her fictional status. Balancing this new
authority exerted by Queneau's name on the title page are the objections raised by
Sally Mara in her preface, which refutes his overall authorship.

Michel Presle's steady decline from the authority he wielded in 1947 culminates
in his death by paratext at Sally Mara's hands in this edition. Emulating Michel
Presle's former paratextual control, Sally Mara relegates him to a metadiegetic level
by quoting in full his preface to *OETTBALF* within the frame of her own preface,
denying all of his claims and stating that as a pseudonym of Queneau he is 'moins
que rien' [less than nothing] (8). However, trying to account for the different
manifestations of Michel Presle leads Sally Mara into grave contradictions. She
states that the Michel Presle who is the pseudonym of the 'soi-disant auteur réel'
[supposedly real author] and the one who appears as a character in the *JI* are
not the same, and that the latter was a figment of her imagination, although she
also accepts that she learnt important lessons from her 'bon imaginaire maître
Michel Presle' [fine imaginary teacher Michel Presle] (9). While insisting that the
biographical information contained in his preface is false, she does not dispute
the dates of her birth and death but rather claims that she was never born at all
(accepting her fictional status) and that she is still alive (insisting on her physical
reality 'à la corpulence près' [right down to her corpulence], 9). Unable to reconcile
her own and Michel Presle's existence on several different diegetic levels, she
exposes her own irreality while demonstrating that of Michel Presle.

Sally Mara responds in a similar way to the threat posed to her diegetic status by
Queneau's name on the front cover. Much like Michel Presle's original preface to
OETTBALF, the very presence of Raymond Queneau's signature (this time with
the explicit claim of authorship rather than as editor or translator) frames Sally
Mara's life and works and relegates them to a metadiegetic level, yet she herself
is capable of framing 'un personnage attaché [aux éditions Gallimard], un certain
Queneau' [a character attached to the éditions Gallimard, a certain Queneau] (7),
by using her preface to quote from a letter he has sent her, justifying the inclusion
in the *OCSM* of the spurious *SPI*: ' "Vous en faites pas, des inédits c'est au poil
pour faire avaler une réimpression, notre clientèle adore ça" et autres niaiseries
ejusdem farinae' ['Do not worry yourself about it, unpublished fragments are just
the stuff for flogging a reprint, our customers love that stuff,' and other nonsense
ejusdem farinae] (7). Raymond Queneau in turn is relegated to a metadiegetic level
by this paratextual framing device, which is used to characterize him as a fraud and
a deceitful profiteer. She also counters the authority of his signature on the front
cover (which also mentions his prestigious status as a member of the Académie
Goncourt) with that of her own signature on the preface:

> Ce n'est pas parce que le nom d'un auteur soi-disant réel figure sur la couverture d'un
> livre pour qu'il soit le véritable auteur des œuvres parues précédemment sous le nom
> d'un auteur prétendu imaginaire. Ce dernier n'a en effet rien d'imaginaire puisque
> c'est moi, signataire de la présente préface, et toute prétention à une plus grande réalité
> est ainsi réfutée *a priori, sine die, ipso facto* et *manu militari*. (7)

[Just because the name of an allegedly real author appears on the cover of a book, that does not mean that he is the genuine author of the works that had previously been published under the name of a supposedly imaginary author. In fact, the latter is not imaginary in the slightest, since it is I, signatory of this preface, and any claim to a greater reality is hereby refuted *a priori, sine die, ipso facto* and *manu militari*.]

Rather than raising her own diegetic status, the effect of this argument is to nullify any claim by Queneau to a greater reality by demonstrating the incapacity of the printed word to authenticate itself, in a way which illustrates Roland Barthes's remarks in *La Chambre claire*:

> le langage est, par nature, fictionnel; pour essayer de rendre le langage infictionnel, il faut un énorme dispositif de mesures: on convoque la logique, ou, à défaut, le serment;[59]

> [language is, by its very nature, fictional; to try to make language non-fictional, we need to call on a huge array of devices: we invoke the forces of logic, or failing that, oaths;]

Sally Mara's terms 'soi-disant' and 'prétendu' indicate that the status of the signatories is assured only by rhetoric, but if the full force of Sally Mara's Latin pseudo-erudition remains unconvincing, Raymond Queneau's own signature cannot claim any greater reality (at least, not from any resources to be found in this printed text).

The other issue at stake for the relative positions of Sally Mara and Raymond Queneau is the attribution of *SPI*. By including it in the collection, Queneau claims that it was written by Sally Mara (in the same fictional sense that he claims that she wrote *OETTBALF* and the *JI*), whereas she refuses to accept her 'droits maternels' [maternal rights] over the work (another authorial posture or metaphor to add to those evoked in the preceding works), and insists that it is Queneau's work (7). There are reasons for associating it with each of them. A reader could easily verify that some of these punning, fragmentary 'foutaises' had been published previously by Queneau,[60] and they bear many traces of his style, especially the 'Arithmétique affective' (344). Conversely, there are close correspondences with Sally Mara's *JI* and *OETTBALF*, both in style (such as the neologisms 'phallussait' and 'Gynéco-logis', 342 and 343) and through quotations ('Écrire pour la postériorité', 350, cf. *JI*, 23). The themes of reality and fictionality ('*Une vie*: Né en...—néant' [*A life*: Born in...—nothingness], 347) and of paratext ('Cette notice biographique l'avait complètement curriculum-vité' [This biographical note had him completely curriculum-vité'd], 341) could also be linked to both Queneau and Sally Mara, since both of them have by this stage demonstrated their awareness of these aspects of the texts.

The ambiguity of the attribution of *SPI* and of its relationship with the other works in the *OCSM* lends itself to several interpretations, which are not mutually exclusive (although in practice this has more often led to *SPI* being ignored even by

---

[59] Roland Barthes, *La Chambre claire: note sur la photographie*, in *OC* ([1980]), V, pp. 785–892, p. 858.

[60] Pouilloux, 'Notice' for *Les Œuvres complètes de Sally Mara*, pp. 1738–9.

those critics who have taken an interest in the other works). Van der Starre remarks upon the paradoxical nature of the title *Sally plus intime* for a work which, unlike the *Journal intime*, contains no personal revelations, and which only uses the word 'je' once.[61] Yet there is a sense in which this apparently impersonal work exceeds the others in *intimité*:

> sur le plan proverbial, c'est dans la troisième partie que Sally se surpasse: être de papier, être de langage créé pour produire du langage, c'est au plus profond de son intimité papetière qu'elle trouve cette quintessence du langage que sont les proverbes.[62]
>
> [Sally surpasses herself in the third part [*SPI*], in the realm of proverbs: a being of paper, a being of language created in order to produce language, it is therefore at the very heart of her papery *intimité* that she finds in proverbs this quintessence of language.]

In this light, *SPI* completes Sally Mara's trajectory as an artist in a way which resembles Faulkner's progression from the 'triple trivialité du recueil de poèmes, de l'autobiographie et du regard sur soi-même en tant qu'artiste' [triple triviality of the collection of poems, autobiography and reflection on oneself as an artist] to writing *The Sound and the Fury*, from which his 'origines "privées"' are absent (this had also been Queneau's trajectory as a writer).[63] This first interpretation treats Sally Mara as an experimental, fictional figure created in order to explore the life and artistic progression of a writer, which find their conclusion and 'consécration' in the unified 'livre unique' of a volume of *œuvres complètes*.

However, a different interpretation is required to take into account Sally Mara's and Raymond Queneau's mutual relationship with regard to *SPI*. The very symmetry of their equally convincing claims, each attributing authorship of the work to the other, reveals the convergence of their style and preoccupations by this point, although they still claim to be *autre*: Sally Mara refers to Queneau as 'l'autre' in her preface (7), whereas Queneau remarks in the introduction to *Moustiques* that 'tout auteur ressent plus ou moins lui-même l'hétérogénéité de son œuvre par rapport à sa "personnalité"' [every author feels to some extent the heterogeneity of his work in relation to his 'personality'].[64] By this interpretation, *SPI* demonstrates the paradoxical end point of literary creation: an identification of the author with the work, which nonetheless remains 'other'. This in turn produces one final complication in the diegetic framework of the Sally Mara works: if the author-figure of Raymond Queneau inhabits the same realm of paratext as Sally Mara and is no less an 'être de langage' than her, the reader is left with a curiosity as to who or what exists at a still higher diegetic level (if a language of diegesis even remains meaningful in this instance), and for whom the author-figure of Raymond Queneau is both same and other.[65]

---

[61] van der Starre, 'Sally Mara romancière?', p. 27.   [62] Ibid., p. 28.
[63] Queneau, '*Moustiques* de William Faulkner', p. 79.   [64] Ibid., p. 83.
[65] A similar distinction is found in Jorge Luis Borges, 'Borges and I', in *Labyrinths*, ed. by Donald Yates and James Irby, trans. by James Irby (London: Penguin, 1981), pp. 282–3.

IMPLICATIONS FOR DIARY-WRITING

In order to consider Queneau's formalist treatment of the legacy of Gide's diary-writing, I have examined what is changed or added to previous readings of these texts when Sally Mara is recognized as an *auteur supposé*, largely constituted by the publication of a *journal intime* and her *œuvres complètes*, rather than as a mere pseudonym for Queneau or the narrator of a diary novel. This approach reveals a complex relationship between the texts' three signatories, who establish their place in the diegetic framework by editing, translating, quoting, interpreting, or characterizing another person or text, and who struggle for authority and control through diverse processes of metalepsis. Their interplay over the course of the three publications leads to Michel Presle's transition from being an authoritative translator, editor, and suspected author to being prefaced ('curriculum-vité'?) out of existence, Sally Mara's maturation as an author and rise through the diegetic levels, and Queneau's eventual confrontation with his own creation. The project as a whole exposes the formal apparatus used in the construction of an author-figure, with the *journal intime* chief among them, yet it is also the *journal intime* that seems to resist the reduction of the author-figure to a purely textual, or fictional existence.

The relations between the three signatories and the metaleptic transgressions of the diegetic framework produce an effect of defamiliarization, which reveals the functioning of the author-figure as a device. This process corresponds closely to a well-known lecture on this subject, not Barthes's 'La Mort de l'auteur',[66] which claims to address a constitutive feature of written texts, but Foucault's 'Qu'est-ce qu'un auteur?', which addresses 'le principe éthique, le plus fondamental peut-être, de l'écriture contemporaine' [the ethical principle, perhaps the most fundamental one, of contemporary writing].[67] Foucault attempts to describe the textual *fonction-auteur* that is made visible, and vacant, by the supposed 'disparition de l'auteur' [disappearance of the author] from contemporary literature:[68]

> On en arriverait finalement à l'idée que le nom d'auteur ne va pas comme le nom propre de l'intérieur d'un discours à l'individu réel et extérieur qui l'a produit, mais qu'il court, en quelque sorte, à la limite des textes, qu'il les découpe, qu'il en suit les arêtes, qu'il en manifeste le mode d'être ou, du moins, qu'il le caractérise.[69]

> [We would finally come to the conclusion that the name of the author does not pass, like a proper noun, from the interior of a discourse to the real and exterior individual who produced it, but rather that it circulates, in a sense, at the boundaries of texts, that it delimits them, follows their ridges, that it manifests their mode of being or, at least, characterizes it.]

This description of the *fonction-auteur* accounts for the failure of the signatories of the Sally Mara works to authenticate their existence by reference to a reality beyond

---

[66] Roland Barthes, 'La Mort de l'auteur', in *OC* ([1968]), III, pp. 40–5.
[67] Michel Foucault, 'Qu'est-ce qu'un auteur?', in *Dits et écrits 1954–1988*, ed. by Daniel Defert and François Ewald, 2 vols (Paris: Gallimard, 2001), I, pp. 817–49, p. 817. First given as a lecture at a session of the Société française de philosophie, 22 February 1969.
[68] Ibid., p. 824.   [69] Ibid., p. 826.

the text (especially Sally Mara's futile attempts to do so in her preface), and also their roles in the paratexts and interstices between diegetic levels, determining the nature of the various narrative instances that make up the project as a whole.

Foucault refers to several of the formal aspects of the *fonction-auteur* that are foregrounded, to comic effect, in the Sally Mara works, but it is strange that he makes no mention of the *journal intime*, the very form that most effectively constitutes Sally Mara as an author-figure (whereas Barthes, in 'La Mort de l'auteur', refers to writers who, like Gide, are 'soucieux de joindre, grâce à leur journal intime, leur personne à leur œuvre' [careful to connect their own person to their work, by means of their *journal intime*]).[70] He does, however, make a comment that limits, or at least complicates, the reduction of the author-figure to a purely textual *fonction-auteur* (in contradiction to the main thrust of his argument), which seems particularly relevant to the Sally Mara works and even to their use of the *journal intime*:

> Il serait tout aussi faux de chercher l'auteur du côté de l'écrivain réel que du côté de ce locuteur fictif; la fonction-auteur s'effectue dans la scission même—dans ce partage et cette distance.[71]
>
> [It would be just as much of a mistake to seek the author on the side of the real writer as on the side of this fictional speaker; the author-function is enacted in the separation itself—in this sharing of roles and this distance.]

This 'partage' and 'distance' closely resemble the convergence and otherness of Sally Mara and Raymond Queneau in *SPI*, as well as the 'identification, sans en être, tout en étant' between the textual Raymond Queneau (an 'être de langage', like Sally Mara) and the imagined, intangible 'écrivain réel' of Queneau outside the works' diegetic structure.[72] Of all the devices of the *fonction-auteur*, it is precisely the *journal intime* that maintains this 'scission', owing to its marginal status—never fully a literary *œuvre*, nor fully under the artistic, authorial control of the diarist.

Even during these years of literary formalism, a literary *œuvre* remained the 'œuvre DE quelqu'un',[73] and the author-figure remained an elusive object for the reader's (perhaps inevitable, and certainly legitimate) curiosity and pursuit. The Sally Mara works share in the contemporary interest in the textual apparatus that produce this *œuvre* and author-figure, but they also intimate that diary-writing (in the forms explored by Gide) resists any complete reduction to a textual *fonction-auteur*, and will be instrumental when the time comes for a return to the writing subject.

---

[70] Barthes, 'La Mort de l'auteur', p. 41.
[71] Foucault, 'Qu'est-ce qu'un auteur?', p. 831.   [72] Queneau, 'Technique du roman', p. 24.
[73] Queneau, '*Moustiques* de William Faulkner', p. 83.

6

The Return of the Diary in Barthes's 'Vita Nova'

RETHINKING BARTHES AS A DIARIST

From Queneau's playful exploration of the diary as a part of the formal apparatus of the author-figure, I pass now to another author who is rarely thought of as a diarist, Roland Barthes.[1] I shall argue that Barthes's diary-writing in the late 1970s, notably the *Journal de deuil* and *Soirées de Paris* (published posthumously in 2009 and 1987 respectively), was central to the projects of the last few years of his life.[2] Barthes revisited his early interest in Gide's *Journal* during his foray into autobiographical writing with the 1975 work *Roland Barthes par Roland Barthes* (*RB par RB*),[3] and his focus subsequently shifted from autobiography towards diary-writing, as a way to consider his own position as an *écrivain* and the relation between his life and his literary work. This was an historical moment when some of the very same figures who had apparently banished the writing subject (or ignored it, or suppressed it, as the case may be) were exploring how it could return to the literary avant-garde, thereby producing some of the most influential and unusual works in the modern literary field of life-writing (which they helped to inaugurate).[4] Barthes's experimental diaries therefore provide a unique insight into the place of the *journal intime* in this return of the writing subject, particularly in relation to the dominant literary claims of autobiography.

Barthes was not alone in his new, or renewed, interest in the *journal intime*. Diary-writing as a private practice had continued unabated during the decades of high theory, but its reappearance as a successful published genre in the late 1970s, amid the more general emergence of life-writing, can usefully be compared with

---

[1] Since this research was undertaken, a collection of essays on Barthes's diary-writing has been published under the title *Deliberations: The Journals of Roland Barthes*, ed. by Neil Badmington (= *Textual Practice*, 30/2 (2016)). This collection involves a version of the present chapter ('Diary-Writing and the Return of Gide in Barthes's "Vita Nova"', pp. 241–66). Some closely related issues are treated in the articles by Antoine Compagnon ('Writing Mourning', pp. 209–19) and Diana Knight ('Barthes Deliberates: Pascal, Ignatius and the Question of the Diary', pp. 221–39).

[2] Roland Barthes, *Journal de deuil: 26 octobre 1977 – 15 septembre 1979* (Paris: Seuil, 2009). Roland Barthes, *Soirées de Paris*, in *OC* ([1987]), V, pp. 977–93.

[3] Roland Barthes, *Roland Barthes par Roland Barthes*, in *OC* ([1975]), IV, pp. 575–771.

[4] Self-reflexive and at least partially autobiographical works from the period include Georges Perec's Oulipian *W ou le souvenir d'enfance* (1975), Derrida's poststructuralist and psychoanalytic treatment in *La Carte postale* (1980), and, by the chief exponents of the *nouveau roman*, Sarraute's *Enfance* (1983) and Robbe-Grillet's *Le Miroir qui revient* (1984).

the 'date charnière' [pivotal date] (in Pierre Pachet's terms) of its success in the 1880s at a time of similar growth in 'littérature personnelle'.[5] At both these points in the diary's history, new, more ambitious editions were published of known diarists (the first 'édition intégrale' of Amiel's *journal intime* was published in twelve volumes from 1976, followed by substantial new editions of Bashkirtseff and Gide), and diaries from earlier periods came to light, both in posthumous publications (Sartre's *Carnets de la drôle de guerre*, 1983) and from living authors (Claude Mauriac's diaries starting from 1925, published in an unusual thematic arrangement under the collective title 'Le Temps immobile' from 1970).[6] Just as the popularity of the *journal intime* in the 1880s led to new forms and uses of diary-writing, Michel Braud finds an important new development in the 1978 publication of the first volume of Charles Juliet's *Journal*: it is 'l'un des premiers journaux, dans le champ littéraire, à avoir été publié par son auteur comme première œuvre et non après plusieurs volumes de fiction ou de poésie' [one of the first *journaux intimes*, in the literary field, to have been published by its author as a first work and not after several volumes of fiction or poetry], and therefore a 'journal-œuvre' in a different way from Gide's *Journal 1889–1939*.[7]

Barthes's importance in the history of life-writing more generally is already established. He played a role in the critique of the subject (in light of the Lacanian concept of the *Imaginaire*) and of the institution of the author (for which his own 1968 essay 'La Mort de l'auteur' is a landmark text).[8] Later in his career he experimented with the forms that life-writing could take in spite of these earlier objections, notably in *RB par RB* and his partly autobiographical reflection on photography, *La Chambre claire*.[9] But this 'death and return of the author', as it is termed by Seán Burke,[10] is also a repression and return of the strong influence that Barthes had received from Gide, manifested in the early article 'Notes sur André Gide et son "Journal"' (1942), and acknowledged again from 1975 onwards with reference to the phantasy of the author and the appeal of the *journal intime*.[11] Just as Gide's diary-writing is, in various forms, placed in relation to the novel as a way of mediating between life, the literary *œuvre*, and the author-figure, when Barthes turns to diary-writing it is inscribed within a global project or phantasy of a *Roman*,

[5] Pierre Pachet, *Les Baromètres de l'âme: naissance du journal intime* (Paris: Hatier, 1990), p. 124. Ferdinand de Brunetière, 'La Littérature personnelle', *La Revue des deux mondes*, 85 (1888), pp. 433–52, p. 434.

[6] Henri-Frédéric Amiel, *Journal intime*, ed. by Philippe Monnier and Anne Cottier-Duperrex, 12 vols (Lausanne: L'Âge d'homme, 1976). Marie Bashkirtseff, *Journal* (Paris: Mazarine, 1980). André Gide, *Journal*, rev. edn, 2 vols (Paris: Gallimard, Bibl. de la Pléiade, 1977). Jean-Paul Sartre, *Les Carnets de la drôle de guerre: novembre 1939–mars 1940* (Paris: Gallimard, 1983). Claude Mauriac, *Une Amitié contrariée* (Paris: Grasset, 1970).

[7] Michel Braud, '"Le texte d'un roman": journal intime et fictionnalisation de soi', *L'Esprit Créateur*, 42/4 (2002), pp. 76–84, p. 76. Charles Juliet, *Journal: 1957–1964* (Paris: Hachette, 1978).

[8] Roland Barthes, 'La Mort de l'auteur', in *OC* ([1968]), III, pp. 40–5.

[9] Roland Barthes, *La Chambre claire: note sur la photographie*, in *OC* ([1980]), V, pp. 785–892.

[10] Seán Burke, *The Death and Return of the Author: Criticism and Subjectivity in Barthes, Foucault and Derrida* (Edinburgh: Edinburgh University Press, 1992).

[11] Roland Barthes, 'Notes sur André Gide et son « Journal »', in *OC* ([1942]), I, pp. 33–46. Barthes, *RB par RB*, pp. 655, 672.

the 'Vita Nova' announced first in his inaugural lecture at the Collège de France on 7 January 1977.[12] This project aims to 'unifier une vie d'écriture' [unify a life of writing] with a new life and way of writing, and it culminates in the actual plans for a novel entitled *Vita Nova*.[13] To avoid confusion in the discussion that follows, I shall use quotation marks and italics respectively to distinguish between the broad project of a 'Vita Nova' that encompassed several areas of Barthes's work (also referred to by Barthes as a 'vita nuova') and the specific, planned work of *Vita Nova*.

My first task will be to demonstrate how the so-called 'death and return of the author' relates to a repression and return of Barthes's interest in Gide and the *journal intime*. This Gidean turn in Barthes's work leads us to the beginning of the 'Vita Nova', which develops over several years in lectures, seminar series, books, articles, journalistic writing, diaries, and the plans for *Vita Nova* itself. The unity of Barthes's work within the overall project of the 'Vita Nova' has not yet been sufficiently recognized, partly owing to the sporadic nature of the posthumous publication of these texts. Having established the context for Barthes's diary-writing, I shall examine his writing experiments across three works: the *Journal de deuil*, 'Délibération' (which, as well as being an essay on the *journal intime*, also contains two samples of his diary-writing),[14] and *Soirées de Paris*. The theoretical reflections of 'Délibération' act as a transition between the two principal diaries, which are also referred to in the plans for *Vita Nova* as forming a part of the projected novel. Using my analyses of the diaries, I shall consider the significance of this pairing within the ambitious imagined *Roman* that would never, in fact, come to fruition.

Barthes's premature death in 1980 interrupted the project of the 'Vita Nova', and had the consequence of leaving *RB par RB* and *La Chambre claire* as his main published contributions to the nascent field of life-writing. This chapter will show that Barthes's diary-writing was the sphere of his last reflections on and experimentation with the writing subject in literature, and can be considered in hindsight as a turning point in the history of the *journal intime*, marking its transition from a form subordinated to the dominant literary claims of the *roman*, towards an equally problematic role in relation to life-writing and its preoccupation with fiction.

'LE DERNIER BARTHES'

The Return of Gide

My discussion in Chapter 4 of Barthes's 'Notes sur André Gide et son *Journal*' characterized Barthes's early appreciation of Gide as follows: the fragmentary form that Barthes values in Gide's *Journal* and practises in his own article persists in

---

[12] Roland Barthes, *Leçon*, in *OC* ([1977]), V, pp. 427–46.

[13] Roland Barthes, *La Préparation du roman I et II: cours et séminaires au Collège de France (1978–1979 et 1979–1980)*, ed. by Nathalie Léger (Paris: Seuil, 2003), p. 32. Roland Barthes, *Vita Nova*, in *OC* ([1995]), V, pp. 1007–18. References are to the edited transcription, but a facsimile is also provided on pp. 994–1001.

[14] Roland Barthes, 'Délibération', in *OC* ([1979]), V, pp. 668–81.

much of his later writing, but his enthusiasm for Gide is formulated in terms of humanism, the author and his *œuvre*, *confession*, and *sincérité*, all of which make it unacceptable to Barthes's later 'sur-moi théorique'.[15] I shall not address here the reasons for the exclusion of the author-figure by critics associated with structuralism and the *nouvelle critique* of the 1950s and 60s, except to note that Barthes's own account in *La Préparation du roman* of an '*incuriosité* à l'égard de l'auteur' [lack of curiosity with regard to the author] followed by a 'retour de la curiosité' [return of curiosity] is a gross understatement of the theoretical principles that were at stake (as observed by Jonathan Culler).[16] However, Barthes seems more justified in presenting it as a '[refoulement] de l'auteur' [repression of the author] followed by a 'défoulement, ou "dé-refoulement" de l'auteur' [re-emergence, or 'de-repression' of the author].[17] An article by Barthes from 1966 responding to Alain Girard's foundational work of 1963, *Le Journal intime*, casts light on a similar 'refoulement' of Gide (whose name is surprisingly, and significantly, absent from the article) and of the *journal intime*.[18]

Barthes's article approves wholeheartedly of Girard's historical and sociological analysis of the *journal intime* leading up to its transformation into a genre with Gide's *Journal* (which Barthes avoids mentioning directly), but the real issue is the present state of the *journal intime*, and its future:

> Bien que le genre soit encore florissant par l'intérêt de lecture qu'il suscite, on peut risquer que la littérature d'aujourd'hui (celle du moins qui cherche des formes nouvelles) ne lui accorde plus beaucoup de crédit; ce sont surtout des écrivains d'une génération déjà ancienne ([François] Mauriac, [Julien] Green) qui tiennent encore leur journal; comme il est fréquent, c'est au moment où le genre est largement accepté par le public qu'il entre en crise au niveau de ses créateurs. (808–9)

> [Although the genre is still flourishing in terms of the interest that readers find in it, there is a risk that contemporary literature (or at least that which seeks new forms) no longer holds it in much esteem; it is mainly writers of a generation that has already passed ([François] Mauriac, [Julien] Green) who still keep their *journal intime*; as often happens, just at the moment when the genre becomes largely accepted by the public, it enters a period of crisis from the perspective of its creators.]

Barthes insists that it is for theoretical reasons that the literary avant-garde has abandoned the *journal intime*, because its *intimisme* and *psychologisme* are unacceptable to writers such as Philippe Sollers, for whom 'le *moi* ne peut plus se raconter parce qu'il n'est plus reconnu comme une entité (si difficile à saisir qu'elle soit apparue aux intimistes)' [the *self* can no longer be the subject of narrative because it is no longer recognized as an entity (however intangible it might have been to the *intimistes*)] (809). However, he also observes that the

---

[15] Barthes, *La Préparation du roman*, p. 276. I have treated this issue in greater depth in 'Forgetting Gide: A Study of Barthes's "Ursuppe"', *Barthes Studies*, 1 (2015). The relation between Gide and Barthes is also discussed by Tiphaine Samoyault in the chapter entitled 'Barthes et Gide' in *Roland Barthes: biographie* (Paris: Seuil, 2015), pp. 125–45.

[16] Jonathan Culler, 'Preparing the Novel: Spiraling Back', *Paragraph*, 31/1 (2008), pp. 109–20, p. 115.

[17] Barthes, *La Préparation du roman*, p. 276.

[18] Roland Barthes, 'Alain Girard: « Le Journal intime »', in *OC* ([1966]), II, pp. 806–10.

journal intime had contained the seeds of modern literary preoccupations, in a 'vaste dialectique qui unit l'écrivain contemporain à son passé' [vast dialectic that connects the contemporary writer to his past] (810). Not only had it '[mis en branle] la problématique de la personne' [set in motion the problematic of the person], which modern literature cuts through like a Gordian knot by an exclusion of the psychological subject, but it is also at the root of its 'réflexivité', or 'le pouvoir qu'a la littérature de réfléchir sur elle-même' [the capacity of literature to reflect upon itself] (809). While this dialectic process acknowledges a debt to the *journal intime*, it also offers the prospect of a return if there should ever be an end to the dogma that 'tient pour acquise la vérité des expériences de dépersonnalisation' [takes for granted the truth of the experiments with depersonalization] (809).

It is difficult to date the return of the subject in Barthes's work with any precision (the author-figure appears as early as 1971 in the fragmentary *biographèmes* of *Sade, Fourier, Loyola*, and Barthes later attributes his 'ébranlement du sur-moi théorique' [shifting of the theoretical super-ego] to the 1973 work *Le Plaisir du texte*), but the return of Gide and the *journal intime* undoubtedly takes place in 1975, with *RB par RB* and an accompanying *dossier* in the February issue of the *Magazine littéraire* (which reprints the 'Notes sur André Gide').[19] Here again I shall leave aside a discussion of the strategies by which this unconventional autobiography addresses the theoretical dogma that '*dans le champ du sujet il n'y a pas de référent*' [*in the field of the subject there is no referent*],[20] and of the writing of subjectivity in the two other works which Tzvetan Todorov identified (not long after Barthes's death) as completing the trilogy of 'le dernier Barthes' [late Barthes]: the 1977 *Fragments d'un discours amoureux* and the 1980 *La Chambre claire*.[21] I shall focus instead on the significance of Barthes's prominent identification with Gide in 1975.

Barthes claims in *RB par RB* that Gide is '[sa] langue originelle, [son] *Ursuppe*, [sa] soupe littéraire' [[his] original language, [his] *Ursuppe*, [his] literary soup], that he is, more than his first influence, his 'première posture' [first posture], and that 'ce premier vœu (je désire et je me voue) fonde un système secret de fantasmes qui persistent d'âge en âge, souvent indépendamment des écrits de l'auteur désiré' [this first vow (I desire and devote myself) establishes a secret system of phantasies which persists from age to age, often remaining independent of the writings of the desired author].[22] These phantasies relate to the author-figure that emerges from Gide's diary-writing, or 'l'écrivain tel que l'on peut le voir dans son journal intime, [...] *l'écrivain moins son œuvre*: forme suprême du sacré, la marque et le vide' [the writer as we see him in his *journal intime*, [...] *the writer without his œuvre*: the supreme form of the sacred, the mark and the void].[23] Accordingly, the texts referred to are all at least partly diaristic in nature: the *Journal* itself,

[19] Roland Barthes, *Sade, Fourier, Loyola*, in *OC* ([1971]), III, pp. 699–868. Barthes, *La Préparation du roman*, p. 276. Roland Barthes, *Le Plaisir du texte*, in *OC* ([1973]), IV, pp. 217–64.
[20] Barthes, *RB par RB*, p. 637.
[21] Tzvetan Todorov, 'Le Dernier Barthes', *Poétique*, 47 (1981), pp. 323–7. Roland Barthes, *Fragments d'un discours amoureux*, in *OC* ([1977]), V, pp. 25–296.
[22] Barthes, *RB par RB*, p. 677.
[23] Ibid., p. 656.

Les Cahiers d'André Walter, *Paludes* ('un grand livre moderne' [a great, modern book]), and *Les Nourritures terrestres*, which inspired Barthes's 1944 travel text 'En Grèce'.[24]

Barthes observes that his own practice of writing in fragments and short forms throughout his career derives from his early attachment to Gide and to his conviction, cited here from the 'Notes sur André Gide', that 'l'incohérence est préférable à l'ordre qui déforme' [incoherence is preferable to an order that would deform].[25] He now uses the fragment as a strategy to write subjectively while avoiding the traps of the *Imaginaire*, in the hope that 'en brisant [son] discours, [il] cesse de discourir imaginairement sur [soi]-même' [by interruping [his] discourse, [he] might cease to spin an imaginary discourse about [himself]].[26] This strategy too derives from Gide's *Journal*, where 'l'authenticité qui se déjoue elle-même, de l'authenticité retorse, qui n'est plus l'authenticité' [an authenticity that subverts itself, a devious authenticity, which is no longer authenticity] addresses the problems of the diary's *intimisme* and *psychologisme*, leading Barthes to the conclusion that 'la thématique du *Journal* est très proche de celle des fragments du *R.B. par lui-même*' [the thematic system of the *Journal* is very close to that of the fragments of *R.B. par lui-même*].[27] Furthermore, he now suspects a latent inclination towards the *journal intime* even in his non-diaristic use of the fragment (undated, unordered, or in an order other than the chronology of composition):

> Sous l'alibi de la dissertation détruite, on en vient à la pratique régulière du fragment; puis du fragment, on glisse au 'journal'. Dès lors le but de tout ceci n'est-il pas de se donner le droit d'écrire un 'journal'? Ne suis-je pas fondé à considérer tout ce que j'ai écrit comme un effort clandestin et opiniâtre pour faire réapparaître un jour, librement, le thème du 'journal' gidien?[28]

> [Under the pretext of disrupting the form of a treatise, we come to the regular use of the fragment: then from the fragment, we slip towards the 'journal'. But then is it not the aim of all this to give oneself permission to write a 'journal'? Am I not justified in considering everything that I have written as a clandestine and dogged attempt to bring back, one day, freely, the theme of the Gidean 'journal'?]

The later project of the 'Vita Nova' would involve identifications with other authors who held a perennial attraction for Barthes (Proust, Michelet, and Dante), but nonetheless the sudden public 'défoulement' of Gide's influence at this point is closely related to the beginning of Barthes's writing of subjectivity, and announces a progression in his experimentation from autobiography (however unconventional) to the *journal intime*.

---

[24] Roland Barthes, 'Dossier', *Magazine littéraire*, 97 (February 1975), pp. 20–37, pp. 26, 35. Barthes, *RB par RB*, p. 677.
[25] *RB par RB*, p. 677.   [26] Ibid., p. 672.   [27] Barthes, 'Dossier', p. 35.
[28] Barthes, *RB par RB*, p. 672.

The 'Vita Nova'

It is still insufficiently recognized, several decades after Barthes's death, how much his late writing in various forms was unified by the guiding aims of the 'Vita Nova' project.[29] The following summary of its development and of the different spheres of its activity will provide the immediate context for Barthes's diary-writing. It will be useful to refer to the timeline of Barthes's composition and publication of the works concerned (figure 6.1, p. 168).

The 'Vita Nova' was first mentioned in Barthes's inaugural lecture at the Collège de France on 7 January 1977, later published as *Leçon*:

> Bref, périodiquement, je dois renaître, me faire plus jeune que je ne suis. À cinquante ans, Michelet commençait sa *vita nuova*: nouvelle œuvre, nouvel amour. Plus âgé que lui (on comprend que ce parallèle est d'affection), j'entre moi aussi dans une *vita nuova*, marquée aujourd'hui par ce lieu nouveau, cette hospitalité nouvelle.[30]

> [In short, from time to time, I must be reborn, make myself younger than I really am. At fifty years of age, Michelet began his *vita nuova*: new work, new love. I am older than him (clearly this parallel is a relation of affection), and I too am embarking on a *vita nuova*, marked today by this new place, this new hospitality.]

The *cours* [lecture courses] at the Collège de France were themselves to play an important role in the 'Vita Nova', often exploring problems that were raised or pursued elsewhere. The project's terms were not fully developed at this early stage, but two ideas from this lecture have far-reaching relevance for Barthes's later work. The first is a desire for a new 'pratique d'écrire' [writing practice] (433), a fundamental change in his way of writing that goes beyond a merely doctrinal or ideological shift. The second is his assertion that 'à l'origine d'un enseignement comme celui-ci, il faut accepter de toujours placer un fantasme' [at the starting point of a teaching process such as this, one must always accept to place a phantasy] (445). He does not yet introduce the particular phantasy that he is to explore, but this pursuit of a phantasy that may not, or perhaps cannot be fulfilled, later comes to govern the whole of the 'Vita Nova'.

One subsequent event gave greater urgency and specificity to the project. On 25 October 1977 Barthes suffered the loss of his mother, and began a period of intense mourning that continued until his own death two and a half years later. In his writing, the most direct response to this event was to begin the *Journal de deuil*, which also led to the composition of *La Chambre claire* and *Soirées de Paris*.

---

[29] The most complete study of the development of Barthes's work at the Collège de France is Lucy O'Meara's *Roland Barthes at the Collège de France* (Liverpool: Liverpool University Press, 2012). Some other perspectives on this work are collected in a special issue entitled 'Roland Barthes Retroactively: Reading the Collège de France Lectures', ed. by Jürgen Pieters and Kris Pint (= *Paragraph*, 31/1 (2008)). The close relation between *Soirées de Paris* and Barthes's eight sheets of plans for a work entitled *Vita Nova* is examined in detail by Diana Knight, 'Idle Thoughts: Barthes's *Vita Nova*', *Nottingham French Studies*, 36/1 (1997), pp. 88–98. The relation between the *Journal de deuil* and *La Chambre claire* is discussed by Éric Marty, *Roland Barthes: la littérature et le droit à la mort* (Paris: Seuil, 2010) and Neil Badmington, '*Punctum saliens*: Barthes, Mourning, Film, Photography', *Paragraph*, 35/3 (2012), pp. 303–19.

[30] Barthes, *Leçon*, p. 446.

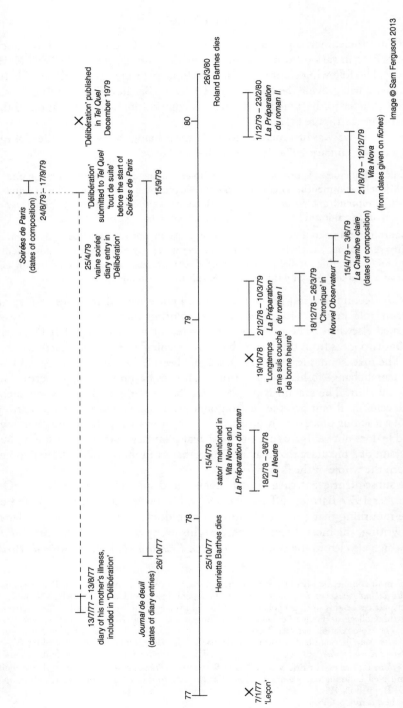

Figure 6.1. Timeline of works relating to Barthes's 'Vita Nova'

Image © Sam Ferguson 2013

Soirées de Paris
(dates of composition)
24/8/79 – 17/9/79

'Délibération'
submitted to *Tel Quel*
'tout de suite'
before the start of
Soirées de Paris

'Délibération' published
in *Tel Quel*
December 1979

25/4/79
'vaine soirée' diary entry in
'Délibération'

15/9/79

26/3/80
Roland Barthes dies

1/12/79 – 23/2/80
*La Préparation
du roman II*

21/8/79 – 12/12/79
Vita Nova
(from dates given on *fiches*)

80

13/7/77 – 13/8/77
diary of his mother's illness,
included in 'Délibération'

Journal de deuil
(dates of diary entries)
26/10/77

15/4/79 – 3/6/79
La Chambre claire
(dates of composition)

18/12/78 – 26/3/79
'Chronique' in
Nouvel Observateur

2/12/78 – 10/3/79
*La Préparation
du roman I*

79

19/10/78
"Longtemps
je me suis couché
de bonne heure'

25/10/77
Henriette Barthes dies

satori mentioned in
Vita Nova and
La Préparation du roman

15/4/78

18/2/78 – 3/6/78
Le Neutre

78

7/1/77
'Leçon'

77

However, since the publication of the *Journal de deuil* in 2009, the echoes between this diary and numerous other works have made it apparent that every part of the 'Vita Nova' is inflected to some extent with Barthes's mourning.

A second lecture at the Collège de France given on 19 October 1978, '"Long-temps, je me suis couché de bonne heure"', gives the most complete account of the aims of the 'Vita Nova'.[31] The lecture introduces the phantasy of writing an ambitious *Roman* that is to guide the *cours* on *La Préparation du roman* beginning the following December, and also establishes that, beyond the *cours*, the project henceforth involves all of Barthes's life and work. A contemporary audience did not have access to all these other areas of his work, but an awareness of their interconnected nature is demonstrated by the fact that those attending the *cours* also followed Barthes's *chronique* in the *Nouvel Observateur*,[32] in which he pursued 'une expérience d'écriture, la recherche d'une forme' [an experiment in writing, the search for a form], and compared his journalistic writing to 'le fragment de journal intime'.[33]

The three authors associated with the radical change of the 'Vita Nova' are now present, Michelet, Dante, and Proust (Gide is important to the project overall, as his frequent occurrence in *La Préparation du roman* attests, but not to the concept of rebirth itself). Dante's influence is felt most strongly in Barthes's plans for *Vita Nova* (not so much Dante's own *Vita Nuova* as the poet's journey in *The Divine Comedy*), but at this point Proust assumes the greatest importance. Barthes identifies his own 'deuil unique et comme irréductible' [unique and as if irreducible mourning] (467) with Proust's period of 'accablement' [despondency] following his mother's death in 1905, when he was 'à la croisée de deux voies, de deux genres, tiraillé entre deux "côtés" [. . .]: le côté de l'Essai (de la Critique) et le côté du Roman' [at the intersection of two paths, two genres, torn between two 'ways' [. . .]: the way of the Essay (of Criticism) and the way of the Novel] (460), and before he succeeded in joining these two 'côtés' in the *Recherche*. Barthes, now viewing all his own past work as essayistic writing varying only by 'théorie' or 'méthode', deems that his 'vie nouvelle' can be realized only by 'la découverte d'une nouvelle pratique d'écriture' [the discovery of a new writing practice] (467), imagined as a 'Roman (fantasmé, et probablement impossible)' [Novel (phantasized, and probably impossible)] (469). The form of this *Roman* develops throughout the 'Vita Nova', but for the moment Barthes wishes for it to convey 'la vérité des affects, non celle des idées' [the truth of affects, not of ideas] and to 'dire ceux qu'on aime, [. . .] témoigner qu'ils n'ont pas vécu (et bien souvent souffert) "pour rien"' [speak of those whom one loves, [. . .] bear witness that they did not live (and often suffered) 'for nothing'], offering as examples the writing of 'la maladie de la mère de Proust' [the illness of Proust's mother] and 'la détresse de Madeleine Gide (dans *Et nunc manet in te*)' [the plight of Madeleine Gide (in *Et nunc manet in te*)] (469).

---

[31] Roland Barthes, '« Longtemps, je me suis couché de bonne heure »', in *OC* ([1978 as lecture at Collège de France, first printed 1982]), V, pp. 459–70, henceforth referred to as 'Longtemps'.
[32] Barthes, *La Préparation du roman*, p. 17.
[33] Roland Barthes, 'La Chronique', in *OC* ([1978–79]), V, pp. 625–53, p. 652.

Near the end of the lecture, Barthes states his new 'méthode' for the 'Vita Nova':

> Je me mets en effet dans la position de celui qui fait quelque chose: je n'étudie pas un produit, j'endosse une production; j'abolis le discours sur le discours; le monde ne vient plus à moi sous la forme d'un objet, mais sous celle d'une écriture, c'est-à-dire d'une pratique (470)

> [I am putting myself in the position of someone who is making something: I am not studying a product, I am undertaking the process of production; I am abolishing discourse on discourse; the world will no longer present itself to me in the form of an object, but in the form of writing, that is, as a practice]

He envisages a new relation between *vie*, *écriture*, and *œuvre*, whereby writing becomes a *pratique* and the world is experienced as *écriture*. This aspect of the project derives from the *satori* which Barthes had experienced on the 15 April 1978, described in *La Préparation du roman* and referred to throughout the plans for *Vita Nova*, a 'conversion "littéraire"' comparable to that of the narrator in *Le Temps retrouvé*, and in which Barthes resolves to 'entrer en littérature, en écriture [...]: image de joie, si je me donnais à une tâche unique, telle que [...] tout instant de ma vie fût désormais travail intégré au Grand Projet' [enter into literature, into writing [...]: an image of joy, if I were to give myself a single task, such that [...] every moment of my life would henceforth be integrated in the labour of the Great Project].[34] This desire to 'unifier une vie d'écriture' makes both the *roman* and the *journal intime* important forms within the 'Vita Nova', both traditionally endowed with a marginal literary status and a closeness to everyday life and language (even if the *roman* had achieved a canonical status, its mythical characteristics are more important in this case, as presented, for example, in Bakhtin's *Esthétique et théorie du roman*).[35] It is therefore unsurprising that Barthes alludes to the complex diaristic and novelistic structure of Gide's *Les Faux-monnayeurs* and *Le Journal des Faux-monnayeurs* when addressing the problem of the 'Rivalité, conflit entre le Monde (la Vie) et l'Œuvre' [Rivalry, conflict between the World (Life) and the Œuvre] in *La Préparation du roman*.[36]

A final note is needed regarding the plans for *Vita Nova*, whose composition coincides with the end of the *Journal de deuil* and the full duration of *Soirées de Paris*. The eight *fiches* of these plans are as many attempts to coordinate the various motifs and forms of the project within a single structure, and I shall discuss their significance for the two diaries at the end of this chapter. However, it is unclear exactly what status to attribute to these documents, and more specifically, to what extent they can be seen as forming a conclusion to the overall 'Vita Nova' project. I shall return to this issue in more detail, but for now it will suffice to say that all we can do is to follow Barthes's writing up to the point when his life and work

---

[34] Barthes, *La Préparation du roman*, p. 32.
[35] Mikhail Mikhaïlovich Bakhtin, *Esthétique et théorie du roman* (Paris: Gallimard, 1978), known in English by the title *The Dialogic Imagination*. See *La Préparation du roman*, pp. 275–80, for a discussion of the integration of an author's life in his or her literary work, including by means of the *journal intime* (a footnote explains that Barthes did not deliver this material in the lecture itself).
[36] Barthes, *La Préparation du roman*, p. 275.

were curtailed by the contingency of the accident that led to his death. This means resisting two distinct temptations. First, it is futile to speculate about where the project might have led Barthes if circumstances had been different, or what role he might have played in the subsequent development of diary-writing (if Barthes were this predictable, he would be a much less interesting writer). Secondly, it would be a fallacy to interpret the abrupt end of his work as a part of the project itself, as if Barthes's death were integral to the project's internal logic. This might seem obvious, but it is at odds with the approach taken by two Barthes scholars, Éric Marty (who reads deeply into an essentially 'posthume' [posthumous] quality of Barthes's writing in the 'Vita Nova') and Marie Gil (whose biography of Barthes is premised on treating the circumstances of his life, and also his death, as a text, and therefore entirely subject to textual interpretation).[37]

THE DIARIES

The *Journal de deuil*

Since its publication in 2009, the *Journal de deuil* has proved to be very useful for the light it casts on other parts of the 'Vita Nova'.[38] However, my immediate concern is with the diary itself, as a writing project that develops from Barthes's Gidean influence in *RB par RB* and pursues the aim of the 'Vita Nova' for a 'nouvelle pratique d'écriture'.[39] The initial terms of this project are established by the choice of form and writing practice, and by the entries of the first two days. From this beginning, the diary explores the possibility of an *écriture* in response to the experience of mourning, which could take two distinct forms: the writing of a separate *œuvre* (these efforts are directed towards the composition of *La Chambre claire*), and the writing of the present diary itself. These two strands of the *écriture* of mourning eventually lead Barthes to an appraisal of his diary-writing in 'Délibération', and then to the very different writing project of *Soirées de Paris*.

The entries of the *Journal de deuil* were written on a series of 331 *fiches* [index cards] that Barthes prepared himself by cutting sheets of paper into four. It was found in a filing cabinet containing 13,000 *fiches* of the same format, which were written and re-ordered in a process of 'perpétuelle recomposition' throughout Barthes's career, and used in the production of his fragmentary works.[40] It is therefore associated with this earlier use of the fragment, but distinguished from it

[37] Marty defines 'l'œuvre posthume' rather expansively as 'ce qui rend plus proches l'œuvre, la littérature et l'espace de la mort' [that which brings closer together the *œuvre*, literature, and the space of death]; Marty, *Roland Barthes: la littérature et le droit à la mort*, p. 18. Marie Gil, *Roland Barthes: au lieu de la vie* (Paris: Flammarion, 2012).

[38] In particular, see two texts belonging to a dossier on Barthes in Le Magazine Littéraire, 482 (January 2009): Laurent Nunez, 'Vie nouvelle, roman virtuel', pp. 74–5, and Valérie Marin La Meslée and Nathalie Léger, 'Journal de deuil: « Chaque fiche est une figure du chagrin »', pp. 84–6.

[39] Barthes, 'Longtemps', p. 467.

[40] Marin La Meslée and Léger, *'Journal de deuil*: « Chaque fiche est une figure du chagrin »', pp. 84–6, pp. 84–5.

by its strictly chronological (and so diaristic) order, and by the unifying effect of the individual *fiches* that provide the work's title and subtitles ('Journal de deuil' [Mourning diary], 'Suite du journal' [Continuation of the diary], and 'Nouvelle suite du journal' [New continuation of the diary]). Yet it is also very different from the diary that precedes it, which coincides with the period of his mother's illness and is cited in 'Délibération'. Whereas this earlier diary is broadly typical of the *journal intime* (a single, fairly long entry for most days, relating banal events and varied reflections), the *Journal de deuil* contains unusually short entries with relatively little narrative of events from the past day, and there are frequently several notes for a single date, without any clear continuity between them. In this respect, it is significant that in the *Journal de deuil* he refers to this earlier diary as his 'journal de cet été' [*journal* from this summer] (72), while the *Journal de deuil* itself is usually referred to as 'ces notes' [these notes] (17, 27, 40, 224) and only once as a 'journal' (163), aside from the title and subtitles. In summary, Barthes's commitment to a chronological arrangement is indisputably diaristic, and his diary-writing practice is even in some ways quite commonplace ('en prenant ces notes, je me confie à la *banalité* qui est en moi' [as I write these notes, I entrust myself to the *banality* that is within me], 27), but by making a clear break with his earlier diary-writing he undertakes a new form of writing, more closely associated with his work as an *écrivain*.

Barthes writes on 26 October 1977, the day after his mother's death, 'Première nuit de noces. / Mais première nuit de deuil?' [First wedding night. / But first mourning night?] (13). This attaches the diary and the *deuil* to the 'Vita Nova' already mentioned in *Leçon* with reference to Michelet's 'vita nuova' starting from his marriage in middle age.[41] The implications of this identification emerge as the diary progresses. First, contrary to the expectations of those around him, his *deuil* is to be a permanent, productive, and creative state, rather than a steady return to normality. Secondly, his *deuil* is to entail an abandonment of his former desires and the construction of new ones, involving not only his affection for his deceased mother, but also his sexual desires and his relation to writing. This first entry also situates the writing of the diary in the night, a time of desires, privacy, and leisure, in opposition to the work of the daytime. This is an important difference from the writing practice of *Soirées de Paris*, to which I shall return.

The nine entries of the diary's second day concisely set out the main elements to be pursued throughout the *Journal de deuil*. I shall comment briefly on each in turn in order to provide an overview of the diary's disparate and discontinuous reflections. The first develops the analogy of his *deuil* with 'noces' ('J'ai connu le corps de ma mère malade, puis mourante' [I have known my mother's body when it was ill, then dying], 14). The second introduces his identification with Proust's mourning for his mother, by a subtle allusion to the opening passage of the *Recherche* ('Elle disait avec soulagement: la nuit est enfin finie (elle a souffert la nuit, seule, chose atroce)' [She would say with relief: the night is finally over

---

41 Barthes, *Leçon*, p. 446.

(she had suffered during the night, a terrible thing)], 15). The third comments on the productive aspect of his *deuil*, his 'construction affolée de l'avenir' [manic construction of the future] (16). The fourth poses the question of what literary use or value the diary might have: 'Qui sait? Peut-être un peu d'or dans ces notes?' [Who knows? Perhaps there is a little gold in these notes?] (17). The fifth opposes his state to the doxa of a psychoanalytic, pathological model of *deuil* and *dépression*: 'S'il y a travail, celui qui sera accouché n'est pas un être *plat*, mais un être *moral*, un sujet de la *valeur*—et non de l'intégration' [If there is labour, the one who would be born is not a *blank* being, but a *moral* being, a subject of *value*—and not one of integration] (18). The sixth introduces a theme which will develop into a reflection on his own mortality and the immortality of an *œuvre* as a 'monument'. The seventh establishes the problem of finding a language for his *deuil* that can convey anything of this private experience to others, from among the 'signes dérisoires, contradictoires' [paltry, contradictory signs] at his disposal (20). The eighth returns to the theme of his mortality, but is also the first example of his use of metalanguage to comment on the repeated words of his *deuil*: 'Et pourtant, contradiction: ce "jamais plus" n'est pas éternel puisque vous mourrez vous-même un jour' [And yet, a contradiction: this 'never more' is not eternal since you yourself will die one day] (21). The ninth entry announces the scale and significance of the *travail* which lies ahead: 'C'est, ici, le début solennel du grand, du long deuil' [This, then, is the solemn beginning of the great, long mourning] (22).

These open-ended beginnings of the diary contain within them a project for Barthes's mourning to be a new start, an active process of construction, in which he will struggle—through some alchemy of writing—to extract the literary gold from the 'signes dérisoires' of his *deuil*. This project is pursued in parallel in two distinct strands, one that aims to produce a separate *œuvre* for which the diary is a preparation, and another that envisages the diary itself taking on this literary status.

Most of Barthes's explicit comments on writing in response to his mother's death belong to a gradual development leading to the composition of *La Chambre claire* (from 15 April to 3 June 1979), and appraising this work once it has been completed. For the first few months of the diary this development is extremely tentative. Barthes initially remarks that, prior to her death, his mother and the writing of his *œuvre* had occupied different parts of his life, and that 'elle se faisait transparente pour qu['il] puisse écrire' [she used to make herself transparent so that [he] could write] (26). He later recognizes that she already occupies a discreet place in his *œuvre*, and he expresses pleasure that 'beaucoup de gens (lointains) avaient perçu ce qu'elle était, ce que nous étions, par son mode de présence dans le "RB"' [many (distant) people had understood what she was, what we were, by the nature of her presence in the 'RB'] (59). A month into the diary he begins to feel 'l'image de l'écriture comme "chose qui fait envie", havre, "salut", projet, bref "amour", joie' [the image of writing as 'something desirable', haven, 'salvation', project, in short 'love', joy] (69). The vagueness of his desire to write at this stage is indicated by the list of terms, the use of asyndeton, and the smattering of quotation marks which distance him from the worn-out concepts of others, but he nonetheless comes to attach this desire to a '*Vita nova*, comme geste radical' [*Vita nova*, as a radical gesture] (84).

In March 1978 Barthes resolves to '[se] mettre au livre sur la Photo' [set to work on the book on Photography] and thereby to 'intégrer [son] chagrin à une écriture' [integrate [his] suffering in a writing project] (115). Over almost a year this project becomes gradually more specific. It is conceived at first as another instance in which 'l'écriture transforme en [lui] les "stases" de l'affect, dialectise les "crises"' [writing transforms [in him] the various 'stases' of affect, dialectizes [his] 'crises'], and he lists the works from his previous *œuvre* which correspond to other crises in his private life (115). He identifies the *travail* of his *écriture* with the '"Travail" au sens analytique (Travail du deuil, du Rêve)' ['Work' in the psychoanalytic sense (Work of mourning, Dream-work)], asserting that, in his case, the *travail* of mourning 'n'est *accompli* que dans et par l'écriture' [is *accomplished* only in and through writing] (143). Having previously become 'reconnu' [recognized] as a *sujet* through his books, he will begin again with the present work, in order to 'faire reconnaître mam.' [make his mother be recognized] in a literary 'monument' (144–5). On 13 June he is 'bouleversé' [overwhelmed] by the discovery of the 'photo du Jardin d'hiver' [photograph from the Winter Garden], and begins to elaborate on the central place it will occupy in *La Chambre claire*. Much remains to be said about the relationship between the *Journal de deuil* and *La Chambre claire*, but it will suffice to note here that it is invested with great importance and high expectations as the single *œuvre* to emerge from the *travail* of Barthes's mourning.[42]

Given these expectations, it is hardly an indictment of the merits of *La Chambre claire* that its completion is followed by disillusionment:

> Tous les 'sauvetages' du Projet échouent. Je me retrouve sans rien à faire, sans aucune œuvre devant moi—sauf les tâches répétées de la routine. Toute forme du Projet: molle, non résistante, coefficient faible d'énergie. 'À quoi bon?'
> —C'est comme si advenait maintenant avec clarté (retardé jusqu'ici par des leurres successifs) le retentissement solennel du deuil sur la possibilité de faire une œuvre.
> Épreuve majeure, épreuve adulte, centrale, décisive du deuil. (22 July 1979, 248)

[All the Project's attempts at 'salvation' have failed. I find myself with nothing to do, without any work ahead of me—except the repeated tasks of routine. Any form of the Project: limp, without resistance, a feeble coefficient of energy. 'Why bother?'
—It is as if my mourning had just clearly rung out the death knell (delayed until now by successive illusions) for the possibility of producing an *œuvre*.
A major trial, an adult trial, the central, decisive trial of mourning.]

The aims of *La Chambre claire* turn out to have been a 'leurre' [lure, trap, illusion], and the few entries leading up to the final note on 15 September, repeating the same words and the same experiences of *deuil* from the earlier parts of the diary, give the strong impression that his *travail* has not been completed,

---

[42] The relationship between these two works is treated at greater length in Badmington, '*Punctum saliens*: Barthes, Mourning, Film, Photography' and Marty, *Roland Barthes: la littérature et le droit à la mort*.

that he has not managed to 'faire passer [son deuil] d'un état statique (stase, engorgement, récurrences répétitives de l'identique) à un état fluide' [make [his mourning] progress from a static state (stasis, obstruction, recurrence of the same thing) to a fluid state] (154). *La Chambre claire* is far from being a failure, but it does not resolve the question of the *œuvre* that is to emerge from Barthes's mourning.

The second strand of Barthes's *écriture* of mourning, the writing of the diary itself, is addressed more obliquely than his plans for *La Chambre claire*, owing to his continuing ambivalence towards the literary status of the *journal intime*. Nonetheless, diary-writing offers a different solution from the attempt to 'dialectiser' his mourning in the more autobiographical form of *La Chambre claire*: the possibility of directly manifesting the *travail* of his *deuil*. This partly explains why the diary reflects the progress of Barthes's mourning itself, 'discontinu' (77), 'chaotique' (41), and 'immobile' (50). However, the specific relationship between the *travail* of Barthes's *deuil* and its manifestation in the language and writing of the diary is more problematic than this. Despite the diary's frequent objections to the psychoanalytic model of mourning (for Barthes this involves not only Freud's 'Mourning and Melancholia' but also the theories of Lacan), his *deuil* is conceived as being a linguistic and partly unconscious process, involving his relation to the loved object:

> Ainsi puis-je cerner mon deuil. [...] Il est là où se redéchire la relation d'amour, le 'nous nous aimions'. Point le plus brûlant au point le plus abstrait... (47)

> Mon deuil est celui de la relation aimante et non celui d'une organisation de vie. Il me vient par les mots (d'amour) surgis dans ma tête... (49)

> [In this way I can grasp my mourning. [...] It is found where our loving relationship is torn apart, the 'we loved one another'. The most painful point at the most abstract point...

> My mourning is that of the loving relationship and not that of an organization of life. It comes to me through the words (of love) that arise in my head...]

Barthes is fully aware of the illusions of the Lacanian *Imaginaire* and of the constitutive alterity of language, yet the act of writing about his mourning is experienced as a movement from the particular to the general, which can bring about both consolation and a sense of alienation:

> Je ne puis supporter qu'on *réduise*—qu'on *généralise*—Kierkegaard—mon chagrin: c'est comme si *on* me le volait. [a footnote elucidates the reference to Kiergegaard: 'Dès que je parle, j'exprime le général, et si je me tais nul ne peut me comprendre.'] (81)

> Mais—sans doute—[mon chagrin est supportable] parce que je peux, tant bien que mal (c'est-à-dire avec le sentiment de ne pas y arriver) le parler, le phraser. Ma culture, mon goût de l'écriture me donne ce pouvoir apotropaïque, ou d'*intégration*: j'*intègre** [footnote: 'faire entrer dans un ensemble—fédérer—socialiser, communiser, se grégariser.'], par le langage. (187)

> [I cannot stand it when someone *reduces*—or *generalizes*—Kierkegaard—my suffering: it seems as if *they* are stealing it from me. [footnote: 'As soon as I speak, I express generalities, and if I remain silent then noone can understand me.']

But—undoubtedly—[my suffering is endurable] because I can, with difficulty (that is, with the impression that I am not succeeding) speak it, put it into words. My culture, my taste for writing gives me this apotropaic power, or a power of *integration*: I *integrate** [footnote: 'make something enter into a whole—federate—socialize, communize, make it gregarious.'], through language.]

The difficulty he faces is therefore in expressing his grief without it being devalued or denatured in the process. This task is made more hopeful by the impression that the particularity of his mourning is peculiarly diaristic in character. His *deuil* is 'l'accomplissement de l'intériorité absolue' [the accomplishment of absolute interiority] (167), while his *chagrin* is 'un bien essentiel, intime' [an essential, intimate possession] (175), and also 'banal' (233). His typically diaristic gesture of renouncing active (autobiographical) self-representation to '[se] confier à la *banalité* qui est en [lui]' [entrust [himself] to the *banality* that is within [him]] (27) therefore raises the possibility for the unconscious *travail* of mourning to make the difficult transition to written language in the *journal intime*.[43]

Whether or not this expression is possible, it is also unclear what its literary status might be:

Je ne veux pas en parler par peur de faire de la littérature—ou sans être sûr que c'en ne sera pas—bien qu'en fait la littérature s'origine dans ces vérités. (33)

[I don't want to speak of it for fear of making literature from it—or without being sure of not doing so—even though literature has its origins in these truths.]

The problem Barthes faces is not that the diary has no literary value, but rather that it might be inappropriate for these 'mots (d'amour) surgis dans [sa] tête' to be placed in a literary context, and therefore to suffer from an extreme form of the generalization and alienation mentioned earlier. This concern is balanced, in a gesture familiar from Gide's use of diary-writing, by suggesting that the 'vérités' of this diary could be central to a new conception of literature. This idea is also developed in 'Longtemps', with reference to the 'moments de vérité' that he finds in *War and Peace* and the *Recherche*, and as an aim of the 'Vita Nova' to convey 'la vérité des affects'.[44]

In practice, these attitudes towards the *écriture* of mourning give a privileged role to the diary's treatment of the words that seem to emerge spontaneously, and painfully, into consciousness, so that the diary becomes the continuation in writing of the unconscious *travail* of mourning. The words that recur most frequently are those of a short remembered dialogue between Barthes and his mother:

Revient sans cesse immobile le point brûlant: les mots qu'elle m'a dits dans le souffle de l'agonie, foyer abstrait et infernal de la douleur qui me submerge ('Mon R, mon R'—'Je suis là'—'Tu es mal assis'). (50)

---

[43] Barthes's expression recalls Éric Marty's account of an essentially diaristic act, when 'le sujet décide de confier au temps le soin de le dévoiler à lui-même' [the subject decides to entrust to time the task of revealing him to himself]; Éric Marty, *L'Écriture du jour: le 'Journal' d'André Gide* (Paris: Seuil, 1985), p. 11.

[44] Barthes, 'Longtemps', pp. 468–9.

Ce que j'appelle *spontanéité*: seulement cet état *extrême* où, par exemple, maman du fond de sa conscience affaiblie, ne pensant pas à sa propre souffrance, me dit 'Tu es mal, tu es mal assis' (parce que je l'évente assis sur un tabouret). (76)

je me mets à pleurer en pensant au mot de mam. qui me brûle et me dévaste toujours: mon R! mon R! (Je n'ai pu le dire à personne). (178)

J'écris mon cours et en viens à écrire *Mon Roman*. Je pense alors avec déchirement à l'un des derniers mots de mam.: *Mon Roland! Mon Roland!* J'ai envie de pleurer. (227)

[This seeringly painful point comes back to me incessantly, unchanged: the words she said to me in the breath of her agony, the abstract and infernal focus of the pain that overwhelms me ('My R, my R'—'I'm here'—'You're not sitting comfortably').

What I call *spontaneity*: only this *extreme* state when, for example, Maman, from the depths of her weakened consciousness, without thinking of her own suffering, says to me 'You're not, you're not sitting comfortably' (because I'm fanning her while sat on a stool).

I start crying when I think of the words of Mam., which always burn and destroy me: my R! my R! (I haven't been able to tell this to anyone).

I'm writing my lecture course and find myself writing *Mon Roman*. I then think with rending anguish of one of the last words of Mam.: *My Roland! My Roland!* I want to cry.]

These successive evocations of the same few words of dialogue illustrate the writing strategies employed for these and other 'mots (simples) de la Mort' [(simple) words of Death] (89), which represent a utopian ideal of a language characterized by 'spontanéité', univocality, and presence.

The gulf separating the diary from this unattainable ideal (although it may come closer than any other language at Barthes's disposal) is acknowledged in several ways. First, the words of mourning cannot be reproduced in their entirety. Barthes claims that he has not been able to repeat the remembered words of his mother to anyone (178, cited earlier), but even in the diary they are only ever written in a partial form. On every occasion but one, Barthes writes 'mon R' instead of 'mon Roland', while the only entry in which the words 'mon Roland' appear omits the rest of the dialogue from the scene (227). Other words of mourning are reproduced with an indication that they cannot be listed comprehensively:

Les mots (simples) de la Mort:
—'C'est impossible!'
—'Pourquoi, pourquoi?'
—'À jamais'
etc. (89)

[The (simple) words of Death:
—'It's impossible!'
—'Why, why?'
—'Forever'
etc.]

An ellipsis or 'etc.' often indicates that the diary's attempt to catalogue his mourning will always fall short.

Not only do the words of mourning resist being fully reproduced in the diary, but they are also resistant to any interpretation:

Maintenant, parfois monte en moi, inopinément, comme une bulle qui crève: la constatation: *elle n'est plus, elle n'est plus*, à jamais et totalement. C'est mat, sans adjectif—vertigineux parce qu'*insignifiant* (sans interprétation possible). (88)

[Now, occasionally I find rising up in me, unexpectedly, like a bursting bubble: the statement: *she is no more, she is no more*, forever and completely. It is flat, without qualification—dizzying, because it is *non-signifying* (without any possibly interpretation).]

The only two things that Barthes can positively say about them are the 'constatation' of their emergence ('beaucoup de neige sur Paris [...]. Je me dis et j'en souffre: elle ne sera jamais plus là pour le voir' [a lot of snow over Paris [...]. I say this to myself and suffer from it: she will never again be there to see it], 103), and the bodily effect that their emergence has on him, whether it 'brûle', 'dévaste', 'déchire', or makes him weep.

Yet the diary cannot completely relinquish a language of interpretation, owing to a further gulf between the supposedly univocal and fully present subject of the words of mourning and the inevitable multiplicity of voices in the diary. Besides the internalized voices of others and the division of the diarist's self by the use of the second person ('vous n'avez pas connu le corps de la femme' [you have never known a woman's body], 'vous mourrez vous-même un jour' [you too will die one day], 14, 21), both typical of the *journal intime* (see the earlier discussion of the 'other' in the *journal intime*, pp. 24–28), there is also, without fail, a form of metalanguage surrounding the words of mourning:

Dans la phrase 'Elle ne souffre plus', à quoi, à qui renvoie 'elle'? Que veut dire ce présent? (25)

'Je m'ennuie partout' (73)

[In the phrase 'She no longer suffers', to what, to whom does 'she' refer? What is the meaning of this present tense?

'I am bored wherever I go']

While this metalanguage often attempts in vain to interpret the words of mourning, its most basic functioning can be seen in the entry on page 73, cited in its entirety above, where it is reduced to the minimal state of a pair of quotation marks. These two small typographic characters relegate the words of mourning to a past time that does not coincide with the moment of writing, frame it within a second voice closer to the linguistic subject of the diarist, and illustrate Barthes's own observation that 'l'étonnant de ces notes, c'est un sujet dévasté en proie à la *présence de l'esprit*' [the astonishing thing about these notes is that they show a devastated subject who is a victim of *presence of mind*] (40).

Given that the diary's *écriture* of mourning follows the course of the 'vrai deuil insusceptible d'aucune dialectique narrative' [true mourning, not susceptible to any narrative dialectic] (60), and seems to reach towards an impossible, utopian, ideal of language, it may be surprising that the *Journal de deuil* does in fact come to a close and attain some of the closure associated with the literary *œuvre*. If any progress takes place across the diary, aside from its comments on the separate writing project that becomes *La Chambre claire*, it is a change towards a minimal state of language and then its eventual extinction, which Éric Marty describes as 'l'Odyssée d'une écriture vouée à s'éteindre' [Odyssey of a writing process destined to fade away]:[45]

> De moins en moins à écrire, à dire, sinon cela [mon R, mon R] (je ne puis le dire à personne). (50)
>
> J'écris de moins en moins mon chagrin mais en un sens il est plus fort, passé au rang de l'éternel, depuis que je ne l'écris plus. (226)
>
> Il y a des matinées si tristes… (255)
>
> [Less and less to write, to say, except that [my R, my R] (I can't say it to anyone).
>
> I write my suffering less and less, but in a sense it is stronger, transferred to the level of the eternal, since I have stopped writing it.
>
> Some mornings are so sad…]

Barthes comments on this process from early on, but towards the end of the diary the reduction of writing takes on a greater significance. It is now conceived as a movement towards an absolute state in which his *deuil* becomes 'éternel' in a different way to the 'monument' that *La Chambre claire* was supposed to be. The last citation above is the whole of the final entry of the *Journal de deuil*, which forms a transition to the silence, or absence of language, which follows it. It comes closer than any other entry to assuming the univocal and fully present subject of the words of mourning, while only the ellipsis suggests that these words do not coincide with the writing of the diary, that they are once again reproduced only in part, and that they continue after the writing of the diary has ceased.

'Délibération'

Barthes's article 'Délibération' constituted his only substantial, published discussion of the *journal intime*, as well as the only publication of his diaries in his lifetime. Upon the publication of *Soirées de Paris* in the 1987 collection *Incidents*, it was recognized that 'Délibération' provided a form of introduction to this diary, which was composed immediately after Barthes had submitted the article to the journal *Tel Quel*.[46] It is a strange work in several ways: it involves a rapid movement between the sort of non-committal formulations that Jonathan Culler describes as 'disposable typologies', and the article also differs considerably in its treatment of the Mallarméen concepts of the *Album* and the *Livre*, compared with the extensive

---

[45] Marty, *Roland Barthes: la littérature et le droit à la mort*, pp. 23–4.

[46] François Wahl, introduction to Barthes, *Incidents*, ed. by François Wahl (Paris: Seuil, 1987), pp. 7–10, p. 9. Samoyault specifies that a letter from Philippe Sollers to Barthes, in which he expressed his appreciation of the second diary excerpt in 'Délibération', motivated Barthes to pursue the diary-writing project suggested by the article, leading to the composition of *Soirées de Paris*; Tiphaine Samoyault, *Roland Barthes: biographie* (Paris: Seuil, 2015), p. 494.

discussion of these same terms in *La Préparation du roman*.[47] I would argue that the peculiarities of 'Délibération' are largely due to its role as a transition between the *Journal de deuil* and *Soirées de Paris*, and the fact that this role has to be obscured, owing to the essentially private nature of the *Journal de deuil*, which was then nearing its conclusion. A brief account of the article's logical progression will elucidate this transitional role.

The ostensible starting point for Barthes's discussion of the *journal intime* is the fairly conventional type of diary-writing that he had previously engaged in, sporadically, and without any 'consistance doctrinale' [doctrinal coherence] (668).[48] The 'envie légère, intermittente, sans gravité' [mild desire, intermittent, without gravity] that motivates this writing evidently does not have anything in common with the writing project of the *Journal de deuil*, nor does Barthes's dissatisfaction with 'l'artifice de la "sincérité"' (an allusion to Gide) and 'la médiocrité artistique du spontané' [the artistic mediocrity of the spontaneous] (668). Nonetheless, the central issue of the article emerges directly from the conclusion of the *Journal de deuil*, or rather from its finding that a direct manifestation of mourning in writing cannot be generalized, published, and turned into a literary *œuvre*. If this form of diary is unpublishable, the question now arises whether Barthes's more conventional practice of diary-writing can pass from being *discours*, or 'une sorte de parole "writée"' [a sort of 'written' speech] with its 'hémorragie de l'Imaginaire' [haemorrhaging of the *Imaginaire*] (678), to the *écriture* of his published works:

> Je n'esquisse pas ici une analyse du genre 'Journal' (il y a des livres là-dessus), mais seulement une délibération personnelle, destinée à permettre une décision pratique: dois-je tenir un journal *en vue de le publier*? Puis-je faire du journal une 'œuvre'? (669)
>
> [I am not attempting here an analysis of the 'Journal' genre (there are books on the subject), but only a personal deliberation, intended to allow a practical decision: should I keep a *journal with a view to publication*? Can I make the *journal* into an 'œuvre'?]

Initially, Barthes asserts that the justification of the diary as an *œuvre* must be '*littéraire*, au sens absolu, même si nostalgique, du mot' [*literary*, in the absolute, even if nostalgic, sense of the word], and elaborates a system of four criteria (a 'disposable typology' to which he does not return): *poétique* ('offrir un texte coloré d'une individualité d'écriture, d'un "style"' [presenting a text coloured with an individuality in writing, a 'style']), *historique* ('éparpiller en poussière, au jour le jour, les traces d'une époque' [scattering the crumbs, day by day, of the traces of an era]), *utopique* ('constituer l'auteur en objet de désir' [constituting the author as an object of desire], so called because 'on ne vient jamais à bout de l'Imaginaire' [one never reaches the end of the *Imaginaire*]), and *amoureux* ('constituer le Journal en

---

[47] Culler, 'Preparing the Novel', p. 110. Culler is speaking specifically of Barthes's rhetorical strategies in *La Préparation du roman*. Lucy O'Meara, *Roland Barthes at the Collège de France*, pp. 183–6.

[48] As Samoyault has remarked, Barthes's archives show that he undertook a wide range of private, daily writing practices throughout his life, but sporadically, and without a direct connection with his public work; Samoyault, *Roland Barthes: biographie*, p. 139.

atelier de phrases' [constituting the *Journal* as a workshop of sentences]) (669–70). The common factor between them is that all four are criteria of *littérarité conditionnelle* rather than *littérarité constitutive* (in Genette's terms).[49] In other words, unlike a poem, which is constitutively literary by generic convention no matter how bad it is artistically, the diary could be literary only on the condition that it adequately satisfies the criteria of literary merit stated above. The article's abrupt transition to the two diaries at this point implicitly puts them to the test of this *littérarité conditionnelle*.

Both diaries undoubtedly have a strong claim to all four criteria, but their importance within the article lies elsewhere. Their very presence indicates that, using his *délibération* as an alibi, Barthes has already decided to publish his diary-writing for the first time, and is in fact deliberating about the path this writing should take. The first diary contains a reflection on 'une sorte de *Journal politique*' that would complete the trilogy of works exploring '[sa] propre bêtise' [[his] own silliness], together with *RB par RB* and *Fragments d'un discours amoureux*. This project never came to fruition, although both its description here and the passage that follows it, recounting social observations from a supermarket, bear a striking resemblance to Annie Ernaux's first published diary, *Journal du dehors* (1993).[50] However, the marked movement from the relative formlessness of the first diary (which lacks a clear beginning or end, at least as it is presented to us here) to the greater unity of the second diary (a single long entry) indicates the direction to be followed in *Soirées de Paris*. The effect is reinforced by the similarity of the second diary to this later work in terms of subject matter (a 'vaine soirée' [futile evening] and 'vadrouille' [wandering, roving] around Paris, 676–7) and its writing style.

When the theoretical *délibération* resumes after the two diaries, Barthes shifts the terms of the problem from a *littérarité conditionnelle* to a *littérarité constitutive*:

> J'ai beau relire ces deux fragments, rien ne me dit qu'ils soient publiables; rien ne me dit non plus qu'ils ne le sont pas. Me voici en face d'un problème qui me dépasse: celui de la 'publiabilité'; non pas 'Est-ce bon, est-ce mauvais?' (forme que tout auteur donne à sa question), mais 'Est-ce publiable ou non?' Ce n'est pas seulement une question d'éditeur. Le doute est déplacé, glisse de la qualité du texte à son image. (678)

> [However much I reread these two fragments, nothing tells me that they are publishable; and nothing tells me that they are not. I am faced here with a problem that goes beyond my own situation: the problem of 'publishability'; not 'Is it good, is it bad?' (the form that every author gives to this question), but 'Is is publishable or not?' It is not only a question for the publisher. The doubt is shifted, slips from the quality of the text to its image.]

In considering the capacity of the *journal intime* to become an *œuvre* on the level of its *image*, Barthes has serious doubts, some of which are more convincing than others. For example, the claim that it is 'inauthentique' amounts to little more than an uncontroversial rejection of its being 'la forme d'écriture la plus 'directe',

[49] Gérard Genette, *Fiction et diction: précédé de Introduction à l'architexte* (Paris: Seuil, 2004), p. 87.
[50] Annie Ernaux, *Journal du dehors* (Paris: Gallimard, 1993).

la plus 'spontanée' [the most 'direct', the most 'spontaneous' form of writing] in any absolute sense (679–80). The objection that matters most here makes use of the theoretical opposition between the *Album* and the *Livre*, but in a very different way from the use of these terms in *La Préparation du roman*. As Lucy O'Meara has shown, Barthes's course at the Collège de France is even-handed in its treatment of these two viable forms of literary *œuvre*, both the *Livre* (possessing a structure that is 'architectural et prémédité'), and the *Album* (with a 'structure fondée sur la nature des choses' [structure based on the nature of things], whose coherence depends on the continuity and rhythm of a method of writing).[51] Of the two, Barthes seems to favour the *Album* for its implicit 'philosophie pluraliste, relativiste, sceptique, taoïste'.[52] Yet in 'Délibération', Barthes denigrates the *Album* as being inessential, lacking the necessity characteristic of the *Livre*:

> L'Album est collection de feuillets non seulement permutables (ceci encore ne serait rien), mais surtout *suppressibles à l'infini*: relisant mon Journal, je puis barrer une note après l'autre, jusqu'à l'anéantissement complet de l'Album, sous prétexte que 'cela ne me plaît pas'. (679)
>
> [The *Album* is a collection of pages that can not only be resequenced (even this would not be a problem) but are above all *infinitely suppressible*: as I reread my *Journal*, I can cross out one note after another, until the whole *Album* is erased, on the pretext that 'I don't like this part'.]

This objection to the diary as *Album*, however disingenuous it might be (when a diary is treated as a unified writing project its entries are neither interchangeable nor suppressible), acts to equate the *œuvre* with the *Livre* alone, as the only possibility for a diary to become a publishable work of literature.

The transitional role of 'Délibération' between the *Journal de deuil* and *Soirées de Paris* helps to explain both the unexpected treatment of the *Album*/*Livre* opposition, and the article's conclusion. The *Journal de deuil* had tended towards an unattainable extreme of the *Album*, in which the writing would be entirely determined by (and indeed produced by) the diary's object, mourning itself. Since Barthes seems to be prohibited from discussing publicly the essentially private writing project of the *Journal de deuil*, in writing 'Délibération' he must instead take as his starting point a conventional form of diary-writing, and direct the argument (by means of sophistry, if necessary) towards the conclusion that the only way for the *journal intime* to become a publishable, constitutively literary text is for it to become a *Livre*. Yet it is difficult to see how the characteristics of the *Livre* can be reconciled with the principal virtue of the *journal intime* (as Barthes sees it), its quality as 'le limbe du Texte, sa forme inconstituée, inévoluée et immature' [the fringe of the Text, its unconstituted, unevolved and immature form], which allows it to embody the 'tourment essentiel' of literature, that of being 'sans preuves' [without proofs], incapable of proving either what it is saying,

---

[51] O'Meara, *Roland Barthes at the Collège de France*, pp. 183–6. Barthes, *La Préparation du roman*, pp. 246, 250.
[52] Barthes, La Préparation du roman, p. 256.

or even that it is worth saying at all (680–1). Its 'tourment' and 'impuissance à la preuve' [incapacity for proof] recuperate the *journal intime*, and when, in the closing words of the article, Barthes formulates the concept of the 'Journal idéal', it must paradoxically combine this instability (characteristic of the *Album*) with a guarantee of its status as an *œuvre* (in the sense of the *Livre*) and as *écriture*:

> Oui, c'est bien cela, le Journal idéal: à la fois un rythme (chute et montée, élasticité) et un leurre (je ne puis atteindre mon image); un écrit, en somme, qui dit la vérité du leurre et garantit cette vérité par la plus formelle des opérations, le rythme. Sur quoi il faudrait sans doute conclure que je puis sauver le Journal à la seule condition de le travailler *à mort*, jusqu'au bout de l'extrême fatigue, comme un Texte *à peu près* impossible: travail au terme duquel il est bien possible que le Journal ainsi tenu ne ressemble plus du tout à un Journal. (681)

> [Yes, that is the ideal of the *Journal*: both a rhythm (fall and rise, elasticity) and an illusion (I cannot reach my own image); a writing, in short, that tells the truth of the illusion and guarantees this truth through the most formal of operations, that of rhythm. I must therefore conclude that I can redeem the *Journal* only on the condition that I work it *to death*, to the point of complete exhaustion, like an *almost* impossible Text: a labour at the end of which the *Journal*, kept in this way, will possibly no longer resemble a *Journal* at all.]

This ideal, perhaps unattainable, is the aim of *Soirées de Paris*. The 'leurre' of an *écriture* that is 'directe' and 'spontanée', and fixes the 'hémorragie de l'Imaginaire', must be accompanied by a comprehensive formal *travail*, resulting in a work that integrates the virtues of the *Album* in a '[Livre] architectural et prémédité'. After the *Journal de deuil*, in which *écriture* tends towards a minimal state of uninterpreted, univocal words of mourning, and its own eventual disappearance, *Soirées de Paris* is imagined as a self-consciously authored *récit* [narrative] or diary novel which also happens to be a real *journal intime*.

Soirées de Paris

Several critics have remarked upon the extremely literary nature of *Soirées de Paris*, describing it with such terms as 'récit', a 'petite fiction d'écriture' [little fiction of writing], and a 'short story in journal form'.[53] The observation is entirely justified, but can obscure what is most remarkable about the text: that it is also a real *journal intime*. James Williams also observes that *Soirées de Paris* resolves an 'anxiety of Gidean influence'.[54] In fact, although it avoids any mention of Gide among its many literary allusions, its form as a novelistic diary draws elements from several parts of Gide's diary-writing: The project's overall movement to 'entrer en littérature, en écriture' (the resolution of the *satori* of 15 April 1978)[55]

---

[53] Roland Barthes, *Incidents*, ed. by François Wahl (Paris: Seuil, 1987), p. 9. Éric Marty, 'La Vie posthume de Roland Barthes', *Esprit*, 174 (1991), pp. 76–90, p. 80. Michael Moriarty, *Roland Barthes* (Cambridge: Polity Press, 1991), p. 5.

[54] James Williams, 'The Moment of Truth: Roland Barthes, "Soirées de Paris" and the Real', *Neophilologus*, 79/1 (1995), pp. 33–51, p. 39.

[55] Barthes, *La Préparation du roman*, p. 32.

resembles André Walter's desire to transcend his diaristic existence to become the novelistic author of his own life, while the narrative's simultaneous status as diary and *récit* problematizes the relationship between life and literature in a similar way to *Paludes*. The problems raised in *Le Journal des Faux-monnayeurs* and Gide's *Journal* concerning the role of the 'écrivain tel que l'on peut le voir dans son journal intime' relative to his or her *œuvre*,[56] discussed in *La Préparation du roman*, are equally at stake in *Soirées de Paris*. Yet it is also a very unusual work, to be understood on its own terms (or rather, the terms announced in 'Délibération') as a *Livre* with elements of the *Album*, and as a part of the 'Vita Nova' project that sets out in a new direction from the conclusion of the *Journal de deuil*.

Two major differences from the *Journal de deuil* explain how Barthes was able, in *Soirées de Paris*, to write a diary that aspires be a *Livre*. First, whereas the *Journal de deuil* was written over almost two years and its development could not be foreseen when it was begun, *Soirées de Paris* consists of only sixteen entries over a period of less than a month. The diarist is therefore far more able in this shorter diary to anticipate what is to follow and, while writing an individual entry, to keep in mind the eventual structural unity of the whole (as we shall see). Secondly, whereas the first entry of the *Journal de deuil* indicates that entries were written in the evening, and the diary tends towards a simultaneity of writing and experience, the entries of *Soirées de Paris* relate the events of Barthes's leisure time in the evenings and weekends, but are systematically written on the following day during the hours dedicated to his work as an *écrivain* (as explained in a note above the first entry, 977). A diaristic *narration intercalée* is maintained, but a greater interval is introduced between the occurrence of the diary's events and their transformation into an *écriture* intended, if not destined, for anthumous publication. This interval creates a (frequently ironic) distance between two perspectives simultaneously present in the text, that of Barthes-as-protagonist engaged in his pursuit of pleasure (an unstructured accumulation of perceptions, associated with the *Album*), and that of Barthes-as-narrator directing the work towards its conclusion as a *Livre*. The relationship between these two figures develops until their apparent unification in the final, concluding entry. I shall follow the course of this secondary plot over the three parts of the work's novelistic structure (alongside Barthes's rovings around Paris and his failed relationships), which is also the plot of Barthes's attempt to 'faire du journal une "œuvre"' ('Délibération', 669).

A preliminary note is needed on the work's epigraph: 'Eh bien, nous nous en sommes bien tiré [*sic*]. / Schopenhauer (*sur un papier, avant de mourir*)' [Well then, we're well out of it. / Schopenhauer (*on a piece of paper, before dying*)] (977). The mere presence of an epigraph presents the diary as a literary work with a certain unity, to which the reference provides some sort of key. This is not unusual for published diaries, and Gide added epigraphs not only to fictional diaries but also to real diaries such as *Numquid et tu...?* (1922) and *Et nunc manet in te* (1951). It is in the nature of epigraphs to lead to highly speculative interpretations, but

---

[56] Barthes, *RB par RB*, p. 656.

James Williams oberves very plausibly that it contains an ironic juxtaposition of colloquial language and a high-brow, philosophical reference (reflecting the ironic distance between the two perspectives identified earlier), and also that the participle's ungrammatical lack of agreement echoes a movement in the text between the individual and the general.[57] I would only add that the reference creates a further similarity with André Walter, for whom Schopenhauer is related to a desire to enter fully into his novelistic illusions, even at the expense of his earthly (diaristic) existence.

The first of the work's three parts consists of five entries, which establish the habits and repetitions of Barthes's evenings spent in *flâneries*, meetings with friends, and observations mediated by his sexual desires. This period corresponds to the phrase 'telles étaient mes soirées' [such were my evenings] in the plans for *Vita Nova* (1014), describing his situation before a transformation takes place. Several aspects of the first entry function both as genuine accounts of experiences from the perspective of Barthes-as-protagonist, and as programmatic comments on the writing project by Barthes-as-narrator, starting from the very first sentence:

> Au Flore où je lis un *Monde* sans événements, à côté de moi, deux garçons (je connais de vue l'un d'eux et même nous nous saluons; il est assez joli à cause de ses traits réguliers, mais a de gros ongles) ont discuté longuement du réveil par téléphone: cela sonne à deux reprises, mais, si l'on ne se réveille pas, c'est tout; tout ça, maintenant, c'est sur ordinateur, etc. (977)

> [At the Café Flore, where I read a copy of *Le Monde* without any news, next to me, two boys (I know one of them by sight and we even greet one another; he is quite handsome because of his regular features, but has coarse fingernails) argued for a long time about telephone wake-up calls: they ring twice, but, if you don't wake up, that's it; nowadays, that's all computerized, etc.]

The diary is going to relate Barthes's social life in Paris centred around the café Flore, where he observes with the relative detachment of a reader (although he greets one of the boys) a '*Monde* sans événements' that is banal and mildly erotically charged. He goes on to relate that, at a dinner among friends later in the evening, 'on a parlé de ce qu'ils appelaient les "histoires plates" ("À la gare de Victoria, en Angleterre, j'ai rencontré une Espagnole qui parlait français")' [we talked about what they call 'shaggy-dog stories' ('At Victoria station, in England, I met a Spanish woman who spoke French')] (978), and indeed the concept of the 'histoire plate' corresponds both to this story of two boys discussing computerized wake-up calls, and to the diary that is to follow.

It is not surprising that, like every one of the diaries discussed in previous chapters, *Soirées de Paris* begins with certain intentions for the writing project, nor that these are expressed with the large degree of literary reflexivity made possible by Barthes's particular writing practice. However, whereas the passages discussed above relate mainly to the stagnant situation of the first part of the diary, there are two ways in which Barthes-as-narrator in this first part anticipates the transformation that will bring about the diary's closure as a *Livre*.

---

[57] Williams, 'The Moment of Truth', p. 35.

This transformation is the 'réforme de vie' announced in the second diary in 'Délibération' (677), referring to his resolution to 'entrer en littérature, en écriture'. First, in opposition to Barthes's leisure time spent in a futile pursuit of pleasure, *Soirées de Paris* manifests the recuperation of his experience through writing, and the increasingly literary nature of this experience itself. For example, his observations are frequently mediated by literary allusions, especially to Proust ('j'ai repéré la rue d'Aboukir, pensant à Charlus qui en parle' [I took the rue d'Aboukir, thinking of Charlus, who talks about it], 977). The incident of the missed meeting with a gigolo whom he has paid in advance shows that he is more 'érotis[é]' by the language of their negotiation than by physical contact (983), and in fact the experience that evokes the strongest feeling in him, and that marks the only real progress in the first part, is his ongoing reading of Chateaubriand at the end of the evening ('je [. . .] reviens avec soulagement aux *Mémoires d'outre tombe*, le vrai livre' [I [. . .] return with relief to the *Mémoires d'outre tombe*, the real book], 980). The second early indication of the transformation that is to follow (again, functioning only from the perspective of Barthes-as-narrator) is another reflexive comment from the first entry:

> j'ai un peu divagué: imaginant une technique qui me permettrait de filmer la scène (une caméra *parfaite* à la place d'un bouton de ma chemise), une autre aussi qui ferait de cette place animée par le mauvais vent un décor où l'on pourrait [transporter/transformer] après coup un personnage. [François Wahl explains in an editorial note that Barthes wrote 'transformer', for which he has substituted 'transporter'.] (978)
>
> [I let my mind wander a little: imagining a technique that would allow me to film the scene (a *perfect* camera in place of one of my shirt buttons), and another that would make this square, with an ill wind blowing through it, into a backdrop where one could [transport/transform] a character afterwards.]

Of the two cameras, the former characterizes (or rather exaggerates) the perspective of Barthes-as-protagonist, comprehensively and perfectly recording his subjective experience, while the latter suggests Barthes-as-narrator's artistic overview of a sequence in which some time is spent in setting the scene (Paris as 'une place animée par le mauvais vent') before a 'personnage' (Barthes himself) is brought on and 'transformé' there.

Up to this point, *Soirées de Paris* reads unlike most real diaries, but its peculiarities are a matter of degree. The work's initial conception and writing practices help to explain its thematic unity, the anticipation of a novelistic structure that is still to emerge, and its literary self-consciousness. Yet this thematic unity still accommodates the diaristic contingency of the *Album* in its many details (difficult to imitate with any fictional *effet de réel*), and there are still considerable limits to the diarist's foresight.

After a short hiatus, the second, central part of the work consists of a single entry recounting a visit to the family home in Urt, strongly associated with Barthes's mourning for his mother. As in the first part, Barthes could not have foreseen the specific events (his being disturbed by his brother and sister-in-law to witness a summer evening that is 'presque étrange à force de perfection' [almost strange in its perfection], 984), yet the observations of Barthes-as-protagonist simultaneously assume a novelistic structural significance from the perspective of Barthes-as-narrator:

> J'ai eu le cœur gonflé de tristesse, presque de désespoir; je pensais à mam, au cimetière où elle était, non loin, à la 'Vie'. Je sentais ce gonflement romantique comme une valeur et j'étais triste de ne pouvoir jamais le dire, 'valant toujours plus que ce que j'écris' (thème du cours); désespéré aussi de ne me sentir bien ni à Paris, ni ici, ni en voyage: sans abri véritable. (984)

> [My heart swelled with sadness, almost with despair; I thought of Mam, of the cemetery where she was, not far away, and of 'Life'. I felt that Romantic impulse as a value and I was sad that I would never be able to speak it, 'always being worth more than what I write' (theme of the lecture course); also in despair at not feeling right in Paris, nor here, nor when travelling: without any real haven.]

A topology is constructed here which situates the mourning of Urt (and so the *Journal de deuil*, never mentioned explicitly) relative to the frustrated desires of *Soirées de Paris*. The value he attributes to his 'tristesse' and his inability to express it publicly are familiar themes from the *Journal de deuil*, but it now seems to be this same 'désespoir' that lies behind the far more public writing of *Soirées de Paris* and, as Diana Knight points out, it is precisely a sense of 'désespoir' that triggers the final act of renunciation with which *Soirées de Paris* ends.[58] Barthes-as-narrator therefore capitalizes on contingent events to create a structurally salient point in *Soirées de Paris*, which makes the present work, and the transformation that takes place in the following entries, into a literary sublimation of an unspeakable *deuil*.

In the third and final part, a series of failed relationships make Barthes more of a 'personnage' than a mere observer, and the ironic distance between Barthes-as-protagonist and Barthes-as-narrator grows wider, until the transformation that brings about the work's conclusion. The seventh entry relates the beginnings of a potential affair which leads nowhere. In the eighth entry, in the context of another unsuccessful relationship, he acknowledges the emergence of a pattern:

> Il me quitte à neuf heures, je me retrouve seul, assez triste – décidé à renoncer (mais comment le lui dire? ne serait-ce pas indigne de ne pas plus le voir, sous prétexte que. . . ? c'est pourtant ce que je voudrais, désirant nettoyer ma vie de toutes ces queues de ratage). (985)

> [He leaves me at nine o'clock, I find myself alone, a little sad—determined to give up (but how to tell him? Wouldn't it be unworthy simply not to see him any more, on the pretext that. . . ? Yet that is what I would like, wishing to clear my life of all these failures trailing on).]

This first, partial act of renunciation is one of very few occasions when *Soirées de Paris* adopts the typically diaristic mode of deliberation and self-interrogation in a present tense attached to the time of writing, a mode that seems to bring

---

[58] Diana Knight, *Barthes and Utopia: Space, Travel, Writing* (Oxford: OUP, 1997), p. 249.

the two perspectives closer together. Nonetheless, while Barthes-as-protagonist remains focused on the contingent details of each case, the perspective of Barthes-as-narrator brings out the repeating pattern of his 'amertume' and 'tristesse' at this failed relationship with Jean-Louis P. (986), 'amertume' again in his envy of Bernard G. and his young Italian boyfriend (988), and 'fatigue' and a lack of desire in his relationship with Saül (990).

The last relationship in this sequence leads in an extremely novelistic fashion towards the work's *dénouement*. In the fourteenth entry, a Tuesday, he meets with Olivier G., feels a greater desire than in any of the other relationships, and announces a further meeting for Sunday lunchtime. A single entry is interposed before this meeting to heighten the narrative suspense, without mention of Olivier, and which contains the diary's most frenetic and uncomfortable 'Vaine Soirée' (991). Éric Marty and James Williams both comment on the closure brought about by the end of this relationship and by Barthes's more general 'renonce[ment] aux garçons' [renunciation of boys] in the final entry of *Soirées de Paris*, a closure which is unusual not only for the diary but also for Barthes's works in general.[59] Surprisingly, both critics mistakenly claim that this entry alone relates events from the afternoon instead of the *soirée* (in fact, weekend afternoons feature in the seventh and twelfth entries as well), but it would be accurate to say that the entry's movement from leisure to *travail* is unique in this diary, and is part of the transformation to which the whole writing project has been leading. However, the most significant part of this transformation is the change that takes place in the relation between Barthes-as-protagonist and Barthes-as-narrator.

The entry begins its account of Olivier's visit with an exterior perspective that, if converted into a third-person narrative, would resemble the narrator of a Realist novel:

> Hier, dimanche, Olivier G. est venu déjeuner; j'avais donné à l'attendre, l'accueillir, le soin qui d'ordinaire témoigne que je suis amoureux. (992)

> [Yesterday, Sunday, Oliver G. came for lunch; in waiting for him, welcoming him, I took all the care which usually indicates that I am in love.]

To emphasize the imminent change, this part of the entry exaggerates the distance between Barthes-as-protagonist blindly awaiting the object of his desire, and Barthes-as-narrator ironically commenting on the former's behaviour and anticipating the thwarting of this desire. The change is precipitated when Olivier politely refuses his advances:

> Une sorte de désespoir m'a pris, j'avais envie de pleurer. Je voyais dans l'évidence qu'il fallait renoncer aux garçons, parce qu'il n'y avait pas de désir d'eux à moi, et que je suis ou trop scrupuleux ou trop maladroit pour imposer le mien; que c'est là un fait incontournable, avéré par toutes mes tentatives de flirt, que j'en ai une vie triste, que, finalement, je m'ennuie, et qu'il me faut sortir cet intérêt, ou cet espoir, de ma vie. [...] Puis je l'ai renvoyé, disant que j'avais à travailler, sachant que c'était fini, et qu'au-delà de lui quelque chose était fini: l'amour d'*un* garçon. (993)

---

[59] Marty, 'La Vie posthume de Roland Barthes', pp. 85–6. Williams, 'The Moment of Truth', pp. 37–8.

[A sort of despair took hold of me, I wanted to cry. I saw quite clearly that I needed to give up on boys, because they did not desire me, and I am either too scrupulous or too awkward to impose my own desire on them; that this is an inescapable fact, borne out by all my attempts at flirting, that I have a sad life because of it, and finally, that I am bored, and that I need to remove this interest, or this hope, from my life. [...] Then I sent him away, saying that I had to work, knowing that it was over, and that besides him something else was over: the love of *one* boy.]

Unlike in the failures of his previous relationships, the particular boy in question is now incidental, and Barthes-as-protagonist sees, behind the immediate circumstances, the terms that structure the whole of *Soirée de Paris*. Behind the contingent pain of this particular rejection he feels the 'désespoir' of his mourning, he becomes fully aware of the 'tristesse' and 'ennui' of his existence, and of the necessity for it to come to an end with a 'renonce[ment] aux garçons'. This is the moment when the perspective of Barthes-as-protagonist joins that of Barthes-as-narrator (and so his leisure time turns to *travail*), with the transformation described in the plans for *Vita Nova* as 'la littérature comme substitut d'amour' [literature as a substitute for love].

Although this transformation brings about the end of the diary, its closure remains incomplete, as Barthes indicates in a parenthesis (situated under the ellipsis in the citation above):

Il ne me restera que les gigolos. (Mais que ferais-je alors pendant mes sorties? Je remarque sans cesse les jeunes hommes, désirant tout de suite en eux, d'être amoureux d'eux. Quel sera pour moi le spectacle du monde?) (993)

[All that will be left for me is hustlers. (But what would I do then during my walks? I constantly notice young men, desiring them straight away, wanting to fall in love with them. What will the spectacle of the world become for me?)]

This closely resembles the parenthetic deliberation in the present tense that follows Barthes's first act of renunciation in the eighth entry, and suggests that the desires through which he experiences the world cannot entirely be sublimated into literary expression. Similarly, the joining of Barthes-as-protagonist and Barthes-as-narrator does not constitute a perfect assimilation of the values of the *Album* into a *Livre*, but rather marks the closest point the diary can reach towards the ideal 'Texte *à peu près* impossible' imagined in 'Délibération'. The two elements co-exist throughout the diary by virtue of a laborious writing process, artificial almost to the point of *autofiction*, that recreates in hindsight the immediacy of expression conventionally associated with the *journal intime*, and accompanies it with a perspective approaching the conflated author-narrator of a Realist novel. But when Barthes-as-protagonist attains the insight and control of Barthes-as-narrator, when he finally 'entr[e] en littérature' and renounces the worldly pursuit of his desires (resembling, at least symbolically, André Walter's end, and the death of Schopenhauer evoked in the epigraph), he brings the *Livre* to completion at the expense of the *Album*, and the diary therefore becomes untenable. Just as the *Journal de deuil* was brought to a close as it approached an ideal writing of interiority, so *Soirées de Paris* brings about its own end as it attempts to realize a fully literary *journal intime*.

The Plans for *Vita Nova*

Before considering Barthes's diary-writing in its entirety, we should also take account of the place of the two principal diaries in the eight pages of plans for a novelistic work entitled *Vita Nova*. This *Roman* seemed to be projected as the ultimate goal of the 'Vita Nova' project, even though Barthes's work over this period gave rise to various forms of texts and *cours*. The plans have been treated in detail by Diana Knight and Maja Zorica, who have discussed their relation with the rest of the 'Vita Nova' project, the correlation of the plans with Barthes's simultaneous composition of *Soirées de Paris*, as well as the particular intertext with Gide's *Journal*.[60] Both Knight and Zorica find that the plans were not simply abandoned, but that a form of programmed failure is 'built into the basic conception' of the work, and so recuperated as a form of success.[61] These readings need to be nuanced in light of Tiphaine Samoyault's more recent revelation of the extent of Barthes's work towards the *Roman*—far more extensive than had previously been thought—before it was interrupted by his fatal accident, and which leads her to assert that 'l'inachèvement ou l'échec de cette œuvre romanesque ne doivent pas être interprétés' [the unfinished state or failure of this novelistic *œuvre* should not be interpreted].[62] It is undoubtedly true that the actual incomplete state of the work is a contingency without any significance of its own, and we will never know precisely what the work might have become, yet the readings of Knight and Zorica remain valid on a thematic level. Furthermore, the excerpts that Samoyault reproduces from Barthes's own notes reinforce the impression that the project was haunted by a sense of impossibility and failure.[63]

The plans for *Vita Nova* twice refer to a progressive sequence of 'Le Fragment. Le Journal. Le Roman.' (1008, 1010), suggesting an intermediate role for diary-writing within the *Roman*. The two diaries are referred to repeatedly in the plans, and without dwelling on their specific place in the structure of the imagined *Roman* it will suffice to remark that they too manifest in their own way a similar failure to satisfy the demands of 'un Texte *à peu près* impossible'.[64] In other words, the diaries are intermediate failures, each testing a certain writing project to its limit, and each forming a part of the greater failure of the *Roman*. While the imagined *Vita Nova* pursues the goal of a literary *Roman* that might express 'la vérité des affects', the diaries create a vast topography for this *Roman* by indicating two cardinal points, always receding over the horizon: one in the direction of the

---

[60] Diana Knight, 'Idle Thoughts: Barthes's *Vita Nova*', *Nottingham French Studies*, 36/1 (1997), pp. 88–98. Maja Zorica, '*Vita Nova* de Barthes', ed. by Véronique and Catherine Viollet (Louvain-la-Neuve: Academia Bruylant, 2009), pp. 127–40 (p. 128 for discussion of the intertext with Gide's *Journal*, which is mainly concerned with the figure of the 'jeune homme inconnu' [unknown young man]).
[61] Knight, 'Idle Thoughts', p. 93. Zorica, '*Vita Nova* de Barthes', p. 128. The quotation is taken from the former.
[62] Samoyault, *Roland Barthes: biographie*, p. 651.   [63] Ibid., pp. 655–6.
[64] Each of the plans begins with a 'Deuil' as prologue, which is expanded to 'Journal de Deuil' on the final page (1018). *Soirées de Paris* is clearly indicated several times under the title *Vaines Soirées*, and on the fifth page the prologue leads directly (by an arrow) onto these *Vaines Soirées* (1014). Knight remarks that both *Soirées de Paris* and the plans for *Vita Nova* end with the same 'self-conscious declaration of abandonment', in the form of a citation from a fable by La Fontaine (p. 93).

direct manifestation of fragmentary 'moments de vérité' in writing (the *Journal de deuil*), the other (*Soirées de Paris*) pointing towards a fully literary sublimation that would not denature these truths.

DIARIES AND LITERARY LIFE-WRITING

It is now possible to follow the development of Barthes's experimentation with diary-writing across the 'Vita Nova' project, and also to situate this relative to his overall contribution to the field of life-writing in the 1970s. Even though Barthes's attitude towards Gide remained equivocal (for example, Gide is almost passed over in silence in 'Délibération'), the effects of this early influence are undoubtedly crucial to these final stages of Barthes's work. The connection with Gide is most visible in the autobiographical project of *RB par RB*, but already at this point the subsequent shift from autobiography to diary-writing is anticipated by Barthes's suggestion that his fragmentary writing practice in this work disguises an 'effort clandestin et opiniâtre' to return to the '"journal" gidien'. The move to diary-writing is also implicit in the initial terms of the 'Vita Nova' as set out in *Leçon* and 'Longtemps', although now without explicit reference to Gide: rather than pursuing an autobiographical account of himself or of his *Imaginaire*, Barthes now finds literary value in 'la vérité des affects', and more particularly in his experience of 'le deuil unique et comme irréductible'. This experience is to be manifested in a new 'pratique d'écriture' that unifies his life and writing, and for which diary-writing seems to offer the greatest potential.

The *Journal de deuil* is the first and most direct attempt to realize this new 'pratique d'écriture', with a form and writing practice very different from Barthes's previous, rather ordinary diaries (as shown in 'Délibération'), but nonetheless pursuing the 'leurres' of the *journal intime*: a joining of experience and *écriture* in a fully present, univocal writing subject, and the possibility of converting an interiority of immeasurable value into a literary *œuvre* without betraying or alienating it. These aims constitute a utopian ideal, but the *Journal de deuil* demonstrates the closest that they can be approached in reality, by leading its *écriture* to a minimal state, and eventually to its vanishing point. However, this conclusion condemns the diary itself to silence (or at least to posthumous publication), and the search in 'Délibération' for a diary that could instead be a fully public literary *œuvre* leads to the project of *Soirées de Paris*. This work's form is as different again from any of Barthes's previous diary-writing, and embraces the essential multivocality of writing by attempting to reconcile the *Album* of a conventionally diaristic voice with the *Livre* of a novelistic narrator. The tense and ironic cohabitation of these voices is tenable in a real diary (maintaining a *narration intercalée*) only for a short duration, and the concluding sacrifice of Barthes-as-protagonist (and therefore also of the *Album* element of the text) marks the limit of the diary's ability to become an *œuvre* in Barthes's terms. Barthes's coordination of these two diaries within the structure of *Vita Nova* reinforces the fact that they are diametrically opposed to one another in their methods and aims, and through this very opposition they become components of the even more ambitious *œuvre* of this imagined *Roman*.

I would argue that, if allusions to Gide are surprisingly sparse across the 'Vita Nova' project as a whole (especially compared with Barthes's allusions to Dante and Proust), it is precisely because this is the point when Barthes moves away from his ironic emulation of a Gidean author-figure in *RB par RB*, towards a more active form of writing in response to Gide's work. This involves both a positive assumption of the role of *écrivain*, and an active mode of writing that seems to pursue the utopian *œuvre* that Barthes had detected much earlier (in 1942) in Gide's *Journal* (this same passage is discussed on p. 131):

> Il y a des phrases qui sont mi-chemin entre la confession et la création; elles ne demandent qu'à être insérées dans un roman et sont déjà moins sincères (ou plutôt: leur sincérité compte moins qu'autre chose, qui est le plaisir qu'on prend à les lire). Je dirai volontiers ceci: ce n'est pas le *Journal d'Édouard* qui ressemble au *Journal* de Gide; au contraire, bien des propos du *Journal* ont déjà l'autonomie du *Journal d'Édouard*. Ils ne sont plus tout à fait Gide; ils commencent d'être hors de lui, en route vers quelque œuvre incertaine où ils ont envie de prendre place, qu'ils appellent.[65]

> [There are sentences that are half way between confession and creation; they could easily be inserted into a novel and are already less sincere (or rather: their sincerity is less important than something else, which is the pleasure that we have in reading them). I would gladly say this: it is not the *Journal d'Édouard* that resembles Gide's *Journal*; on the contrary, many passages of the *Journal* already have the autonomy of the *Journal d'Édouard*. They are no longer entirely Gide; they are on their way towards some uncertain *œuvre* where they long to be, which they call into being.]

It is particularly relevant to the 'Vita Nova' project that Barthes's attention here turns from the issue of *sincérité* (which was the important element in *RB par RB*) to a concept of literary creation, a form of writing grounded in personal experience but which attains the autonomy and literary nature of the *roman*, or at least of some 'œuvre incertaine' which remains to be found. Indeed, this search for an 'œuvre incertaine' is also relevant, more broadly, to the situation of life-writing at this particular moment when diverse experimental works were being undertaken by writers such as Perec, Derrida, Sarraute, and Robbe-Grillet (all cited at the beginning of this chapter) who were acutely aware of the theoretical objections to a psychologically coherent writing subject. In this sense, Barthes's diary-writing within the 'Vita Nova' project can be seen as indicative of the place of the diary in life-writing at this time: a real diary appears unable to accomplish the ambitious aims for an *œuvre* (closely associated with the *roman*), and it might even be considered a marginal form, but it is also the ideal form for addressing the theoretical and practical problems that these writers faced. The diaries in the 'Vita Nova' project tested two opposite approaches to their practical limit, and although these texts were not published until much later, they nonetheless mapped out a horizon of possibility for subsequent life-writing.

---

[65] Barthes, 'Notes sur André Gide et son « Journal »', pp. 34–5.

7

Annie Ernaux
The Place of the Diary in Modern Life-Writing

Since the late 1970s the return of the subject heralded by Barthes, among others, has grown steadily into a field of writing that is abundantly published and read, and has also been granted an unprecedented literary status. These texts are referred to in English by the term 'life-writing', which offers the advantage of encompassing the great breadth of writing practices among these texts.[1] Their diversity is found both in their varying approach to truth and fictionality (sometimes embracing the hybrid forms of *autofiction*), and in their eclectic use of, or disregard for established genres.[2] The diary has shared in this success (some examples of recent and contemporary diarists are given on p. 138), but no writer of real *journaux intimes* has achieved the critical or commercial success that is enjoyed by many autobiographical works, and in fact diaries seem to attract the most interest when they constitute a part of a broader autobiographical project, such as the diary publications of Hervé Guibert and the diaristic elements of Jacques Roubaud's vast, open-ended project 'Le Grand incendie de Londres'.[3] Despite its relative success, the diary has effectively exchanged one type of marginality for another: while it is no longer generally a supplement to an author's fictional or poetic works, it is instead subordinated within the field of life-writing in relation to the dominant literary claims of autobiography (although an opposition between these two forms is already present in the work of Gide and Barthes). The present chapter will

---

[1] Antoine Compagnon offers the terms 'l'écrire la vie' and 'l'écriture personnelle' as equivalents to the English term 'life writing', in the introductory text for his lecture series 'Écrire la vie' at the Collège de France, beginning 6 January 2009; <http://www.college-de-france.fr/site/antoine-compagnon/course-2009-01-06-16h30.htm> [accessed 31 August 2017].

[2] The different meanings attributed to the terms 'autofiction' are discussed on p. 29. Among many possible examples of the eclectic mixing of genres, I shall merely point to Assia Djebar's 1985 work *L'Amour, la fantasia*, which combines autobiographical accounts, more lyrical modes of writing, testimonies of women from the Algerian War of Independence, historical accounts from the French conquest of Algeria, and historiographical reflection on the written sources available; Assia Djebar, *L'Amour, La Fantasia* (Paris: J.-C. Lattès, 1985).

[3] Jean-Pierre Boulé cites an interview with Guibert from 1992 in which the latter claims that his *journal intime* is the generative centre of his writing, or 'la colonne vertébrale, la chose essentielle' [the backbone, the essential substance]; Jean-Pierre Boulé, *Hervé Guibert: Voices of the Self*, trans. by John Fletcher (Liverpool: Liverpool University Press, 1999), p. 4. Guibert's *Cytomégalovirus: journal d'hospitalisation* was published posthumously in 1992, followed by *Le Mausolée des amants: journal 1976–1991* in 2001. The six parts of Roubaud's project that have been published so far are grouped in a single volume, *"Le Grand Incendie de Londres"* (Paris: Seuil, 2009).

therefore examine the place of the diary within life-writing, and more specifically, the role that the diary plays in relation to the author-figure and collective *œuvre* in a context where the writer might be known exclusively as a creator of works of life-writing. Rather than studying any of the numerous authors who have come to write and publish their diaries with the 'consistance doctrinale' that Barthes claimed to lack[4] (such as Renaud Camus, who appears in *Soirées de Paris* and might be considered the continuer of Barthes's experiments with the diary), I shall approach the question through the work of Annie Ernaux. This corpus offers the unusual advantage of including several different types of diary-writing that engage progressively with the question of the writer's authorial posture, but each of them published as if reluctantly, and in the face of significant resistance from an overall writing project that addresses the full breadth of life-writing. These tensions within Ernaux's work will cast light on the problematic place of diary-writing in modern life-writing more broadly.

The timeline of Ernaux's work in figure 7.1 (p. 195) helps to illustrate the place of diary-writing in the development of her writing career. Ernaux's first works, beginning with *Les Armoires vides* (1974), were labelled as *romans*, and although they draw heavily on the author's life experience, they were published without any autobiographical pact.[5] Siobhán McIlvanney's 2001 study of Ernaux's *œuvre* demonstrates various continuities from these early works, especially the preoccupations with class and gender,[6] but her career is nonetheless marked most strongly by the rejection of fiction in *La Place* (1983). Ernaux relates in this work how she had previously begun writing a *roman* about her complex relationship with her father, but then came to the conclusion that this use of fiction was a bourgeois convention which exacerbated the very betrayal of her working class origins that she was seeking to redress.[7] Her former use of fiction is replaced by a strict commitment to truthfulness in her depictions of the personal and social reality that she recalls or finds around her, however difficult this might be in practice. In seeking the means to achieve this truthfulness, *La Place* inaugurates a broad life-writing project that is also largely inimical to the subsequent publication of diaries. Its politically engaged conception of writing is pursued above all in the long series of retrospective nonfictional works, characterized by a '*valeur collective* du "je" autobiographique et des choses racontées' [*collective value* of the autobiographical 'I' and of the things that are related],[8] a focus on the 'signes objectifs' of people's lives, such as 'les paroles, les gestes, les goûts' [the words, gestures, tastes] (thereby rejecting psychological introspection),[9] and an 'écriture

---

[4] Roland Barthes, 'Délibération', in *OC* ([1979]), V, pp. 668–81, p. 668.

[5] Annie Ernaux, *Les Armoires vides* (Paris: Gallimard, 1974).

[6] Siobhán McIlvanney, *Annie Ernaux: The Return to Origins* (Liverpool: Liverpool University Press, 2001), pp. 14–15.

[7] Annie Ernaux, *La Place* (Paris: Gallimard, 1983), pp. 23–4.

[8] Annie Ernaux, *L'Écriture comme un couteau: entretien avec Frédéric-Yves Jeannet* (Paris: Stock, 2003), p. 79.

[9] Ernaux, *La Place*, p. 24. Ernaux reserves particularly criticism for psychoanalysis; Ernaux, *L'Écriture comme un couteau*, pp. 59–60.

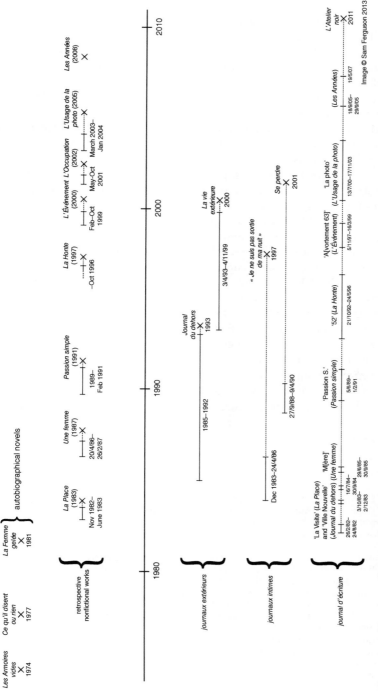

Figure 7.1. Timeline of principal works by Ernaux

Crosses indicate publication, solid horizontal lines indicate periods of composition. *L'Usage de la photo* is grouped with retrospective nonfictional works despite its *narration intercalée*, as in other respects it belongs to this series of works. The timeline of the *journal d'écriture* (*L'Atelier noir*) shows, for each period of writing, the name given to the project at hand, and the work which issued from each project. The main omission is the project referred to most often as 'RT (roman total)', eventually issuing in *Les Années*, and which runs throughout the whole diary.

Image © Sam Ferguson 2013

de la distance' [distanced writing method][10] that aims at the 'vie enfin découverte et éclaircie' [life finally revealed and enlightened] evoked in Proust's *Le Temps retrouvé*.[11] This does not amount to a condemnation of the actual writing of diaries (which Ernaux has done for her whole adult life), but it does mean that her *journal intime*, in which 'la spontanéité l'emporte sur la distanciation' [spontaneity takes precedence over distancing] and which lacks any 'achèvement' [completeness, closure],[12] cannot transcend its individuality to take on the political role which Ernaux demands of her published, literary work.

Despite the obstacles that this posed to the publication of diaries, three distinct types of diary-writing have emerged in Ernaux's career, accompanied in each case by a paratext that attempts to justify their place in the overall project. The *journal extérieur*, undertaken in 1985 and first published in 1993 as the *Journal du dehors*, claims to replace the interiority of the *journal intime* with a focus on the material and social reality that the diarist finds around her.[13] It was therefore surprising that Ernaux later published relatively conventional *journaux intimes*, *"Je ne suis pas sortie de ma nuit"* in 1997 followed by *Se perdre* in 2001, both justified by the supplementary relationship that they established with earlier publications in the series of retrospective nonfictional works (*Une femme* and *Passion simple* respectively).[14] In 2011 Ernaux published *L'Atelier noir*, the *journal d'écriture* that had accompanied her deliberations regarding her writing career since 1982.[15] This last work, building on the publication strategy of the earlier *journaux intimes*, acts as a supplement to the whole life-writing project that was undertaken in *La Place* and is now manifested in Ernaux's single volume of *œuvres complètes* (published in the same summer-autumn period of the *rentrée littéraire* of 2011), entitled *Écrire la vie*.[16] *L'Atelier noir* and *Écrire la vie* both belong to a stage of summation in Ernaux's career, which constitutes Ernaux as an author-figure in a form familiar from André Walter, A.O. Barnabooth, Gide, and Sally Mara, despite the suspicion with which Ernaux regards this role, which she sees as part of a bourgeois literary institution.[17]

---

[10] Ernaux, *L'Écriture comme un couteau*, p. 79.

[11] Fabrice Thumerel and Annie Ernaux, 'Ambivalences et ambiguïtés du journal intime: entretien avec Annie Ernaux', in *Annie Ernaux: une œuvre de l'entre-deux*, ed. by Fabrice Thumerel (Arras: Artois Presses Université, 2004), pp. 245–51, p. 248.

[12] Ibid., pp. 248, 246.

[13] Annie Ernaux, *Journal du dehors* (Paris: Gallimard, 1993). References are made to the second edition in Gallimard's Folio collection (actually published in 1997, but still dated 1993), which is the first to contain the 'avant-propos inédit de l'auteur' (dated 1996).

[14] Annie Ernaux, « *Je ne suis pas sortie de ma nuit* » (Paris: Gallimard, 1997), henceforth referred to as *Je ne suis pas sortie*. Annie Ernaux, *Se perdre* (Paris: Gallimard, 2001). Annie Ernaux, *Une femme* (Paris: Gallimard, 1987). Annie Ernaux, *Passion simple* (Paris: Gallimard, 1991).

[15] Annie Ernaux, *L'Atelier noir* (Paris: Busclats, 2011).

[16] Annie Ernaux, *Écrire la vie* (Paris: Gallimard, 2011). The title refers to Antoine Compagnon's *séminaire* of the same name at the Collège de France in 2009–10 (as stated in the introduction, 7), and thereby characterizes her whole writing project as a self-conscious engagement with the problems and possibilities of life-writing.

[17] Ernaux, *L'Écriture comme un couteau*, pp. 15–16.

After providing a brief account of the contexts for Ernaux's writing career (particularly the prevalence in modern life-writing of *autofiction*, which Ernaux herself rejects), I shall proceed quite simply by examining the chronological development of published diary-writing in her work. For each of the three types of diary—the *journal extérieur, journal intime*, and *journal d'écriture*—a reader's approach is conditioned by the paratextual presentation of the work, which attempts to reconcile its publication with the overall aims of Ernaux's life-writing project. These paratextual claims often do not bear comparison with the main text, and consistently understate the implications of diary-writing in her work. Ernaux's strategy of marginalizing diary-writing within her *œuvre* reaches its conclusion with the almost simultaneous publication of *L'Atelier noir* and *Écrire la vie*, whose ambiguous relationship demonstrates how the diary and the restored writing subject of modern life-writing differ from their precursors in Gide's *Œuvres complètes* and *Journal*.

CONTEXTS FOR ERNAUX'S DIARY-WRITING

While the diary has benefited from the rise of life-writing by attaining a higher literary status in its own right, it has also come to be characterized by its anomalous position within the field of life-writing, which has been strongly marked by a preoccupation with fiction since the return of the writing subject in the late 1970s. It is not necessary here to follow the development of this preoccupation, including but not limited to those works adopting the hybrid generic label *autofiction* first used on the back cover of Serge Doubrovsky's *Fils* (1977),[18] but it can be seen to emerge from the theoretical and literary concerns that preceded it: the fictional nature of the Lacanian *Imaginaire* (such that Barthes presents the writing subject of his 1975 *Roland Barthes par Roland Barthes* as 'un personnage de roman' [a character from a novel]),[19] the artificiality of any narrative structure, the essential inability of language to transcribe the *Réel* or authenticate itself (Barthes again, in *La Chambre claire*, 'le langage est, par nature, fictionnel' [language is, by its very nature, fictional]),[20] and finally the high literary status attributed to fiction (Ernaux later explained her choice of a fictional frame for her early works: 'dans le mot roman, je mettais littérature' [in the word novel, I used to put all of literature]).[21]

Michel Braud finds that diary-writing does not share in this tendency towards *autofiction*, and he demonstrates the point by discussing two examples that, at least superficially, seem to be exceptions to this rule:[22] in *L'Apprentissage du roman*

[18] Serge Doubrovsky, *Fils* (Paris: Galilée, 1977).
[19] Roland Barthes, *Roland Barthes par Roland Barthes*, in *OC* ([1975]), IV, pp. 575–771, p. 575.
[20] Roland Barthes, *La Chambre claire: note sur la photographie*, in *OC* ([1980]), V, pp. 785–892, p. 858.
[21] Ernaux, *L'Écriture comme un couteau*, p. 26.
[22] Michel Braud, '"Le texte d'un roman": journal intime et fictionnalisation de soi', *L'Esprit Créateur*, 42/4 (2002), pp. 76–84, pp. 78–9.

(1993), Jean-Benoît Puech presents the diary of the fictional Benjamin Jordane, which is effectively Puech's own diary of time spent with Louis-René des Forêts substantially rewritten in the manner of a *roman à clé*.[23] Conversely, in *Mémoires d'Aramis ou l'Anti-journal* (1999), Christophe Deshoulières writes a diary concerning events one year in the past, whereby the position of hindsight makes possible a 'fictionnalisation du diariste' comparable to autofictional techniques in retrospective autobiography.[24] In both cases a form of *autofiction* is achieved by a deviation from the procedure of a conventionally real diary (composition by means of a *narration intercalée*, published with minimal subsequent editing), and in fact the diary that is most literary and 'écrit' [written, crafted] while still fulfilling these requirements remains Barthes's *Soirées de Paris*, which maintains a (nonfictional) autobiographical pact throughout. The diary's claim to truthfulness is therefore related to its fundamentally unchanged form and writing practice, and although this claim has been made throughout its history (Braud provides an example from Benjamin Constant in 1804),[25] in the face of *autofiction* the diary assumes a more specific role than before as 'antifiction' (to borrow a term from Philippe Lejeune).[26]

One further context for Ernaux's publication of diaries is its relation to issues of gender. As I discussed in the introductory chapter (pp. 35–38), the gendered nature of diary-writing is not uniquely an issue for Ernaux, as the only female writer that I am studying at length, and I do not intend to treat her work primarily from this perspective. Nonetheless, gender is one of the major recurring themes of her work (as Siobhán McIlvanney has remarked), and its relevance to her practice of publishing diaries has been addressed specifically in a conference paper by Philippe Lejeune, and in the discussion immediately following it between Lejeune and Ernaux herself.[27] Lejeune's own research indicates that more diaries are written in total by women than by men, but that more diaries by men come to be published. He also finds that, among professional writers, women are more likely than men to consider their *journal intime* and their professional writing as constituting 'deux activités autonomes et sans rapport' [two activities that are autonomous and without relationship] (253). When Lejeune invites Ernaux to reflect on how her own experience of writing and publishing diaries corresponds to his findings, her response suggests that there are some similarities with the observed pattern. Ernaux claims that, at the time of writing the *journaux intimes* that would later become *Je ne suis pas sortie* (1997) and *Se perdre* (2001), she had no thought of publication, and this only became possible after a period of forgetting and then rereading had made them seem distanced, as if the work of '*une autre*' [an other], and therefore potentially literary (256–7). In this respect, Ernaux's publication of her *journaux intimes* avoids the 'publication brute, originale, [l']entrée *directe*

[23] Jean-Benoît Puech, *L'Apprentissage du roman: extraits du "Journal d'apprentissage" de Benjamin Jordane* (Seyssel: Champ Vallon, 1993).

[24] Christophe Deshoulières, *Mémoires d'Aramis ou l'anti-journal* (Paris: Fayard, 1999).

[25] Braud, 'Le Texte d'un roman', p. 77.

[26] Philippe Lejeune, 'Le Journal comme « antifiction »', *Poétique*, 149 (2007), pp. 3–14.

[27] Philippe Lejeune, 'Un singulier journal au féminin', in *Annie Ernaux: une œuvre de l'entre-deux*, ed. by Fabrice Thumerel (Arras: Artois Presses Université, 2004), pp. 253–8.

dans l'intimité' [raw publication of the original text, *direct* entry into the *intime*] that Lejeune associates with male diarists (255). However, the case is much less clear with regard to the earlier publication of the two *journaux extérieurs* (*Journal du dehors* and *La Vie extérieure*, 1993 and 2000 respectively), both undertaken with publication in view, and clearly the *journal d'écriture* (*L'Atelier noir*) was never 'autonome' in relation to Ernaux's professional writing. It may well be that established gender norms within diary-writing play a role in Ernaux's publication of diary texts, and moreover in her apparent resistance to this publication, but there are also many other factors involved, some of which are addressed explicitly in the works' paratexts, and some of which remain implicit.

THE *JOURNAL EXTÉRIEUR*

Despite the apparent contradictions between Ernaux's overall life-writing project inaugurated with *La Place* and the diary-writing published in *Journal du dehors*, it is now apparent that these works emerged from two projects being considered simultaneously in the *journal d'écriture* in 1982, entitled 'La Visite' and 'Ville Nouvelle' respectively. The project of the 'Ville Nouvelle' only gradually took on its diaristic nature as a *journal extérieur*, which was acknowledged at the point of its publication by a title that offers a number of different interpretations, but all of them establishing programmatically the various ways in which this *journal* is 'du dehors' [of the outside] rather than 'intime'. The 'avant-propos', dated 1996 and added to editions from 1997 onwards, provides much more abundant paratextual guidance for readers, and particularly emphasizes two models for the text, which are nonetheless present from the first edition:[28] first, a model of an anonymous *transcription* of the world that Ernaux sees around her in the *ville nouvelle*, and secondly, a form of diary in which the diarist is manifested in her relations with others, rather than through introspection. These two models are difficult to reconcile (the former strives for anonymity whereas the latter constitutes the diarist as a writing subject), and most critical works solve the problem by emphasizing either one or the other. It is not a question here of judging which of the two is correct, nor of dismissing both as alibis for a secret or repressed reality in the text, but rather I shall examine how the models function in practice, and how their apparently contradictory co-existence leads to a first diaristic, authorial posture in Ernaux's work.

The *transcription* model

The *transcription* model of the *journal extérieur* is summarized by the account of the work on the back cover (of the Folio editions): 'De 1985 à 1992, j'ai transcrit

---

[28] Michael Sheringham's reading of *Journal du dehors* chooses to ignore this 'avant-propos' in order to emphasize the open-ended quality of the writing project; Michael Sheringham, *Everyday Life: Theories and Practices from Surrealism to the Present* (Oxford: OUP, 2006), p. 320.

des scènes, des paroles, saisies dans le R.E.R., les hypermarchés, le centre commercial de la Ville Nouvelle, où je vis' [between 1985 and 1992, I transcribed scenes,
words, overheard in the R.E.R., supermarkets, the shopping centre of the New
Town, where I live]. The concept of a *transcription* eliminates the writing subject
entirely leaving only an anonymous writing hand, and suggests an interpretation
of the title whereby the work is the diaristic writing produced spontaneously by
the outside world, or the world of social outsiders, and granted entry into the
literary sphere for the first time through Ernaux's intercession. This largely satisfies
the requirements for her wider writing project, as there is an emphasis on 'signes
objectifs', the problem of the '"je" autobiographique' is removed entirely, and a
critical distance is provided by writing 'de façon impersonnelle' [impersonally].[29]
This concept of the *journal extérieur* is espoused by Françoise Simonet-Tenant
(using the term 'journal externe'), for whom 'la diariste [. . .] se fait écrivain public
[. . .] parce qu'elle prend en charge et recueille une parole dispersée, qui ne bénéficie
ni de reconnaissance ni de légitimité, et qu'elle lui prête un vecteur écrit pour se
faire entendre' [the diarist [. . .] makes herself a public *écrivain* [. . .] because she
takes in hand and gathers together a dispersed body of speech, which does not
have the benefit of either recognition or legitimacy, and because she provides it
with a written form so that its voice can be heard].[30]

 This model of a faithful recording of a diary produced by the outside world
(the diary of the 'dehors') presupposes that this world is linguistic in nature,
whether it consists of 'des scènes, des paroles, des gestes d'anonymes' [scenes,
words, gestures of anonymous individuals] (8), or of the mortal remains of a cat
left on the road 'comme inscrit dans le goudron' [as if inscribed in the tarmac]
(29). It also involves an effort on the part of the diarist not to 'se mettre en scène'
[put herself in the scene], nor to express the emotion that influences her selection
of certain scenes (9). The explicit aim of the transcription is to 'atteindre la réalité
d'une époque—cette modernité dont une ville nouvelle donne le sentiment aigu'
[grasp the reality of an era—this modernity of which a new town provides a
strong impression] (8), a transient reality that is unlike 'les marques du passé et de
l'histoire' [the traces of the past and of history] found in older cities (6). This diary
of the 'dehors' is established by the very first entry's uncommented reproduction of
words of graffiti from an RER station carpark, and it is also reflected in the overall
form of *Journal du dehors*: just as the entries are not dated individually but merely
grouped by years, so there is little or no causal connection between the scenes
involved, and the 'réalité d'une époque' seems to develop by years rather than days.
As the *ville nouvelle* is experienced as fragmentary and formless, 'juste des instants,
des rencontres' [only moments, meetings], it renders useless any 'description' or
'récit' [narrative] (64).

---

[29] Marie-Madeleine Million-Lajoinie and Annie Ernaux, 'Au sujet des journaux extérieurs: entretien d'Annie Ernaux avec Marie-Madeleine Million-Lajoinie', in *Annie Ernaux: une œuvre de l'entre-
deux*, pp. 259–65, p. 261.
[30] Françoise Simonet-Tenant, *Le Journal intime* (Paris: Nathan, 2001), p. 84.

The particular desire to make present the 'réalité d'une époque' is expressed by the frequent comparison of the *transcription* with photography, which conflicts with the impression of this reality as being already linguistic in nature:

> J'ai cherché à pratiquer une sorte d'écriture photographique du réel, dans laquelle les existences croisées conserveraient leur opacité et leur énigme. (Plus tard, en voyant les photographies que Paul Strand a faites des habitants d'un village italien, Luzzano, photographies saisissantes de présence violente, presque douloureuses—les êtres sont là—, je penserai me trouver devant un idéal, inaccessible, de l'écriture.) (preface, 9)
>
> [I tried to practise a sort of photographic writing of the real, in which the beings that I encountered would keep their opacity and their enigma. (Later, when I saw the photographs that Paul Strand took of the inhabitants of an Italian village, Luzzano, photographs that struck you with their violent, almost painful sense of presence—the beings are right there in front of you—, I had the impression of being stood before an inaccessible ideal of writing.)]

A photographic ideal of language that sacrifices all possibility of interpretation in favour of complete presence is familiar from Barthes's *Journal de deuil* and *La Chambre claire*, and will recur in Ernaux's other diaries, but in the present context two observations are necessary. First, the utopian ideal is only ever realized imperfectly, and so the initial words of graffiti from the RER, 'DÉMENCE [...], JE T'AIME ELSA et IF YOUR CHILDREN ARE HAPPY THEY ARE COMUNISTS [*sic*]' (11), while certainly enigmatic, also implicate other signifiers and contexts and permit some, speculative, interpretation. Secondly, the ideal is in itself insufficient, the entries' 'caractère instantané, hors de tout récit' [momentary, snapshot character, outside any narrative] leaves Ernaux 'insatisfaite' [dissatisfied], and she finds herself writing them '*pour eux-mêmes, sans qu'ils servent à quoi que ce soit*' [for their own sake, without them serving any purpose at all] (85).

The Diary of the *vrai moi* (*extérieur*)

Although the *transcription* model of the *journal extérieur* remains problematic and, in itself, dissatisfying, it is more compatible with Ernaux's overall writing project than the second model is (a record of the diarist's relation towards others and the outside world), and the former is accordingly given greater prominence both in the diary and in the paratext. Nonetheless, the second model, presented as a historical development of or replacement for the *journal intime* ('lequel, né il y a deux siècles, n'est pas forcément éternel' [which, born two centuries ago, is not necessarily eternal], 10), is reinforced by the epigraph citing Rousseau ('Notre *vrai* moi n'est pas tout entier en nous' [Our *true* self is not entirely within us], 6), and has led to several studies of the question of alterity in *Journal du dehors*.[31] This diary of the

---

[31] For example, Mariana Ionescu, 'Journal du dehors d'Annie Ernaux: "Je est un autre"', *The French Review*, 74/5 (2001), pp. 934–43, and Monika Boehringer, 'Paroles d'autrui, paroles de soi: *Journal du dehors* d'Annie Ernaux', *Études Françaises*, 36/2 (2000), pp. 131–48. Michael Sheringham also demonstrates how it contributes to the development of the important concept of the 'je transpersonnel' in Ernaux's work; Sheringham, *Everyday Life*, pp. 321–2.

vrai moi has two distinct ways of functioning. The former is less contradictory with regard to the *transcription* model: while Ernaux acknowledges that her selective recording of scenes is always motivated by 'une émotion, un trouble ou de la révolte' [an emotion, confusion, or indignation] (8), or by 'obsessions, souvenirs' [obsessions, memories] (9), these are deliberately omitted from her writing and, furthermore, it is 'inconsciemment' [unconsciously] (9) that they determine the choice of scenes. It is therefore at a subsequent stage of rereading that the *vrai moi* appears, and specifically at the point when Ernaux diegetically and paratextually frames a section of the diary under the title 'Journal du dehors' and presents it to the reader for interpretation. Only from this perspective can the three initial phrases of graffiti cited earlier be related to the 'obsessions' present in her earlier published works, the 'démence' of her mother in *Une femme*, sex in *Passion simple*, and social class in *La Place*.

The second way in which the model of the *vrai moi* functions is less consistent with the *transcription* model, as it involves an active search at the moment of the diary's composition:

> Qu'est-ce que je cherche à toute force dans la réalité? Le sens? Souvent, mais pas toujours, par habitude intellectuelle (apprise) de ne pas s'abandonner seulement à la sensation: la 'mettre au-dessus de soi'. Ou bien, noter les gestes, les attitudes, les paroles des gens que je rencontre me donne l'illusion d'être proche d'eux. [...] Peut-être que je cherche quelque chose sur moi à travers eux, leurs façons de se tenir, leurs conversations. (36–7)

> [What am I looking for at all costs in reality? Meaning? Often, but not always, owing to an intellectual habit (which has been learnt) not to give myself over to sensation alone: to 'put it above oneself'. Or again, noting down the gestures, manners, words of the people I meet gives me the illusion of being close to them. [...] Perhaps I am looking for something in myself through them, the way they act, their conversations.]

This search for herself in others, or interpretation of her own traits which she recognizes in others, often manifests itself in entries that begin with an observation or *transcription* before moving towards personal recollection (of the working-class culture of her youth, 70, 72–4, of her nascent sexuality, 81–2, of words spoken by her parents, 87–8), and explanation of the connection between the two. More simply, she projects her own thoughts and desires onto others, such as a man looking into his shopping trolley ('satisfaction de posséder bientôt ce qu'il désirait, ou crainte d'en "avoir pour trop cher", ou les deux' [satisfaction of soon possessing what he desired, or fear of having 'paid over the odds', or both], 13). Far from an impersonal recording of an opaque reality, this process involves the diarist reading for parts of herself in the diary of the *dehors* which she finds all around her, re-writing this diary, and presenting it for further interpretation and appropriation by the reader.

A Diaristic Authorial Posture

The third model for the *journal extérieur*, which emerges from the inconsistencies of the *transcription* model and of the diary of the *vrai moi*, can be identified as a first diaristic authorial posture in Ernaux's work. Although this authorial posture is not described explicitly, it involves the whole process from the diary's conception as a literary project to its eventual reception by readers, and it is also addressed obliquely by several entries that express anxiety about the various modes of presence of an author (although the word is never used, preferring instead 'écrivain', 'artiste', and 'intellectuel'). These include comments on the material signs of an author's life (a cat, a 'carnet (de notes)', 52), the artifical, televised presentation of Marguerite Duras and Jean-Luc Godard as if in private intellectual conversation (67–8), the hypocritical public performance of a woman 'jouant longuement à l'écrivain maudit' [playing to excess the role of the cursed writer] (93–4), and the thought of her own works in the future lying neglected among the dusty tomes of the Sorbonne library (96–7). Similarly, Ernaux herself occupies a number of different roles in the *journal extérieur*. Aside from being a transcriber of reality (albeit an imperfect and dissatisfied one), she is inscribed in various scenes as an observer (12) or as an actor (her irresistible desire for 'toutes les fringues' [all the clothes] in the shopping centre, 31–2), she is both subject and (indirect) object of her search for herself in others, she is present in the distinct continuities of her programmatic reflections on the diary (18–19, 36–7, 46, 85, 106–7) and of her changing relationship with the *ville nouvelle* starting from her initial 'expérience bouleversante' [overwhelming experience] (7), and finally she signs her name as author in the paratextual frame of *Journal du dehors*. It might be common for a diaristic subject to be divided and dispersed in the text, but Ernaux's avatars are unusually numerous, and they all exist simultaneously as a subject striving to read and understand (the world around her, or another part of herself) and as an object of reading and interpretation by others (other parts of herself, or readers of Ernaux's books).

The authorial posture of the *journal extérieur* is therefore characterized by the stratification of the writing subject and its dual existence as subject and object, but it also assumes the implications of the two models discussed above. First, despite her desire to reproduce an opaque presence of the reality around her, Ernaux finds this reality to be linguistic, always already caught in a 'chaîne symbolique', and even already literary ('je m'aperçois que je cherche toujours les signes de la littérature dans la réalité' [I realize that I always look for the signs of literature in reality], 46). It follows that even her most faithful citation of this linguistic reality will be an interpretation, and yet one whose meaning is deferred indefinitely through her own re-interpretations and those of her readers (*Journal du dehors* is, by any account, a very *scriptible* text, to borrow Barthes's term). Secondly, the realizations that lead her to the concept of the *'je' transpersonnel*[32]—that her past life is 'déposée' [stored up] in the strangers around her and that she is herself 'porteuse de la vie des autres' [a vector for the life of others] (107)—concern not only her relation to the world around her but also her relationship as an author with her readers. The *vrai moi* that she has found in others can be appropriated in turn by readers, but more fundamentally the *je* of this writing subject has a porous

---

[32] Annie Ernaux, 'Vers un « je » transpersonnel', *RITM*, 6 (1993), pp. 219–21.

boundary with the *je* of the reader, as she remarks after making the embarrassing admission of having read her horoscope:

> La troisième personne, il/elle, c'est toujours l'autre, qui peut bien agir comme il veut. 'Je', c'est moi, lecteur, et il est impossible—ou inadmissible—que je lise l'horoscope et me conduise comme une midinette. 'Je' fait honte au lecteur. (18–19)
>
> [The third person, il/elle, is always the other, who can act just as they wish. 'Je', is me, the reader, and it is impossible—or unacceptable—that I would read the horoscope and behave like a silly young woman. 'Je' brings shame on the reader.]

By this means the diary seems to achieve the '*valeur collective* du "je" autobiographique' required by her broader writing project.[33]

La Vie extérieure

If this first diaristic authorial posture is arrived at only cautiously and implicitly in *Journal du dehors*, it is pursued more confidently in *La Vie extérieure*.[34] However, since Ernaux's publication of a *journal intime* with *Je ne suis pas sortie* in 1997 predates the publication of *La Vie extérieure* (2000), and also constitutes a more important development in her diary-writing, I shall comment only briefly on this second instalment of the *journal extérieur*. *La Vie extérieure* generally pursues the same strategies that are found in *Journal du dehors*, but with greater self-assurance and with the addition of some new themes. There are still many passages which follow the *trancription* model established by *Journal du dehors*, starting from the overheard dialogue in the first entry (9–10). The diary of the *vrai moi* is developed through explicit discussion of the diarist's identification with others (12–13, 14–15), and in particular by several allusions to the circumstances of Ernaux's personal experience of an abortion, which is described directly in the almost contemporary publication of *L'Événement* (96, 133, 146). There are more reflections on the hypocrisy of authors, intellectuals, and their literary *milieu* (37–8, 53–5, 55–6, 115), and more programmatic discussion relating to issues of truth and fiction (17–19, 99–101). Ernaux's authorial posture is given still greater presence by the main formal difference of *La Vie extérieure* in comparison with *Journal du dehors*: whereas entries in the earlier publication are merely grouped by year, which reflects the temporality of the *ville nouvelle*, the entries in *La Vie extérieure* are individually and specifically dated, producing much the same impression of quotidian, personal experience as does the *journal intime*. This has the effect of grounding the diarist's reflections in a more individualized, continuous, and historically specific chronology (particularly with regard to her political comments on the ongoing wars in Bosnia and Chechnya, 11–12, 146). Despite these changes in *La Vie extérieure*, as a piece of diary-writing it is more a prolongation of the initial project of the *journal extérieur* than a radically new departure.

---

[33] Ernaux, *L'Écriture comme un couteau*, p. 79.
[34] Annie Ernaux, *La Vie extérieure* (Paris: Gallimard, 2000).

THE *JOURNAL INTIME*

Given that the publication of the *journal extérieur* is justified by opposition with the implicitly unacceptable (or unpublishable) *journal intime*, Ernaux's publication of the two volumes of *journaux intimes*, *Je ne suis pas sortie* (1997) and *Se perdre* (2001), is an unexpected development in her writing career. These two works are even described as possessing to an extreme degree the very characteristics that make the *journal intime* unfit for Ernaux's life-writing project. They were initially composed without any politically engaged 'valeur collective' in view (unlike the *journal extérieur*), and in place of the clarity of an 'écriture de la distance' or of a 'témoignage objectif' [objective testimony] Ernaux writes 'dans la violence des sensations, sans réfléchir ni chercher d'ordre' [in the violence of her feelings, without pausing for thought or seeking any order] to produce 'le résidu d'une douleur' [the residue of a pain] (preface to *Je ne suis pas sortie*, 13) or 'quelque chose de cru et de noir' [something raw and black] (*Se perdre*, 15). This is by no means the necessary condition of every *journal intime*, and in particular Ernaux places herself in opposition to both Gide and Sartre, for whom the diary is (in her view) 'à la fois un outil intellectuel rigoureux et un lieu de vérité' [both a rigorous intellectual tool and a place of truth].[35]

Rather than attenuating these aspects of the *journaux intimes*, Ernaux recuperates them by means of a new publication strategy with two main strands, both resting on the fact that *Je ne suis pas sortie* and *Se perdre* depict events that have already featured in earlier retrospective works (*Une femme* and *Passion simple* respectively). First, a critical distance is established that is analogous to the writing of *La Place*, but in this case the separation is between the supposedly unreflective 'violence des sensations' of the diary and the authorial voice associated with the paratextual frame and the act of publication. This separation is greater than for most published diaries, as the delay of ten years and the intervening composition of the retrospective work (during which time the pages of the diary were 'comme interdites' [as if forbidden]; *Je ne suis pas sortie*, 12) allow Ernaux to 'jeter sur le journal un regard objectif, froid, de considérer le "je" comme un autre, une autre' [to look with a cold, objective eye on the *journal*, to consider the 'je' as an other, an other woman].[36] This paratextual voice (particularly in the prefaces to the two works) also assumes a greater magnitude than in most volumes of diaries, not just that of an *écrivain*, but of an author-figure orchestrating the relations between different parts of her *œuvre*.

The second strand of her publication strategy concerns the relationship between the retrospective work and the diary. Ernaux explains in the preface to *Je ne suis pas sortie* that she had initially wanted to leave 'une seule image, une seule vérité' [a single image, a single truth] of her mother (in *Une femme*), but has now decided that the publication of the diary provides the opportunity to '[mettre en danger]

---

[35] Thumerel and Ernaux, 'Ambivalences et ambiguïtés du journal intime', p. 248.
[36] Ernaux, *L'Écriture comme un couteau*, p. 39.

l'unicité, la cohérence auxquelles aboutit une œuvre' [[endanger] the uniqueness and coherence that an *œuvre* produces] (12), while in *Se perdre* she proposes to present 'une "vérité" autre que celle contenue dans *Passion simple*' [a different 'truth' from that contained in *Passion simple*] (15). Ernaux later describes the ability of the two diaries to 'faire "jouer" le premier texte' [set the first text 'in motion'] and to 'démystifier aussi la clôture de l'œuvre' [demystify the closure of the *œuvre*].[37]

Whereas the writing of the *journal extérieur* involves the gradual creation of a diaristic authorial posture, the published *journaux intimes* are more deeply integrated into Ernaux's life-writing project by means of these relations between several narrative instances. It will therefore be useful to consider this *jeu* of supplementarity by first examining the programmatic claims, contradictions, and insufficiencies of *Une femme*, then the additions or compensations offered by the diary of *Je ne suis pas sortie*. Finally, the paratextual frame of *Je ne suis pas sortie* seems to constitute a diaristic author-figure which, if fully assumed by Ernaux, would significantly change the nature of her whole life-writing project.

Une femme as *œuvre*

The specific date and place given in the first sentence of *Une femme* inscribe it in the series of retrospective nonfictional works established by *La Place* (all the works in this series are indicated in the timeline on p. 195). Many of Ernaux's stated aims in *Une femme* resemble those of *La Place*, such as the intention to write 'à la jointure du familial et du social, du mythe et de l'histoire' [at the intersection of the familial and the social, of myth and history] (23), and to be an impersonal 'archiviste' of a culture that she has long since abandoned (26). The analogy between the two works also implies that, for *Une femme* as for *La Place*, 'il n'y aura jamais aucun autre récit possible, avec d'autres mots, un autre ordre des phrases' [there will never be another possible narrative, with other words, another sequence of its sentences] (73). However, two major differences between these projects account for the specificities of *Une femme* that apparently necessitate the publication of a supplementary work: whereas *La Place* was written several years after her father's death, Ernaux composed *Une femme* in the midst of a mourning process that does not allow 'la distance qui facilite l'analyse des souvenirs' [the distance that allows the analysis of memories] (22), and unlike her father, Ernaux's mother has a timeless constitutive importance as 'la femme de [son] imaginaire' [the woman of [her] imagination] (22–3) or 'la seule femme qui ait vraiment compté pour [elle]' [the only woman who has really mattered to [her]] (22). The composition of *Une femme* is therefore an attempt to 'saisir la femme qui a existé en dehors d['elle], la femme réelle' [grasp the woman who existed outside [her] imagination], the real woman] by presenting a chronological 'histoire' of her life (22–3), and so to 'la mettre au monde' [place her in the world] (43), to grant her an ideal, literary existence in 'le monde dominant des mots et des idées' [the

[37] Ibid., p. 39.

dominant world of words and ideas] (106) with 'un ordre idéal [des mots], seul capable de rendre une vérité concernant [sa] mère' [an ideal sequence [of words], the only one capable of producing a truth about [her] mother] (43–4).

Despite a claim of completion and success towards the end of the book ('maintenant, tout est lié' [now, everything is tied up], 103), certain insufficiencies of the text are manifest even before being revealed by the supplement. First, Ernaux is unable to realize fully the intended 'vérité' and 'signification plus générale' [broader meaning], as her attempt to use a neutral and abstract language to grant her mother an existence separate from her own *Imaginaire* is often defeated by the emotional effect of certain familiar expressions spoken by her mother (such as the phrase '"s'il t'arrive un malheur"' ['if anything should happen to you'], 62). Secondly, she is even unwilling to transform her own memories into this generalized form, as she experiences a conflicting desire to 'conserver de [sa] mère des images purement affectives, chaleur ou larmes, sans leur donner du sens' [hold on to purely affective images of [her] mother, warmth or tears, without attributing any meaning to them] (52).

Besides her inability and unwillingness to pursue the project to its logical conclusion, Ernaux encounters a particular problem with regard to the period of her mother's dementia, which is to be precisely the subject of the supplementary work. At the start of the book she expresses confusion about how to relate to this part of her mother's life (22), and incomprehension towards the conviction of others that these years of declining health were without any value ('"ça servait à quoi qu'elle vive dans cet état plusieurs années"' ['what was the point of her living in that state for several years'], 19). Furthermore, when the narrative arrives at the point of her mother's illness, Ernaux states that this is the point when 'son histoire s'arrête, celle où elle avait sa place dans le monde' [her story comes to an end, that story in which she had her place in the world] (89). If a certain correspondence exists between the *histoire* that Ernaux is constructing and the way a life is lived as *histoire* in practice, in society, and over time, this correspondence does not apply to the life her mother led on the geriatric ward of the hospital. Accordingly, the following part of the book struggles to depict this institutional environment 'sans saisons [...] ni temps, juste la répétition bien réglée des fonctions, manger, se coucher, etc.' [without seasons [...] nor time, just the well regulated repetition of mundane tasks, eating, going to bed, etc.] (97), or to integrate this experience into a whole in which, supposedly, 'tout est lié' (103).

The *journal intime* as Supplement

The *journal intime* presented in *Je ne suis pas sortie* supplements *Une femme* most clearly in its temporality, both in the chronology of its composition and with regard to the tenses that Ernaux uses to write about her mother. The composition of the diary itself continues from Ernaux's first fragmentary observations of her mother's decline, accompanies a first, abortive attempt at a *livre* on her mother (97, 99), claims later to be in a state of 'rupture' or 'disjonction' between the diary and the intended *livre* following her mother's death (111–12, 114), then overlaps briefly with the composition of *Une femme* (115–16). However, most entries also refer back to a visit to the hospital ward preceding the moment of writing—an experience which excludes thought ('le plus souvent, je ne pense à rien, je suis auprès d'elle, c'est tout' [most often, I do not think about anything, I am in her presence, that is all], 84), time ('le temps a disparu' [time has disappeared], 41), and therefore writing itself—and they refer forwards to the point when 'tout sera lié, comme une histoire' [everything will be tied up, like a story] (112), whereas we know by this point that it is precisely the shortcomings of the supposedly unified *histoire* of *Une femme* that called for the publication of *Je ne suis pas sortie*. The chronology established by the diary therefore serves not only to extend that of *Une femme*, but also to open up a broader space which both works inhabit, but cannot entirely fill.

Within this chronology, it might be expected that the diary, supposedly complementing the generalized *histoire* of *Une femme* (narrated in perfect and imperfect tenses) with the presence of a 'résidu de la douleur' [residue of pain], would be orientated towards the unthinking, timeless experience of the visits to the hospital ward, even as an ideal that is impossible to attain in writing (this would resemble the general trend of Barthes's *Journal de deuil*). Indeed, most entries begin with observations of the diarist's mother in the present tense (and to a lesser extent the perfect tense), first at home and later in the hospital, but the movement of the diary's reflections then leads elsewhere. The present tenses usually either turn out to refer to an ongoing, habitual state, or lead directly to an observation of such a state ('Elle veut voir la télé tout de suite. [...] Maintenant elle ne comprend plus rien, que son désir' [She wants to watch the television straight away. [...] She now understands nothing except her own desire], 15). Sometimes a comparison of these states gives an impression of the passage of time over the course of the illness, which was one of the difficulties encountered in *Une femme* ('Elle perd toutes ses affaires personnelles, mais elle ne les cherche plus. Elle a renoncé' [She loses all her personal possessions, but she does not look for them any more. She has given up], 35). More often, however, the present is joined by a recollection from the distant past, such that the two events produce a timeless observation concerning her mother, or their relationship:

> M'accueille très mal. Renfrognée: 'Tes visites ne me font pas plaisir! Comment tu te conduis, tu n'as pas honte?' Je suis dans une stupeur sans nom, je viens de passer la nuit avec A., à faire l'amour. Comment SAIT-ELLE? La croyance de mon enfance me submerge, son œil capable de tout voir, comme Dieu, dans la tombe de Caïn. (22)

> [Gives me a very cold welcome. Sullenly: 'Your visits give me no pleasure! How you carry on, aren't you ashamed?' I am struck with an indescribable astonishment, I have just spent the night with A., making love. How does she KNOW? I am filled again with the belief from my childhood, her eye all-seeing, like God, in Cain's grave.]

As the diary advances, these recollections and observations become more frequent, and Ernaux also begins to comment without any introduction on apparently permanent qualities of her mother ('Une femme violente, avec une seule grille d'explication du monde, celle de la religion' [A violent woman, with a single way of viewing the world, that of religion], 37). Rather than an orientation towards the absolute presence experienced on the hospital ward, the writing of the diary seems to move in the direction of a *livre* on her mother, but one that has not in fact been written, and which describes 'la femme de [son] imaginaire' that is purposely avoided in *Une femme* (which instead pursues a depiction of 'la femme réelle').

In this way, the diary could be considered to be providing just another possible 'vérité' in addition to that found in *Une femme*, yet it also addresses a fundamental question of presence in writing, in terms that invite comparison with Barthes's *Journal de deuil*. Not only does Ernaux recognize that 'écrire sur sa mère pose forcément le problème de l'écriture' [writing about one's mother necessarily poses the problem of writing] (49), owing to the complex relationship of identification with her mother (19–20, 23, 29, 37, 41), but also the gradual loss of self caused by Alzheimer's disease leads to a real and present mourning, as has been recognized by psychoanalytic literature on dementia:

> The pattern of psychological distress and nature of the disease would fit more easily into a paradigm of present grief for actual, not anticipated, loss: current loss with current grief. Recently a colleague was distressed after visiting her mother in a nursing home. Her mother had forgotten her. She felt she had lost not only her mother, but also that part of herself invested in her mother, carried in her mother's memory.[38]

The diary is very lucid in this regard, and Ernaux recognizes that with the onset of the illness her mother 'a commencé de "partir"' [began to 'leave'] (68), leading to a painful and confusing situation of undecidable presence and absence ('c'est ma mère et ce n'est plus elle' [it is my mother and it is no longer her], 26). Like Barthes, in her mourning process Ernaux attempts to realize a linguistic presence of the particular essence of her mother, through a '[tentative éperdue de fixer] des expressions qui [...] se confondent avec son être unique' [[desperate attempt to pin down] the expressions that [...] are conflated with her unique being] (80). But whereas Barthes's diary moves gradually towards a utopian ideal that is inaccessible to language, Ernaux's project finds greater possibilities in writing itself, precisely because the object of her writing is the constitutive '*elle*' (76, 80) of her *Imaginaire* that is implicated in the relationship of mutual identification with her mother. This *Imaginaire* appears to be essentially linguistic in nature, and so to be open to exploration through writing, without any possibility of being exhausted, finalized, or fixed.

The publication of *Je ne suis pas sortie*

While both Barthes's and Ernaux's diaries of mourning were written without the intention of publication, the latter did in fact come to be published anthumously, and it is the diegetic instance of this act of publication that effectively establishes an author-figure to a much greater extent than the *journal extérieur*. This diegetic voice is constituted by the paratextual frame of the diary, notably the choice of title, the preface, the back cover, and a single explanatory footnote (28),

---

[38] Jane Garner, 'Dementia: An Intimate Death', *British Journal of Medical Psychology*, 70 (1997), pp. 177–84, p. 179. This article aims to 'link some of the psychoanalytic literature of grief and the experience of clinicians in old age psychiatry working with patients and their relatives' (177).

all of which are signed by or attributable to Annie Ernaux (or 'A.E.', on the back cover). The paratext establishes a substantial third point of reinterpretation regarding the problem of writing on Ernaux's mother, by providing a factual account of the composition of *Une femme* and the diary (9–12), and by presenting their relationship of supplementarity from a more recent perspective:

> Je crois maintenant que l'unicité, la cohérence auxquelles aboutit une œuvre— quelle que soit par ailleurs la volonté de prendre en compte les données les plus contradictoires—doivent être mises en danger toutes les fois que c'est possible. En rendant publiques ces pages, l'occasion s'en présente pour moi. (12–13)
>
> [I believe now that the uniqueness, the coherence that an *œuvre* produces—whatever the intention might be to take into account the most contradictory elements—should be put in danger whenever possible. By making these pages public, I am taking the opportunity to do just this.]

Far from claiming finally to have concluded this particular writing process, the third stage is marked by the same problem that is explored in the diary, that of the undecidable presence and absence of her writing, a paradoxical state that is reflected in Ernaux's dreams of her mother as being 'morte et vivante à la fois, comme ces personnages de la mythologie grecque qui ont franchi deux fois le fleuve des morts' [dead and alive at the same time, like those characters from Greek mythology who have twice crossed the river of the dead] (14). The continuing irresolution is also reflected in the title, a citation from the author's mother that remains enigmatic (thereby fulfilling her father's prediction, 'tu n'auras pas le dernier mot avec elle!' [you won't have the last word with her!], 75), and which, given the strong identification between the two women, suggests that the author-figure too is still in the 'nuit' of her mourning and of partial ignorance.

As the supplementary role of the diary opens up a space of writing and interpretation that is broader than the two main texts, so the paratext extends this space indefinitely in the author's work, and infuses it with the diary's 'inconscience de la suite—qui caractérise peut-être toute écriture, la mienne sûrement' [unawareness of what is to follow—which perhaps characterizes all writing, certainly my own] (12). This has the potential to institute a diaristic author-figure, whose literary *œuvre* is dominated by her continuing reflections and successive reinterpretations of her own life, and also (building on the work of the *journal extérieur*) maintains a *'je' transpersonnel*, open to the lives and identities of others, and to the reinterpretations of readers. This diaristic author-figure would invite comparison with the concept of the 'espace autobiographique' [autobiographical space], which Philippe Lejeune suggests as the organizing principle of Gide's *œuvre*.[39] However, the implications of Ernaux's publication of *Je ne suis pas sortie* do not necessarily extend to her whole *œuvre* in a way that would replace the distanced, impersonal authorial posture established in *La Place*, nor is this fully accomplished with the publication of *Se perdre* in 2001.

---

[39] Philippe Lejeune, 'Gide et l'espace autobiographique', in *Le Pacte autobiographique* (Paris: Seuil, 1996), pp. 165–96.

Se perdre

Just as for the *journal extérieur*, Ernaux's second publication of a *journal intime*, *Se perdre*, continues the same general strategy while developing some elements that had remained implicit in *Je ne suis pas sortie*. The overall form of *Se perdre* is the same as that of *Je ne suis pas sortie*, preceding the diary with a preface (13–16) that explains the circumstances and relationship of the two texts, the diary itself and the retrospective *livre* treating the same material, which had been published in 1991 as *Passion simple*. This new paratextual frame once again establishes itself as a third point of interpretation. The experience of mourning and of her *passion* are closely linked throughout the diary ('je sais que je *vis* un deuil, celui d'une passion' [I know that I am *living* a mourning, the mourning of a passion], 210). Like her mourning, Ernaux's *passion* is a process of anticipation, recollection, and interpretation (therefore associated with writing and absence), which relates to a repeated experience of absolute presence that is inaccessible to writing—respectively, the hospital visits in *Je ne suis pas sortie* and the sexual encounters in *Se perdre*, of which she writes that 'à chaque minute, je *suis* ce présent qui fuit' [every minute, I *am* this present that is passing] (35). The diary is preoccupied with the same problem of presence and absence, and if her mother's death, her abortion (alluded to in *La Vie extérieure*), and her *passion* all result in 'la même perte, [...] que seule l'écriture peut élucider vraiment' [the same *loss*, [...] which only writing can truly elucidate] (173), her desire in writing is still 'par-dessus tout, de sauver la vie, sauver du néant ce qui, pourtant, s'en approche le plus' [above all, to save life, to save from the void that which, nonetheless, comes closest to it] (13).

The main development that takes place with the publication of *Se perdre* is indicated by the epigraph, '*Voglio vivere una favola* / (Je veux vivre une histoire)' [I want to live a story]: the diary emphasizes the linguistic nature of the *passion* (as opposed to the supposedly non-linguistic experience of the sexual encounters themselves), and Ernaux self-consciously aims to live and write this *passion* as a 'roman de la vie' [novel from life] (15) or 'la "belle histoire d'amour"' [the 'great love story'] (23), with the ultimate goal of 'la perfection de l'amour comme [elle a] cru atteindre en écrivant *Une femme* la perfection de l'écriture' [the perfection of love, as [she] thought [she] had achieved, with *Une femme*, the perfection of writing] (22). Once again, a comparison with Gide is invited by this desire to 'faire de sa vie une œuvre d'art' [make his life into a work of art] (281), and the relationship with Gide's authorial posture will reappear in the later publication of the *journal d'écriture*, *L'Atelier noir* (2011), which sets out far more positively the place of diary-writing in relation to Ernaux's whole life-writing project.

THE *JOURNAL D'ÉCRITURE*

Following the publication of *Les Années* in 2008, whose breadth of subject matter and ambition as 'une forme nouvelle d'autobiographie, impersonnelle et collective' [a new form of autobiography, impersonal and collective] (*Les Années*, back cover) make it a culmination of the life-writing project undertaken in *La Place*,[40] Ernaux's career arrived at a stage of summation with the almost simultaneous publication in 2011 of *Écrire la vie* and the *journal d'écriture, L'Atelier noir*. This resembles the progression in Gide's career from *Les Faux-monnayeurs* (as a culmination of his fictional writing in a *roman* 'somme')[41] to the summation of his author-figure in his *Œuvres complètes* and the *Journal 1889–1939*, and indeed certain allusions to Gide in Ernaux's 2011 publications draw attention to parallels between their respective situations. However, the most striking similarity between them is that, for both authors, their *œuvres complètes* and the diary offer different, even contradictory images of the *œuvre* and author-figure, while in each case the two publications avoid referring to one another. The overall effect of the paratext, additional material, and arrangement of works in *Écrire la vie* is to present a collective *œuvre* devoted to life-writing, a complete, finalized, and objective account of a *vie*, from which the writing subject is elided. The relation of *L'Atelier noir* to the apparent self-sufficiency of *Écrire la vie* is homologous to the publication strategy of *Je ne suis pas sortie* relative to *Une femme*: whereas Ernaux's *journaux intimes* provide a diaristic account of life experience that is related in a separate, retrospective work, *L'Atelier noir* is the diary of the experience of writing, and therefore provides '"l'autre côté" [des] textes publiés' ['the other side' [of the] published texts] (*L'Atelier noir*, 7) and constitutes the very writing subject that is excluded from *Écrire la vie*.

Just as for *Je ne suis pas sortie*, it will be useful to follow the structure of supplementarity through its several stages: first the claims of *Écrire la vie* to constitute a coherent, self-sufficient whole, then the way in which the *journal d'écriture* supplements the works that it discusses (from *La Place* up to *Les Années*), and finally the way the very publication of *L'Atelier noir* destabilizes and opens up the model of the *œuvre* proposed by *Écrire la vie*. This is not only a more complex structure than that of the *journaux intimes*, but it also demonstrates the place of diary-writing in Ernaux's whole life-writing project, a place that is once again marginalized relative to the dominant literary form of autobiography, but with an important role in qualifying and subverting the latter's totalizing claims.

Écrire la vie as *œuvre*

At the risk of being trivial, one can say that *Écrire la vie* consists of two elements, *écrire* and *la vie*, of which the former is consistently de-emphasized in favour of the latter. *Écrire la vie* includes a preface, most of Ernaux's works printed roughly in the chronological order of the experiences that they relate (unlike the conventional arrangement of *œuvres complètes* either by genre or by order of original publication), and a 'photojournal' (a chronological series of photographs

---

[40] *Les Années* was also recognized as Ernaux's magnum opus by a number of literary prizes, including the Prix Marguerite Duras, Prix François Mauriac, and Prix de la langue française.
[41] Alain Goulet, 'Notice' for *Les Faux-monnayeurs*, in André Gide, *Romans et récits*, II, pp. 1201–20, p. 1201. As discussed earlier (p. 41), Gide had also initially conceived of *Les Cahiers d'André Walter* as being '[sa] somme'.

of Ernaux and her family, accompanied by thematically linked fragments of *journal intime* which lack any chronological continuity). Whereas most collections of *œuvres complètes* make a corpus cohere around the author-figure as the strongest unifying element, the *photojournal* and the arrangement of works in *Écrire la vie* serve to 'bouscul[er] l'évolution de l'écriture' [disrupt the evolution of the writing] (preface, 8), and so to move emphasis from the development of the author-figure over time to the quite separate life that is depicted in order and in many different narrative forms. In these respects, the volume corresponds to her long-standing desires to tell the whole, finalized truth about her life (or *la vie*, more generally) with such objectivity that the writing subject is elided entirely (or rather dispersed among 'la diversité des formes, l'écart des voix et des styles' [the diversity of forms, the gaps between voices and styles], 8).

This separation between *vie* and *écriture* is a continuation of the 'écriture de la distance' established at the start of Ernaux's life-writing project in *La Place*,[42] and runs counter to some of the developments that had taken place in the diary publications. As early as the publication of *Journal du dehors*, the *journal extérieur* had begun to reconcile the separation between the writing subject and the material being narrated, by means of the authorial posture that it gradually adopts. Whereas the *journaux intimes* had demonstrated Ernaux's need in her writing project to 'sauver' aspects of her life (*Se perdre*, 13), embracing the particularity that makes them so important for her, the preface of *Écrire la vie* describes this life as being extremely generalizable, or even abstract:

> Non pas ma vie, ni sa vie, ni même une vie. La vie, avec ses contenus qui sont les mêmes pour tous mais que l'on éprouve de façon individuelle: le corps, l'éducation, l'appartenance et la condition sexuelles, la trajectoire sociale, l'existence des autres, la maladie, le deuil. (7)

> [Not my life, nor one's life, nor even a life. Life itself, with its contents that are the same for everyone but which we experience in an individual way: the body, education, gender and sexual preference, social life, the existence of others, disease, mourning.]

Unlike the impression given by the published diaries of relating to an existence that is always already linguistic in nature, *Écrire la vie* conceives of life as being 'muette et informe' [silent and formless], requiring the writer to 'l'inscrire dans une forme, des phrases, des mots' [inscribe it in a form, with sentences, words] (8). Finally, *Écrire la vie* directly refutes the Gidean desire expressed in *Se perdre* to 'faire de sa vie une œuvre d'art' (*Se perdre*, 281):

> Je n'ai pas cherché à m'écrire, à faire œuvre de ma vie: je me suis servi d'elle [...] comme d'une matière à explorer pour saisir et mettre au jour quelque chose de l'ordre d'une vérité sensible. (7)

> [I have not set out to write myself, to make an *œuvre* of my life: I have made use of it [...] as if it were material to be explored in order to grasp and make known something in the order of an intuitive truth.]

---

[42] Ernaux, *L'Écriture comme un couteau*, pp. 79–80.

Écrire la vie therefore appears to forget the lessons learnt from the earlier diary publications, despite the fact that they are included (except for *La Vie extérieure*) in this same volume.

In effect, *Écrire la vie* returns to a structure that is by now familiar from Ernaux's work, but which is applied for the first time to her whole *œuvre*: the dominant autobiographical model of her writing project makes certain totalizing claims—here, to fix the 'muette et informe' material of a whole life in a definitive and generalizable linguistic form—while simultaneously calling for another work to compensate for ('suppléer à') its insufficiencies. This contradictory structure is reflected in the problematic aim of the *photojournal* to 'ouvrir un espace autobiographique différent' [open up a different sort of autobiographical space] (8), for the very reason that an *espace autobiographique* is not, by any definition, autobiography. The *espace autobiographique* in Gide's work, as conceived by Philippe Lejeune, involves the orchestrated failure of the autobiography *Si le grain ne meurt*, which thereby opens the rest of his *œuvre*, fiction and nonfiction alike, to autobiographical readings which cannot be finalized or fixed.[43] If the *photojournal* opens an *espace autobiographique* in Ernaux's work (including the two early *romans* contained in *Écrire la vie*) by virtue of 'la réalité, matérielle, irréfutable des photos' [the material, irrefutable reality of photographs] and 'la réalité subjective du journal' (8), it follows that this *vie* has not been finalized or fixed in its present form, and furthermore, that both the *vie* and the writing subject (obscured and elided as it is) lack the 'réalité' or presence claimed by the *photojournal* itself. This sentiment is expressed most directly in the opening sentence of the preface, where Ernaux finds that the collection inspires in her 'une espèce d'incrédulité, voire d'irréalité' [a sort of incredulity, even a sense of unreality] (7).

The *journal d'écriture* as Supplement to the Previous Works

The supplementary relation of the *journal d'écriture* to the works on which it reflects is largely established, just as in *Je ne suis pas sortie*, by its chronology. The diary is begun in a 'période de désarroi' [period of disarray] following Ernaux's abortive attempt to write a *roman* about her father, a period when she 'hésitai[t] entre plusieurs projets' [wavered between several projects] (8). This opening section is dominated by a deliberation on 'le problème du réel et de l'imaginaire' (17), or between '"l'authentique" ou "la fictive"' (21), which gives rise to the life-writing project established in *La Place*. The diary contained in *L'Atelier noir* ends immediately before the completion of *Les Années*, and although this conclusion is created artificially by Ernaux's editorial decision not to include any subsequent entries from the ongoing *journal d'écriture* (14), it is also anticipated by the diary's frequent discussion of this very project, as highlighted by the preface:

> Par-dessus tout apparaîtra la gestation de ces *Années*, texte envisagé dès 1983—'ce serait une sorte de destin de femme'—, désigné sous les appellations successives de

---

43 Lejeune, 'Gide et l'espace autobiographique'.

'RT' (roman total), 'Histoire', 'Passage', 'Génération', 'Jours du monde', et que je ne poursuivrai réellement qu'à partir de 2002. (13)

[Above all, the gestation of *Les Années* will be apparent, a text imagined from 1983 onwards—'it would be a sort of life of woman in general'—, denoted successively by the terms 'RT' (roman total), 'Histoire', 'Passage', 'Génération', 'Jours du monde', and which I would only really pursue from 2002.]

The diary therefore reveals a continuity in Ernaux's writing from the inauguration of her life-writing project in *La Place* up to a conclusion or 'somme' (28) in *Les Années*, an authorial 'engage[ment] [...] au fil des années' [commitment [...] across the years] that is alluded to but otherwise obscured in *Écrire la Vie* (8), and it situates itself relative to this continuity as a distanced but also instrumental point of reflection.

Within this continuity, the development of Ernaux's writing projects is governed by the totalizing aims of the project that eventually leads to *Les Années*, and which I shall refer to by its most common name of 'RT' ('roman total'). As 'une somme' or an 'autobiographie totale' (151), the 'RT' aims to depict a life in its entirety, but this life is to be completely generalized by a form that is 'anonyme' (20), 'tout à fait impersonnelle' [completely impersonal] (169), and narrated in the third person (69). As a 'livre "total"' (107)—recalling the concepts of the *Livre* and the *Album* that Barthes adopts from Mallarmé[44]—the 'RT' aspires towards an ideal, unified, and timeless 'vérité', which is related to a device that Ernaux terms 'la vie palimpseste' (115, 140, 145), a process of 'suppression du temps par l'art' [supression of time through art] (33) by evoking 'deux temps à la fois' [two moments at once] (140), such as two points of intense 'jalousie' in her life (29–30). This second aim presents one of the principal difficulties of the project, as Ernaux admits that '[avec] une histoire palimpseste—hors du temps—[elle se sent] morte' [[with] a palimpsest, rewritten story—outside of time—[she feels] dead] (145), and that the impression of 'permanence' must somehow co-exist with a sense of 'le *déroulement* du temps' [the *passing* of time] (33).

The overall movement of Ernaux's writing consists of a series of smaller projects gradually splitting off from deliberations about the 'RT', and consequently at any one time she has '2 projets, toujours le grand et un petit' [2 projects, always the big one and a little one] (140). It is often a cause of regret that she succumbs to the 'tentation du "second texte"' [temptation of the 'secondary text'] (145), and these intermediate works with more modest aims than the 'RT' can appear as a 'manœuvre de retardement' [delaying strategy] (60), although she is also sometimes resigned to being 'condamnée à n'écrire que ce qui naît de [son] désir, que le "nécessaire"' [condemned to write only what arises from [her] desire, only what is 'necessary'] (101). However, the distinction between the intermediate works and the 'RT' gradually changes in a way that calls into question whether *Les Années*, apparently the realization of the 'grand roman total' (111), is

---

[44] Roland Barthes, *La Préparation du roman I et II: cours et séminaires au Collège de France (1978–1979 et 1979–1980)*, ed. by Nathalie Léger (Paris: Seuil, 2003), pp. 246–58.

really fundamentally different from the partial, qualified successes of the earlier publications:

> Tout le problème est de résoudre cela: ce que j'ai envie de faire (livre beau, une génération) et ce que je peux faire (venu de mes profondeurs, de mes désirs). (63)
>
> Au fond, à part 'Dans le temps', je n'ai fait jusqu'ici que des débuts. Je n'ai donc pas trouvé ma méthode et mon vrai désir. (169)
>
> [Je sais] bien que le désir de poursuivre [le RT] est tiré non du sentiment de réussite esthétique mais du désir venu de l'émotion. (187–8)
>
> [The whole problem is to reconcile this: what I want to do (a great work, story of a generation) and what I am capable of doing (arising from my depths, my desires).
>
> Essentially, aside from 'Dans le temps', I have so far made only beginnings. I have not, therefore, found my method and my real desire.
>
> [I know] that the desire to pursue [the project of RT] is motivated, not by a sense of aesthetic accomplishment, but from a desire arising from emotion.]

From the initial opposition between the conscious, theorized 'envie' for the 'RT' and the obscure, unconscious 'désirs' behind the intermediate works, the 'RT' comes to be seen as the 'vrai désir' which needs to be clarified together with its corresponding 'méthode', until finally the 'RT' resembles the prosaic emotional necessity of the intermediate works more than the aesthetic concerns of a 'livre "total"'.

If the *journal d'écriture* acts as a supplement to the earlier published works, it reveals their insufficiencies by means of this image of the *œuvre* (including *Les Années*) as so many incomplete realizations or intermediate 'investissements' [investments] (60) of desires that cannot be fully known, and it is the diary's own pursuit of these desires that offers some compensation. Like other forms of supplement, the diary both distances itself from the object being supplemented, and in other respects demonstrates a continuity between the two. This distance, which depends on the autonomy of the *journal d'écriture* as a coherent series of dated entries (9), is conceived as an opposition between the diary's blind, hesitant, 'travail de taupe creusant d'interminables galeries' [work of a mole digging endless tunnels] (7), written on scrap paper to eliminate any 'caractère solennel' [solemn character] (8), and the clarity of the real writing process of the published works:

> C'est un journal d'avant-écriture, un journal de fouilles, qui m'accompagne encore un peu en début de rédaction, mais que j'abandonne aussitôt que je suis happée par la certitude d'aller jusqu'au bout du texte entrepris et que, dès lors, un regard en arrière, un repentir ou une hésitation ne sont même plus concevables. D'où ces grands blancs, de plusieurs mois, voire d'années, qui correspondent à des périodes pendant lesquelles j'écris 'vraiment'. (9–10)
>
> [It is a *journal* of pre-writing, a *journal* of excavations, which accompanies me for a short while at the start of the real writing process, but which I abandon as soon as I am seized by the certainty that I will see through to completion the text that I have undertaken, and from this point on, a glance behind me, any regret or hesitation are no longer even imaginable. That is the reason for these large gaps, of several months, even years, which correspond to periods during which I am writing 'for real'.]

Yet there is a sense in which it is the supposedly real *écriture* of the individual works that is blind, since the 'certitude d'aller jusqu'au bout du texte entrepris' is in fact a decision to embrace an individual 'désir' or 'nécessité' (10), and although Ernaux 'écri[t] pour construire, comprendre en même temps' [writes to construct something, and to understand as well], this writing is also an 'acte de foi' [act of faith] (60). In contrast, the *journal d'écriture* is Ernaux's attempt to 'connaître le désir qui est en [elle]' [know the desire that is within [her]] (93), in the expectation that the diary can '[l']éclaire[r] sur ce désir' [shed light on this desire] (11), and on the assumption that each work has a necessary 'poétique [qui] est dictée par l'inconscient, la vie de l'auteur' [literary form [which] is determined by the unconscious, the life of the author] (116). As a search for the unconscious (including the interpretation of her own dreams, 19), this process can never be completed, and the metaphor evoked in the preface of 'autant d'échelles adossées au vide' [so many ladders propped up against the void] and of a 'sensation accablante de tourner en rond dans un lieu noir' [overwhelming feeling of going round in circles in a dark place] (10) is effectively manifested in the diary's potentially endless rereadings of itself (93, 133, 134, 140, 158).

Like the *journaux intimes*, the *journal d'écriture* opens up a diaristic space that contains and extends beyond both the previously published works and *L'Atelier noir* itself, but the author-figure that this creates now takes on a very different appearance:

> 'Chercher comment je suis devenue écrivain' est mal poser la question. Plutôt, mon imaginaire de l'écriture à mettre au jour (et de ce fait, je supprime l'aspect narcissique et particulier de la recherche de soi-écrivain). (88)
>
> Ce qui sera bouffon, si on publie un jour ce journal d'écriture, en fait de recherche à 99%, c'est qu'on découvrira à quel point, finalement, la forme m'aura préoccupée. Bref, ce qu'ils appellent la littérature. (125)
>
> ['To explore how I became a writer' is to ask the wrong question. Rather, I should take stock of my imaginary conception of writing (and in this way, I get rid of the narcissistic and individual aspect of the search for the writer-self).
>
> It would be bizarre, if this *journal d'écriture* were published one day, in an effort to exhaust every avenue of research, that they would discover just how much, ultimately, I have been preoccupied with matters of form. Or in fact, with what they call literature.]

Ernaux finds the *journal d'écriture* 'le plus effrayant' [the most frightening] of her diaries (133), not because of any revelation of details of her private life, but because of its 'mise à nu de [ses] processus d'écriture' [revelation of [her] writing processes] (14), which produces a formal, literary, author-figure, reminiscent not only of the exposition of an authorial *Imaginaire* in *Roland Barthes par Roland Barthes*, but also of the authorial 'être de papier' [being of paper] that emerges from the Sally Mara works.

L'Atelier noir and *Écrire la vie*

The absence in *L'Atelier noir* and *Écrire la vie* of any direct reference to one another allows for a fundamental ambiguity as to the relationship between these two published volumes: whether they are joined by a relationship of supplementarity (which builds on the supplementary role discussed earlier of the actual text of the *journal d'écriture*), or whether they provide two mutually exclusive ways of concluding and unifying the whole life-writing project. It will be possible to examine these two possible relationships individually, how they are constructed, and their implications, before considering the significance of this very ambiguity for modern life-writing more broadly.

The role of *L'Atelier noir* as a supplement is based on the premise that, since *Les Années* fails (for all its merits) to satisfy the exacting requirements of the 'RT', *Écrire la vie* itself becomes the embodiment of this project. Just as in Gide's *Journal des Faux-monnayeurs*, Ernaux initially imagines within the diary itself that she could 'l'intégrer au récit' [integrate it into the narrative] (while reflecting on *La Honte*, 134), and later that she could 'publier ce journal en même temps que le texte' [publish this *journal* at the same time as the text] (vaguely attached to the project of the 'RT', 158), but when the diary is finally published it accompanies *Écrire la vie* rather than *Les Années*. The justifications of the preface to *L'Atelier noir* also allow this supplementary relation with *Écrire la vie*, without confirming it:

> D'avoir publié plusieurs des textes en travail dans ce journal joue peut-être comme une autorisation d'en dévoiler les cheminements chaotiques, les tourments préalables, comme si toute cette peine obscure, dépourvue de la grandeur qu'on prête à la création littéraire, se trouvait rachetée et valorisée par l'existence, hors de moi, du livre. (14)

> [The fact of having published several of the texts whose labour is related in this *journal* perhaps acts as a an authorization to expose their chaotic paths, their initial torments, as if all this suffering in darkness, without the grandeur that we associate with literary creation, were redeemed and given value by the existence, outside myself, of the book.]

While the plural 'textes' evoke the diary's relationship with the individual works in question, the singular 'livre' suggests the role of *Écrire la vie* as the 'livre "total"' (107) of Ernaux's life-writing project, or—in Barthesian terms—as the *Livre* that gives value to the *Album* of *L'Atelier noir*. By this reading, *Écrire la vie* makes the strongest claim yet to achieving the aims of the 'RT', to depict a whole life in an impersonal form, a 'vie palimpseste' producing a timeless 'vérité' and a sense of 'permanence', while *L'Atelier noir* compensates for the resulting sense of 'irréalité' with the presence and 'déroulement' over time of an author-figure.

However, whereas the role of *L'Atelier noir* as a supplement to *Écrire la vie* resembles the *Journal des Faux-monnayeurs* by using diary-writing to qualify and open up the 'roman total', its nature as an alternative summation of Ernaux's life-writing project corresponds to the claims of Gide's *Journal 1889–1939* for a unification of the literary *œuvre* with the diaristic presence of the author-figure. In Ernaux's case, this would make the authorial diaristic subject of the *journal d'écriture* into the organizing principle of her *œuvre*, so that her other works would be situated within the diaristic space of the pursuit of her life-writing desires, as a series of intermediate 'investissements'. First of all, we must recognize the limitations of this comparison: evidently, *L'Atelier noir* does not possess the scale or boldness of Gide's *Journal*, and very few readers would find as much interest in *L'Atelier noir* as they would in the contents of *Ecrire la vie*. This alternative model of Ernaux's *œuvre* and author-figure therefore inevitably remains marginal, or secondary in relation to the claims of *Écrire la vie*. Ernaux also suggests, in a phrase from Nietzsche cited twice in the diary, a strong ambivalence towards adopting the same authorial posture as Gide: 'le meilleur auteur sera celui qui aura honte d'être homme de lettres' [the best author will be the one who is ashamed of being a man of letters] (135, 155). Gide might be considered the very model of the 'homme de lettres', and this particular term suggests several of the reasons for Ernaux's resistance towards a Gidean model of authorship. It evokes the bourgeois literary institution of the author-figure as well as the hypocritical public performance of writers that is criticized in *La Vie extérieure*. The individualism implicit in this role is also characteristic of the bourgeois culture that Ernaux treats with considerable irony throughout her work (observed from her position as a 'transfuge de classe' [defector from her social class]),[45] and conflicts with her own concept of the *'je' transpersonnel*. Finally, Gide is not just 'de lettres' but also an 'homme', and therefore more inclined, according to Lejeune's analysis of gender in diary-writing, to connect the life related in his *journal intime* to his literary work.[46]

Nonetheless, Ernaux reflects in the *journal d'écriture* itself on her adoption of a Gidean authorial posture, in a form of citation which manifests her continuing anxiety in this regard:

[1] Jette mon livre; dis-toi bien que ce n'est là *qu'une* des milles postures possibles en face de la vie. Cherche la tienne. [2] Ce qu'un autre aurait aussi bien fait que toi, ne le fais pas. Ce qu'un autre aurait aussi bien dit que toi, ne le dis pas, aussi bien écrit que toi, ne l'écris pas.—Ne t'attache en toi qu'à ce que tu sens qui n'est nulle part ailleurs qu'en toi-même, [3] et crée de toi, impatiemment ou patiemment, ah! le plus irremplaçable des êtres.

[[1] Throw away my book; assure yourself that it is *only one* of a thousand possible postures to adopt in life. Look for your own. [2] Whatever another would have done just as well as you, do not do it. Whatever another would have said as well as you, do not say it, written as well as you, do not write it—Only concern yourself with that part of you that you feel exists nowhere except in yourself, [3] and make yourself, impatiently or patiently, ah! the most irreplaceable of beings.]

I have divided the passage above, originally found in Gide's *Les Nourritures terrestres*,[47] into three sections, although it is important to note that it forms a coherent development of a single idea. This passage is found at the end of *Les Nourritures terrestres* in an 'envoi' addressed by the narrator to the reader-disciple Nathanaël, exhorting him to find a distinct path from his Gidean mentor, to act, speak, and write in a new way. Ernaux initially cites section two (48), then she later cites sections two and three together (57). On both occasions the passage is given without any further comment (they are separated typographically from the rest of the entry, with which they have no evident relation), and section one remains excluded throughout. Section two, taken by itself in the context of

---

[45] McIlvanney, *The Return to Origins*, p. 1.   [46] Lejeune, 'Un singulier journal au féminin'.
[47] André Gide, *Les Nourritures terrestres*, in *Romans et récits* ([1897]), I, pp. 347–444.

Ernaux's *journal d'écriture*, could relate unproblematically to her desire to find 'une forme nouvelle d'autobiographie' and to address in her own way the fundamental issues of modern life-writing. Ernaux only later, and reluctantly, acknowledges that this project entails the creation of a unique (and undoubtedly individualist) author-figure, 'le plus irremplaçable des êtres', which is obscured in *Écrire la vie* but placed centre-stage by *L'Atelier noir*. Section one, which remains unquoted, if not repressed, suggests a truth that is more difficult still for Ernaux to accept: she may, like Barthes before her, reject the Gidean 'homme de lettres' and 'jette [son] livre', but in forming her own authorial 'posture en face de la vie' she finds herself to belong inescapably to a development of the very desires, practices, and forms exemplified by Gide's own diary-writing.

THE PLACE OF THE DIARY IN MODERN LIFE-WRITING

Ernaux's programmatic commitment to truthfulness from the beginning of her life-writing project in *La Place* is unrepresentative of modern life-writing's preoccupation with fiction, and perhaps goes some way to explaining her interest in publishing diaries (given their role as 'antifiction').[48] It is significant, then, that her *œuvre* still manifests the common marginalization of the diary relative to the dominant literary claims of autobiography. In itself, this suggests that the diary's marginal position in life-writing is not simply a matter of its truth status appearing naïve or redundant after the discoveries of high theory, and that it is rather a development of earlier structures whereby the diary—by virtue of its marginality—plays an important role in the construction of a literary *œuvre* and an author-figure. Ernaux's diary-writing can therefore be viewed as a gradual exploration of the role of the diary in a new situation, where the writer's life is already the material of his or her principal works, and where it is autobiography that confers literary status on the collective *œuvre*.

The initial terms of this exploration are recognizable in the single volume of *Journal du dehors*. Mindful of the hypocrisy of the literary figures she finds around her, Ernaux cautiously develops in the *journal extérieur* an authorial posture which implicates the writing subject, the individual who inhabits and observes the *ville nouvelle*, and the paratextual subject who presents the diary to the reader. This posture is characterized by a diaristic process of successive, inexhaustible, reinterpretations of experience that is always already linguistic in nature. However, this posture also remains tentative (somewhat less so in *La Vie extérieure*), and is limited to the specific writing project of the *journal extérieur*. In contrast, Ernaux's *journaux intimes* were initially written without assuming any authorial posture, but upon their publication they take on a greater significance than the *journal extérieur* for Ernaux's whole writing career. The supplementary role of

---

[48] Lejeune, 'Le Journal comme « antifiction »'.

the *journaux intimes* relative to biographical and autobiographical works (*Une femme* lies somewhere between these two categories) leads to the creation of an author-figure characterized once again by the diary's 'inconscience de la suite' (*Je ne suis pas sortie*, 12), and which allows Ernaux's works to be read as belonging to a diaristic space.

However, it is the ambiguous role of *L'Atelier noir* in Ernaux's *œuvre* that is most revealing with regard to the place of the diary in life-writing more generally. It may be surprising that *Écrire la vie* forgets the developments of the published diaries and returns to the model of an impersonal, timeless account of reality, but this apparent shortcoming creates the possibility for the two functions of *L'Atelier noir*: as a supplement to *Écrire la vie*, and as an alternative summation of the *œuvre*. The implications of the two possibilities are quite different. The first case results in a complementary relationship between autobiography and diary as *Livre* and *Album*, in which the diary—with the paradoxical logic of the supplement—supports the totalizing literary claims of the autobiographical *œuvre* (as 'livre "total"') by qualifying it and opening it up to reinterpretations. The second case echoes the claims of Gide's *Journal* for the diary to adopt pride of place in a literary *œuvre*, although for *L'Atelier noir* it is a question of opening an authorial diaristic space encompassing the *œuvre*, rather than of consecrating an 'homme' or 'femme de lettres' in literary form.

This ambiguity in the diary's role remains in a state of suspension in Ernaux's work, and we are faced with the task, not of artificially resolving it, but of interpreting it. It would undoubtedly be useful to extend our enquiry to some of the other, varied uses of diaries in modern life-writing—including works mentioned earlier by Renaud Camus, Hervé Guibert, or Jacques Roubaud—but we can draw several conclusions from Ernaux's own diary publications. With regard to the legacy from earlier generations of diarists, it is the question of an authorial posture, or the construction of an author-figure, that connects Ernaux's diary-writing to the desires, problems, and strategies of Gide, even as she expresses her ambivalence towards this archetype of the diaristic 'homme de lettres'. Ernaux also continues to address similar problems to those that Barthes had theorized and experimented with at the early stages of modern life-writing, such as the dynamics of presence and absence when writing from personal experience, and the opposition between the diaristic *Album* and the *Livre* ('livre beau', 'livre "total"', 'roman total').[49] The major difference in Ernaux's situation relative to these precursors is the greater prestige that is now attributed to life-writing, and to autobiography in particular, which in turn changes the situation of diary-writing: whereas diaries have long been criticized for their naïve adherence to certain mythic ideals (including the familiar myths of absolute spontaneity, sincerity, and privacy in writing), the diary now plays a salutary role in qualifying the totalizing claims of autobiography, or even a subversive role in pricking the arrogance of

[49] Ernaux, *L'Atelier noir*, pp. 63, 107, *passim*.

autobiography's new-found literary status. Yet the ambiguity in the diary's role is itself a mark of continuity from the point in the 1880s when diary-writing positively assumed its contradictions and its literary potential. Even at this time of a relative proliferation of life-writing, diaries of all forms retain their quality as (in Barthes's terms) 'le limbe du Texte, sa forme inconstituée, inévoluée et immature' [the fringe of the Text, its unconstituted, unevolved and immature form],[50] and draw from this undecidable, marginal state their capacity for perpetually reinventing themselves.

[50] Barthes, 'Délibération', pp. 680–1.

Conclusion

It was not my intention in this study to prove that real and fictional diaries participate in a single inter-related history of diary-writing, but if proof were needed, it is amply demonstrated by the many relations between them that have emerged throughout the preceding chapters. These relations include the complex structures formed by real and fictional diaries within an author's *œuvre*, the models established by *auteurs supposés* such as André Walter or Sally Mara for real authors' anthumous publication of their own *journaux intimes*, and the particular role of diary-writing as 'antifiction' (in Lejeune's terms)[1] with regard to modern life-writing's fascination with fiction. On the other hand, the broad approach that I have adopted—positively seeking out unconventional texts that do not fit the established critical models—has revealed the considerable extent to which truth and fictionality are, in themselves, central preoccupations of diary-writing throughout the long twentieth century. This is apparent from the very beginning of this study, in André Walter's project to transform his diaristic reality into a transcendental, literary state of fiction, right up to Annie Ernaux's use of diary-writing to find 'une "vérité" autre' [another 'truth'] in her life experience and an alternative model for conceiving of the author and *œuvre*. Evidently, this preoccupation can be followed in all its diversity only by using the flexible method that I described in the introductory chapter, accommodating diverse concepts of truth and fictionality, and recognizing that in literary practice these different models tend to be reconfigured or conflated (a process which has great potential for literary invention). These findings also raise a number of questions requiring further study. It remains to be seen whether truth and fictionality became more pressing issues at the historical moment in the 1880s at which I began my enquiry, or if these same issues might be found to be no less significant in works of diary-writing from earlier in the nineteenth century. In more recent history, it is still unclear to what extent the *journal intime* has participated in the hybrid mode of autofiction, and the texts identified by Michel Braud as possible examples of this (by Jean-Benoît Puech and Christophe Deshoulières) warrant closer attention.[2]

Besides the issue of fictionality itself, certain themes have emerged throughout this study which cast the history of diary-writing in a different light. Although Pierre Pachet, who ends his study of the *journal intime* at the pivotal date of

---

[1] Philippe Lejeune, 'Le Journal comme « antifiction »', *Poétique*, 149 (2007), pp. 3–14.

[2] Michel Braud, '"Le texte d'un roman": journal intime et fictionnalisation de soi', *L'Esprit Créateur*, 42/4 (2002), pp. 76–84, pp. 78–9.

1887–88, regrets the diary's apparent loss of its private and non-literary nature at this time,[3] this moment now appears to have a different significance as the point when writers embraced an 'otherness' inherent in diary-writing, and began to pursue its literary potential with great ingenuity. As I discussed in the introductory chapter, this 'otherness' includes the inevitably shared nature of language, the textual construction of self in opposition to imagined 'others', and the material reality of the circulation of diary texts beyond the diarist's writing desk, where they become subject to the interpretations of other readers. These claims could be made of many, and perhaps all forms of writing, but the diary texts that I have examined from across the twentieth century make use specifically of the conflict between this 'otherness' and a persistent myth of the *journal intime* as a spontaneous, entirely private, manifestation of a diarist's supposedly coherent self. Two general outcomes of this conflict can be observed. The first involves the multiplication of voices, modes of writing, and authorial roles. A textual plurality is created which opens up many possibilities for problematizing the relations between reality, author-figure (however this might be defined in the specific case), and *œuvre*. Gide's work offers several models for this: in *Les Cahiers d'André Walter*, the complex relations of same and other between André Gide (as *auteur supposant*), André Walter, and Allain, each with their own diaristic and literary texts; in *Paludes*, the interactions between Gide, the diaristic writer of *Paludes I*, and the author of *Paludes II*; then in *Le Journal des Faux-monnayeurs*, Gide's creation in a real diary of apparently independent fictional characters, corresponding to Édouard's own diary and literary creation within the novel *Les Faux-monnayeurs*. These relations are played out in a new literary and intellectual context in Queneau's works attributed to Sally Mara, and there is a different dispersal of authorial roles again in Barthes's *Soirées de Paris* (the co-existence of novelistic and conventionally diaristic modes of writing) and in Annie Ernaux's life-writing project (a number of authorial postures are developed, from the *journal extérieur* up to the publication of the *journal d'écriture*). The second outcome—closely related to the first—is a conceptual opposition between a spontaneous, sincere writing of psychological interiority, and a process of generalization and literary sublimation that risks destroying or betraying the initial, individual experience. This can be seen most clearly in André Walter's desire to pass from the banal existence manifested in his *journal intime* into a transcendent state of literary fiction (his excessive ambitions lead to his own death and even the end of his existence as an *auteur supposé*), and in Barthes's opposition between the pursuit of an immediate, fully present writing of mourning in *Journal de deuil*, and a fully literary sublimation of his grief in *Soirées de Paris* (both of these turn out to be impossible, or utopian, in their own way). Crucially, my readings of works from across the twentieth century do not indicate a steady

---

3 'Mais cette date marque aussi une fin. Le journal intime cesse d'être aussi privé, aussi secret, aussi intime qu'il l'a été. Sa vocation publique désormais le surplombe et le précède' [But this date also marks an ending. The *journal intime* ceases to be as private, as secret, as *intime* as it has been. From this point on its public role dominates and precedes it]; Pierre Pachet, *Les Baromètres de l'âme: naissance du journal intime* (Paris: Hatier, 1990), p. 126.

process of enlightenment or a complete rejection of the illusions of diary-writing: from Gide to Ernaux, all the works that I have examined have shown some lucidity regarding the illusory nature of the mythic qualities of the *journal intime*, yet these same illusions, even as utopian desires, continue to serve their purpose and to stimulate new diary-writing projects.

Another aspect of diary-writing that has been assumed and exploited by writers since the 1880s is its very marginality and uncertainty as a literary genre, or as Barthes describes it, its status as 'le limbe du Texte, sa forme inconstituée, inévoluée et immature' [the fringe of the Text, its unconstituted, unevolved and immature form].[4] This question of literary status poses the greatest problem regarding the overall history of the diary in twentieth-century French writing, which can be summarized as follows: if the *journal intime* takes on an inescapable 'vocation publique' in the 1880s (according to Pachet) and is transformed into a fully literary genre in 1939 with the publication of Gide's *Journal* (according to Girard), one would expect the diary to continue after Gide as a constitutively literary genre (like poetry or the novel), yet my own readings have demonstrated that the marginality of diary-writing persists after Gide and even up to the recent past. A possible explanation would be that Girard's assessment of the literary status of Gide's *Journal* was mistaken, or alternatively that the *Journal* was an anomaly without historical importance, but these explanations are not borne out by the continuing interest that subsequent diarists took in Gide's *Journal* (as well as in his other diary works). A more satisfactory solution to this problem is that the marginality of diary-writing plays a similar role to that of its 'otherness': just as diarists have made varied use of the very tension between the 'otherness' of the *journal intime* and its mythic value as a private, spontaneous, univocal form of writing, a great deal of use has also been made of its uncertain status between the literary and the mundane, and in a similar way the diary has succeeded in holding these apparently contradictory values in suspension. In *Les Cahiers d'André Walter*, *Paludes*, and *Le Journal des Faux-monnayeurs*, and again in Queneau's Sally Mara publications, the literary status of the diary (principally the *journal intime*) is problematized by placing it in opposition to the constitutive literary claims of fiction and the novel, to which it remains secondary. In Barthes's writing projects it is conceived in the more abstract framework of the *Album* and the *Livre* (it cannot attain the literary ideals of the latter), and in Ernaux's work the diary remains marginal in relation to the dominant literary status of autobiography. In every case the diary's very marginality complicates and enriches the concept of the literary, sometimes acting as a supplement to qualify the claims of an *œuvre* for unity, coherence, and finality, but it would not do so simply by displacing the novel (or autobiography) and asserting its own importance. What should we make, then, of Gide's *Journal*, and the symbolism of its publication in Gallimard's prestigious Bibliothèque de la Pléiade? It undoubtedly makes strong claims as a literary *œuvre* in its own right, and in this respect it lays the ground for later writers for whom the *journal intime*

---

[4] Roland Barthes, 'Délibération', in *OC* ([1979]), V, pp. 668–81, pp. 680–1.

was their principal form of literary production (such as Charles Juliet and Renaud Camus), but it also polemically proposes a new form of *œuvre* that derives its unity and value from an author-figure. If we consider that it claims this literary status despite the fact that the contents of this volume had mostly already appeared in Gide's *Œuvres complètes*, it can even appear as an *œuvre* devoid of content, a strange sort of anti-*œuvre*, or in Barthes' terms '*l'écrivain moins son œuvre*, forme suprême du sacré: la marque et le vide' [*the writer without his œuvre*: the supreme form of the sacred, the mark and the void].[5] Gide's *Journal* may well be unique, a hapax, but this is not the same as a historical anomaly, since it plays a meaningful role in the history of diary-writing as a marginal form.

A more general observation regarding the sorts of formal variation that I have found in works of diary-writing may help to identify areas for further enquiry. Throughout the wide range of works under discussion in this study, the actual practice of diary-writing and the substance of real diaries have shown surprisingly little variation over the twentieth century, and the same is true even going back as far as the origins of the *journal intime*. In this respect, there is a strong formal resemblance between such chronologically distant *journaux intimes* as those of Maine de Biran and Annie Ernaux, and conversely it would be difficult to find two diaries that are more different from one another than Barthes's *Journal de deuil* and *Soirées de Paris*. This relative consistency may be related to a certain continuity in practices of introspection since the broad epistemological shift described by Foucault as taking place in the late-eighteenth century,[6] or it may be due to the stability of its use in educational and pedagogical contexts, or again it may be that the basic form of the diary—fragmentary, dated, and with a *narration intercalée*—simply does not permit a great deal of variation. On the other hand, there is a large diversity in the structures by which real and fictional diaries have been placed in relation to other texts, or in relation to each other, sometimes within a single volume and sometimes across multiple publications, and there is a corresponding diversity in the effects produced by these structures. There are many other works of diary-writing that would be worth examining from this perspective, from across the whole period addressed in this study,[7] but in particular there is much more work to be done in order to understand the role that diary-writing has played in the context of modern life-writing from the 1970s up to the present. My reading of works by Barthes and Ernaux focused on the marginal position of diary-writing relative to certain literary ideals (such as the *Livre* and a particular conception of autobiography), but given the great wealth of thought and writing practices that

5 Roland Barthes, *Roland Barthes par Roland Barthes*, in *OC* ([1975]), IV, pp. 575–771, p. 656.
6 Michel Foucault, *Les Mots et les choses: une archéologie des sciences humaines* (Paris: Gallimard, 1966), pp. 13–15.
7 I shall mention only a selection of the works that I would like to have had the time to discuss at length: Valery Larbaud's works attributed to A.O. Barnabooth, published from 1908 and gathered in *A.O. Barnabooth, ses Œuvres complètes: c'est-à-dire un conte, ses poésies et son journal intime*; Jean-Paul Sartre, *La Nausée* (Paris: Gallimard, 1938); Claude Mauriac's 'Temps immobile' series of diary publications, beginning in 1970 with *Une amitié contrariée* (Paris: Grasset, 1970); Françoise Sagan, *Des Bleus à l'âme* (Paris: Flammarion, 1972); Hervé Guibert, *Cytomégalovirus: Journal d'hospitalisation* (Paris: Seuil, 1992) and *Le Mausolée des amants: journal 1976–1991* (Paris: Gallimard, 2001).

have emerged in the field of life-writing as a whole, it is to be expected that the very marginality of diary-writing has also been put to new and varied uses, which largely remain to be explored.

With regard to the future of diary-writing in France, there are certain ongoing questions that will be extremely interesting to follow, and whose development I would not dare to predict. Owing to the strange chronology of the publication of diaries—the path from *cahier* to print can be very short (as is the case for the regular publications of Charles Juliet and Renaud Camus) or long and difficult (as it was for Sartre's *Carnets de la drôle de guerre*)—new diary publications may substantially change our understanding of the history of this form, as well as its present. The greatest changes in the material circumstances of diary-writing are undoubtedly the use of computers for the composition and storage of diaries, and the growth of the Internet as a means of their dissemination.[8] Of these two, the shift from pen and paper to keyboard and hard drive seems the less significant, and it may have little more impact on the practice of diary-writing than did the invention of the typewriter. It does, however, give rise to serious concerns about the preservation of diaries in digital form, which could easily be destroyed or overlooked after the diarist's death (or even before it), or become inaccessible owing to the obsolescence of file formats. The same concerns exist with regard to the change from handwritten correspondence to email, and the archives of writers in general. Yet the consequences for diary-writing of the growth of the Internet are both more far-reaching and harder to predict, since they involve rapidly shifting attitudes towards such fundamental concepts as privacy, authorship, intellectual property, and the unity or permanence of a literary work.[9] It is reasonable to suppose that the diary will continue to capitalize on its marginal status as 'le limbe du Texte', but the ways in which it might construct this marginality, and in relation to which new dominant literary forms, allow for practically limitless possibilities.

[8] These questions were addressed by Philippe Lejeune as early as 2000; Philippe Lejeune, *"Cher Écran... ": journal personnel, ordinateur, Internet* (Paris: Seuil, 2000).

[9] A useful discussion of the implications of technological change for the concepts of literature and the *livre* is found in François Bon, *Après le livre* (Paris: Seuil, 2011).

Bibliography

Dates given in square brackets indicate the date of first full publication, when this is different from the edition that is being referred to (often the most recent Pléiade edition).

Abbott, Hans Porter, *Diary Fiction: Writing as Action* (Ithaca: Cornell University Press, 1984).

Alblas, Anton, *Le 'Journal' de Gide: le chemin qui mène à la Pléiade* (Nantes: Centre d'études gidiennes, 1997).

Alblas, Anton, 'Le n'importe quoi, le n'importe comment et le n'importe où: trois dimensions de l'écriture du *Journal* de Gide', in *André Gide et l'écriture de soi: actes du colloque organisé à Paris les 2 et 4 mars 2001 par l'Association des Amis d'André Gide*, ed. by Pierre Masson and Jean Claude (Paris: Presses Universitaires de Lyon, 2002), pp. 153–64.

Albouy, Pierre, '*Paludes* et le mythe de l'écrivain', *Cahiers André Gide*, 3 (1972), pp. 241–51.

Alexandre, Didier, 'Les Écrivains français et le roman américain 1943–1951: histoire d'un désamour?', *Romanic Review*, 100 (2009), pp. 81–92.

Allen, Woody, *Complete Prose* (New York: Picador, 1980).

Amiel, Henri-Frédéric, *Journal intime*, ed. by Philippe Monnier and Anne Cottier-Duperrex, 12 vols (Lausanne: L'Âge d'homme, 1976).

Angelet, Christian, 'Ambiguïté du discours dans *Paludes*', in *André Gide 3: Gide et la fonction de la littérature*, ed. by Claude Martin (Paris: Revue des lettres modernes, 1972), pp. 85–96.

Arland, Marcel, 'Sur un nouveau mal de siècle', *NRF*, 125 (February 1924), pp. 149–58.

Badmington, Neil, '*Punctum saliens*: Barthes, Mourning, Film, Photography', *Paragraph*, 35/3 (2012), pp. 303–19.

Badmington, Neil (ed.), *Deliberations: The Journals of Roland Barthes*, ed. by Neil Badmington (= *Textual Practice*, 30/2 (2016)).

Bakhtin, Mikhail Mikhaïlovich, *Esthétique et théorie du roman* (Paris: Gallimard, 1978).

Barthes, Roland, *Œuvres complètes*, ed. by Éric Marty, 5 vols (Paris: Seuil, 2002).

Barthes, Roland, 'Notes sur André Gide et son « Journal »', in *OC* ([1942]), I, pp. 33–46. First printed in *Existences* (journal of 'Les Étudiants au sanatorium'), 27 (July 1942), and reprinted in *Le Magazine littéraire*, 97 (February 1975), pp. 24–8.

Barthes, Roland, *Sur Racine* (Paris: Seuil, 1963).

Barthes, Roland, 'Alain Girard: « Le Journal intime »', in *OC* ([1966]), II, pp. 806–10.

Barthes, Roland, 'La Mort de l'auteur', in *OC* ([1968]), III, pp. 40–5.

Barthes, Roland, 'L'Effet de réel', in *OC* ([1968]), II, pp. 25–32.

Barthes, Roland, *Sade, Fourier, Loyola*, in *OC* ([1971]), III, pp. 699–868.

Barthes, Roland, *Le Plaisir du texte*, in *OC* ([1973]), IV, pp. 217–64.

Barthes, Roland, 'Dossier', *Magazine littéraire*, 97 (February 1975), pp. 20–37.

Barthes, Roland, *Roland Barthes par Roland Barthes*, in *OC* ([1975]), IV, pp. 575–771.

Barthes, Roland, *Fragments d'un discours amoureux*, in *OC* ([1977]), V, pp. 25–296.

Barthes, Roland, *Leçon*, in *OC* ([1977]), V, pp. 427–46.

Barthes, Roland, 'La Chronique', in *OC* ([1978–79]), V, pp. 625–53.

Barthes, Roland, '« Longtemps, je me suis couché de bonne heure »', in *OC* ([1978 as lecture at Collège de France, first printed 1982]), V, pp. 459–70.

Barthes, Roland, 'Délibération', in *OC* ([1979]), V, pp. 668–81.

Barthes, Roland, *La Chambre claire: note sur la photographie*, in *OC* ([1980]), V, pp. 785–892.

Barthes, Roland, *Incidents*, ed. by François Wahl (Paris: Seuil, 1987).

Barthes, Roland, *Soirées de Paris*, in *OC* ([1987]), V, pp. 977–93.

Barthes, Roland, *Vita Nova*, in *OC* ([1995]), V, pp. 1007–18.

Barthes, Roland, *La Préparation du roman I et II: cours et séminaires au Collège de France (1978–1979 et 1979–1980)*, ed. by Nathalie Léger (Paris: Seuil, 2003).

Barthes, Roland, *Journal de deuil: 26 octobre 1977 – 15 septembre 1979* (Paris: Seuil, 2009).

Bashkirtseff, Marie, *Journal* (Paris: Mazarine, 1980).

Benda, Julien, *La Jeunesse d'un clerc* (Paris: Gallimard, 1936).

Benda, Julien, *Les Cahiers d'un clerc (1936–1949)* (Paris: Emile-Paul Frères, 1949).

Benveniste, Émile, *Problèmes de linguistique générale* (Paris: Gallimard, 1966).

Blanchard, André, *Entre Chien et loup: carnets, avril–septembre 1987* (Paris: Le Dilettante, 1989).

Blanchot, Maurice, 'Gide et la littérature de l'expérience', in *La Part du feu* (Paris: Gallimard, 1949), pp. 208–20.

Blanchot, Maurice, 'Kafka et la littérature', in *La Part du feu* (Paris: Gallimard, 1949), pp. 20–34. First printed in *Cahiers de la Pléiade*, 7 (July 1949), pp. 93–105.

Blanchot, Maurice, 'La Lecture de Kafka', in *La Part du feu* (Paris: Gallimard, 1949), pp. 9–19. First printed in *L'Arche*, 11 (November 1945), pp. 107–16.

Blanchot, Maurice, 'Le Journal intime et le récit', in *Le Livre à venir* (Paris: Gallimard, 1959), pp. 224–30.

Boehringer, Monika, 'Paroles d'autrui, paroles de soi: *Journal du dehors* d'Annie Ernaux', *Études Françaises*, 36/2 (2000), pp. 131–48.

Bon, François, *Après le livre* (Paris: Seuil, 2011).

Borges, Jorge Luis, 'Borges and I', in *Labyrinths*, ed. by Donald Yates and James Irby, trans. by James Irby (London: Penguin, 1981), pp. 282–3.

Boswell, James, *An Account of Corsica, the journal of a tour to that island, and memoirs of Pascal Paoli* (Glasgow: Edward and Charles Dilly, 1768).

Boswell, James, *The Journal of a tour to the Hebrides with Samuel Johnson, LL.D.* (London: Charles Dilly, 1785).

Boswell, James, *Boswell's London Journal, 1762–1763* (London, W. Heinemann, 1950).

Boulé, Jean-Pierre, *Hervé Guibert: Voices of the Self*, trans. by John Fletcher (Liverpool: Liverpool University Press, 1999).

Boylesve, René, *Feuilles tombées* (Paris: Éditions de la Pléiade, 1927). Published in the 'Écrits intimes' series, directed by Charles Du Bos.

Brasillach, Robert, 'André Gide, *Pages de journal (1929–1932)*', *BAAG*, 74–5 (1987), pp. 53–8. First printed in *L'Action française*, July 1934.

Braud, Michel, '"Le texte d'un roman": journal intime et fictionnalisation de soi', *L'Esprit Créateur*, 42/4 (2002), pp. 76–84.

Braud, Michel, *La Forme des jours: pour une poétique du journal personnel* (Paris: Seuil, 2006).

Bretonne, Nicolas-Edme Restif de la, *Monsieur Nicolas, ou le cœur human dévoilé*, 16 vols (Paris, 1794–97).

Brunetière, Ferdinand de, 'La Littérature personnelle', *La Revue des deux mondes*, 85 (1888), pp. 433–52.

Burke, Seán, *The Death and Return of the Author: Criticism and Subjectivity in Barthes, Foucault and Derrida* (Edinburgh: Edinburgh University Press, 1992).

Butler, Judith, *Gender Trouble: Feminism and the Subversion of Identity* (New York: Routledge, 1990).

Butor, Michel, *L'Emploi du temps* (Paris: Minuit, 1956).

Butor, Michel, 'Le Roman comme recherche', in *Essais sur le roman* (Paris: Minuit, 1964), pp. 7–14. First printed in *Les Cahiers du sud*, 334 (April 1956).

Campana, Marie-Noëlle, *Queneau pudique, Queneau coquin* (Limoges: Presses universitaires de Limoges, 2007).

Camus, Renaud, *Journal romain: 1985–1986* (Paris: POL, 1987).

Chevalier, Anne, 'Le même et l'autre dans *Les Cahiers et les Poésies d'André Walter*', *BAAG*, 110–11 (1996), pp. 177–8.

Cohn, Dorrit, *The Distinction of Fiction* (Baltimore: Johns Hopkins University Press, 1999).

Cohn, Dorrit, 'Métalepse et mise en abyme', in *Métalepses: entorses au pacte de la représentation*, ed. by John Pier and Jean-Marie Schaeffer (Paris: EHESS, 2005), pp. 121–30.

Colonna, Vincent, *Autofiction et autres mythomanies littéraires* (Paris: Tristram, 2004).

Compagnon, Antoine, introductory text for lecture course 'Écrire la vie' at the Collège de France, beginning 6 January 2009, <http://www.college-de-france.fr/site/antoine-compagnon/course-2009-01-06-16h30.htm> [accessed 31 August 2017].

Compagnon, Antoine, 'Writing mourning', trans. by Sam Ferguson, in *Deliberations: The Journals of Roland Barthes*, ed. by Neil Badmington (= *Textual Practice*, 30/2 (2016)), pp. 209–19.

Cornick, Martyn, *The "Nouvelle Revue Française" Under Jean Paulhan, 1925–1940* (Amsterdam: Rodopi, 1995).

Cross, Máire and Caroline Bland, 'Gender Politics: Breathing New Life into Old Letters', in *Gender and Politics in the Age of Letter-Writing, 1750–2000*, ed. by Caroline Bland and Máire Cross (Aldershot: Ashgate, 2004), pp. 3–14.

Culler, Jonathan, 'Preparing the Novel: Spiraling Back', *Paragraph*, 31/1 (2008), pp. 109–20.

Dabit, Eugène, *Journal intime: 1928–1936* (Paris: Gallimard, 1939).

Dawson, Deirdre, *Voltaire's Correspondence: An Epistolary Novel* (New York: Peter Lang, 1994).

Defoe, Daniel, *The Life and Strange Surprizing Adventures of Robinson Crusoe, of York, Mariner* (London: W. Taylor, 1719).

Defoe, Daniel, *A Journal of the Plague Year* (London: E. Nutt, J. Roberts, A. Dodd and J. Graves, 1722).

Delay, Jean, *La Jeunesse d'André Gide*, 2 vols (Paris: Gallimard, 1956–57).

Deprun, Jean, 'Gide, Leibniz et le Pseudo-Virgile', *in Lettres et réalités: mélanges de littérature générale et de critique romanesque offerts au professeur Henri Coulet par ses amis* (Aix-en-Provence: Université de Provence, 1988), pp. 29–38.

Derrida, Jacques, *La Carte postale: de Socrate à Freud et au-delà* (Paris: Flammarion, 1980).

Derrida, Jacques, '« Ce dangereux supplément »', in *De la grammatologie* (Paris: Minuit, 1985), pp. 203–34.

Derrida, Jacques, 'Le Facteur de la vérité', in *La Carte postale: de Socrate à Freud et au-delà* (Paris: Flammarion, 2014), pp. 421–509.

Deshoulières, Christophe, *Mémoires d'Aramis ou l'anti-journal* (Paris: Fayard, 1999).

Dethurens, Pascal, 'L'Ironi(qu)e mise en abyme dans *Paludes*', *BAAG*, 96 (1992), pp. 411–24.

Didier, Béatrice, *Le Journal intime* (Paris: PUF, 1976).

Djebar, Assia, *L'Amour, La Fantasia* (Paris: J.-C. Lattès, 1985).

Doubrovsky, Serge, *Fils* (Paris: Galilée, 1977).

Du Bos, Charles, *Approximations* (Paris: Plon, 1922).

Du Bos, Charles, *Extraits d'un journal, 1908–1928* (Paris: Éditions de la Pléiade, 1928).

Due, Reidar, '*Paludes* and the Subversion of the Moral Subject', *Orbis Litterarum*, 57 (2002), pp. 259–74.

Dällenbach, Lucien, *Le Récit spéculaire: essai sur la mise en abyme* (Paris: Seuil, 1977).

Ernaux, Annie, *Les Armoires vides* (Paris: Gallimard, 1974).

Ernaux, Annie, *La Place* (Paris: Gallimard, 1983).

Ernaux, Annie, *Une femme* (Paris: Gallimard, 1987).

Ernaux, Annie, *Passion simple* (Paris: Gallimard, 1991).

Ernaux, Annie, *Journal du dehors* (Paris: Gallimard, 1993). References are made to the second edition in Gallimard's Folio collection (actually published 1997, but still dated 1993), which is the first to contain the 'avant-propos inédit de l'auteur' (dated 1996).

Ernaux, Annie, 'Vers un « je » transpersonnel', *RITM*, 6 (1993), pp. 219–21.

Ernaux, Annie, *La Honte* (Paris: Gallimard, 1997).

Ernaux, Annie, *« Je ne suis pas sortie de ma nuit »* (Paris: Gallimard, 1997).

Ernaux, Annie, *La Vie extérieure* (Paris: Gallimard, 2000).

Ernaux, Annie, *Se perdre* (Paris: Gallimard, 2001).

Ernaux, Annie, *L'Écriture comme un couteau: entretien avec Frédéric-Yves Jeannet* (Paris: Stock, 2003).

Ernaux, Annie, *L'Atelier noir* (Paris: Busclats, 2011).

Ernaux, Annie, *Écrire la vie* (Paris: Gallimard, 2011).

Ferguson, Sam, 'Metalepsis and the Auteur Supposé in Raymond Queneau's *Œuvre Complètes de Sally Mara*', *French Studies*, 66/2 (2012), pp. 178–92.

Ferguson, Sam, 'André Gide's *Paludes*: A Diary Novel?', *French Studies*, 68/1 (2014), pp. 34–47.

Ferguson, Sam, 'Forgetting Gide: A Study of Barthes's "Ursuppe"', *Barthes Studies* 1 (2015).

Ferguson, Sam, 'Diary-writing and the Return of Gide in Barthes's "Vita Nova"', in *Deliberations: The Journals of Roland Barthes*, ed. by Neil Badmington (= *Textual Practice*, 30/2 (2016)), pp. 241–66.

Foucault, Michel, *Les Mots et les choses: une archéologie des sciences humaines* (Paris: Gallimard, 1966).

Foucault, Michel, 'Qu'est-ce qu'un auteur?', in *Dits et écrits 1954–1988*, ed. by Daniel Defert and François Ewald, 2 vols (Paris: Gallimard, 2001), I, pp. 817–49. First given as a lecture at a session of the Société française de philosophie, 22 February 1969.

Garner, Jane, 'Dementia: An Intimate Death', *British Journal of Medical Psychology*, 70 (1997), pp. 177–84.

Gasparini, Philippe, *Autofiction: une aventure du langage* (Paris: Seuil, 2008).

Genette, Gérard, *Figures III* (Paris: Seuil, 1972).

Genette, Gérard, *Seuils* (Paris: Seuil, 1987).

Genette, Gérard, *Fiction et diction: précédé de Introduction à l'architexte* (Paris: Seuil, 2004).

Genette, Gérard, *Métalepse: de la figure à la fiction* (Paris: Seuil, 2004).

Gide, André, *Journal 1887–1925*, ed. by Éric Marty (Paris: Gallimard, Bibl. de la Pléiade, 1996).

Gide, André, *Journal 1926–1950*, ed. by Martine Sagaert (Paris: Gallimard, Bibl. de la Pléiade, 1997).

Gide, André, *Essais critiques*, ed. by Pierre Masson (Paris: Gallimard Bibl. de la Pléiade, 1999), pp. 836–54.

Gide, André, *Souvenirs et voyages*, ed. by Pierre Masson (Paris: Gallimard, Bibl. de la Pléiade, 2001).

Gide, André, *Romans et récits: œuvres lyriques et dramatiques*, ed. by Pierre Masson, 2 vols (Paris: Gallimard, Bibl. de la Pléiade, 2009).

Gide, André, *Les Cahiers d'André Walter* (Paris: Librairie de l'Art indépendant, 1891).

Gide, André, *Les Cahiers d'André Walter* (Paris: Librairie académique Didier Perrin et Cie, 1891).

Gide, André, *Les Cahiers d'André Walter* and *Les Poésies d'André Walter*, in *Romans et récits* ([1891–92]), I, pp. 1–166.

Gide, André, *Le Traité du Narcisse* (Paris: Librairie de l'Art indépendant, 1892).

Gide, André, *Les Poésies d'André Walter* (Paris: Librairie de l'Art indépendant, 1892).

Gide, André, *La Tentative amoureuse* (Paris: Librairie de l'Art indépendant, 1893).

Gide, André, *Le Voyage d'Urien* (Paris: Librairie de l'Art indépendant, 1893).

Gide, André, *Paludes* (Paris: Librairie de l'Art indépendant, 1895).

Gide, André, *Paludes*, in *Romans et récits* ([1895]), I, pp. 257–326.

Gide, André, 'Préface pour une seconde édition de « Paludes »', *Mercure de France*, 16 (1895), pp. 199–204.

Gide, André, *Feuilles de route (1895–1896)* (Brussels: N. Vandersypen, 1897).

Gide, André, *Le Voyage d'Urien, suivi de Paludes* (Paris: Mercure de France, 1897).

Gide, André, *Les Nourritures terrestres*, in *Romans et récits* ([1897]), I, pp. 347–444.

Gide, André, *Réflexions sur quelques points de littérature et de morale* (Paris: Mercure de France, 1897).

Gide, André, *Philoctète, Le Traité du Narcisse, La Tentative amoureuse, El Hadj* (Paris: Mercure de France, 1899).

Gide, André, 'Oscar Wilde', in *Essais critiques* ([1902]), pp. 836–54.

Gide, André, *Amyntas* (Paris: Mercure de France, 1906).

Gide, André, *Les Caves du Vatican: sotie par l'auteur de Paludes*, 2 vols (Paris: NRF, 1914).

Gide, André, *Morceaux choisis* (Paris: NRF, 1921).

Gide, André, *Pages choisies* (Paris: Crès, 1921).

Gide, André, *Les Faux-monnayeurs* (Paris: NRF, 1925).

Gide, André, *Les Faux-monnayeurs*, in *Romans et récits* ([1925]), II, pp. 173–517.

Gide, André, *Le Journal des Faux-monnayeurs* (Paris: Éos, 1926).

Gide, André, *Le Journal des Faux-monnayeurs*, in *Romans et récits* ([1926]), II, pp. 519–82.

Gide, André, *Numquid et tu?...* (Paris: Éditions de la Pléiade, 1926).

Gide, André, *Si le grain ne meurt*, in *Souvenirs et voyages* ([1926]), pp. 79–330.

Gide, André, *Essai sur Montaigne* (Paris: Éditions de la Pléiade, 1929).

Gide, André, *L'École des femmes* (Paris: NRF, 1929).

Gide, André, *Œuvres complètes*, ed. by Louis Martin-Chauffier, 15 vols (Paris: NRF, 1932–39).

Gide, André, *Pages de journal (1929–1932)* (Paris: Gallimard, 1934).

Gide, André, *Nouvelles Pages de journal (1932–1935)* (Paris: Gallimard, 1936).

Gide, André, *Journal 1889–1939* (Paris: Gallimard, Bibl. de la Pléiade, 1939).

Gide, André, *Les Pages immortelles de Montaigne: choisies et expliquées par André Gide* (Paris: Corrêa, 1939).

Gide, André, *Pages de journal: 1939–1942* (New York: Pantheon Books, 1944).

Gide, André, *Thésée* (New York: Pantheon Books, 1946).

Gide, André, *Thésée*, in *Romans et récits* ([1946]), II, pp. 983–1028.

Gide, André, *Récits, roman, soties*, 2 vols (Paris: Gallimard, 1948).

Gide, André, *Et nunc manet in te* (Paris: Ides et calendes, 1951).

Gide, André, *Romans, récits et soties, œuvres lyriques* (Paris: Gallimard, Bibl. de la Pléiade, 1958).

Gide, André, *Journal*, rev. edn, 2 vols (Paris: Gallimard, Bibl. de la Pléiade, 1977).

Gide, André, *Les Cahiers et les Poésies d'André Walter*, ed. by Claude Martin (Paris: Gallimard, 1986).

Gil, Marie, *Roland Barthes: au lieu de la vie* (Paris: Flammarion, 2012).

Gilot, Michel, 'Quelques pas vers le journal intime', in *Le Journal intime et ses formes littéraires: actes du colloque de septembre 1975 (Grenoble)*, ed. by Victor del Litto (Geneva: Droz, 1978), pp. 1–25.

Girard, Alain, 'Kafka et le problème du journal intime', *Critique*, 1 (1946), pp. 21–32.

Girard, Alain, *Le Journal intime* (Paris: PUF, 1963).

Godard, Henri, 'Préface' to Raymond Queneau, *Romans I (Œuvres complètes II)*, ed. by Henri Godard (Paris: Gallimard, Bibl. de la Pléiade, 2002), pp. IX–LVIII.

Goulet, Alain, 'Notice' for *Les Caves du Vatican*, in André Gide, *Romans et récits*, I, pp. 1463–83.

Goulet, Alain, 'Notice' for *Les Faux-monnayeurs*, in André Gide, *Romans et récits*, II, pp. 1201–20.

Goulet, Alain, 'De la Contingence et de la rhétorique dans *Paludes*', *BAAG*, 54 (1982), pp. 191–206.

Goulet, Alain, 'Mme André-Walther', *BAAG*, 61 (1984), pp. 107–12.

Goulet, Alain, 'Une Enquête sur l'influence de Gide en 1975', in *Actualités d'André Gide: actes du colloque international organisé au Palais Neptune de Toulon et à la Villa Noailles à Hyères les 10, 11 et 12 mars 2011*, ed. by Martine Sagaert and Peter Schnyder (Paris: Honoré Champion, 2012), pp. 106–30.

Green, Julien, *Journal: 1928–1934* (Paris: Plon, 1938).

Green, Julien, *Journal II: 1935–1939* (Paris: Plon, 1939).

Guéhéniau, Florence, *Queneau analphabète: répertoire alphabètique de ses lectures de 1917 à 1976*, 2 vols (Brussels: F. Guéhéniau, 1992).

Guibert, Hervé, *Cytomégalovirus: Journal d'hospitalisation* (Paris: Seuil, 1992).

Guibert, Hervé, *Le Mausolée des amants: journal 1976–1991* (Paris: Gallimard, 2001).

Głowiński, Michał, 'On the First-Person Novel', *New Literary History*, 9/1 (1977), pp. 103–14.

Hellens, Franz, 'Le *Journal* d'André Gide', *BAAG*, 59 (1983), pp. 422–5. First printed in *Le Soir*, 2 February 1940.

Hogan, Rebecca, 'Engendered Autobiographies: The Diary as a Feminine Form', in *Autobiography and Questions of Gender* ed. by Shirley Neuman (London: Cass, 1991), pp. 95–107.

Holdheim, Wolfgang, *Theory and Practice of the Novel: A Study on André Gide* (Geneva: Droz, 1968).

Hollier, Denis, 'Notice' for *L'Âge d'homme*, in Michel Leiris, *L'Âge d'homme, précédé de L'Afrique fantôme*, ed. by Dennis Hollier (Paris: Gallimard, Bibl. de la Pléiade, 2014), pp. 1212–38.

Ionescu, Mariana, 'Journal du dehors d'Annie Ernaux: "Je est un autre"', *The French Review*, 74/5 (2001), pp. 934–43.

Jeandillou, Jean-François, *Supercheries littéraires: la vie et l'œuvre des auteurs supposés* (Paris: Usher, 1989).

Jefferson, Ann, *Biography and the Question of Literature in France* (Oxford: OUP, 2007).

Johnson, Alexandra, *A Brief History of Diaries: From Pepys to Blogs* (London: Hesperus, 2011).

Jones, Percy Mansell, *French Introspectives: From Montaigne to André Gide* (Cambridge: Cambridge University Press, 1937).

Juliet, Charles, *Journal: 1957–1964* (Paris: Hachette, 1978).

Kafka, Franz, *La Colonie pénitentiaire: nouvelles, suivies d'un Journal intime*, trans. by Jean Starobinski (Paris: Egloff, 1945).

Kafka, Franz, *Journal intime, suivi de Esquisse d'une autobiographie*, trans. by Pierre Klossowski (Paris: Grasset, 1945).

Kafka, Franz, *Journal: texte intégral, 1910–1923*, trans. by Marthe Robert (Paris: Grasset, 1954).

Keypour, David, *André Gide: écriture et réversibilité dans 'Les Faux-monnayeurs'* (Montreal: Presses de l'Université de Montréal, 1980).

Keypour, David, 'Le Journal fictif dans l'œuvre d'André Gide', *BAAG*, 82–3 (1989), pp. 217–24.

Knight, Diana, 'Barthes Deliberates: Pascal, Ignatius and the Question of the Diary', in *Deliberations: The Journals of Roland Barthes*, ed. by Neil Badmington (= *Textual Practice*, 30/2 (2016)), pp. 221–39.

Knight, Diana, *Barthes and Utopia: Space, Travel, Writing* (Oxford: OUP, 1997).

Knight, Diana, 'Idle Thoughts: Barthes's *Vita Nova*', *Nottingham French Studies*, 36/1 (1997), pp. 88–98.

Lacan, Jacques, 'Le Séminaire sur "La Lettre volée"', in *Écrits I* (Paris: Seuil, 1999), pp. 11–61.

Lacan, Jacques, 'Le Stade du miroir comme formateur de la fonction du Je telle qu'elle nous est révélée dans l'expérience psychanalytique', in *Écrits I* (Paris: Seuil, 1999), pp. 92–9.

Lacan, Jacques, 'Jeunesse de Gide ou la lettre et le désir', in *Écrits II* (Paris: Seuil, 1999), pp. 217–42.

Lacretelle, Jacques de, *Colère: suivi d'un journal* (La Haye: Le Bon Plaisir, 1926).

Lacretelle, Jacques de, *Aparté* (Paris: NRF, 1927).

Landheer, Ronald, 'Queneau et la rhétorique du sous-entendu', in *Études sur Les Œuvres complètes de ~~Raymond Queneau~~ Sally Mara*, ed. by Evert van der Starre (Groningen: Institut de langues romanes, 1984), pp. 74–104.

Larbaud, Valery, *Poèmes d'un riche amateur: ou Œuvres françaises de M. Barnabooth*, *précédées d'une introduction biographique*, published without mention of Larbaud's name (Paris: Léon Vanier, 1908).

Larbaud, Valery, *A.O. Barnabooth, ses Œuvres complètes: c'est-à-dire un conte, ses poésies et son journal intime* (Paris: NRF, 1913).

Larbaud, Valery, *Journal inédit I: 1912–1920* (= *Œuvres complètes* IX) (Paris: Gallimard, 1954).

L[efèvre], F[rédéric], 'Le *Journal des Faux-monnayeurs* par André Gide', *Les Nouvelles littéraires*, 13 November 1926, p. 3.

Leibniz, Gottfried Wilhelm, *Nouveaux essais sur l'entendement humain*, in *Sämtliche Schriften und Briefe* (Berlin: Akademie-Verlag, 1962–), Reihe 6: *Philosophische Schriften*, VI: *Nouveaux essais* (1990).

Leiris, Michel, *L'Âge d'homme*, in *L'Âge d'homme, précédé de L'Afrique fantôme*, ed. by Denis Hollier (Paris: Gallimard, Bibl. de la Pléiade, 2014), pp. 751–942.

Lejeune, Philippe, *Le Moi des demoiselles: enquête sur le journal de jeune fille* (Paris: Seuil, 1993).

Lejeune, Philippe, *Le Pacte autobiographique*, rev. edn (first published 1975) (Paris: Seuil, 1996).

Lejeune, Philippe, 'Gide et l'espace autobiographique', in *Le Pacte autobiographique* (Paris: Seuil, 1996), pp. 165–96.

Lejeune, Philippe, *L'Autobiographie en France* (Paris: Armand Colin, 1998).

Lejeune, Philippe, *"Cher Écran…"*: *journal personnel, ordinateur, Internet* (Paris: Seuil, 2000).

Lejeune, Philippe, 'Un singulier journal au féminin', in *Annie Ernaux: une œuvre de l'entre-deux*, ed. by Fabrice Thumerel (Arras: Artois Presses Université, 2004), pp. 253–8.

Lejeune, Philippe, *Signes de vie: le pacte autobiographique 2* (Paris: Seuil, 2005).

Lejeune, Philippe, 'Le Journal comme « antifiction »', *Poétique*, 149 (2007), pp. 3–14.

Lejeune, Philippe, 'Marc-Antoine Jullien, contrôleur du temps', *Lalies*, 28 (2008), pp. 205–20.

Lejeune, Philippe, 'The Story of a French Life-Writing Archive: "Association pour l'Autobiographie et le Patrimoine Autobiographique"', *Forum: Qualitative Social Research* 12/3 (2011).

Lejeune, Philippe, *Aux Origines du journal personnel: France, 1750–1815* (Paris: Honoré Champion, 2016).

Leleu, Michèle, *Les Journaux intimes* (Paris: PUF, 1952).

Leleu, Michèle, 'Une « Météorologie intime »: le « Journal » de Charles Du Bos', *Cahiers de l'Association des études françaises*, 17 (1965), pp. 133–50.

Lionnet, Françoise, *Autobiographical Voices: Race, Gender, Self-Portraiture* (Ithaca: Cornell University Press, 1989).

Le Journal intime et ses formes littéraires: actes du colloque de septembre 1975 (Grenoble), ed. by Victor del Litto (Geneva: Droz, 1978).

Léautaud, Paul, *Journal littéraire I: 1893–1906* (Paris: Mercure de France, 1954).

Lévi-Strauss, Claude, *Les Structures élémentaires de la parenté* (Paris: PUF, 1949).

Magny, Claude-Edmonde, *L'Âge du roman américain* (Paris: Seuil, 1948).

Magny, Claude-Edmonde, 'Le *Journal* de Gide à la Pléiade', *BAAG*, 139 (2003), pp. 389–92. First printed in *Esprit*, February 1940, pp. 306–10.

Marchal, Bertrand, 'Notice' for 'Notes en vue du « Livre »', in Stéphane Mallarmé, *Œuvres complètes*, ed. by Bertrand Marchal, 2 vols (Paris: Gallimard, Bibl. de la Pléiade, 1998), I, pp. 1372–83.

Marin, Robert, review of André Gide, *Les Faux-monnayeurs*, *Sélection*, 5/2 (1925–26), pp. 156–8, reprinted in *BAAG*, 65 (1985), pp. 122–4.

Marin La Meslée, Valérie and Nathalie Léger, *'Journal de deuil*: « Chaque fiche est une figure du chagrin »', *Magazine littéraire*, 482 (2009), pp. 84–6.

Martens, Lorna, *The Diary Novel* (Cambridge: Cambridge University Press, 1985).

Martin, Claude, *La Maturité d'André Gide: de 'Paludes' à 'L'Immoraliste' (1895–1902)* (Paris: Klincksieck, 1977).

Marty, Éric, *L'Écriture du jour: le 'Journal' d'André Gide* (Paris: Seuil, 1985).

Marty, Éric, 'Gide et sa première fiction: l'attitude créatrice', in *L'Auteur et le manuscrit*, ed. by Michel Contat (Paris: PUF, 1991), pp. 177–97.

Marty, Éric, 'La Vie posthume de Roland Barthes', *Esprit*, 174 (1991), pp. 76–90.

Marty, Éric, 'Notice', in André Gide, *Journal 1887–1925*, ed. by Éric Marty (Paris: Gallimard, Bibl. de la Pléiade, 1996), pp. 1297–321.

Marty, Éric, *Roland Barthes: la littérature et le droit à la mort* (Paris: Seuil, 2010).

Masson, Pierre, 'Préface' to André Gide, *Romans et récits: œuvres lyriques et dramatiques*, ed. by Pierre Masson, 2 vols (Paris: Gallimard, Bibl. de la Pléiade, 2009), I, pp. XI–XLVII.

Matzneff, Gabriel, *Cette Camisole de flammes: 1953–1962* (Paris: La Table ronde, 1976).

Matzneff, Gabriel, *Les Moins de seize ans: suivi de Les Passions schismatiques* (Paris: Scheer, 2005). First printed in 1974.

Maubel, Henry, 'Notes en marge de *Paludes*', *Le Coq Rouge*, 3 (June 1895), pp. 97–9. Reprinted in *BAAG* 54 (1982), pp. 212–15.

Mauriac, Claude, *Conversations avec André Gide: extraits d'un journal* (Paris: Michel, 1951).

Mauriac, Claude, *Une Amitié contrariée* (Paris: Grasset, 1970).

May, Georges, *L'Autobiographie* (Paris: PUF, 1979).

McIlvanney, Siobhán, *Annie Ernaux: The Return to Origins* (Liverpool: Liverpool University Press, 2001).

Meyer-Minnemann, Klaus, 'Un procédé narratif qui « produit un effet de bizarrerie »: la métalepse littéraire', in *Métalepses: entorses au pacte de la représentation*, ed. by John Pier and Jean-Marie Schaeffer (Paris: EHESS, 2005), pp. 133–50.

Million-Lajoinie, Marie-Madeleine and Annie Ernaux, 'Au Sujet des journaux extérieurs: entretien d'Annie Ernaux avec Marie-Madeleine Million-Lajoinie', in *Annie Ernaux: une œuvre de l'entre-deux*, ed. by Fabrice Thumerel (Arras: Artois Presses Université, 2004), pp. 259–65.

Mok, Q.I.M., 'L'Art de faire des fautes', in *Études sur Les Œuvres complètes de ~~Raymond Queneau~~ Sally Mara*, ed. by Evert van der Starre (Groningen: Institut de langues romanes, 1984), pp. 57–73.

Montherlant, Henry de, *Carnets XXIX à XXXV: du 19 février 1935 au 11 janvier 1939* (Paris: La Table ronde, 1947).

Moriarty, Michael, *Roland Barthes* (Cambridge: Polity Press, 1991).

Morino, Lina, *La Nouvelle Revue Française dans l'histoire des lettres* (Paris: Gallimard, 1939).

Moutote, Daniel, *Le Journal de Gide et les problèmes du moi (1889–1925)* (Paris: PUF, 1968).

Moutote, Daniel, *Réflexions sur 'Les Faux-monnayeurs'* (Paris: Champion, 1990).

Murray, Gilbert, *The Four Stages of Greek Religion* (New York: Columbia University Press, 1912).

Nabe, Marc-Édouard, *Nabe's dream: juin 1983—février 1985* (Monaco: Rocher, 1991).

Neuman, Shirley (ed.), *Autobiography and Questions of Gender* (London: Cass, 1991).

Nobécourt, René-Gustave, 'Le *Journal* d'André Gide', *BAAG*, 59 (1983), pp. 407–22. First printed in *Journal de Rouen*, 15 and 22 August 1939.

Nunez, Laurent, 'Vie nouvelle, roman virtuel', Magazine Littéraire, 482 (January 2009), pp. 74–5.

O'Meara, Lucy, *Roland Barthes at the Collège de France* (Liverpool: Liverpool University Press, 2012).

Oura, Yasusuke, 'Introduction aux romans journaux français' (unpublished doctoral thesis, Paris VII, 1986).

Oura, Yasusuke, 'Roman journal et mise en scène « éditoriale »', *Poétique*, 69 (1987), pp. 5–20.

Oura, Yasusuke, 'Étude sur le roman journal français', *Études de Langue et Littérature Françaises*, 52 (1988), pp. 100–17.

Pachet, Pierre, *Les Baromètres de l'âme: naissance du journal intime* (Paris: Hatier, 1990).

Pepys, Samuel, *Memoirs of Samuel Pepys, esq., F.R.S., secretary to the Admiralty in the reigns of Charles II and James II: Comprising his diary from 1659 to 1669*, 2 vols (London: Henry Colburn, 1825).

Perec, Georges, *W ou le souvenir d'enfance* (Paris: Denoël, 1975).

Pier, John and Jean-Marie Schaeffer, 'Introduction: la métalepse aujourd'hui', in *Métalepses: entorses au pacte de la représentation*, pp. 7–15.

Pier, John and Jean-Marie Schaeffer (eds), *Métalepses: entorses au pacte de la représentation* (Paris: EHESS, 2005).

Pieters, Jürgen and Kris Pint (eds), 'Roland Barthes Retroactively: Reading the Collège de France Lectures' (= *Paragraph*, 31/1 (2008)).

Poirot-Delpech, Bertrand, « *J'écris Paludes* » (Paris: Gallimard, 2001).

Pouilloux, Jean-Yves, 'Notice' for *Les Œuvres complètes de Sally Mara*, in Raymond Queneau, *Romans II (Œuvres complètes III)*, ed. by Henri Godard (Paris: Gallimard, Bibl. de la Pléiade, 2006), pp. 1719–37.

Prince, Gerald, 'The Diary Novel: Notes for the Definition of a Sub-Genre', *Neophilologus*, 59/4 (1975), pp. 477–81.

Puech, Jean-Benoît, 'L'Auteur supposé: typologie romanesque' (unpublished doctoral thesis, EHESS, 1982).

Puech, Jean-Benoît, *Du Vivant de l'auteur* (Seyssel: Champ Vallon, 1990).

Puech, Jean-Benoît, *L'Apprentissage du roman: extraits du "Journal d'apprentissage" de Benjamin Jordane* (Seyssel: Champ Vallon, 1993).

Puech, Jean-Benoît, 'Présentation', in *L'Auteur comme œuvre: l'auteur, ses masques, son personnage, sa légende. Colloque des 25 et 26 avril 1997, Université d'Orléans*, ed. by Nathalie Lavialle and Jean-Benoît Puech (Orléans: Presses universitaires d'Orléans, 2000), pp. 9–12.

Queneau, Raymond, *Chêne et chien* ([1937]), in Raymond Queneau, *Romans I (Œuvres complètes II)*, ed. by Henri Godard (Paris: Gallimard, Bibl. de la Pléiade, 2002), pp. 3–36.

Queneau, Raymond, 'Technique du roman', in *Bâtons, chiffres et lettres* ([1937]), pp. 22–7.

Queneau, Raymond, Introduction to William Faulkner, *Moustiques* (Paris: Minuit, 1947), pp. 7–14.

Queneau, Raymond, *Exercices de style* (Paris: Gallimard, 1947).

Queneau, Raymond, *On est toujours trop bon avec les femmes*, originally published under the name Sally Mara (Paris: Éditions du Scorpion, 1947).

Queneau, Raymond, *Bâtons, chiffres et lettres* (Paris: Gallimard, 1950).

Queneau, Raymond, '*Moustiques* de William Faulkner', in *Bâtons, chiffres et lettres* (1950), pp. 77–84.

Queneau, Raymond, *Journal intime*, originally published under the name Sally Mara (Paris: Éditions du Scorpion, 1950).

Queneau, Raymond, *Cent mille milliards de poèmes* (Paris: Gallimard, 1961).

Queneau, Raymond, *Entretiens avec Georges Charbonnier* (Paris: Gallimard, 1962).

Queneau, Raymond, *Les Œuvres complètes de Sally Mara* (Paris: Gallimard, 1962).

Queneau, Raymond, *Les Œuvres complètes de Sally Mara* (Paris: Gallimard, 1979).

Queneau, Raymond, *Journal 1939–1940: suivi de Philosophes et voyous* (Paris: Gallimard, 1986).

Queneau, Raymond, *Journaux 1914–1965*, ed. by Anne Isabelle Queneau (Paris: Gallimard, 1996).

Queneau, Raymond, *Romans I (Œuvres complètes II)*, ed. by Henri Godard (Paris: Gallimard, Bibl. de la Pléiade, 2002).

Queneau, Raymond, *Romans II (Œuvres complètes III)*, ed. by Henri Godard (Paris: Gallimard, Bibl. de la Pléiade, 2006).

Ramuz, Charles-Ferdinand, *Journal 1896–1942* (Paris: Grasset, 1945).

Rannoux, Catherine, *Les Fictions du journal littéraire: Paul Léautaud, Jean Malaquais, Renaud Camus* (Geneva: Droz, 2004).

Raoul, Valerie, *The French Fictional Journal: Fictional Narcissism/Narcissistic Fiction* (Toronto: University of Toronto Press, 1980).

Rivière, Jacques, 'La Crise du concept de littérature', *NRF*, 125 (February 1924), pp. 159–70.

Robbe-Grillet, Alain, *Pour un nouveau roman* (Paris: Gallimard, 1963).

Robbe-Grillet, Alain, *Le Miroir qui revient* (Paris: Minuit, 1984).

Robert, Marthe, *Kafka* (Paris: Gallimard, 1960).

Robinson, Lillian, 'Foreword' to *Revealing Lives: Autobiography, Biography and Gender*, ed. by Susan Bell and Marilyn Yalom (Albany NY: State University of New York Press, 1990), pp. vii–ix.

Rod, Édouard, *La Course à la mort* (Paris: L. Frinzine, 1885).

Rod, Édouard, *Le Sens de la vie* (Paris: Perrin, 1889).

Rouart, Eugène, *La Villa sans maître*, preface by David Walker (Paris: Mercure de France, 2007).

Roubaud, Jacques, « *Le Grand Incendie de Londres* » (Paris: Seuil, 2009).

Rougemont, Denis de, *Journal d'un intellectuel en chômâge* (Paris: Albin Michel, 1937).

Rousseau, Jean-Jacques, *Les Confessions*, in *Œuvres complètes I: Les Confessions et autres textes autobiographiques*, ed. by Bernard Gagnebin and Marcel Raymond (Paris: Gallimard, Bibl. de la Pléiade, 1981), pp. 1–656.

Rousseau, Jean-Jacques, 'Préambule du manuscrit de Neuchâtel', in *Œuvres complètes I: Les Confessions et autres textes autobiographiques,* ed. by Bernard Gagnebin and Marcel Raymond (Paris: Gallimard, Bibl. de la Pléiade, 1981), pp. 1148–55.

Rousseau, Jean-Jacques, *Les Rêveries du promeneur solitaire*, in *Œuvres complètes I: Les Confessions et autres textes autobiographiques*, pp. 993–1099.

Rousset, Jean, *Le Lecteur intime: de Balzac au journal* (Paris: Corti, 1986).

Roy, Claude, *Permis de séjour: 1977–1982* (Paris: Gallimard, 1983).

Ryan, Marie-Laure, 'Logique culturelle de la métalepse', in *Métalepses: entorses au pacte de la représentation*, ed. by John Pier and Jean-Marie Schaeffer (Paris: EHESS, 2005), pp. 201–23.

Rysselberghe, Maria van, *Les Cahiers de la Petite Dame: notes pour l'histoire authentique d'André Gide*, 4 vols (Paris: Gallimard, 1973–77).

Sagan, Françoise, *Des Bleus à l'âme* (Paris: Flammarion, 1972).

Sainte-Beuve, Charles-Augustin, *Vie, poésies et pensées de Joseph Delorme*, ed. by Gérald Antoine (Paris: Nouvelles Éditions Latines, 1956).

Samoyault, Tiphaine, *Roland Barthes: biographie* (Paris: Seuil, 2015).

Sarraute, Nathalie, 'De Dostoïevski à Kafka', in *L'Ère du soupçon*, pp. 67–94. First printed in *Les Temps modernes*, October 1947.

Sarraute, Nathalie, *L'Ère du soupçon: essais sur le roman* (Paris: Gallimard, 1956).

Sarraute, Nathalie, *Enfance* (Paris: Gallimard, 1983).

Sartre, Jean-Paul, *La Nausée* (Paris: Gallimard, 1938).

Sartre, Jean-Paul, *Qu'est-ce que la littérature?* (Paris: Gallimard, 1948).

Sartre, Jean-Paul, *Les Mots* (Paris: Gallimard, 1964).

Sartre, Jean-Paul, *Les Carnets de la drôle de guerre: novembre 1939–mars 1940* (Paris: Gallimard, 1983).

Sartre, Jean-Paul, *Les Carnets de la drôle de guerre: septembre 1939–mars 1940*, in *Les Mots et autres écrits autobiographiques*, ed. by Jean-François Louette (Paris: Gallimard, Bibl. de la Pléiade, 2010), pp. 143–679.

Savage Catharine, '*Le Journal des Faux-monnayeurs*: œuvre accessoire ou œuvre autonome', *BAAG*, 88 (1990), pp. 535–44.

Seys, Élisabeth, *Ces Femmes qui écrivent: de Madame de Ségivné à Annie Ernaux* (Paris: Ellipses, 2012).

Sheringham, Michael, *Everyday Life: Theories and Practices from Surrealism to the Present* (Oxford: OUP, 2006).

Shônagon, Sei, *Les Notes de l'oreiller,* trans. by Kuni Matsuo and Émile Steinilber-Oberlin (Paris: Stock, Delamain et Boutelleau, 1928).

Shônagon, Sei, *The Pillow Book,* trans. by Arthur Waley (London: George Allen & Unwin, 1928).

Simonet-Tenant, Françoise, *Le Journal intime* (Paris: Nathan, 2001).

Simonet-Tenant, Françoise, *Journal personnel et correspondance (1785–1939) ou les affinités électives* (Louvain-la-Neuve: Academia-Bruylant, 2009).

Starre, Evert van der, 'Sally Mara romancière? Exercices de style?', in *Raymond Queneau romancier: actes du 1ᵉʳ colloque international Raymond Queneau, Verviers, 27–30 août 1982,* 2 vols (= *Temps mêlés: documents Queneau,* 150 + 17–19, 20–1) (Verviers: Temps Mêlés, 1983), II, pp. 85–107.

Starre, Evert van der, 'Sally Mara romancière? Exercices de style?', in *Au ras du texte: douze études sur la littérature française de l'après-guerre* (Amsterdam: Rodopi, 2000), pp. 9–28.

Starre, Evert van der, *Curiosités de Raymond Queneau: de « l'Encyclopédie des Sciences inexactes » aux jeux de la création romanesque* (Geneva: Droz, 2006).

Thumerel, Fabrice and Annie Ernaux, 'Ambivalences et ambiguïtés du journal intime: entretien avec Annie Ernaux', in *Annie Ernaux: une œuvre de l'entre-deux,* ed. by Fabrice Thumerel (Arras: Artois Presses Université, 2004), pp. 245–51.

Todorov, Tzvetan, 'Le Dernier Barthes', *Poétique,* 47 (1981), pp. 323–7.

Topia, André, 'Sally Mara ou le sexe a-t-il une âme', in *Études sur Les Œuvres complètes de ~~Raymond Queneau~~ Sally Mara,* ed. by Evert van der Starre (Groningen: Institut de langues romanes, 1984), pp. 1–21.

Vian, Boris, *J'Irai cracher sur vos tombes, traduit de l'américain par Boris Vian* (Paris: Scorpion, 1946). Published under the name 'Vernon Sullivan'.

Walker, David, 'Notice' for *Le Journal des Faux-monnayeurs,* in André Gide, *Romans et récits,* II, pp. 1248–54.

Walker, David, 'L'Écriture et le réel dans les fictions d'André Gide', in *Romans, réalités, réalismes,* ed. by Jean Bessière (Paris: PUF, 1989), pp. 121–36.

Walker, David, 'En relisant le *Journal des Faux-monnayeurs*', in *André Gide et l'écriture de soi: actes du colloque organisé à Paris le 2 et 3 mars 2001 par l'Association des Amis d'André Gide,* ed. by Pierre Masson and Jean Claude (Lyon: Presses universitaires de Lyon, 2002), pp. 89–101.

Watt, Ian, *The Rise of the Novel: Studies in Defoe, Richardson and Fielding* (London: Chatto & Windus, 1974).

Williams, James, 'The Moment of Truth: Roland Barthes, "Soirées de Paris" and the Real', *Neophilologus,* 79/1 (1995), pp. 33–51.

Wilson, Adrian, 'Foucault on the "Question of the Author": A Critical Exegesis', *Modern Language Review,* 99/2 (2004), pp. 339–63.

Wynchank, Anny, 'Métamorphoses dans *Les Cahiers d'André Walter*: essai de rétablissement de la chronologie dans *Les Cahiers d'André Walter*', *BAAG,* 63 (1984), pp. 361–73.

Zorica, Maja, '*Vita Nova* de Barthes', ed. by Véronique and Catherine Viollet (Louvain-la-Neuve: Academia Bruylant, 2009), pp. 127–40.

Zwanenburg, Wiecher, 'Aux Frontières de la formation des mots', in *Études sur Les Œuvres complètes de ~~Raymond Queneau~~ Sally Mara,* ed. by Evert van der Starre (Groningen: Institut de langues romanes, 1984), pp. 33–56.

Index